CW01647048

Calamity Spain

Fulfilling the Dream

By
Charlotte Moore

Copyright © 2016, Charlotte Moore

All rights reserved.
No part of this publication may be reproduced,
stored in a retrieval system or transmitted
in any form or by any means
without the prior written permission of the author

Enquiries; calamityspain@outlook.com

Cover design by Charlotte Moore

Edited by Matt Nunn

The following story is based on true events.
Names of some characters may have been changed
to preserve anonymity.

www.calamityspain.com

Like any true story, this has been hard to write.
It has been shelved
many times and then dragged out and added to.
I often lost faith in myself as a writer
as to whether it would ever be completed.
It has been rewritten at least three times,
each time I have gone through
the roller coaster of emotions all over again
and each time I came through stronger.

It is the book it is today because of perseverance.
It's also a nicer book to read now the
dark days are gone.

I did it for me.

What was I doing here?

I stood on my little terrace looking into the darkness nursing a glass of wine. It was almost midnight and I had just driven into Lanjarón; my second home. Everywhere was pretty much silent apart from a light chatter of Spanish coming across from a neighbouring terrace and the scrape of plastic chairs on tile as someone got up to get more wine. The light from the myriad of stars twinkling above in the velvet blue sky highlighted the deep black mounds of the Sierra de Lujar in front of me. But it wasn't making my heart leap like it should. Over the last few years people had come and gone. Bars had closed, others had moved premises. Those who were true friends were still my friends and the views were as awe inspiring as they were the very first time I saw them. But I didn't feel at ease. There was a large part of me that was incredibly sad.

After a holiday in the area, I had saved hard to buy my own small part of paradise here. I had been single for a few years and was happy and relaxed at home in the UK after a long marriage. The ex is the ex because; well, we grew apart as much as anything else. Together from the age of 14 there was only so long that you could keep reworking things before you both realised that the sticking plaster was not going to hold things together any longer. A 24 year marriage does not fall apart over night but the 'anything else' was his dalliances and the one with the next door neighbour was one too many. It was the clincher. Despite him shouting out in the road that he was not having an affair, 'me thought he doth protest too much'. He was lucky not to get himself beaten to a pulp from her husband who was a bruiser of a guy and already suspected that they were playing away. I stuck up for him when questioned, I was too proud to admit that my husband would do such a thing when I already had my suspicions. But someone else was saying it? That was tough to take.

He had always been a charmer. I suppose it was what had attracted me originally, but then I was also 14 going on 20 and he was 17 and had a car. I knew my own mind and was older and wiser than my years. Didn't we all think like that? My closest friends were in steady relationships and I felt left out. Here was the man of my dreams, the man to make me feel equal with my peers for however long it lasted. We met a few days before Christmas so we neatly skipped over that period to Boxing Day when he was going to pick me up to go for a drive. I spent the intervening few days trying to build up the courage to tell my parents, not just that I had a boyfriend but that I had a boyfriend with a car. I had only ever had one other boyfriend and my mother knew him as he worked for the local butcher. So telling them about John was a massive hurdle but somehow I managed it, using the excuse that we were going up the Lickey Hills with my normal group of friends and that he and another friend were picking us all up. We were together from that day forward.

He was a handsome guy and was naturally charming and fun. After four years together which went mostly smoothly, we got married. Living together wasn't an option in the early 1980's and my father was certainly not letting us live 'over the brush.' In the September of '82 we managed to secure the purchase of a small terraced house and in the October we were married. It was a hard slog from the beginning. Neither of us earned much money, the house we bought was cold and draughty with no heating other than an open fire and only single glazing that the wind would whistle merrily through, and affording a bag of coal for the fire was sometimes not possible. I spent many an evening using wall filler paste to try to seal off gaps where the glass met the frame in the windows in an attempt to stop the cold air sneaking its way in. Draught excluders were at the bottom of every door and thick curtains made and hung. More than once I went to loosen a net curtain from the misted window to find it wasn't condensation but was ice. The net remained iced to the window till the sun released it. Washing clothes was done in a single tub and wrung out with a mangle in the back yard. Technology had yet to reach us and before it did I was washing clothes in the bath and even those froze solid on occasions.

As with most young couples, we had more going out than coming in and balancing the bills was also my responsibility. Because of our limited resources, I made use of the old way and had bags for each utility with a precise amount in it each week rather than direct debits from a bank account. In March we could splurge a little as the rates were paid over 10 months not 12 so that money either went towards a holiday at the coast or on repairs for our old car. It took us 10 years before we had double glazing and then a telephone and eventually central heating that John actually fitted himself. He was a dab hand at DIY and friends often asked him to do odd jobs for them. I tried to encourage him to go to night school to get new skills but he couldn't be bothered. At least with heating installed, the old Victorian terrace became less damp and hacking-off damp plaster to re do it became a thing of the past. I did actually become a dab hand at plastering though!

We both worked hard and long hours and were for the most part happy. When we met he was a very sociable person but now he was more interested in sitting in front of the TV every evening and often refused to go to a party or event. I found it embarrassing to attend on my own and often had to use the excuse that he was working. He didn't like mixing with certain people, those who were at or had been to university and were eloquent and what I'd call rounded. He said that they used big words to confuse him and that included me. I changed my usage of vocabulary so that he didn't feel belittled in any way, not that I felt he was and no one was talking down to him, but it was easier to do than be blamed for something and nothing. Around the home we worked well as a team and it was great to achieve something on our tight budget. Over time we made a comfortable home. With the death of my parents we managed to move upwards in the property chain and into our 'forever home.' Again it needed work...a lot of work. A quarter of the structure had dry rot and damp. It had no central heating but at least was double glazed. The gas fire was condemned, but we loved the house and were undaunted by the work it needed. My inheritance would be used wisely. John was working away in London only coming home at weekends, I was a partner in a small business where the other partner had now got Alzheimer's [although we just thought he was behaving oddly at the time] and I was also moving the business to better premises and not one full of damp and fungus. I juggled this with sorting out the builders and specialist, chasing solicitors and project managing all the workmen. It was a staged workload with retention of funds until those elements were completed. A strange situation as the vendor could have pulled the sale at any time and our money could have been lost, but to get a good house in a great area we had to push on. The place was full of builders and electricians along with bible quotes behind wall boarding in the kitchen. Moving in day and the builders were still in situ. Furniture was stored in the ramshackle garage in the back garden and in the lounge. Even when the workmen had gone there was much work to be done. There were no carpets anywhere and no wallpaper that was suitable to stay, but at least we no longer had water dripping from the circuit board, but we didn't have any plaster on the kitchen walls yet either: nor a ceiling, a floor above that or a ceiling above that. The roof had yet to be done too, but now we were in, in a fashion, we could crack on with what needed doing.

I pressured the workforce, who were now behind schedule by a week, to crack on. John could not build the kitchen until they had left and when they did, the house was eerily quiet. After work and weekends John began fitting the kitchen and I worked on the master bedroom. Cooking was done with a small microwave and we slept on the floor in the lounge; it wasn't good. Thankfully a friend of ours had a large house and offered a spare room which we gratefully accepted. After eating plaster dust for weeks it was heaven. My skin felt dry and dirty and I had a constant cough.

There was also a smell.

A strange smell of old man, you know the one? We searched everywhere for something rotting. Even lifting floor boards to see if the workmen had left a half eaten sandwich and sniffing the fresh plaster in case something was leeching out of that, but no. Then the smell went. It would then appear in a different room. The day we saw a shadow walk past the patio doors we knew we had a ghost. The previous owner had died in front of the condemned gas fire and as he was the only owner since the house was built, we figured it was him; Bill. Bill stayed around. Roaming the house and flitting past the window to the lean-to green house. But Bill seemed to like following me around. The day he followed me into the shower I shouted at him to get lost. The smell disappeared for a few days and eventually went altogether. We assumed he was happy we had settled in and had merrily gone on his way to, well, wherever the smell of ghosts go.

Sadly it seemed that with the house completed the relationship got worse. Our neighbours had moved in six months after us and were about ten years younger. We got on well and would often have joint barbeques in the summer or the guys would have fires at the top of the garden. John had stopped working away so much now so was quite often home before me. I came home one day to find a fence panel removed between our gardens. I can't even remember why now. He was chatting with a cup of tea on their patio with Claire. I said hello and went inside to prepare dinner. Unfortunately this seemed to form a pattern and I asked that the fence panel be put back up. The requests were ignored so I put it up myself, I wasn't prepared for the anger I was greeted with and it was taken back down again. I still hadn't twigged. Curry night at theirs seemed to be getting frosty and I talked with John about why Claire was so off with me; I had no idea why. But instead of supporting me, he defended her; I must have done something or said something to hurt her and I must be nice to her. The penny dropped. I'd had this before when I found out John was seeing my best friend. The pattern was formed but I wasn't sure as it was only a hunch. He began to be sullen when he came in from work. He wouldn't talk to me about what was wrong but would just eat his dinner and fall asleep. I began drinking too much. Soon it was a bottle of wine a night to blot out the pain I was feeling. I didn't know what to do. It wasn't until one day when I was putting the ironing away that I found a card, not very well hidden, in his t-shirt drawer. The words turned my stomach, love and longing, and I recognised the hand writing immediately. I replaced it and carried on as normal.

I made the decision to look and see what else I could find. I knew if I found anything else, it was over. What I wasn't prepared for were photos of an ex girlfriend on the PC, emails to another ex girlfriend with arrangements for a week's holiday when I thought he was working and his subscription to a dating site. I was floored. To this day he doesn't know I know all about these things. It was the nail in the coffin and I was sitting in the coffin: our forever home that I had spent my inheritance on.

I kept a brave face and my silence. I didn't know what to do. The gym got more visits than it should have. Often I would just drive somewhere and sit in the car and think. I decided to tell my best friend

Ian what I'd discovered. Ian and I rarely saw each other as we lived on opposite sides of the Midlands, but that allowed us to talk freely on the phone with each other and we were honest to a fault. In all the time we talked, he never judged or accused he just allowed me to vent my emotions and my confusion. John still had no idea I knew what he was up to, neither did Claire. But both myself and her husband [I found out afterwards] were noting their trips to the supermarket or the petrol station, one after the other and not coming back for an hour or more. How stupid did they think we were?

Then came the night at the local pub: the four of us walking down to see a band. Claire was as frosty with me as ever and John was treating me like I did not exist. I didn't want to drink. I didn't even want to be there and we had argued about it before leaving. I'd got enough pressure with the business, I didn't need silly arguments. Claire was buying the drinks and didn't get me one. I bought my own soft drink and was berated for it, that I wasn't being sociable by not having alcohol. In reality I wanted to stay sober and not get angry in public. I'd had enough. I turned and left the pub. I heard my name bellowed and took no notice. John caught up with me. I ignored him. He was calling me all the names under the sun and then shouted at the top of his voice that he wasn't having an affair with Claire. I hadn't even mentioned it.

His last dalliance whilst he shared my bed. I wasn't having it any more.

We didn't argue after that. He moved into the spare room and we functioned quite well. I rarely argue; I don't see the point. I'd seen too many couples eaten away by the bickering getting out of control. We had been together for nearly 30 years. There were some happy times that I did not want to tarnish so we existed side by side and continued to do the same chores week in and week out whilst we had the house valued and I found one to move into. That day 6 months later was bizarre in itself. John picked up the keys for me and moved my half of our stuff in with my nephew helping. I left one house in the morning and slept in my new home that night.

Over the coming year I realised I wasn't the one who should carry all the blame for everything that went wrong in our marriage. I realised he had laid his own guilt at my door and that I had scooped it up like a loyal trusting wife would. I never talked about our problems with anyone other than a doctor when he said I was frigid. We had been married for a few years and he expected to come to bed at one in the morning and have sex. It wasn't pleasant and left me fearing the act. The doctor wasn't much help either but the blame was always thrown at my door. He was the only man I'd ever slept with so I assumed I was at fault. It's a mental scar I still have to this day. I was at last in charge of just me and it was bliss; although I did have to go back to see him a few times to explain how bills were paid and what he had to do. He had never taken charge of anything however much

I had pleaded with him to do so. The load was never shared.

Even booking holidays was a pain. He never had any ideas of where to go or what to do. I booked and paid for the lot. He only wanted to go to places where they spoke English or that he knew well from going with a previous girlfriend. It's surprising we were together for so long but I felt I couldn't give up whilst my parents were alive as I would feel like I'd failed. Silly I suppose when separation and divorce had become a normal occurrence. But I thought that deep down I had not wanted to be a failure in my parent's eyes. They had been happily married since their late teens and had provided my brothers and I with a happy and stable home, yet both my brothers had divorced and I had not wanted to admit to having a failed marriage too. Not that I regard 24 years of marriage a failure.

Splitting up was the hardest but best move I'd ever made and now I dealt with my own demons and started finding myself again. John rang me regularly, he was lonely. I listened on many occasion but as much as he was telling me all his woes and problems, it was leaving him with a clear conscience and me feeling troubled and sad. This had to stop. The phone calls got ignored and I settled into my single life decorating and improving the place. I relaxed. I began to enjoy intelligent conversation and used words that were tucked in the recesses of my mind. I dusted those off and my opinions about world affairs and anything else I could now talk freely about with no fear of him feeling disparaged.

I fell madly in love with someone I shouldn't, a client called Colin. An incredibly intelligent and caring man who showed me what I had been missing in my marriage but sadly after a few years that ended when his children decided that they would withhold their affections from him if he moved in with me. I was not wanted in their life and he would not stand up to them. But I had maintained my independence throughout and although splitting up was hard; playing second fiddle to 4 teenage daughters dictating to their father wasn't my idea of a relationship. If it was meant to be it would be, I lived in hope for a while after the tears had been shed and then slowly realised it was never going to happen.

Life as a single woman in her 40's wasn't the biggest shock to the system that it would have been for most people. As the ex husband had worked odd hours, I was adept at living the solo life within a marriage. Once I had found and purchased a home, I was free to do my own thing as and when I wanted. What really surprised me that I was financially so much better off now I was paying for everything rather than 50% of everything.

I had, when sorting my finances for the house, ensured I did not go to my full mortgage allowance. Apart from needing a cushion in case I needed to inject funds into the business, [oh the joy of self employment] I wanted to still be able to travel and have holidays abroad. But going abroad alone for a holiday was a nerve jangling experience. I'd spent most of my life travelling around the UK for holidays enjoying the green and pleasant land that we have around us so I hadn't been abroad much. I had got the travel bug though and now enjoyed picking places to go that were for me to enjoy and who cares if they didn't speak English, I got by. I treated myself to some nice hotels but found a lot of the time that the other tourists were many years older than me and seemed to look at me a bit strange. Although I am a gregarious person, inside I am quite shy. So many a holiday was spent with little interaction with other tourists unless it was on a trip out. But it was ok, books by the pool or walking and exploring were fine by me.

My first solo holiday abroad was straight in at the deep end. Colin suggested I use his family apartment in Mojacar, Spain. Not a bad idea really and as I was so besotted with the man at the time I thought it would be another step closer together. I still paid for it though; I didn't want any favours. In one giant leap I went from package holidays with a partner to independent flights and car hire, plus driving on the wrong side of the road in a country where I didn't speak the language. It was a nerve jangling day to say the least but in hindsight it was the start to a more self-sufficient me. It wasn't my ideal location for a holiday as I'm more country than seaside, but it was very much a week I needed. To spend time with myself and let go of the past and the stress that had been building up over the last few years. I had spent my days either on the terrace reading or forced myself to go out in the car to places I really wasn't interested in seeing. Evenings were spent sitting solo in some lovely restaurants feeling miserable before going back to the apartment where I drank more wine than was good for me and diluting it with tears. That holiday was a great healer and also boosted my confidence as a solo traveller. Lanzarote, Fuerteventura and Tenerife were visited where I always stopped in quality hotels. Now I was only paying for myself and not myself and my husband I was enjoying some luxury. There was sumptuous food at every meal and delightful champagne receptions at Christmas 'Black Tie' banquets. These would have been lovely but for the fact that I had struggled to interact with the other guests. For the most part they were very much older than me and ignored my smiles and hellos. The odd few couples befriended me, sadly usually, just a day or so before I was due to leave. Part of me thought the ladies thought I was about to steal their octogenarian husband! I lazed by pools reading books by day and sat in the hotel lobby or lounge by night again with a book. I was and felt, very alone. I am good at talking to strangers but not the best at foisting myself into their company in such situations.

I decided I needed to change my destinations and type of accommodation in an attempt to mix easier with fellow guests and hopefully to find people in a similar age group to enjoy things with. This I did when I visited Tossa de Mar and stayed in a more rustic 2* hotel and what an amazing difference. A broader mix of guests who were easy to chat to and whom I enjoyed spending time with. It was one of my favourite holidays. My next holiday was to inland Spain and up into the mountains away from the normal tourist destinations and it was here I was to fall in love again.

It was a lovely little town situated in the Sierra Nevada in Spain. I had an outside room at the Alcadima Hotel which opened onto a secluded little terraced area and when I walked to breakfast, the view across the Spanish countryside was of rolling hills in every direction and the ruins of a Moorish castle across the road. A walk down Lanjarón main street revealed buildings hundreds of years in age nestled next to low rise apartments of fifty years old. Little side streets with trailing plants off balconies, drinking water fountains every so often with tiled backdrops and inscriptions' by Federico Garcia Lorca and little dogs yapping on leads or running free. Ruddy complexioned old people milling up and down and men in trilby's and flat caps seated on benches, many leaning on sticks, watching the world go by. I was mesmerised by this life so different from the tourist parts of Spain I had been to in the past. It had the charm of a small Spanish village as there was a mere 4,000 population and it had traditions and family values that I admired so much. It was not touristy like coastal resorts but it did have the most amazing views in every direction.

Apart from spraining my ankle on the second day, I spent an idyllic week staring at the views and imagining what life would be like to actually live in a community like this. There was no large supermarket, no burger bars or take-aways. There were independent butchers, bakers, fishmongers, and ironmongers. A real community that traded with each other and I loved it.

It was a surprise to me that I felt so passionately about the place. The only other place I had felt so much passion for was The New Forest in Hampshire, England-again a rural idyll but of heath land and wildlife rather than mountains. How could I feel so attached to a place I had known so little about?

When I got back home I was not only telling friends about the wonderful views but also how wonderful it must be to live in such a wonderful location steeped in traditional values and did not have the trappings of materialism that we all tended to live with on a daily basis.

Over the next few years, Lanjarón didn't leave my mind for very long. I enjoyed holidays to other destinations but I was always comparing them to Lanjarón and its simple way of life. It was a lifestyle I had begun to feel connected with. After being alone for a few years, I had found my character as I had not had to flex myself to suit someone else.

I questioned my life and wondered why I had bought a two bedroom semi detached house when something smaller would have suited me better. I reflected that I was guilty of the materialism that I had begun to dislike, although not in a grand way. I had always desired a more rural life; more simplistic, but the business sadly had always dictated what and where I should have been. I wanted to be free of the manacles of modern life and retreat back to something, not just closer to nature, but to a quality of life that would suit me: a more frugal and meaningful life where the stress of work did not overshadow everything else.

I had then begun to look more seriously at moving to Spain as a way of achieving that peace. But how would I do it, could I even afford to do it? Those were just two of the myriad of questions that I was firing at myself once the seed had been planted in my mind.

Property prices across Andalucía were noted not just Lanjarón as it did seem the more expensive area so I had to widen my search area. I wasn't interested in coastal locations as I preferred rolling hills over rolling waves. I had to do the research to see if it was viable. The financial aspect was like one of those Mensa puzzles where you had to find the values of x and y. Except that my known figures for a, b and c were also variable depending on whether I sold or rented my home in the UK and whether I sold or closed my small business.

If I sold my house I had thought of buying a small guest house with a bit of land for camping. Or I could have bought a small property in addition and then made the choice to move at a later date. Those were the two prime options I had in mind. The savings pot was small so I had to be sure whatever I did was right. Research was a necessity and there was no rush or pressure, just desire. I had to form a plan and see how I felt along the line.

This was something I was doing for me and me alone.

*

Morning broke and the chatter of the sparrows in the tree outside my bedroom window awoke me far earlier than I would have liked and pulling the blind up revealed the beginnings of a glorious day. I stepped onto the balcony to drink in the view I had been longing to see, the hills and mountains of the Alpujarra with the rising sun starting to light up the striations in the rock bringing them to life. I was feeling good.

Over the coming days, the weather was not its best but then it was October. I had my research list and wanted to see why some houses that were selling for as little as 12k. I had bored my friend who lives in Órgiva to death asking about different areas and once she realised I was serious, she gave me as much information as she could, leading me away from the higher areas that were snowbound and freezing in winter and the most isolated places that would have driven me mad with their solitude. I marked up my short list of eight towns and villages to visit on the map. I was ready to explore.

Having conquered the nerves about the drive from the airport I felt comfy about exploring the other villages nearby on my list. Although my heart had beaten wildly for the first few days as I drove up and down the 9km of twisting road from Lanjarón to the motorway. Suddenly when faced by a lorry and forgetting which side of the road I was on I feared a head-on collision. In reality there was plenty of room to manoeuvre. Some of the local drivers though were impatient at my careful driving and they were not going to stick to the speed limits and overtook me on the blindest of bends. There were flowers attached to various sections of Armco that reminded me to stick with my careful approach.

It continued to rain most days so the time that I spent looking around was done in real weather, which had its advantages; it stops the romantic notions and channels you into the gritty reality of day to day life. Although I did look like a drowned rat at the end of the day and was glad of a cosy hotel room and a hot shower.

Dúrcal was a definite possibility; all roads seemed to lead to the centre, the streets were clean and the atmosphere friendly. Plenty of cafe bars to while away the hours except I found it was a little too 'townie' for me even though it only has around 7000 inhabitants. It also seemed dark compared to

Lanjarón. The buildings here were brown rather than white and it seemed to be a working, bustling place, certainly not relaxing. I wanted a slower pace of life, the chance to kick back and relax; I suppose the Spanish version of the villages in the Cotswolds.

A trip into Órgiva was getting close: this was the next town over from Lanjarón with a very mixed population of residents and travellers. The main square was the hub of life here as you seem to have to pass through it on each visit from the Pharmacia to La Caxia bank; it also made a great stage area for fiestas which were an important part of Spanish life. Its Baroque church rose proudly above the town with steeples iced with dots. It has a bohemian air and the travellers who settle here make a wide range of goods for the market. Again the population is not huge by British standards but I wasn't feeling the vibe that I felt in Lanjarón.

By the time I had visited Lecrín, Padul and Torvizcón I was definitely feeling like Goldilocks; too big, too small, too hilly [not necessarily in that order]. But there was one place I needed to visit out of curiosity, Ízbor. Only a few hundred inhabitants, you drive past it on the way up the motorway to Lanjarón; time to divert. Ízbor like so many villages in Spain is visible from the main road but the drive into it seems to snake around forever, it's very easy to lose your bearings. I sat in the car on the bottom road looking up at its perch on the side of the mountain. The houses seemed to sit precariously on the side of the hill, with one I could see having the biggest staircase I have ever seen to get up to it; seven sets! I only hoped they could actually drive there along the high street. Some of the village would only get sun in the morning and would then be cast in shadow for the rest of the day. That was not an idea that appealed to me so I went no further into this little village. This may sound wrong as I'm sure the spirit of the south and beautiful houses would line the streets, but I didn't want to buy a house that I felt sorry for; I had to love it and the town or village it was in. I needed to have sunlight. I had to face facts. Nowhere ticked the boxes like Lanjarón; my heart was firmly wedged there and wasn't going to be moved.

It was a relief to have made that decision and I now felt I could move on to the next step. It had to be Lanjarón. But what was the next step? For this visit, I think I had achieved what I wanted to do so it was time to relax and once more walk the higgledy-piggledy streets of Lanjarón and see where the majority of the people lived, and work out where I could fit in and of course, if I could afford it. It was time to take a drive to the coast and spend a day on the beach. The body could relax whilst the mind went over the details.

This home was for me. Somewhere for me to grow into the person I knew I was. To relax and develop my artistic side once more. To begin again with a clean sheet amongst new people and I was so excited. But were there now too many hurdles that had been created in the last few years for me to be able to settle here and enjoy it for what I hoped it was meant to be?

Things in the UK were getting worse and when it was announced that I would not be able to draw a state pension until I was sixty seven possibly seventy, I knew I had to act now if I was going to give myself a better life. It was also dawning on me that I wasn't about to be getting a man in my life anytime soon: there seemed to be a dearth of available and suitable partners. I had some amazing friends to socialise with but finding 'the one' to share my life didn't seem to be on my radar.

I have worked for myself since I left college. Starting off in the screen printing and design trade, I've grown up planning and budgeting. As my business had developed and I had branched out into corporate embroidery to expand my business services, I got involved with the local Chamber of Commerce as a Business Advisor, mentoring and being a support for people starting up on their own. This was an unpaid post but it brought me a lot of satisfaction to help people achieve their dreams. This led me also into a project called Young Enterprise where students in secondary school started a business and had to manufacture a product and sell it. All this was crammed into a full term and they had to comply by all the normal regulations any other start up business would. I would go into school as their mentor and open their eyes to life as a small business. As much as

I gave to these students, I received as much back in return. On a personal level, I'm quite strict with myself over what I spend on anything. I've never been one for fancy bits and bobs; I was brought up to believe that if I didn't have the money to buy something, then I had to save until I had. My odd splurges were on a camera that would also be helpful with work and my campervan to give me cheap holidays. Following my own crazy principles, I had forward planned and had given myself a strict budget to buy a house in Spain and make my dreams a reality.

All the time I had been doing my planning, all my hopes and dreams were sounded out on my friend Julie. Ours was an unusual friendship as in the ten years we had known each other; we had only ever met once. Julie worked for one of my suppliers and it was always her that sorted my orders out or who called me with offers. She later went on to run her own business and we always kept in touch. Conversations on the phone getting longer and more frequent, we developed a very trusting friendship. If I've had a bad day or a job has gone wrong she is the first person I call to discuss It with or to just have a good cry to release the tension, the same in reverse. She had listened for hours as I told her about Lanjarón again and again, [not to mention my marriage breakup] She'd put up with me sending her estate agent details of little ramshackle places in towns that we knew not where they were nor could pronounce the name of. She went through my budgeting sheets to ensure I hadn't made a mistake in my figures and she played devil's advocate to make me question every single one of my decisions. Never pushing me one way or the other, but offering sound reasoning. Two straight forward Scorpio's being, well, straight forward!

Behind the scenes

Although small in size, it was a pleasure to walk the streets as there was so much to look at in Lanjarón, quaint little shops and crooked side streets and on almost every side street there were effigies of the Saint of whom the street was named after set in a display window. Some are small, barely a foot high but others are around four foot high. Some have the same little windows with silk flowers instead. I was very self conscious taking photographs of these things as I was usually the only person in the street other than a local going about their business. There were no tourists wandering around, they were all at the coastal resorts so I was conscious that I stuck out like a sore thumb. In exploring, you would come across small squares lined with houses and cobblestones, balconies to the upper windows that overlooked the courtyard area and a small round fountain burbling away in the centre. While the street cleaner sweeps rhythmically with his besom broom at a steady slow pace, a little old man would put a bundle of willow into the fountain to soak before returning back to his home to weave more baskets. It was all so *tranquilo*.

After walking through the barrio which is the ancient quarter of the town, I dropped into a bar for a coffee. Before I first came here I had explored the area online, bought a few travel guides and rather cheekily contacted Mountain House Holidays who organised walking tours in the Sierra to pick their brains about the suitability for a single person with a renewed interest in walking and they had also recommended this place as a good point of contact for expat locals and great food. As I was newly single, walking had come back into my life but I felt I wasn't yet fit enough to be going anywhere at altitude, especially on my own. The majority of my walking had been English countryside fields and lanes and I was happy pottering off with maps and camera rather than being part of a group. I appeared to be forgetting that the previous year I had been in Slovenia doing just that but I have to admit that they were well signed and cleared routes around the Kranjska Gora region. Mike and Jane came back to me with a plethora of information not just about walking but about Lanjarón and its people and the surrounding towns and villages, hence why I ended up at the Ambienza. I still hated going into a bar or restaurant alone, in fact it was something I had rarely done back home. In foreign countries it seemed easier to do. Knowing there were English in this bar though made it harder not easier but I gritted my teeth and went in. I need not have been worried. The people who ran the bar were English speakers and smiled warmly as I entered. Nursing my glass of wine I began to look through the photographs I had taken. First one person began talking to me, then another. Although all English men, they were a friendly bunch and there was a good rapport between them all and the girl behind the counter. I was invited to join them at the table and listened to their tales of how they had all ended up here. Some lived here, others had second homes here, but they all had the same passion that I felt about the place and how life was.

Like most tourist destinations the world over, these people had heard it all before, but thankfully, the more we talked, the more we drank and so the more we talked and the more I discovered. Amongst the locals was a guy called Dom, an expat of ruddy complexion with a tan and a wonky smile, slim and charming: I fell without realising it when he said he lived in this wonderful place. He woke up every morning to the stunning blue skies and mountainous countryside that surrounded us; he was glad to be alive and blessed the day he made the leap. He also owned a town house. How envious was I?

Out of the group of friends he was with, he seemed the most sober, quieter and most in control. He had moved abroad from the UK and rebuilt his own house in the town. He got by on virtually nothing, doing the odd job here and there to pay the bills and would never return to the UK to live; his quality of life here was too good to leave. I listened to his tales of the area and his own building experience and felt like I was getting a sneak behind the scenes preview of what life was like as an expat in this lovely place. I leapt in with both feet about my love for the area and how much I wanted to live here. That I was a writer and artist and wanted to come here to have the peace and inspiration to sit, gazing out from a sun drenched terrace that would never cease to inspire me and be creative. Dom smiled and continued to put up with my chatter. I couldn't shut up!

My vision was coming back to earth with a bump as the bar we were in shut [but it's only 1am!] and we had to move onto the next one. Along with Dom and a number of others I had yet to remember the names of, I stumbled across the road to another bar; a ramble of countryside-loving Brits on what I thought was 'a session' headed 200 yards without backpack or navigational equipment to get the beers lined up and continue the chat. Little did I know this was normal drinking here. My alcohol limit was at its peak. No more for me thanks. By the time I weaved my way to bed that night I had invited myself to Dom's townhouse so that I could get a feel of what lay behind those shuttered doors.

Come 4 pm the next day I turned up on Dom's doorstep. I rang the bell and was pleasantly greeted by a yapping puppy as the door swung open. Oh my god, how many stairs were there? In I went up a small staircase with doors leading off, bedrooms, and up I went to the middle level of a large open kitchen dinner, bright white and light, and then up again to the open lounge and the terrace and the view.

The view.

So captivating, breathtaking and many other clichéd superlatives. The rolling peaks and troughs of the Lujar and you could see it all from the lounge. After a beer, I got the grand tour and tried to work out the layout. I couldn't. The second floor bedroom ran under the lounge and some of the kitchen, but the downstairs rooms weaved their way into the neighbour's space. Poke your head out of the bedroom window and you see a little square that is reached by a gate at the side of the houses, leading to more doors of other houses. It reminded me of the centre of a rhiad in Marrakech with the lush planters but sadly no pool. What I did feel was comfortable in the space. With the white wavy walls and upside down living, I felt I could cope with something like this but didn't need it to be quite as big. My plans were changing yet again but it was all positive. Dom had reformed the house a few years back and was happy to be living in this idyllic place and away from the pressure of the rat race in the UK. He confirmed my ideals for my own future. We met a few times whilst I was there on that visit. During the day I was driving around the area looking at other small towns and villages and in the evening I was back in town eager to hear more tales of Lanjarón and its people. For the insider information I was getting, I didn't mind paying the tab in the local bar or for some food as we chatted away until the small hours, it seemed the right thing to do at the time.

I have to admit that at this point I had already seen, on paper, a little place I liked the look of. From the details and the location, it was just off the town centre, it ticked all the boxes and it had been reduced in price. But for some reason I didn't mention it to any of the guys nor did I make any attempt to locate it.

December

Once I got back to the UK I was straight on the phone to Julie. Work was forgotten that Monday morning as I felt so excited about Lanjarón being the place for me. It didn't take Julie long to pick up on the fact I was mentioning Dom a lot. "So who's this Dom guy then?" "Oh he lives there, reformed his own house. He's a builder and we got along just great." I gabbled away. "In fact I'll probably have a chat with him later on Skype. He's done exactly what I want to do and wouldn't change a thing."

The chat with Dom went on for many hours. Not without interruption from his slow broadband. But one night's chat led to two then three. All going on into the early hours of the morning and by the end of the week I was a zombie from lack of sleep. But I had a smile on my face. We were getting on great. He had a great sense of humour and was telling me more and more about the area. It didn't take much more than that week for me to book a long weekend in December.

I continued my research into houses within the town and also into the history of Lanjarón, translated it meant 'place abundant in water'. For a town of so few inhabitants it had a lot crammed into a small space. As well as the expected bars and hotels there was the Spa that attracted quite a wealth of Spanish visitors to ease their aches and pains: a very high end establishment with its own luxury hotel attached. There is a tourist information centre, a large market hall, various small shops selling clothing and fresh produce, a laundromat and a hardware shop that sold a mind boggling array of things that you could ever need. Go in there with a broken 'thing' and come out with a brand new one for just a few cents. For leisure there's a swimming pool and a football pitch plus as you come into town a range of exercise equipment with a view no other gym could compete with over the Lujar. Plus there were the castle ruins. There was something for everyone.

Lanjarón is recognised by the world health organisation as one of the places with the greatest longevity on the planet with many of the inhabitants living to over 100 years old. The waters, the pure mountain air and the diet are the main contributors. It surprises me considering the amount of alcohol that can be consumed here in any of the 53 [evidently] bars of which I have still only visited a few, but that's by the expats and rarely the Spanish. They can stomach coffee and brandy at 6am before they go to work and drink in moderation, we don't seem to be able to do that. The town is protected by cannons at either end; remnants of its long history which is catalogued back to the 10th century. After resurgent battles in the 16th Century and the expulsion of the Moors, the captain who defended the town, refused to surrender preferring to throw himself from the Castle tower. In the aftermath and the population being decimated, Lanjarón was repopulated with fifty new settlers whose families continue to have special rights to this day. During the War of Independence, Lanjarón made a heroic defence of the town and residents have since been known as cañoneros. (If I moved there, I too would become one).

As for the Castillo, it remained on its rocky promontory near to town. Its location was superb because it dominated on one hand the access road to the Alpujarra and on the other it links Granada with the coast. The castle was surrounded by a wall defended by two great semicircular towers of rubblework, one to the north, and one to the south. It stood proud, even if covered in scaffolding and offered a pleasant walk across from the park with a magnificent view back across to town and of the surrounding hills and mountains.

My long weekend came around very quickly. It would have been cheaper to hire a car but I wanted the romance of being picked up at the airport, so happily agreed to cover the fuel costs for his clapped out motor. I made an effort to travel smartly so that when Dom saw me I was looking nice rather than crumpled and casual. I was greeted with a mild hug but knowing he wasn't the demonstrative type I didn't have a problem with this. A stop off at Lidl in Salobreña for supplies including dog and cat food: oh and a case of cheap beer and some wine, and we were off. €35 seemed a cheap shop and worth the cost of not having to pay for a hotel. We dropped off my bag, got licked to death by a very excited dog and then headed straight for the Ambienza to sit in the lovely winter sunshine.

"It's so good to be back." I said as I leant against the wall.

Dom gave a small snort as he rolled a cigarette. "So are you going to get the drinks in then?"

I squinted open my eyes, "When he comes out I'll order, *no problemo*".

Dom tittered, "you know *'no problemo'* doesn't exist in Spanish?"

"Really? So you speak Spanish too?"

"A little. Enough to get by." He lit his cigarette as the waiter came out to serve us.

"Er...*un vino blanco y una cerveza, por favor*." He smiled and walked away. Dom was laughing and I didn't know why. I looked at him sternly, I wanted in on the joke.

"*Que pasa*?"

"What's the big joke?" I frowned.

He drew on his cigarette looking me in the eye; I noticed that his left eyebrow was twitching. "We don't say *cerveza*, its *tubo*, as in a half pint glass. No one drinks in bigger glasses as the beer always gets warm in the sun. If you want a smaller beer it's a *caña*. Also.."

At that point the waiter came back out, "Hey Dom, you going to introduce your friend?" now I knew why he was laughing, the waiter spoke perfect English. I had the idea I was never going to win with this man!

I was feeling decidedly tiddly before I realised it was 7pm and we had not eaten much other than a little tapas. With getting up at 5.30am for the flight too, I was shattered. Food was needed before going back onto the wine. Neither of us could be bothered to cook so I ordered from the menu. After a lovely day we sauntered back up the road and I was asleep before my head hit the pillow: evidently snoring loud enough for the whole house to shake!

I'm not usually a morning person but to be able to get up in the morning and see the view from the terrace got me out of bed straight away. To sit there, wrapped in thick pjs and a dressing gown, nursing a cup of tea as you watched the sunrise was bliss. By 9.30am the terrace was basking in sunlight and the dressing gown was too much. As my cheeks were now glowing it was time to start the day. As a weekend treat it was breakfast the Spanish way at Alberto's; coffee and brandy with tostadas. I raised an eyebrow at the brandy bit but did tip a little into my coffee.

A stroll down to the Ambienza where I was introduced to Martin and Brenda, more friends of Dom's. I was welcomed warmly and we chatted for a while before Brenda invited us up for dinner the next day. Dom offered to bring up a chicken that evidently I would be cooking whilst he was at work, but I was more excited that I was going up the mountain and would be seeing a real cortijo! Did I have any idea what to expect? Well of course I did. I had seen enough property web sites and relocation programs on the TV to know what these places would be like.

Dom said we would have to be there on time because of the light and getting down again. A little puzzled but nevertheless, the chicken was put on to cook and I strolled to the Ambienza for a glass of wine. I felt comfortable already wandering along to this bar and seeing if there was anyone to chat to. Kindle in hand, just in case there wasn't, I headed down the street to sit and enjoy the morning sun. The couple who ran the bar are two of life's beautiful people; genuinely friendly and open and they also served great food.

A van pulled up and out stepped Dom and the guy he had been working for, Doug, for a quick beer after a dusty morning's work. Workdays are workdays everywhere in the world, but here they ended at 2 and always it seemed with a beer. I picked up my drink to join them at the bar "Hi, good day?"

Dom looked surprised that I was there, "er yes, this is Doug the boss."

"Hi Doug, good to meet you, what have you been doing this morning?" I was standing there like a spare bookend. Neither man offered me a seat or gave the impression I was welcome into their chat. I felt uncomfortable. “Well I’ll go back to my table and see you in a bit.” I was confused but I’m sure there was an explanation. Doug left and we wandered back to the house. Dom still a little off. I tried to take his hand and he shook me off “Don’t do that.”

“What?”

“Hold hands.”

“Why not?” I got no reply and just assumed he was in a bad mood.

With the chicken out of the oven, wrapped in foil and popped in a casserole for easy transit, we headed to the car; and then the back streets of town. I had assumed for no valid reason that all people that live up the mountain, had an access road out on the edge of town, I certainly didn’t expect to be going through the warren of streets in the middle of town then off up a concrete track that wound its way up the mountainside: Rough ridged concrete that went from mountainside to, well, fresh air. Dom kept looking at me and I kept looking over the edge; it was a long way down. He laughed; I grimaced! Tight twists and turns were interspersed with dirt tracks leading off to other cortijos deeper into the mountain, whilst some people lived just off the track.

Calming myself down, I began to enjoy the view of the mountain [Caballo] with a good dusting of snow along the ridge, until we pulled in and stopped. A car was coming the other way and we had to find a space to squeeze past each other. We had thankfully just done a left hand bend so had the rock in our favour, the guy coming down had to brush with the edge to get by. My heart was in my mouth and by the time we got to Martin and Brenda's I was sighing with relief. We rounded another bend and another cortijo when we came to a stop by some gates. But realisation that I was driving down made me gulp.

Dom turned the car around in a very tight gap before parking. Dogs gathered around the car and were barking like mad at us; mountain dogs. In my naivety I assumed they were Martin and Brenda's but they weren't! Thankfully they were ok. We entered the gates and Brenda gave me a tour of the property including the knowledge of how to use the toilet; I thought this was a cantankerous idiom at the time but I was just green between the ears to compost loos. Living off grid as you are when you are in the campo is a completely different lifestyle to living down in the main town and even that is so far removed from living in the UK it is hard to comprehend. You are in isolation for the most part, you could have a neighbour across the track or you could be completely on your own. You have no piped water, gas or electricity: You have your allotted water from the mountain: providing there is any and for drinking you have to drive down into town and collect some from one of the many *fuente* [fountains]. You have gas; providing you have been into town to replace the gas bottles. Electricity is usually by solar power so if the sun's not out or the mountain is shrouded in cloud, its cold showers. They are something you really do have at times; invigorating! Then frugality comes into play along with not watching TV, not doing any washing or even at times living by candle light. I'm not sure how many people could actually live life like that with today's reliance on gadgets. I knew immediately that as a single person I would struggle.

The only way I can describe the cortijo is like going into a Cornish cottage. Compact and well planned out and of course, being on a mountainside, its single level seems to cover many. Wood, stone and natural fabrics made for a very cosy dwelling; much nicer than I anticipated having never been in one. As the afternoon sun was still warm, we went back outside where I toured their terrace of vegetables and fruit trees before we sat outside in the afternoon sun and drank wine whilst Martin peeled the vegetables he'd just pulled from the garden. Can you get a more perfect environment that this in which to live? Most people who live in the campo grow their own produce. Back breaking work that always ends up with a glut of zucchini by all accounts, but the pleasure of fresh produce. After all, it's what the terraces are for and most people have olive and almond trees so seasonal production of olive oil goes on too. I love the thought of cooking with all my own produce from start to finish; very satisfying. Sanitation is interesting with compost toilets and septic tanks. I knew I couldn't cope up there on my own with the seclusion, or the drive down into town on a regular basis as I was still a little nervy after the ride up. But the quality of life, eating your home grown food is idyllic. I was like a sponge. Absorbing any information that anyone was giving me. Brenda and her no nonsense approach to life in general and Martin, a mountain and walk guide had much information to pass on regarding buying here versus letting for a time first. It was by coincidence that I found out that Martin worked with Mike and Jane too. Renting seemed a sensible idea at the time and I was wondering if that would be the best thing to do. But, I knew that once I left England for Spain, I could not afford to go back, so would I be doing myself any favours in the long term? The pros and cons were debated over dinner but sadly, with food eaten and now having overstuffed bellies, we needed to leave and get down the mountain before darkness set in.

Having completely forgotten I was driving down the mountain it was a rude awakening to realise why the car had been turned down. It was dark. Pitch black: couldn't see the hand in front of your face black and on a cloudy night, no stars to light the way either. Stepping outside I found this out. No halogen lights lit the track, you had your headlights and that was it. Complete blackness cloaked the mountain. It was as dark as dark could be.

Probably for the best on the first drive to the town.... I thought.

In first gear I crawled along, totally oblivious to the sheer drop, my concentration was on the concrete and hoping against hope that no one was coming up. I counted off the progress by remembering who lived where on the track, wobbled occasionally as the track seemed to disappear, going from 10mph to 0 in a second. Whatever it costs at a funfair is not as adrenaline inspiring as this, believe me. I began to relax as I knew we were nearing the lower section, but then we got to a rise on the track and I had no idea if the track went left, right or straight on. Terrified once more I eased forward and trusted instinct and the drop of the headlights as we crested the brow; straight on with a little move left. Dom stayed quiet all the way down but I knew he would alert me if he thought we were in danger. I could have cried once I saw the halogen lights of town and was actually glad of the two glasses of wine I had drank earlier. To do that drive daily? Not on your life.

Sadly the early morning came too soon and we had to be up at 6 so that I could get to the airport. Both of us not being morning people the first half hour in the dark was silent. Both thinking our own thoughts but it seemed to have gone well. Even in such a short time, we seemed to have developed a comfortable bond so I felt sure we would be seeing each other again. I didn't know what the attraction was for me with Dom, but there was something there that drew me even though he wasn't the most tactile guy. I knew a large part was a moving on process after John, a need to feel free of that relationship as it had meant so much to me. I wasn't even sure I could deal with another relationship so a man showing me attention but also contrary and feisty seemed a good option. I certainly wasn't in it for a full on love story so his detachment was an attraction in itself. Saying that, if it had developed further, it would have been the icing on the cake to have gotten my own house and the man both in a place that I love.

On the plane journey home, I was thinking about the last few days. As I had stayed with Dom, it had been a good opportunity to live the life. I had met local English people who were living the dream and even though times were tough, they all would do the same again. I already felt like I fitted in as I somehow knew I would, but my brain was telling me to do more visits before jumping in at the deep end. With Christmas already booked in Malta I was not going to get back till the end of January. I'd done a deal with myself that I would go over on a regular basis. Dreams don't happen on their own, they have to be chased and nurtured. It was time I did something for myself after years of putting other people first.

January

It had been six weeks since my last visit and we'd had Christmas in between. I'd had a lovely break in Malta with minimal contact with Dom as there was no wifi in the hotel until I had a message asking me to call him urgently. He had no electric: he'd been cut off for an unpaid debt by a previous lodger whilst he was in the UK, could I help out?

All the time I was away, I tried not to think about Lanjarón but it was constantly in my thoughts. When I got home I intensified my search but I could still only find the one in Lanjarón that was within my price bracket. I reviewed all the plans I had made over the last 18 months or so and was sure I could do this. With the way the economy was going it was a buyer's market and what good were any savings doing in the bank? I knew where I wanted to be I now just had to make it happen. It was time for my next visit.

Flight time came and I felt like I was home before I even started the drive from the airport. Yes it is nearly a two hour drive but it was beautiful all the way whether early morning or late at night. The mountains guide you along with the lights from the towns as you drive along the motorway that runs parallel to the coast and then, once you get to Motril, you turn left and start the last half hour up to Lanjarón. It never fails to amaze me in its beauty: every seasonal change seems to spotlight on another piece of landscape that looked amazing.

Dom greeted me and was speechless at the gift of teabags. Yes teabags. You would not believe how happy a packet of decent English teabags makes people. I had sent some over after my first visit but they hadn't arrived until just before I arrived on this trip. They had gone to Grenada in the Caribbean not Granada as I didn't put Spain on the envelope; lovely postage marks though! There are a number of things that you have to learn to live without but teabags are the one thing that everyone asks for when relatives are visiting. Then there is milk, or UHT milk, the only thing sold locally which I find revolting so if you are doing the run up in daylight hours a stop in Salobreña at the Lidl is a must for fresh milk. I was beginning to feel very fortunate, the locals had taken me in immediately and treated me as one of their own and I was grateful for that; it felt like I'd never been away. Friendships were being forged on social media so I could keep up with events. But what do you do when you have no work here: when the romance has worn off and it's down to the nitty gritty? A week of being in town and believe it or not, that can open your eyes a lot.

As it's out of tourist season, there are only locals around so Lanjarón is sleepy. But the sun is out, so you go to the bar with the sunny patio for a coffee and then a beer, then another and another. Friends will pass on their way to the mini market and sometimes stop to chat. More beer consumed and before you know it, the day is gone. It's lovely that you are fed a light diet of tapas and it's also a great way to meet more of the people that live in the area and understand their way of life. Everyone has a story to tell-not always theirs though. I'd yet to discover the negatives of being in a small town and that gossip spreads like wildfire. The jungle drums are always beating. Domestic arguments, who is dating who, business deals, all manner of 'news' is spread around over a beer and not all of it is the truth. Sitting around is ok in holiday mode and for the odd day and I've had some good times sitting chewing the cud with some fantastic people but I do feel like I'm wasting my time doing nothing and pickling my liver in the process. I certainly couldn't do this if I lived here. Although beer is cheap, the money to pay for it is hard earned and would be limited once I was here.

Something needed to be done, I needed to escape the barfly culture and see more of Andalucía; so to make the most of my little hire car I suggested we drive to the white villages. Off through Órgiva and a sharp left and we were soon twisting and climbing quite quickly; my first time driving on the high mountain roads. The temperature was soon dropping, we drove through Pampaneira and on to Bubion where we stopped to walk the streets and admire the view. The air took my breath away as I got out of the car; there was a sharpness to it that was freezing the inside of my nostrils. But the view down the valley and across to the sea was amazing. The locals were going about their business at their own steady pace, used to the altitude and the chill factor; we were not, it was about 20' colder up there than it was back in town. Off we went again up to Capileira, 1400m high. It was bright and crisp with amazing views up to Mulhacén, which stood proud with a capping of snow. I stood and marveled, making my mind up there and then that I would do the two day climb at some point. Mulhacén is the highest mountain in mainland Spain and is part of the Sierra Nevada range with an elevation of 3478.6m and it would be on my doorstep.

Meandering the streets we passed shops selling home-made trinkets and the specialty of the area, Andalucía 'Jarapas' rugs. I wanted one in every size and every colour Imaginable; thick hand woven rugs that you knew would insulate you from the cold in the depth of winter. Bright oranges with stripes of golden yellow, blues marbled with purples and heavy rich reds woven with golds and greens. Bright and brilliant like the country and the people. We stopped at a bar where the sun was shining on the terrace and enjoyed a café con leche, wrapped in our winter coats enjoying the sun beating down on our faces and looking at the snow cover mountain. Could life really get any more perfect?

The drive down revealed the ploughed terraces with perfect rows of olive and almond trees lined this way and that, following the curve of the hills: terraced to catch the sun and the best of the water when the *acequias* [water channels] were open for watering. A farmer tending his trees seemed to be in total isolation from any other life form; where did he live, how far had he come, and how? Every time a new sight was open to me, more questions remained unanswered. Bubion and the white villages in reality were not many miles from Lanjarón but it took an age to traverse the mountain roads when you are not used to them. Hopefully I wouldn't remain a novice at it! We dropped back into town and headed down to the bar. But it wasn't the Ambienza, we went to Bar Health. Were we going on a health kick with smoothies? I was puzzled. But on entering the Bar it was obvious it was a regular bar. Then it clicked. This was the bar we had staggered into when I first met Dom. I was warmly greeted by Fernando who worked the bar whilst his partner Karen cooked the food in the tiny kitchen. I was impressed with Fernando's humour, he certainly knew how to crack a joke. A couple of Spanish guys sat at the head of the bar. One old and wizened in a flat cap nursing a brandy and a well dressed guy in a suit, "who's he?" I tilted my head towards the guy.

Dom looked over, "Diego, owns a few places around here but you rarely see him." At the other end of the bar there was a small group having an animated conversation, "Have you met Sarah?" asked Dom.

"No, why?" all I could see were backs of people wrapped in warm fleeces.

"Oh. She runs the local stables up over the

other side of the campo. Come on I'll introduce you."

Collecting our drinks I lagged behind Dom as we went over to them. A gap opened and Dom introduced me. "I'd like to introduce you to Charlotte, a friend from England who'd like to live here." He then went around the group, "this is Sarah from Caballo Blanco, Tracy, Ruth and Andy." Pleasant conversation ensued then I had an idea.

"Dom, do you ever go riding?"

"Never done, it. Why?"

"Do you fancy it?"

"Yeah, why not."

I leant over to Sarah, "Any chance of a ride for us this week?"

And so, the next morning we were off up yet another track in my little hire car. When this one ran out of tarmac, the clay soil was deeply rutted from the rain. Thankfully I had let Dom drive and was very glad we didn't bottom out at any point. Punto's seemed to have good ground clearance! It had been ten years since I had last ridden. I was just a holiday rider but always felt at ease on horseback but this would be a new experience as we would hopefully go up towards the snow line. Given helmets we were helped onto our horses. I had a beautiful Andalucían called Cielo. He seemed completely bored by the whole thing as Sarah adjusted my stirrups. We were introduced to Tracy our guide and off we went. Sadly not going upwards. There was a huge black cloud coming over and we did not want to end up caught in a snow fall. We were already at 1200m at the ranch and going up would have taken us to 2000m so too risky. It was another of the things that was talked about incessantly here, the weather. Not for the same reason we talk about it in the UK as most times the weather really doesn't affect us other than taking an umbrella or not, but here it mattered. Most people's lives depended on what the weather was doing from the ranch to mountain guides to olive workers and I was getting used to the difference in discussions. We trekked down, mostly on the track we had driven up, which gave me chance to see an almost aerial view of Lanjarón, it looked magnificent. I could see wiggly lines of houses, the church with its clock tower and a massive spruce tree in front of it. Plus, in the distance, a handful of wind turbines rotating as they stood like lollipops on the undulating landscape. Conversation wasn't really necessary, there was too much to take in. We cut off right and went across some open ground and a goat farm. Hundreds of brown goats in a pen herded around by three massive Spanish Mastiff dogs. Along we went again, seeing shepherds and farmer working on the land. We seemed to tiptoe along a narrow track, how the horses kept their footing I do not know before we turned to head back upwards. Ahead of us was a narrow grass track next to a waterfall. With one hand on grasping the reigns and the other taking a firm grasp of mane we were out of our seat leaning forward as we galloped up the side of the water: it was exhilarating. The air was getting colder and snow was starting to fall as we got off our mounts and drove back down to town with a rosy glow. "Well for someone who couldn't ride, you did a fair old job Dom."

He smiled, "It was great, and I really enjoyed it, thanks for the treat."

"I have to say, it's the first time I've seen anyone roll a cigarette whilst riding a horse though!"

All too soon the week was over. I felt dissatisfied that I had achieved little in my time there but in reality I had managed a lot. I had lived like a local and I was making some very solid friendships with a wide range of people. I knew open and closing times of local shops, where to buy fresh rabbit and order hot chicken on a Sunday: such a delight to go and fetch a roasted chicken with vegetables and chips without any washing up. Which mini market to use before all others and I managed to get the locals' rate in the panaderia. Which bars served the best tapas and who closed when. I could recognise the sound of a scops owl and became familiar with booted eagles. It seems most people get hooked on the local birdlife at some point, especially if you like to take photographs and I knew I would too.

* * *

Leaving Dom asleep, at six the next morning I got up to head down the mountain. Goodbyes were easier that way. The town was quiet as I wiped the dew off my windscreen and slowly headed out of the car park, a lump in my throat; I did not want to leave. The nine kilometers down the mountain were getting harder to bear already. The sun was rising behind me as I left, bringing out the most amazing colours in the rock faces; ochre's, reds, purples streamed across in front and to the right of me; a colourful end to my week.

*

Why didn't I look at that house?

The closest I can think to a reason is that I did not want my dreams to be shattered; if I didn't look then it would stay a pleasant dream to fantasize about. If it turned out to be a money pit and not what it seemed on paper I would have to start again as I did not have the capital for a reform. At some point I had to make a decision about my future. I was not getting any younger and with the stress of work, long hours and other recent issues, my health was suffering. I had worked for myself doing the same thing for 30 years and although things were doing ok, I would never be rich. Added into this that standing and doing screen printing was playing havoc with rheumatism in my hip and knee joints leaving me with swollen joints and in pain for days on end and at the same time I was having breast lumps checked out which thankfully turned out to be nothing more than cysts. I had too many stresses going on and needed to change my working life to suit my health better: work was not my passion any more, but making a better life for myself was.

On Skype a few nights later I mentioned it to Dom. "Why hadn't you mentioned it, why hadn't you looked at it?"

"I don't know" I muttered, "maybe... maybe it's not right and I feel so much like I want it to be." I was flustered. "I just don't know."

"Well you can't make a decision blind can you?"

"Well, no."

"So book an appointment and I will go and look at it for you."

With support like that, I rationed that it was the right thing to do. After all, in his previous life in the UK, Dom had been a builder, so along with reforming his own house in Lanjarón, he knew what he was looking for. I emailed the agent whose details I had taped to my office wall along with the basic particulars. It was a quaint little place but very outdated. From the pictures it looked certainly liveable and clean and tidy. All rooms came either complete with beds and wardrobes or settee, TV, sideboard etc. Yes the kitchen and the bathroom looked a bit dated but as long as it was habitable I didn't really care too much about that; it could all be changed in time. Garish tiles in both the kitchen and the bathroom put to one-side; it seemed like a suitable place for me to call home at some point in the near future. The bonus being the mule shed below that was a space I was hoping to turn into a workspace as many of the Spanish do. It was laughably advertised as a studio flat conversion but I suggest any standard sized person would struggle, but for a workspace it was perfect and as it was isolated from my main house that had a great advantage too plus it had its own little courtyard at the back and electricity. It ticked all the right boxes and it was giving me a good feeling. It could be mine if I could get it in on budget.

I checked my emails constantly and within two hours I had a call on my mobile, 'could I make tomorrow?' Well I couldn't but my friend could.

I called Dom, "you can go tomorrow at 3pm, is that ok?"

"Sure. Leave it to me and I'll let you know what I think." My heart was in my mouth and my stomach flipping somersaults. I was actually putting into practice the dream I had held for a number of years. But I was scared stiff. All those hopes and dreams were finally, possibly becoming a reality. Within a short space of time I may have a new reason to live, a new lease of life. I pulled down the details off my office wall and looked at this little place that could be my home; I felt it in my bones. I emailed Julie, “Dom is going to look at that little house for me.”

‘”The one with the mule shed? Didn't you think to go look at that when you were last over?”

“No...”

“Silly sod, good luck and let me know what he thinks. Don't buy it on his say so though, you've got to go and look at it yourself.” she said cautiously

“Yes I know, but if it's a mess and not worth looking at, this will save me the heartache.”

I couldn't concentrate on work and fortunately there was nothing urgent to be done.

The next day he went to view it. “You’d better call me.”

My heart was in my mouth as I dialed his number.

“Hi, it's pissing down here, how's it with you?”

“DOM! Whatever: what's the house like?”

“Well” there was a pause and I waited impatiently. “I want to word this so that it comes across unbiased.” I'm drumming my fingers on the desk but knew the more impatient I became the more he would tease the whole thing out.

“Well, as I said it’s raining and this was good as I got to see that it doesn’t leak. It's..” again a pause, "it's you; it's quirky." I think that was a compliment.

"It's basically sound and liveable in, although you'd have to do something with those tiles." I could hear him draw on a cigarette. "Yeah, it's good. You need to come over and see it, but I'd put in an offer to account for the work that needs doing and put it subject to sight." I was now getting as excited as Dom was; my dreams were moving forward at last.

The heart had settled, so had the stomach. DIY wasn't a problem really. After a chat later on Skype, we discussed what needed doing and I drew up a proposal email to tender to the agent detailing renewal of the bathroom and a canopy that needed doing over the patio door to link the bedroom and lounge, and two days later I put in an offer at well under the asking price. I spent the following hours once more doing battle with my own conscience about whether this was the right thing to do or not.

Within three hours it was accepted!
I had just verbally bought myself a little bit of paradise; now I needed to pay for it!

Booking a flight over was far more stressful than necessary. School half term holidays were coming up and the flights had jumped in price. I was chasing my dream on a restricted budget so could not afford to squander money on expensive flights.

Leaving work again so soon would I thought be professional suicide, only a couple of my clients were privy to what I had planned so I couldn't get over until after the school holidays, if it was meant to be then it would be ok and I reasoned to myself that it had been on the market for a while so I was hardly going to be pipped at the post. I emailed the agent and told her the problem; would it be a deal breaker? She said not and I booked another long weekend break for the viewing. Thank heavens for Dom as if I'd had had to pay hotels too then it would have been costing me much more, but then, the shopping in Lidl was mounting up too!

Prior to returning to Lanjarón to view the house myself, I had been running around to get finances in place. I'd decided on a small extension to my UK mortgage plus savings leaving me with enough capital to do any emergency repairs and the odd undiscovered one. But trying to get the bank to give the final agreement on paper was proving nerve jangling. It was such a small sum that they had hardly given it a glance but I'm not one to assume under any circumstance. I was calling my contact daily and he must have been crawling under his desk to hide! Eventually, on the afternoon before I was due to fly, I had written approval that I was good to go.

The bliss of getting off that cheap flight mid morning was fantastic. My skin tingled as it sucked up the heat from the sun. I just couldn't stop smiling. I picked up the rental car and hit the road, a short stop

before going up the A44 for fresh supplies and then the mountain road to Lanjarón. This is nine kilometers of climbing twisting road but it's well asphalted and is a pleasant drive as long as you relax and remember that some bends are tighter than others! The views are fantastic as ever, even if it is a little scary when the Lanjarón water articulated lorry comes thundering towards you when you are in a tiny car!
I came into town past the Balnearo and down the deserted street, turned right at the island over a few speed bumps on the town bypass and turned left into the municipal car park. I pulled up next to Dom's car, got out and stretched my legs. Before I knew it, Dom's puppy was running across the car park towards me, jumping all over me, her tail wagging in excitement; what a lovely greeting [lets gloss over the white paw marks all over my black trousers!] Of course, once my backpack was dumped, the fridge filled and the animals fed, it was off down to the Ambienza. The viewing of the house was the next day and I was tired but as ever, we were rooted to the seats outside the bar, getting steadily sozzled in the sun. My logic had been cast away with any reason as it was all a big adventure and I was doing what I wanted to do for the first time in my life.

I couldn't sleep. I was analysing whether I was doing the right thing and I was coming back to the same answer every time. Yes.
With bleary eyes, morning broke and we enjoyed the sunrise with the customary cup of tea.

Mi Casa

It was viewing day. I couldn't eat and had barely slept.

We turned into the side street and walked down the hill, twisting left then right until the house came into view. After seeing the place on paper for months I was actually going inside. I already knew that bar it being a wreck, it was mine; I felt it had my name on it for some reason.

The agent and vendor were waiting for me, basking in the winter sunshine. I had Dom with me who assured me he would highlight any problems as we went around. With no further ado, we were in through the gates and up a tiny set of steps to the front door. I don't know what I was expecting but I immediately felt at home and began to grin. A spacious hallway that was currently set as a dining room with a door off to a cool dark master bedroom; light was filtering down from a roof light above the stairs and drawing us up into the main living space.

A sufficient kitchen in vintage Spanish style with the most garish style tiles as a splash back. The bathroom knocked us for six, more of the garish brown and cream tiles on every wall! What were they thinking when they put these in with the part avocado part champagne bathroom suite? It was certainly clean and usable but not one for keeping that was for sure, and the bath...oh my... it was about a metre long maximum! On the other side of the kitchen was another bedroom which seemed odd at the time except for the fact you could slide open the door and see the most amazing views whilst having your morning cuppa or sit in bed at night watching the stars. But where was the lounge? I was confused.

We went out through the sliding door, down some steps and onto a small functional terrace; a set of steep steps led up to the roof terrace but there was also a door. On opening this, more stairs down and we were in a beautiful little room with a traditional fireplace and again with a stunning view; this was the lounge. Exposed beams treated and painted were above, and there was a cosy two seater sofa. It was easy to imagine nights sitting there watching TV with a glass of wine after a day out in the sun or simply sitting on the steps gazing out of the window and watching the clouds roll over the Sierra de Lujar. Back up the wonky and badly tiled steps and onto the terrace it was time to go up to the roof terrace. A precarious climb up what can only be described as a set of ships ladders led onto a spacious terrace and what a view. Apart from the corner of a neighbouring building knocking out a few degrees, there was a 360' view of the surrounding mountains that sheltered Lanjarón. The brain was devoid of all function other than to help me keep up the inane smile. All around were views of the Sierra Nevada, snowy peaks meeting a clear blue sky. I did not want to leave this terrace, it was magnificent. Giddy with happiness it was an interesting descent down the steps and not for the faint hearted. It all felt so right. Despite the work I could see needed doing, and not even thinking about the possibility of what was to come, I felt at home.

Trying to temper the grin factor, we went down to the mule shed, the 'studio apartment' room which was semi derelict but would be a worthy workspace. The walls were bare terracotta brick with some white paint slapped on them, no plastering or render and cement poked out from in between each brick. On the low ceiling, original chestnut beams ran left to right, front to back and Dom assured me that they had been treated and were ok. I poked at them and little bits of wood and paint flaked off, he knew best. The door at the back led into a tiny courtyard the width of the building and about 2meters deep. This really did have the makings of a good studio. I'd made my mind up before I walked in the door. This was my piece of heaven and I wanted it. Shaking hands with the vendor and agent, we left and went to the bar to discuss the offer that I had already made. Those tiles had made an impact on me but tiling was an easy job. The water heater seemed broken so that would have to be replaced. The mule shed conversion could wait. Although it was a space that excited me, it was also the least important. No point in doing anything in there until it was necessary. The key could stay firmly turned on that. "Dom, should I just offer a few thousand less than I'd previously offered just like we would do in the UK?" I looked at him as he was scribbling on bits of paper.

"Eh?"

"Should I drop the offer a bit?"

"Don't be daft. What justification have you got to do that?"

I shrugged. "None, other than its normal practise."

He put his pen down and looked over his glasses. "No. It's not done the same here. Are you happy with the offer you've already made?"

"Well yes."

"And why?"

"I snorted. " Because I love the place and it suits me. Its right in town but it's quiet. It's got good views and it's big enough for me to do all I want to do."

"Then?"

I grinned.

"Just one thing." He looked me in the eye, "Don't buy it if it has anything to do with me and you. That would be the wrong thing to do." He picked his pen back up and carried on scribbling.

I wasn't quite sure how to put this but simple is best, "No, that would be bloody daft. It's far enough away from yours for us not to be overlooking each other so no, that would be silly. Apart from the fact that your place is big enough to house a big family so I wouldn't need to buy if I had ideas of marital bliss." I said this with a hint of humour but the eyebrow shot up. Nothing more was said on the matter. Whether Dom and I worked out long term or not, a rental property was a good source of income if we were together. I mentally stepped back and thought it through again. I got my notepad out and checked the figures then picked up the phone. When I put the phone down I was shaking and my stomach was churning.

What had I done? This was probably the biggest decision I had ever made in my life and I was doing it with no back up from anyone. It was strange not having my parents there to discuss things with or to lean on. My brothers, well, we aren't that close so no real support there sadly. My sounding boards were my friends and thankfully they knew me well enough to be honest in their opinions for me. But the final choice was mine and I'd just made it. This decision was to change my whole life.

Within the afternoon my final firm offer was accepted.

After an evening of celebration drinking, I was expecting to wake up in the morning with a major hangover and the feeling that I had made a huge mistake, but I was still feeling buoyant and eager to get things moving, the hangover was another matter. There is not the bureaucracy and red tape that we have in England so things are processed a lot quicker. With recommendations from Dom and a few others, I called the conveyances and set the wheels in motion. I now needed to rush through obtaining my NIE number too as I could not purchase anything without it; nor could I open a bank account! I needed to sober up fast as I had a lot to get done in a short time.

An NIE number is an identity number that you use when purchasing anything and is also your identity and should be carried at all times. To obtain this I had to fill in a few forms and accompanied with a passport photo, visit the police station in Motril. But as with any legislation in Spain, this changes with regularity. The most recent change had been that it was now forbidden for anyone else to collect your NIE number other than yourself which was a bit of a pain when you are a non resident. Having to drive past Motril late at night after arriving on a flight into Malaga then having to drive back down again does feel like a wasted journey. But, the system is the system so having gone through a metal detector and being given a number we entered a room to wait, not sure where to sit we did a scatter tactic and kept our eyes peeled for people leaving. Number called and we approached a desk, I answered a couple of questions, the sheets of paper were stamped with a great heavy flourish and I was given a copy with my number on. Simple? No, not really. I had the number but not the official bit of paper. The number would get the wheels in motion but I needed the official copy which would take a week or two. That would have to be collected on the next visit then!

Whilst down in Motril I decided I may as well get a phone card so complete with my NIE and passport it was into Alcampo and again, identity needed to purchase a phone sim card; yes honestly. I really did start to feel like Big Brother was now watching me but no one seems to moan about it like in the UK when identity cards are mentioned. The philosophy being that if you have nothing to hide, you have nothing to worry about. More paperwork to fill in and half an hour later, I was presented with my forms and a sim card by a smiling young lady. Stashing everything safely, Dom decided it was time for a hair of the dog and a coffee before heading back up to town. With the amount I'd consumed in celebration the night before, a coffee was the only thing I wanted for the next 24 hours! Starting to feel less delicate there was one more stop back up in town before the 2pm closing and siesta time, the conveyance agency: time to introduce myself in person.

We drove back up and into Órgiva. I hadn't been here since I had done my research visit so it was nice to stop. There was no way I was going to attempt to purchase a house without legal representation and this company had been recommended to me by a number of people. In England we would call them conveyancers but in Spain they also provide lawyers, surveyors, translation services amongst other things. Anything that, as a foreigner, you need to do right, they helped you with. So it was with them I had booked an appointment with to help me buy a house after chatting to them via email over the previous weeks. Crossing the square we climbed the stairs to

Alpujarra Conect to leave a deposit and let them get on with their job. It was nice to meet Inma and Lisa at last. Halfway through doing paperwork, Dom's phone rang, he was chatting in Spanish and I heard my name mentioned; now that was confusing. I couldn't understand anything that was being said and was completely confused. A rather thunderous look came across his face. My heart sank; what had happened? Had I lost the sale? Had there been an accident? But why would anyone who wanted me call Dom? He ended the call and glared at me; "where's your passport?"

"In the side pocket of my trousers....oh...oh." I ferreted in my handbag, then my folder, then again in the pocket I was sure it was in; no passport.

"You haven't got it because you left it at the phone stand in the Alcampo store." I wilted under his gaze biting my lip; a night of celebrating had left us both somewhat thick headed but not one to argue about it, I took it on the chin as I could already feel Lisa squirming as Dom's condescending tone. Thankfully I saved my own bacon as I always copy everything so was able to leave a colour copy of my passport with Lisa but boy did I feel stupid.

Dom settled himself in the sun with a *tubo* whilst Lisa and I headed across to the bank where Lisa managed to offer this photocopy as identification when we went over to open my bank account on the proviso I popped in the next day to show them the real thing. Last time I opened a bank account I did it online and within minutes I had it there on the screen in front of me. Not in Spain; and it wasn't going to be free either. The beauty of using a conveyancer/solicitor is having one that is fluent in Spanish and English, even if you speak some Spanish, it smoothes things through much quicker. Alpujarra Conect came recommended by a few people so that was an easy choice to make and so far so good even thought the bank manageress spoke good English. Data inputted, paper spewed from the printer; 4 sheets. 2 sheets signed and 2 pieces for me, 3 for the bank. More typing, more cancelling out, a sign, a few words with Lisa that I couldn't make head nor tail of, more paper out of the printer, more signatures. I helped myself to a bank embellished mint and wondered why I was there at all! 2 more signatures and I was done. I had my Spanish bank account. I had no card [cheque books don't occur in Spain] but I had sheaves of paper, a monthly bank payment as I was a non resident and a dental plan. Yes a dental plan; it was part of the deal...evidently (!). Leaving the friendly staff to do their job, we went back to the office, copied some papers [mislaying my passport did not make the best first impression] and I went off to round up Dom to drive back down to Motril. We made it with 5 minutes to spare before closing and Dom couldn't resist emphasising my mistake.

By the time we had got back to Lanjarón, it was time to enjoy the sun so over yet another beer and coffee I began redesigning the layout and forward planning. Both of us scribbling layouts and mentally working out measurements. The other strange thing with Spanish house purchases, and there are many, is that the house comes complete with a certain amount of furniture. Beds, sofas, cupboards, wardrobes are all commonly left in situ but I wouldn't know what until I got the keys. This benefitted me greatly as it meant I could save money and didn't need to solve the conundrum of getting big furniture up awkward stairs in 40' heat and beg my new friends for favours of help. As the Ikea store was 2 hours drive away you can't just nip out for an hour. But we weren't talking about the furniture, we were busy discussing the wonderful view from my top terrace and how I must have one of the best views in town. Ah Dom, if anyone could sell sand to the Arabs, I think it would be him; but as I'd fallen in love with Lanjarón before I met Dom, I didn't need convincing that my heart was here, whatever was to happen in the future. From the Ambienza we were across to the Bar Health, this was already a familiar pattern. Breaking the good news as we went along that I had bought the house and would soon be a regular visitor and in the fullness of time, a resident.

I remained in a daze for the rest of the week, not quite believing that all the years planning in my head, scouring the internet and dreaming had come off. My five year plan was about to be completed in three. For once I was praising myself for the research and effort I had put into the whole thing and so pleased it was a house where I wanted to be. The buying pattern was the same as any house I had purchased in England; do the research, have a wish list and the rest is gut instinct. But it was frustrating that there was nothing I could do until the sale had gone through other than work out what modernisation to do first.

The kitchen definitely needed replacing but at the moment it was serviceable. The bathroom was an eyesore so I decided that would be first on the list. But I kept getting distracted by the stunning view, it was amazing, it was really all I could talk about, think about, dream about.

A new chapter in my life was just beginning and I couldn't wait to get started on it.

It felt all too soon that I was to leave again, but not for long.

It's in the details

Back in the UK I was routinely spending the Monday back at work fielding phone calls from clients as to how I had got on and what the progress was. The joy of being self employed is that you do get the chance to build up a good rapport with your clients and they become friends as well as professional colleagues. A number were eager to hear what I had got up to in the previous week, had everything gone ok and where were the latest photographs. It was nice to have the support of my friends and work colleagues and everyone was behind me if not a little envious of my capability to branch out as I approached 50. On a number of occasions I was referred to as brave, but why? We all live our lives differently and the best we can. I was planning at the outside for my retirement but optimistically I was hoping to move sooner than that. I didn't have a big house in the UK or a private pension scheme so I had to try to cover my bases now whilst I could. A nice juicy lottery win would always be the dream so that it would make life easier but in all honesty, if that win ever came, I would still work and I'd still want to be in Lanjarón; what the extra money would do is ease the everyday stresses, but would probably bring more of its own: but I'd like to try it!

The conveyance system in Spain is far quicker than in the UK. One of the big reasons why is that you don't have a survey done. Searches yes but structural surveys are rare. It is usually deemed that a builder can tell you all you need to know. I'm not sure on the procedure if you are having a mortgage but as I was a cash buyer, it should move along quite swiftly, in fact a matter of weeks. I had left Lisa to deal with everything and Dom and I had headed back to the UK. As work was so scarce, he was going to do some work for me. It was very strange to now be in my environment. Days were back into a monotonous routine and it was strange to either have someone in work with me or to have someone at home when I returned: unless he had gone to the local pub of course! Dom came along to meet some friends at my Poetry Pub night and we also met up with an old school friend and her husband for a Sunday drink. After a week of Dom being quite surly I was relieved to have him back as his charming intelligent self. It was a lovely afternoon. But the UK life really didn't suit Dom and I wasn't finding it easy to find work for him to do.

I was in daily contact with Spain as they tried to sort out the sale. There was an issue that they had to work hard on, the vendor had a mortgage on the property but instead of it being with a bank in either Órgiva or Lanjarón, it was down on the coast in Salobreña. Phone calls were made daily as we needed to know what the bank was deeming as a settlement figure and that changed daily. All the other legal searches were complete and we pencilled in a date for the notary. I had got a great deal from a money transfer agency and my Sterling was in the process of being transferred across to my bank in Órgiva in euros. I was most surprised that my own personal bank in the UK would not match their rate but they would not budge from the advertised daily exchange rate.

The notary was in Órgiva on Mondays and Thursdays and Lisa had booked a Thursday. I wasn't particularly keen on this. If anything was wrong and the papers needed to be amended then we would have no time to do it as I tended to be there from one weekend to the next rather than mid week to mid week. We agreed to go for the following week which gave Lisa more time to ensure all the paperwork was in order so I booked our return flights and added extra hold luggage as Dom had got some stuff he wanted to take back with him. Three weeks from start to finish; when have you ever heard of that in the UK?

So, after those mad weeks back at work, we were off again. I was wondering when I was going to get pulled aside at the airport. I had become an erratic but regular flier over the last four months; less than a month ago I had gone out with hold luggage, two days later I was back with hand luggage and a companion, three weeks later I was going back with a companion and hold luggage again. My creative mind was in overdrive; what did they think I was doing? Smuggling t-bags across the border to expats? No matter, it hadn't happened and I was perfectly legitimate, just taking over all those little essentials I was going to need that I had either double of or too many.

As ever, we landed, drove along the coast and up the A44, dropped the baggage and headed for the bar to catch up, Dom was relieved to be back as he was getting twitchy in the UK, too cold and too dark. I can't say I blame him to be honest as I felt the same. Before the house purchase, we had St Patrick's Day to enjoy; another fiesta to add to the many that are happening throughout the Spanish year, but why not? Bar Health as ever was the venue being the only bar in town to sell Guinness and the fact that there was Irish in the genes. Shamrocks festooned the place and everyone, including little old Spanish men, were wearing St Patrick's Day hats. It was a celebration for people to come down from their mountain hideaway and mingle: people I had never met before or since and for the life of me I can't remember their names. We all mingled, catching up on news, drinking beer and each running up a bar tab that would probably be paid tomorrow in most cases rather than tonight! A little live music supplied by local guys set the evening off and a great celebration of singing, dancing and chatting was had by all. This was how to celebrate and it was a great evening to take my mind off the house purchase.

I was still checking my feelings on the whole thing and questioning whether I was doing the right thing in buying the house. This was a big step I was taking and taking alone with no fall back at all should anything go wrong. I was always factoring in questions like, what is the health service like in Spain if I were to fall ill, what would happen to me if my business took a turn for the worse at home, what if there was something wrong with the house and I couldn't afford to repair it. But we can't live life on 'what if's.' I'd done as much homework as I could and was doing it as safely as I could. I'd done research, I was buying legally and I felt good about the whole thing.

Gone were the days of under the table deals on houses, this was going to be all legal and up front, including house insurance! It was a fraught few days prior to the arranged date with the Notary to complete the sale. Pressure was being put on the vendor's bank to supply us with a settlement figure as the majority of what I was paying out was to pay off her mortgage. But they were incredibly slow. They refused to freeze at the rate they had given her a few months ago and had insisted on calculating a daily rate increase. Whilst all this was going on, I refused to walk past the house at all. I didn't want to tempt fate in any way. Until I had the keys I refused to believe it was mine so we had the rest of the weekend to relax and enjoy the weather. Not that curling up in front of a wood fire at Dom's was doing me any favours; I don't think its flue was removing the smoke so we were, if the truth be known, probably sitting in a whole cloud of carbon monoxide, plus I was coughing incessantly. Never mind, some heat was better than no heat. The days were sunny, bright and warm but the nights were cold!

Exchange day arrived and I was up bright and early to get to Órgiva on time, Dom on the other hand was in relaxed mode and refused to believe that being on time was necessary so I had to drag him out the door. It was lovely to sit in the square having coffee but my nerves were jangling the way they did on house purchase day. Thirty minutes later I went across the square in the morning sunshine, rang the bell, trotted back up the cool marble staircase to meet with Lisa and get the proceedings started with a visit to the bank.

This took two attempts as the bank manager was obviously as relaxed as Dom and was late for our appointment! Dom meanwhile stayed sitting in the sun whilst I got on with things.

In the bank manager's office the conversation started off in English, and then went to Spanish, then back to English. Lots of typing on the computer, but even though I could see figures on the screen I had no idea what they were.

Lots of sighs and frowns, then fingers racing across a calculator again, what was going on? The monitor was swivelled and figures being pointed at. I had a feeling that bad news was coming but was unsure what it was going to be. Were the calculations wrong and I couldn't have the house? Had I not done something I should have? [after the passport fiasco I was vigilant but...]. My stomach was churning in fear of the unknown. More furious typing and I began to zone out and wondered if I should have stayed at the cafe with Dom. There was a sad look on the manager's face and I was getting more nervous. She turned her back and picked up the phone.

Lisa had turned to me "It seems there's a problem with paying the money across to the bank of the vendor, they still haven't agreed a settlement figure so we have to wait."

I sighed. It was frustrating just having to sit there whilst someone else does everything for you and you can't understand the majority of it. It's not a role I was used to playing.

The phone went down and the news given that the bank wanted the extra daily rate to be added on and they had at least given a final figure of settlement; unfortunately this did not agree with the figure that Lisa and the manager had arrived at! Three of us then began independently scribbling figures and making the calculations to try to work out where the bank had got their figures from; eventually getting there bar a few cents. That agreed, we sat back whilst the manager typed up then printed off all the paperwork we needed for me to sign to allow the money transfer to take place. Initially the bank were insisting that I personally take the paperwork down to Salobreña and hand deliver it, get it signed for, then go back down to make the payment in person.

Thankfully I didn't have to do this. The typing was fast and furious; typing, deleting, browsing and then starting over again. I was getting a little deflated by now. It was a hindrance not to understand the language fully and
wondered what this new hold up was. The manager spoke. Lisa coughed and nodded then turned to me. "It appears there is a charge for transferring the money from bank to bank."

"Yes that's fine," thinking it would be €50 or so for the admin.

"It's €360." If this was a cartoon, my eyes would have come out on stalks I'm sure. "How much? €360? How do they justify that?"

Lisa shrugged apologetically. Fortunately I had transferred extra funds across for 'emergencies'. Seems like this was one of those: non-negotiable. I shrugged and accepted it, what else could I do; pay in cash and then that would not be traceable and I could get into all sorts of problems. I had no choice other than a cheque in a cheque book I didn't have because they don't have them in Spain and taking it all the way to Salobreña then awaiting its clearance before going to the notary and getting the house. But a bank cheque would have cost a staggering €800! Catch 22.

More paperwork was produced [everything in Spain comes with paperwork], a copy for me, Lisa and the bank.

Signature.

Signature

Signature.

The manager pressed the return key and the money flew out of my account and down to the bank in Salobreña.

What next?

Lisa got up to leave. Now I was puzzled and was rooted to my chair. "We've got to wait now for the phone call from the bank in Salobreña to say that they have received and banked the money."

With a shrug, Lisa went back across the square and I went for yet another cup of coffee. The excitement had well and truly worn off now but Dom was happily sitting in the sun but this time nursing a *tubo*, chilled as ever.

Eventually my phone rang and I met up with Lisa again to go to the Notary and complete the process.

The Notary's Office was nothing very special at all. A long counter with people typing furiously one side and various Spanish people sitting the other, awaiting their turn to be seen. We were ushered into a side office on the right. A man behind the desk was surrounded by neat stacks of paper. To the left blank, to the right printed. All embossed and numbered. And a printer was hiding behind these stacks. Lisa handed over the paperwork and this guy began to type, type and type. It seems a lot of typing goes on in Spain! But they crack on with it at a furious pace. A woman who was working on a PC outside came in and passed him some details, he typed some more. All the while, the printer was churning out sheets of paper. It took me about ten minutes to realise what was happening. This was the *escritura*, the title deeds for the house, being typed up with all the details from myself and the vendor on it. He was following through the legal template and any information he didn't have to hand was being brought to him from the lady in the outer office who was working in tandem with him; it was very efficient. Questions asked, passports and NIE numbers checked. More typing. Then stapling and we were out of the office and off to the other end and another office along with the vendor and her agent, now this was it!

With us all seated the Notary began reading through the paper work, Lisa translating bits for me that I didn't catch and then, with the usual round of signatures the keys were handed to me. I had my house!

Thank you very much time to celebrate. Not quite.

I thanked Lisa and walked to where I could see Dom chatting with the vendor and her husband and father. Dom had consumed far too much beer to drive back to Lanjarón so my celebrations had to wait till I had driven back. A swift drink in the Ambienza before packing my few bits and pieces and turning the key in my new home.

I dragged my bags around in the afternoon heat whilst Dom went to bed, I wasn't impressed. I cleared his fridge to fill my fridge leaving just the dog food and with my fourth trip, I was in. Although only March I was sweating like it was mid-summer. First things first, I headed to the top terrace. The view was just fantastic and I wanted to drink in what little bit of it was now mine. Yes I had to share it with everyone else but it felt like mine. With the light drawing in and the chill, I set to giving the bedroom a quick clean up before I opened up the new bedding that dwarfed the Spanish bed; typical opposite of Swedish furniture! But I didn't care, I was in this lovely little place and it was mine. All I had to do now was enjoy it and improve it as time went on. The last three years plans were now a reality, I could plan what I wanted to do and hopefully transfer my business over when the bits and bobs were done and work from here. Smiling, I left 'home' to go for dinner and a proper celebration drink.

Tormenta

A little the worse for wear, I stumbled up my steps in the dark and eventually managed to get the key in the lock. In the excitement I had not found the switch for the porch light or left an internal one on for guidance. I had to do the drunken feel around for the lock and eventually guided the key in. Where was the light switch? I ran my hand along the wall and eventually illuminated the hall. Thankfully I could now see well enough to get up to the kitchen and bedroom. Shrugging off my coat, I slid open the door to see the view just one more time before I went to bed. The darkness of the facing ridge was crisp against the skyline, the stars lighting up the icy blue hue of the night sky, bad weather was predicted overnight.

I got into bed and turned off the light, not only enjoying the bliss of crisp sheets and duvet but being in a new home, listening for those sounds you only hear when the lights are off. It was silent. I was woken by a deafening noise and bright flashes bouncing off the wall. I lay frozen for a minute not realising where I was. A mighty boom and I was out of bed. I slid the door open slightly to see a flash of lightening light up the ridge of the Lujar. Hailstones were hammering down and my green terrace was a gravel pit of gobstoppers at least 1cm in diameter. I held my hand out to catch one and quickly pulled it back in as I was stung by the ferocity of them tumbling down. I looked up and as the roof appeared not to be leaking so the best place was back in bed.

The morning brought a less than bright sky but nevertheless, the storm had ceased and I was intact. The hailstones had dispersed and the terrace drying out. From the top terrace I could see that the storm had brought some fresh snow to the surrounding peaks of the Sierra and the Lujar, just a small highlight along the top of the ridges. The air was crisp and as far as I was concerned it was a beautiful day, a day to be spent cleaning and clearing out junk. I had inherited more than just furniture, the vendor had left the bathroom as if she had just popped down to the local store. Shampoos, cleaners, soaps, toothbrushes were left there. I thought this rather odd but as she hadn't lived there for a couple of years having got married and moved to the coast, I shrugged my shoulders and set too with rubber gloves and bin liners.

The bathroom was quite a dizzying sight; floral brown tiles were on every wall from floor to ceiling. Combine that with the standard Spanish terrazzo tiling and avocado and beige suite and it's all a bit much. All was functional but the bath was minuscule. I have yet to ask a Spaniard why they have such tiny baths; I don't see the point, it's neither bath or shower as the shower doesn't hook on the wall, you have to hold it: another question I have yet to ask and see the logic of.

It seemed obvious to me that the bedroom by the kitchen would be a perfect lounge; I wanted to enjoy the view as much as I could. As I only needed one bedroom, I decided to swap the lounge that had come complete with TV, video, DVD player and couch and chair with the upper bedroom. Sounds simple and it would be in most houses but not in this one! Moving stuff was on the agenda for Dom to do when I went back to the UK and evidently, when they came to move stuff up or down the staircase there was a tight spot it wouldn't go through. Plan B was to then remove the lounge window and hoist things up and down. Only a distance of about 10 feet but quite precarious and things needed careful tying. Tempers frayed and simple bed base and frame were not going to go. Never mind I didn't need it anyway. A bed settee in there was a better option as there was enough room for it to double up as an office, so the spare bed was dropped down, out through the mule shed and walked around to Dom's for his spare room. It was a lovely room with a small fireplace but sadly this was taken out as it stopped the room being used to its full potential. I was sad to see it be smashed out but only because I didn't have one in the upstairs room. I did have something no one else had though, ceramic radiators. These were the cause of much envy when friends came around as they all had wood burners or open fires. I could just plug in and have a steady warmth heat the room. I have to say they are perfect in the small rooms that I have.

Once the swap was complete, I would use the downstairs bedroom by the front door as my own and once rid of the computer desk [complete with computer] and dining table the hall would then be a lovely entrance with the Spanish dresser in it. The downstairs bedroom was the least appealing as a room as it had a very small window at head height that was a traditional Spanish wood with shutters and a second on the wall by the front door which was the more modern, maybe 60's style aluminium with frosted glass and decorative security bars. But the temperature was constant so rugs in winter and marble tiles in the summer. Dark at night for a good sleep and a decent light if needed in the day. Turning the ceiling fan on was a mistake though as years of dust began to fly off before I scrambled back to the switch; add that to the cleaning list! The rest of the house was so bright that it wasn't a worry. The bedroom came with a good double bed, albeit a Spanish size mattress [easy enough to replace in time] and a large dark wood double wardrobe; one woman and a double wardrobe: heaven. The puzzling thing was the head height window... when you looked out of it you were at ground level...how could that be? I was confused!

Clearing the kitchen took longer but only because I had also inherited a whole host of pots and pans and bits and bobs. Why had she not taken these with her? I love my cooking pots and wouldn't dream of leaving them behind. Nor my little nicks and nacks that make cooking go smoothly. I kept what I felt I needed and threw away anything tired, worn or just too personal to use. This included the dirty frying pan in the oven, the mouldy plate in the microwave and eventually the microwave when I discovered that it burned in a certain spot. I'm not one for microwaves anyway so not a great loss. Bags and bags got humped down the stairs and into the porch and with every bag the place got cleaner.

It took me a few days after my initial euphoria to realise why I wasn't feeling as settled here as I expected. It was all these inherited things. Not so much the big bits of furniture like beds and wardrobes but all those little bits and bobs that had been left behind, even down to the plastic and wire coat hangers that I would never have in a million years. I felt like I was living in someone else's home not my own and that they would come back at any minute and turf me out. I hoped that this would pass as time went by and I put my own stamp onto the place. When Dom appeared the place had undergone something of a transformation.

Over many *tubos* we discussed what would need to be done, in what order and at what cost before my next trip. It seemed logical for Dom to do the work especially as he had done his own house. There was not much to do other than modernisation and general improvements. With the layout being so quirky, I could understand why the vendor had her bedroom next to the kitchen on the same level and the lounge in what was originally a chicken shed. It would have made more sense though to level up the steps before tiling them and add a hand rail. In the middle of town a chicken shed complete with a traditional Spanish fireplace but by this time I had got use to having a mule shed, so the fact the chicken shed was now a lounge just didn't seem confusing at all.

Happy with the plan, I invited my friends around for a look and get their opinions on my new home with a snack menu direct from Lidl of wine, beer, crisps and nuts, a traditional English buffet. So on a lovely sunny afternoon a great bunch of people came together and endorsed my love of my little quirky house, gave helpful hints and interesting ideas and more than that, welcomed me into their community. All of them either lived in old houses, hade reformed old places or built from scratch so between them, they were a mine of information that I would learn to rely on when I needed to. I'd left the invites to Dom really as he had the phone numbers so it was lovely to see Martin and Brenda again who were eager to see the place and apart from all the steps, loved it! The entrance to my little house is not for the feint heated as it is four tight spiral steps to the door then the fumble for the tiny key hole. Then there was Bella who I'd only briefly met, another expat and an artist who came on the arm of Diego the Spaniard I'd seen in Bar Health, then Annie who lived in cortijo just outside of town with her dog Flopsy and Doug the carpenter; who bore an uncanny resemblance to the young John Wayne. It was lovely to get time to chat with everyone and ask opinions on the house. Bella and Brenda were deep in discussion and looking at the steps up to the top terrace. "That's a bit steep, how are you going to get up there with wine?"

"I hadn't really thought of that why?"

"We were thinking" they looked at each other, "Why not attach a pulley to the wall and a bucket at the end? Save you trying to carry stuff up."

"That's not a bad idea at all, thanks."

"And I'm sure that Martin and Dom could sort it easily?"

"I'll stick it on the list of 'To Do's."

I was interested to chat with Bella about her art. She was a sculptor working mostly in metal. The more we chatted about art and our preferred artists and styles the more we seemed to warm to each other. I hoped that she would become a firm friend in the future and I was glad she had been invited along.

Doug came out with fresh beers for everyone after nearly tripping over Flopsy who had taken root in the doorway. He'd overheard me saying to the other that some furniture must go. "I'll have the sideboard if it's going" he said cheekily knowing full well that a traditional Spanish sideboard was going nowhere.

"Oh no you won't, but you are welcome to make an offer on the dining table and chairs."

"Don't you want it?"

"Way too big for me and I'd not use it

downstairs. Seems a shame for it to just sit there gathering dust."

"We've been after one. How about a trade?"

"For what?"

"Double oak doors for the back of the mule shed? Beautiful doors that need a bit of TLC but they would look lovely if you are planning to use downstairs."

"Done. Providing the size is workable it would be great."

"Now we've drunk those beers, where's the next round?"

A knock on the door and I wondered who it was, Mike and Jane! I didn't realise they were in town and I had not met them since my original holiday here when they had been so helpful to me, but Martin had mentioned it to them so it was a lovely surprise. It had been 3 years or more since I had met with them, talked about the area and discussed the local walking at the start of what should have been a lovely week of exploring. Painfully, it was the day after that chat that I went out walking and badly twisted my ankle and had to be rescued by the local taxi driver and hotelier. All at the time of San Juan as well, so I missed so much on my first visit as I was only able to hobble to the lounger by the pool.

This time as I left it was with excitement. I was pleased that the purchase had gone well and I was happy that I had made a great choice of home in a beautiful place and couldn't wait to get back again to see what improvements were made. I had left Dom with a detailed plan of work with prices agreed on the work and staged payments over the coming months to cover materials and labour as needed. A ceiling was agreed on expenditure too; I didn't have the cash to spend on things that were not necessary.

Out with the old

The worse thing about the out of season months was the early flight times; great if you are a morning person but I'm not. It was very strange to creep out of my own house and not know what I would be coming back to on my next visit in two months time. The drive down with the sunrise coming up to my left was as lovely as ever and when I got to the coast it was burning its way across the sea. Another bright and beautiful day was dawning on the Costa Tropical and I was once more leaving it behind. The flights were already becoming nothing more than a bus journey and I was getting adept at being in the right place at the right time on these cheap flights. The joy of flying solo is that you can normally get a decent seat anyway but I had discovered the benefits of the window seat after years of preferring the aisle; sleep! Would I ever manage to sleep the whole way though? That had yet to be mastered.

Back home and it was straight back into work mode with almost nightly chats on Skype. Dom was buoyant and eager to crack on and was starting in the bathroom. Not sure yet whether to rip off the old tiles for fear of what lay underneath or tile over the top. An exploratory tile or two needed removing. But first the old 70's bathroom suite needed ripping out. Sink and toilet were useless and went down the tip. "Can you call me?"

My stomach sank.

'"What's up?"

"Well, we've been working all day to get this bath out and we're struggling. It's going to take a couple of days as it's cemented in."

"Ok." I didn't really see a problem other than it was a pain in the arse.

"Crack on then as it's not stopping!"

Couple of days later.

"Finally got the bath out."

"Great."

"But there's a problem I'm afraid."

"Oh. What?"

"We've found lead piping so that's got to be changed."

"Well, yes of course, how much?"

"Not a lot, Juan can sort it."

"Ok fine. You have enough in the budget and there's no point in having lead piping."

"No, no not at all and I want you to have the best."

"Ok, just do what needs to be done and keep me informed, there's no point in doing a botch job and to have to rip it out in a few years because it's broken or leaking."

"Ok, I've taken pictures so you can see what's what."

Once out, the bath was hijacked by someone

in the night and now housed probably in someone's garden as a pond, I'm sure I will find out one day. The pink frilly shower curtain went by the way of the local refuse collection. I'd already noticed that things left out could disappear overnight but that stayed where it was put!

Skype was used almost daily now. Although Dom's internet was too slow for pictures, it saved a fortune on phone calls.

"I've started on the mule shed, knocked the hole out for the new doors."

"Good. I can't wait to see those."

"Have had to hire a kango too to dig some of the floor back too."

"Really why?"

"Well, it needed levelling like and to do that we need to dig it back some to refill."

"Well, ok but shouldn't you be getting on with the bathroom?"

"Oh it's ok, I'm waiting for concrete to set and I've got the electrician in as well to increase the *potencia*."

"Weren't we going to do that later?" Spanish electricity came in a variety of Amps depending on the age of the property; mine was minimal and needed increasing so that more than a couple of things could be used at once. Otherwise the fuse board would have kept tripping out.

"Oh its ok it'll be fine."

In my head I am totting up the work and the

money: assuming in my head that there was enough in the pot to include everything. I was concerned though that Dom was stretching himself a bit thin and doing too much in one go. For a one man band with specialist work outsourced, I was a little concerned but he said he was ok so I trusted him. I had no reason not to.

"Look, leave the kitchen or I'll have no place to do anything when I come over."

"Ok, fine. Err, can you forward some more money though as we've been working all hours and with Juan here as well, it's costing more that was expected?"

"Yeah sure, I'll do it tomorrow."

It sounded like work was progressing well even if there were a few hiccups.

A few days later via Skype.

"How's it going?"

"Yeah good, slow but lots getting done. I've got Doug coming in tomorrow to help me get the couch up from downstairs into the lounge. I've taken the double bed down to mine. Once the lounge is sorted, I can start on the fireplace."

"Can you finish the bathroom before you start anything else please?"

"I'm still waiting for some of the concrete to set. I'm hanging around so I might as well carry on. Don't worry, it'll all be fine." And I didn't worry. I had complete faith in him and that everything that was being said was being done as it all seemed perfectly reasonable.

"Skype?" Dom wanted to chat.

"Phew, taken all day to get the settee into the upstairs lounge."

"Why?"

"Wouldn't go up those stairs so we had to rope it out of the bedroom window and haul it up over the terrace balcony. Bloody hard going I'll tell you, nearly killed me and Doug doing it. But it's up now and we can start on the chimney breast tomorrow and then it'll be much better. Looks a great room without all the TV and settee in it."

The next day Dom wanted to chat again.

"Hey, how you doing?"

"I'm good, you?"

"Yeah, yeah. Think I've got you a good deal."

"Oh yeah?"

'"Yeah. There's a guy in Órgiva that's moving out and he has some furniture to sell. I've got you a shower base, shelves, smaller fridge, IKEA sofa bed, cooker and a blind for a couple hundred bucks plus fifty delivery."

"Fifty delivery? That sounds a lot ?

"Well, it's gotta be in a van and it'd cost that to borrow one with the fuel."

"But its only 10k away?"

"Yeah but it's the right money to get it all here

in one piece, trust me."

"And is everything ok, all working?"

"Yeah. What I thought was, the cooker has the compartment for the gas bottle and is too big for your place so if I have that and you have mine."

"Sounds logical if it's all ok then fine."

"Good, I've got it coming over tomorrow."

"And how's everything else going?"

"Fine but slow. Waiting for materials and for people to turn up. Not managed to get anything done much this week as had to keep waiting for the electrician and then cable and wire. I'll start chiselling out for a rewire while I'm waiting next week."

"No leave that."

"But it'll be fine and will save you money as I can do most of the wiring and then the electrician can pass it off."

"I thought it was going to be cheaper to let the electrician do the lot? I'd rather it that way as I can't see the point of paying both of you to do work when I only need to pay one. Leave a rewire for now until I see where we're at. I can't keep sending money over until I know what's what. How much are we up to?"

"Oh don't worry I'll sort it out with you when you come over. When are you coming over?"

"Two weeks time."

"Oh great, we should have the bathroom finished by then."

"That'd be nice, and you can treat me to the bottle of champagne I never had when I got the house!"

Laughter. "Right, must crack on."

Phone pinged. A text.

"Call me."

My stomach sunk as I pressed his number in the middle of the day. What had he unearthed now?

"What's up?"

"Do you still want a car?" I'd figured that if I were there as often as I wanted to be, having my own car would save me money.

"Yes of course why?"

"Well how about a nice Golf?"

"Yes great but how much?"

"600 euros"

"What? What's wrong with it?"

"Nothing."

"Oh, is it on English plates?"

"Yeah but you don't have to register it for 3 months so if it's no good you can flog it. It's a real beauty."

"Ok, test drive it and see what you think."

"I have its great."

"And what colour is it?"

'"Silver why?"

"Just asking." A golf for 600 euros? Must have a few dents and dings but as long as it was mechanically sound I didn't see a problem for that price.

"Can you send me the money over as I need to pay him."

"Can't it wait till I come over in a couple of weeks?"

"No, cos someone else will snap it up and anyway I've already given him 100 deposit."

"Oh,ok."

"Oh and I've got some lovely mosaic tiles for the bathroom, much nicer than the ones we bought."
Sigh.

A few hours later.

"This car is a real beauty you know, it drives like a dream, and you'll love it."
Dom's enthusiasm and confidence was catching and I felt myself getting excited at the thought of having my own car. Well. It would be best if we split it between us as he would be using it more than me and as he normally treats cars like sheds, I thought it would give him a bit more respect for the thing if he was partly responsible for it.

I got a European fully comp insurance for it and he was legal as can be.

*

I then started to wonder how come there was a pattern of Dom being on FB up until 11 am, back on late afternoon and then on Skype to me even later. How hard a day was he having? I began to get even more suspicious when he said that his internet was down. What was going on?

I reasoned that all would be fine with the building but I wasn't feeling particularly good about the relationship anymore and I didn't really know why. Or was it just because I wasn't there hands on with the building work? I was so used to being involved with renovation that it was hard to let someone else control what I wanted without being there to guide it.

2 days before I was due to go.
Skype.

"Hi, how are we doing, are you ready for my arrival? Is the bathroom finished?"

"Nearly, when you getting here?"

"Two days time? You know that, I keep telling you."

"Oh you know what it's like here, one day leads into the next and you forget."

"Well I hope it's done when I get there as I'll be dying for a shower."

"Well, you may as well stay at mine the first night as it's no good seeing the work at midnight is it?"

"Well no, suppose not, and I will be knackered.

I'll text you when I've landed."

"Ok, I'd better crack on."

"Don't forget you are picking me up at the airport too."

"Oh yeah. See you soon."

*

I hope I never tire of that feeling when you step out of the airport into that lovely warmth. I immediately relax and smile, probably looking like and inane idiot from the UK and I was excited to see what had been done to the house. Would it at last feel like it was mine rather than like I was squatting? I called Dom. 'Hiya, I'm here, where are you?'

"Oh you're early. Won't be long. Make your way up to the arrivals and I'll see you there in about 15 mins." I knew exactly where he was and was sure it involved a coffee and a brandy.

The car was good but Dom was not. Cap pulled firmly on his head, unshaven, he looked like someone I didn't know. No hug, no kiss, not even a welcome more of a feeling of this is a pain to have to drive down here to pick me up. Thank God for the puppy on the back seat who licked me to death! My intuition was right. We had no future together, I could cope with no outward emotion in public but to not even be greeted warmly was just not right and to be honest it was upsetting. But, let's make the most of this and get on with it. I got in the driver's seat and headed off for the drive to Lanjarón. We barely spoke on the journey other than occasional pleasantries when we were on the last leg. I put it down to the work he was doing and he said he had been working into the night which would account for his dishevelled appearance. I pulled into the car park with relief. Although the night run isn't arduous at all, I'm not a lover of night driving. I was looking forward to a glass of wine.

The next morning dawned and I was eager to get round to the house. After a stop at Albertos for coffee, *tostadas* and a brandy for you know who, I went off to the house. Dom suddenly remembered he had to see someone about a job.

There was a spring in my step as I walked down the street and excitement in my tummy. At last, I returned to my pretty little house nestled in the middle of town with the fantastic views. But what I found? A squat, a tip, a great mess, a hell hole. Whatever words I used to describe it cannot describe what my stomach was doing when it came into view. The front gates were propped against the wall and a mini skip was in the entrance way piled high with rubble and rubbish. A grotty brown cooker had wire piled on it and I had to take care not to trip over breeze blocks that had tumbled across the floor and that was just the porchway. Well there was no denying that work had been going on that's for sure!

I unlocked the front door and headed upstairs. Layers of cement dust covered everything from mould laden mugs in the kitchen to the sofa. The front of the

TV could be used to leave messages it was that dusty. Someone with bad body odour had been here too. I walked through each room and mentally checked off what had or had not been done, gathering cigarette butts, beer cans and wine bottles along the way. Even a new window and frame that had been put in had whistling gaps around it; would it stay in place or would it just fall out if I touched it? At least the vines outside had been pulled down and the window was a bargain buy at €20, plus the glass and the frame though! My beautiful Spanish sideboard was hiding behind a sofa bed and had shelves and brackets piled on it. 2 bathroom sinks were propped in front; no pedestals, just sinks. I only have one bathroom! A 'new' fridge stood its ground and dared me to open the door. It could wait; I really didn't want to see what it could possibly hold. The master bedroom was relatively untouched other than a sleeping bag and blanket on top of the quilt. A sad reminder of the person that had been in my life for the last six months. I was numb.

The next morning, I set to, cleaning up more mess in my Spanish home. There was a pile of rags next to the TV. I moved them and a heady stench hit my nose: someone's smelly work clothes covered a pair of boots kicked into the corner and I knew they weren't Dom's. Old bedspreads acted as dustsheets over my couch but bits of rubble and fag ends were flicked underneath the edges.

The middle terrace was covered in sawdust,

builder's rubble and cement dust, no wonder I was coughing in the night, the dust had been blowing into the bedroom as the window was level with the terrace. This was the window that had puzzled me on my first visit. Because the house is twisted in its layout, the levels for each floor are uneven hence the window at floor height.

The kitchen was what can only be described as a builder's yard. Tile offcuts were on every work surface from where the builder had been cutting them whilst doing the bathroom, all my plates were stacked, filthy dirty amongst the debris along with a grease laden frying pan; it was like someone had been living here whilst I was away. With the clothes in the lounge, maybe they had. The rubbish bag was in the same place it had been five weeks previously and was oozing something from the bottom onto the marble floor. A line of empty wine bottles snaked its way around the base of one cupboard and for some reason, there was a gaping hole where the cooker should have been. I later found this down in the entrance way, snuggled up to the over-laden mini skip, old door frames, breeze blocks and *yeso* bags full of rubble. The neighbour's rubber tree plants were coated in a thick layer of cement dust; she must have been cussing me since the day I moved in.

I was not going to cry, in fact the thought never entered my head. I was more disappointed that my trust had been betrayed. I steadily worked my way through the rubble and mess, bagging it up, carting it down the two flights of stairs and tried to find a place in the skip for it. More moving of rubble to clear a space for more rubble, it was madness as it should have all been clear. Slowly my hard work revealed a kitchen once more but a new layer of dust was already settling on the surfaces. At 1.30, sweaty and weary I decided to go down to the bar for a coffee; I'd had enough for now. I looked down at myself; dusty from head to toe, I wasn't going to get changed just to go for coffee, so I sauntered down town and seated myself in the sun. I didn't give a damn how I looked. Café con leche, tostadas, fresh air and sun to repair the mind.

The week dragged as I was avoided by Dom and phone calls remained unanswered. The daily routine was cleaning and cleaning again. The minute I finished cleaning one room, the dust would settle again. Every time I sat down, a cloud of dust rose off the couch, there were no such things as a vacuum cleaner here. To make a sandwich I had to wash everything immediately beforehand; it was tiresome. Then Juan the builder who was working on the house under Dom's supervision would appear and the mess would start again. I hadn't got the energy to tell Juan that I hated smoking and that I wished he wouldn't do it in the house, but he was working so hard to right the wrongs that were not his fault that I don't think I cared much anyway. Considering we did not speak each other's language, there was empathy between us. The bathroom was a big issue as I had no sink to wash in or shower to use. But with Juan coming in daily, at least the bathroom was being completed. And contrary to popular belief about the Spanish, Juan was there every morning at 9.15 ready to crack on. Daily washing could be done in the kitchen but I was desperate for a shower. It was May and hot. Cleaning day in day out was hard work when you are not used to doing it in the heat. The sweat was pouring off me but the only thing I could do was have a strip wash with a bucket of warm water. I had even thought of hiring a hotel room for the night just so I could feel clean.

Dogs always make me laugh when they have done something wrong, they pop their paw over their nose to cover their eyes; if they can't see you, you can't see them and tell them off. And so it is with some human beings. I set about trying to find Dom and find out what had been going on. Searching the usual haunts I eventually found him. A *tubo* in one hand, a cigarette in the other.

He wanted more money to do more work.

He couldn't understand my concerns.

There was no problem, work was on schedule.

He'd been working through the night. Digging the floor up in the mule shed and the bathroom.

He was sacked.

He got up and walked away.

I had no idea what to do now. Then I decided to call the first person I thought of, Bella. "Can you come down?"
"What's up?"
"The house. It's a mess"

An hour later, Bella arrived at the door. Kettle on and ignoring the debris, we went through the receipts that I had managed to get from Dom and what were scattered around the house, listed and collated them and factored in the money that had exchanged hands. The doorbell went, it was Juan, here to carry on in the bathroom. Thankfully Bella knew Juan and could converse with him as she was fluent. Juan had done all the work in the bathroom, Dom had done close to nothing. From gesticulations I could work out what was happening, Dom would let Juan in and then he would head off to the nearest bar. This had evidently been going on since a week or so after I had left and Juan was not happy. For now I let Juan continue with the work in the bathroom whist Bella and I assessed the damage; at least from my list I knew Juan had been paid.

Time for new list or should I have said damage limitation exercise.

The spare bedroom had the least issues. The fire place had been knocked out and the new window put in, badly. Both of those could be easily remedied and neither was urgent. The lounge was just a ruddy mess so that was easy enough to remedy. The kitchen was a major mess and as the leaky *calentador* had been ripped out, I had a mass of tiles missing, but it was liveable with for the short term. If I could not get any finances back, it was all going to need repairing in the short term. The bathroom? Well, it had a toilet and a shower basin and one short wall tiled and as Juan was working on that it should be finished within days.

I had been so careful. I'd read books, articles and planned ahead. But the figures and the work done did not add up. With a heavy heart that I had been so stupid and foolish, we walked down to the mule shed which was to be my little work space when I moved here. It was all planned and measured in my head that I could fit necessary machinery into the space to provide a print, design and embroidery service. With its tiny little courtyard at the rear I would get some lovely daylight in too. The plan was to leave the 'rustic' clay brick walls as they were and the lovely exposed chestnut beams that were the house's foundations as a feature. From my first viewing I could imagine me being very happy working in this space, it was perfect. I turned the 6 inch long key and knocked back the hasps and pulled open the door. I think I must have gone white. Bella, not normally short for words could only say one, 'oh.' Rubble was strewn everywhere, half the floor had been dug up with a kango hammer for some reason and worse still;

the majority of the back wall had been knocked out to put the replacement double oak doors in. But there was nothing in its place. Just fresh air and daylight. No supports, no lintel, nothing. As for the doors, they had not been stripped and varnished they were in fact, lounging across some building blocks and tiles that had been dumped in the corner, a sorry state for something so beautiful. Another job started and not finished. I'm not a shouty angry person by nature but I was now feeling like I needed to vent my anger.

Bella was a rock: a master of organisation and knowledge. A Scouser built of solid stuff. Having lived in Spain for a good number of years, she knew the system and the right tradesmen to use. Forget using English trades, bring in the Spanish. Juan was to become my new best friend. From local stock he was Alpujarran through to the core: which also meant he spoke not one word of English! His guttural dialect harsh on the ears and not easy to translate to a lowly Spanish beginner. Even the Spanish/English dictionary was little use... thankfully my drawings were more helpful but not whilst we were in the mule shed.

We went upstairs and came back down with Juan and that's when the dream did fall apart. His Spanish became even louder. His screw driver poking into the chestnut beams with little effort and a down falling of sawdust and shards of rotten wood began to float down to the floor. He moved along to another beam and the same happened. I was mute. That's when the arms started flailing and we were shooed out of the mule shed. He didn't want us in there until the beams were replaced. Seven of them in total. The main support to the house and the neighbour's houses was in danger of collapse. I had to find more money to get this essential work done or my dream would be literally in tatters.

I felt more of a fool to have trusted someone and felt it was my fault. My guts were churning that all the hard earned money I had injected into my little bit of paradise had gone and it wasn't spent on the work in my house. But of course I blamed myself totally.

I had trusted.

On a good note, I had kept the local alcohol economy buoyant at what was starting to be a rough time for any business in Spain to the tune of €...... no, the amount is immaterial and only known to a few. It's not like I would ever get it back. In fact the cheeky beggar was asking for more saying that I still owed him for work he had done. Thankfully my stupidity stopped there and no more was handed over to him at all!

Now I had to re-budget what I could afford to have done. Gone were the initial dreams of a canopied mid terrace and bespoke bench seating and sail like covers on the roof terrace. No new furniture straight away. No luxuries at all, just practicalities. Anything that worked could stay and be used until a time that I could afford to replace it. I was going to struggle now to replace the necessities. For now there was no more that Bella or I could do. Declining her offer of going up into the mountains for the night, she left me to it.

As I gazed out I could just see through the mountains to Morocco on my left and to my right the sweeping undulations of the Lujar. The sun was going down on what should have been another beautiful day in May but I felt like it was my last day on the planet. I couldn't face clearing up any more of the debris that surrounded me, I needed to run and escape what was happening. But I wasn't at home. I couldn't just call up a friend and escape into their lives with my tales of woe. I had to face this on my own. A drink was required and some company and light banter; time to let Fernando tell me his worst jokes.

The joy of a small town was that everyone knew your business or thought they did. Dom had started with good intent and had taken to the project with gusto. But evidently, the further into the project he had gone, the more time he had spent in the bar. So it was a natural assumption that all the work was not being done to schedule. So rumour was rife before my arrival that things were 'awry'. What they didn't know was how much off schedule things were. But at least when I walked in the bar, everyone was ready for me but was unsure as to how I would react.

How would they know? They hardly knew me. It was a blessed relief that everyone already knew that there would be fall out one way or another. As everyone knew Dom better than me, I wasn't sure what to expect at all but to be honest, I was not even considering any reaction I might have off the locals, I just wanted the escape. A few glasses of wine, lovely tapas and some corny banter from Fernando and I was feeling less battered than when I walked in. With my senses slightly numbed by the wine, I gritted my teeth and went back to the house. I grabbed a bottle of wine from the fridge, washed off a glass and headed outside for the rickety chair on the terrace and got what can only be described as well and truly drunk.

I didn't sleep well that night. I constantly awoke sweaty and frightened having just dreamed that the middle terrace had collapsed into the mule shed as the beams had finally given way. Then I dreamt I was buried under a pile of rubble as the lounge collapsed on top of me, choking on the dust and debris. I was trapped in a surreal state of fright and worry. But I still refused to get upset. No one had the right to steal my piece of paradise and come hell or high water, I was not going to allow him to take away the beauty of this place. Never. With what limited funds I had left, this place was going to be made safe and habitable.

Juan was working in the bathroom the next day, determined to have it finished for me. There was a settled coexistence when you can't communicate much. I would clean, Juan would work.

I spent evenings in solitude.

Thankfully the house had a good stock of wine and beer. I was eating very little and drinking far too much and it wasn't blotting out the worry.

I was working in the bedroom when Juan yelled me. From his tone I couldn't tell if it was good or bad so I scampered upstairs. I flew up the steps and across to the bathroom. I must have looked scared stiff as Juan put both hands towards me and said *tranquillo, tranquillo.* He took my hand and led me into the bathroom and turned me towards the shower. He held the shower head and raised the lever. A spray of water came out. I went towards it and felt the warm water run over my hand, tiny little bubbles forming on my skin. Heaven! A smile spread across my face and gave Juan a big hug. I could have a shower at last! But Juan wasn't going to let me. It was celebration time. The bathroom was finished and it was time for the topping out ceremony. Off to the bar we would go. Dirty and stinky as you like but did it matter? No, no one in Lanjarón would bat an eyelid. I was given the best seat on the terrace and a glass of wine put in my hand. Friends of Juan who I had seen around town joined us and I was introduced. More wine was brought forth as the tale was told and then another wine. I was decidedly wobbly now. Juan bellowed for a change in the music and then they were trying to get me up to dance. Me and three Spaniards; what could I say? After the fourth glass of wine I managed to give my thanks to them all for celebrating with me and I staggered back up the road to the house for my much longed for shower. Oh that moment was so luxurious that I'm sure I audibly groaned at the pleasure. The hot dry dust went down the plug hole and I felt clean inside and out. I had achieved something and I felt just a little bit happier with life.

The next day was Juan's last on the job and he was finished by lunch time. I thanked him but he didn't leave but jabbered on in Spanish. Eventually in his best Spanish to help me understand. He needed to be paid.

"But hasn't Dom...?"

"No."

"But," I grabbed my list and pointed to a payment with his name by the side.

Juan took my hand and took me to the Calentador and the pipe work.

Ah, I understood. He'd been paid for one job but not the tiling.

Thankfully I had the money and paid him only then to find myself dragged downstairs and out the door. Juan was darned sure I wasn't going home unhappy, he felt sorry for what had happened and if he could buy me a drink to cheer me up then he would. Off we went again!

Car

Sadly I needed to locate Dom again as I had no car keys, car or paperwork. I eventually cornered him in a bar.

"Where's the car?"

"Up the mountain."

"What's it doing up there?" A shrug. "Well I want it here and now and I want all the paperwork."

"You have to pay for it first."

"What, it's paid for. I sent the money to your bank!" he looked at me and I held his glare. His left eyebrow was twitching, for the first time ever I could see anger brewing. I was looking into the eyes of a man I didn't know. What had happened to the intelligent, clean shaven, well dressed charming man I had met? It was like there were two of him. Neither of us giving in to the glare he walked off. I was later to find the car on the high street and the keys in the Ambienza. Over coffee and *tostadas* I had to work out how to find the true owner of the car.

All I knew was that he was also new in town and from London, I didn't even know his name. I was making notes as I was eating and by coincidence heard a London accent as a couple came in for breakfast. My appetite went immediately. I had to approach them and explain who I was. With apologies I passed the keys to his car across the table explaining I couldn't afford to pay him twice and that I was sorry for the trouble. With no hesitation, he pulled out his wallet, gave me my deposit back and threw the keys back at me; "use it whilst you are here, we don't need it." I filled up with tears.

*

It was Thursday and I was flagging. I was actually looking forward to the flight home on Saturday, then I realised I had no way of getting to the airport.

"Bella, I've got a problem."

"Go on."

"I'm going home on Saturday."

"Yes."

"But I have no transport!"

"Oh don't worry, I'll take you to the airport."

I could have cried then. This was no 30 minute trip down the road, it was a 4 hour round trip. She was giving me the support and confidence to carry on and get my love back for my little house. We hardly knew each other but I felt I could trust her. I had to trust, I couldn't let Dom ruin my trust in people.

Locks were changed and plans made for the next stage of work on the house. The beams. I would send over a prepaid credit card to Bella who would then administer funds only as and when work was on schedule. She assured me she would have a receipt for the smallest washer to the labour involved so all the money would tie up. No more lies and no more English builders.

The journey down to Malaga was pretty quiet. I was back to feeling numb. Replacing beams was a big job, plus I had just spent a week in a house with a gaping hole in the main back wall that was unsupported. We were on to the next stage but this was the biggie. Seven beams were having to be replaced and it would cost. Would they discover anything else? Figures were running through my head; what I could rob from A to fund B should anything else crop up.

On a bright sunny hot afternoon, we two *amigas* headed down to the coast and along to Malaga. I had to face facts on what the build was going to cost now we had the figures from Juan. Never once did Bella ever suggest I sell up and move on. I was pretty low but I wanted to push forward too so was glad of her strength of character in helping me do just that when all I wanted to do was bury my head in a bucket. So that journey to the airport was one of decisions and lists and hopefully an end to a painful episode in my life and the cementing of a great friendship.

Beams

Juan was starting the work on Monday.

I was back at work and my nerves were on edge. Concentrating on anything was hard. I kept my eye on Skype expecting Bella to call at any moment but all was quiet. I had got so used to the routine Skype calls with Dom about hiccups that I was expecting more, especially with this work being so major. I was snappy with anyone who happened to come in the firing line. All I could see in my mind was the house collapsing or more work needing doing and my dream of a stress free life falling down around my ears. I had no backup financially and no one to turn to for a hug of support. Thankfully the moral support from friends was constant and for that I was truly grateful.

I drove into work on Monday and called Julie. It was only then that I let the flood gates open and I sobbed my heart out. In-between sobs and snuffles I explained what had happened. I could hear her fuming the other end of the phone. All the time I am blaming myself and she is telling me that it wasn't my fault. I've never felt anyone get so angry on my behalf and in a weird way I was grateful for it as I was totally broken and exhausted. I locked the door to the unit and concentrated on catching up on emails and post: all the time waiting for bad news.

Tuesday

Juan had decided to put the new doors in the unsupported opening first so that the back wall was now safe and the house would not fall down.

Wednesday

Old beams were out and acro props in place.

Friday

New beams were in.

I cried.

The house was secure and the relief I felt was immense. The extra cost was immaterial. It did now make sense of the vendor's attitude when I bought it. When I first viewed the house it had all her knick-knacks around. Plus, when I made an offer on the property it had been accepted straight away and I had offered well under the asking price. When we had met at the notary I was sure she had wanted to tell me something but her agent was ruling her with a rod of iron and diverted her.

The relief I felt also that the neighbours would be happy now that their properties were not at risk too. If they knew the beams were rotten then she must have. Ironically they were the first thing I had asked Dom about and he had reassured me that they were ok. What a fool I was.

I couldn't plan any further ahead at the time, I needed space to breathe and get myself feeling normal. I was constantly shaking internally. Too many things had been uncovered over that week there that I couldn't just brush it off. There were so many things I needed to address in my head and to face telling people as so many people were following my progress with as much excitement as I was initially feeling. This was a great boost to my confidence in what I was trying to achieve but now I was feeling so low it wasn't easy to say what had happened.

Slowly over the next couple of months I returned to an even keel. My next visit was planned and booked and I could begin to work out what to do next and relax. I was brushing off the fact that Dom was still in town. I couldn't see any point in getting angry with him-it wasn't going to help matters and nor would it get my money back. I could face his scowls of contempt; I knew I had done no wrong.

That intervening time before my next trip was a roller coaster. As ever I blamed myself for everything that had gone wrong. Kicked myself for falling for the wrong man and being smooth talked. Kicked myself for losing so much money that I couldn't afford to lose. Fretted over whether I had bought something that was never going to be habitable and would shortly resemble a few of the places in town; pulled down into a pile of rubble because of rot. Inwardly I was distraught and feeling foolish. Outwardly I was level headed and putting on a true British brave face. But could I bear to go back?

I kept in touch with a number of new friends via social media and never mentioned a thing. A number of them knew that the relationship had broken down but no one knew why, they only had the gossip flying around and that varied depending on who you spoke to. I could have shouted it loud across the town, but what was the point? What would it achieve? It wouldn't get me my money back, nor would it make my house secure; that could only be done with a proper builder.

But how would the town's folk react when I returned and Dom had told his side of the story? It was still the talk of the town and I assumed that they would take Dom's side of things as the truth. After all, I was a newcomer, why believe me? So as I pulled into the car park in town, I sat for a few moments to get my thoughts together. I had come this far, I could carry on. All I was guilty of was giving someone a chance.

New Beginnings

It was nice to enter the house and find it in the same condition as when I had left-plus an extra layer of building dust that had settled. I ignored it for that night and opened a bottle of wine and sat on the terrace and remembered why I thought this place was the best place on earth.

*

"Before Juan starts the kitchen, I have an idea." My brain was back in gear and as the kitchen was a complete disaster zone, it had to be replaced. I had already done the design for a traditional simple Spanish kitchen with a tiled surface, Belfast sink and curtains to the fronts of the units rather than doors. In fact I had done a complete file of designs for the whole house.

"Go on." said Bella.

"Knock this doorway wider to allow better access to the kitchen," I pointed to the adjoining door between lounge and kitchen, "or take the door out, knock half the wall down to make a counter between the two rooms... or just knock the wall out completely and have a through lounge?" Even as a through lounge it would only measure about 20' x 9' but it would feel far more spacious. I needed to make the decision before the end of the week. Bella was 100% with the wall out.

I looked at my layout designs and reworked them. Planning and re-measuring with each of the choices. Whichever choice I made, space was at a premium. The major thing to do was to make the tread space at the top of the stairs safer. Currently you walk out of the lounge into the kitchen with the space of a 12" tile underfoot. One wrong step and you were heading down the stairs. It really was a no brainer. "Ok, let's whip out the wall and if necessary put a support beam in."

Gulp... here I go again. Should I really play safe and leave the wall there? No, it had to go. I had finally taken control of my project on my house and that felt good.

Decision made it was time to relax, meet up with what I hoped were still friends and have a drink or three.

I had played this scene over and over in my head and it unnerved me every time. I wasn't sure what would happen. I had to admit it, I was scared.

Every step down the street was a struggle. I didn't know what reaction I would receive or how I would react. As for bumping into Dom…well, I'd address that when it happened. I still could see no point in getting angry with him, it would most likely upset me more that make me feel any better. Better to just nod hello and walk on; the sooner I did that the better.

Deep breath and I walked into Bar Health.

"Hey Charlotte, you meet my friend Paulo, he's single." I glanced to where Fernando was pointing. A spry octogenarian sat on the end bar stool.
"No gracias Fernando!"
"Vino blanco?"
"Si."
"Karen, tapas for Charlotte."
A smiling face appeared from behind the beaded curtain "Yes you're back, how long for?" Karen turned back to preparing the tapas.
I smiled. Maybe things would be more normal than I thought.

The week was thankfully uneventful and dare I say relaxing. I managed a trip into Granada and walked so much my feet hurt, but it was great to have the freedom and confidence to drive away from the centre of my new universe without someone guiding the way.

I love Granada, a busy bustling city with a huge amount of history and a thriving Arab quarter plus the Alhambra; and it still shuts for siesta at 2pm, a fact that I struggle to get my head around. I milled around the main shopping streets and visited El Corte Ingles the department store, struggled to leave all the little Souks without buying up almost everything and found a fabulous five level material shop and marvelled at the fabric available for home and dress making; including all the frilled and three dimensional fabrics for making flamenco dresses. It was heaven. The only issue with buying fabric was the lack of a sewing machine. Never mind, I was way off soft furnishings yet. I took a leisurely lunch and people watched in the sunshine.

I was even smiling as I set off back down the motorway home.

I think Julie heaved a sigh of relief when I got home and called her on the Monday morning.
"It's ok; it's all going to be ok."
"You sure, no problems with that idiot?"
I smiled, "No, that idiot was nowhere to be seen thank heavens." I had seen him, but only in the distance. I'd also heard a lot of things about him that I previously didn't know, but now wasn't the time to repeat those things, I just wanted to bury them and move on.

Fire.

It was nearly the end of June and time for me to be heading back off to Lanjarón. I was working from home on a Saturday afternoon and as usual had social media open, having the odd chat with friends here and there. Pictures came on screen of the hillside smoking, then ablaze. The hillside around Lanjarón was on fire.

It was horrible to see the place I loved being engulfed in black smoke. It spread. The wind was blowing it uphill towards Caballo Blanco. I was unsure of who was taking the photos and the video but they must have been in danger too. I could see Bella's house on the left hand side. She was just on the edge of the smoke but you could not see where the flames were, I hoped she was safe. I would have been no help had I been in Spain but I felt completely useless sat at home in the UK.

The *bomberos* were flying overhead in helicopters dousing the flames from buckets slung beneath them before disappearing again to refill in the nearest reservoir or *albercas*. Then the little yellow plane flew over that was loaded with fire retardant powder and skillfully dropped this onto *cortijos*. It was mesmerizing to watch. What you couldn't see were the brave *bomberos* [firemen] on the ground fighting the fire in the thick of it.

Social media was alive with people tracking

what was going on. People checking in that the fire was heading this way and that. Others saying that they were safe but were evacuating for safety. A call went out for volunteers to gather the horses from the ranch should it be necessary. Sadly others saying that their property had been caught, even worse, the people that no one could reach.

As quickly as it flared, it was out. The plumes of black smoke had gone, the *bomberos* were still dousing any hot spots but we could now see the landscape again. Except now it was a charred blackness. There was a mildly funny side to this event, one house had a 100% hit with the retardant powder so this one white cortijo turned bright pink. How long it stayed that way for would remain to be seen!

Sadly the next day it flared again. Once more I sat rooted to social media and relied on friends to keep me up to date with the news. The wind had risen and taken the fire in the opposite direction and away from homes, but not before claiming the life of some animals and a home. This time it was quickly brought under control but not before it had cut a path around Bella's house not 3 foot from her building. It had burned her olive and almond trees but thankfully left her home intact.

San Juan

The staff at Marbesol, the car hire company, now recognised me and it was a short operation to sign, sign, sign and get a set of keys ahead of the forming queue as I was a gold card member; cost nothing but worth at least an hour of your time in the busy season. The drive was a pleasure. With windows open [the air con was redundant on a beautiful evening] I felt the warmth and enjoyed the pleasure it had brought of immediate relaxation. Before I got to town I found cars parked on the side of the mountain road. In my naivety, I had assumed someone from outside of town was having a party, I hadn't actually equated the parking complexity that an extra 20k people has on a small town in the mountains. As I entered town the barriers were across the entrance to the high street which was a shame as I had hold luggage that would have been easier to drop off by the front door. Thankfully the car park was only a few minutes' walk away so it wouldn't be too much of a struggle. But the bypass was crammed with cars and the car park too. The level of the car park [read shingle flattish space or waste ground] nearest my house was full so up to the next level. 4x4's were slewed over the edge of the drive up and it was rammed up there too but I manage to sneak into a space on my second circuit, just beating a Renault Clio to the coveted prize. Thank heavens. I opened the car door and absorbed the rhythms of the music blasting from the street and the warmth of the night. I heaved my case out of the boot and carted it slowly to my house. It was 1am and the fiesta was in full swing.

San Juan: a celebration of fire and water which was normally a coastal celebration with fires along the beaches and all night parties. In Lanjarón the festival of water and ham for which the area is renowned occurred annually on the 23rd June, and spreads either side of it with bank holidays...to recover from constant partying. The majority of the high street was cordoned off for a few days preceding and stalls were erected along with even more 'temporary' bars that were mostly selling mojitos, which come in varying strengths of 'mmmm, minty', 'eye popping intoxicating' and 'where's my legs gone?' Word soon passed around as to who was crushing the best mojito in town, they were so refreshing that you never seemed to stop at one! The scent of food drifted across the packed square where there was a stage erected and various singers and bands played to entertain in the evenings.

Home. No Dom, no fags, just me and my *casa.* I could have gone and partied, but no, partying was the following night with my friends and I was so looking forward to being drenched in the water fight that I was amazed at myself; but then I had just left a very cold and wet UK.

I hauled my bags inside and dumped them in the hall before I headed upstairs for the wine I had left chilling on my last visit. The place was just a dusty mess and not a chaotic disaster zone this time. The cleaning and looking at the work would wait for the next day. I had faith in Bella and builder Juan, at that moment I just wanted to feel what it was like to be sat in my house on my own without someone else trying to influence me. I sat with a glass of wine on my terrace, listening to the music as a Spanish family jabbered on as they walked home down the side street, and I smiled. I was part of all this and I didn't need to rush out and see it like a tourist, I could come and go as I pleased year after year and that made me feel content. Just then a live rendition of Whitney's 'I will always love you' drifted over town. I wandered downstairs to bed with the music still thumping away like an annoying neighbour; but this is San Juan and everyone was happy and having fun. Let them party.

Morning dawned with a shaft of sunlight coming in through the shutters, I had had the best night's sleep in a long while. I heard three strikes from the church bell and knew that it was quarter to something. A quarter to what didn't matter as I was back where I felt at home; and home was still standing despite what others may have done in error. But I was shaking a little from nerves, from expecting the unexpected and fearing the worst, it would take time to relax here again. I buried my head back into the pillow and slept a while longer.

Curiosity ensured it was not much longer. I opened the sliding door of my lounge to reveal the

Sierra de Lujar in its morning glory and I smiled and relaxed as I held the beaded curtain to one side. Nature was a wonderful thing when its beauty had this calming effect on you. It was so good to take time to breathe and absorb it. I turned to look inside and surveyed the layer of dust in the kitchen and then my new bathroom sink. It was a bit large but hey, I had two others I could swap it over with if I had to. On the middle terrace I sat and gazed at the view. That view was priceless. It changed every minute of every day in every season and was one of the reasons I wanted to be here. I glanced down to the lower terrace, and saw the rotten beams leant forlornly up the wall alongside a set of ladders I didn't recognise. I leant a little further out to see the render work that has been done at the back but didn't tempt fate by trusting the little wall too much. The plan was back on track. My next deep breath would be going down to the mule shed and seeing what Juan had done in my absence. I was going to wait a little before going there; I needed to build up the courage as the thought of it still made me feel sick.

I needed to escape Lanjarón for a couple of hours to get some supplies and if I wasn't back before noon I would never get a parking space. The car park was still quite full as I head off up to Ortura to ransack Lidl.

It's was a pleasant drive up towards Granada and already hot at 10 am. Shopping list forgotten, I loaded the trolley with stuff, including of course a case, well two, of Conde Noble white wine; noting with disgust that it has risen in cost to 80c! Then I spied some deck chairs but was shocked at the €17.99 price tag for a bog standard chair, but next to it a folding lounger at €29.99 caught my eye; relaxation on the terrace beckoned. Struggling through the till I then wondered if it would actually fit into the Kia Picanto. Just, but it was a struggle. In fact with all the shopping in, there was room for little else. I headed back down to Lanjarón and was relieved to see the main road was still open. Great, I could get the car down to unload and decide to leave it parked there rather than drop it into the car park. I parked in tight to the front gates so that the neighbour's two cars could get out if need be.

The music was drawing me out of the house by mid afternoon; I had to go and see what was going on. It was complete and utter madness, there were people everywhere. The smell of fresh mint drifted from people's drinks as they sipped mojitos. The calico sails were strung across the road to give shade and line after line of Spanish flags weaved their way as far as you could see. After a rather sleepy start to the day, there was excitement in the air. Kitchen and dining chairs lined the kerbs: old tatty ones, new high backed leather ones, raffia stools all from homes and bars to mark where everyone would sit later as they awaited the procession to start. Some Spanish people were already sitting, chatting to their neighbours, their fans wafting away as they talked. Some seats were empty, awaiting the owner's occupation; no one would dream of moving them to one side. Smiling, happy, laughing faces were enjoying the afternoon sun even though the parade was still hours away. Family and friends mingled amongst strangers, drinks in hand, this was the biggest occasion in the village calendar and no one missed it.

Music started to boom as the first of the parade vehicles came down the street. The theme as ever was 'water' and floats and costumes were bold and bright having been prepared many months in advance. The children came though first; boys and girls dressed in bright pinks, blues and yellows, danced along with their parents in tow. A group of what appeared to be cupcakes in powder blue and cerise pink with a cherry on the top for a hat passed by. An adult 'cake' wandered over to chat; a young man with more make up on than I'd seen in a long while! The music changed as a Viking ship [on wheels] came along. Leather clad men in horned helmets and some dressed as serving wenches; it seems men are completely liberated here and are happy to dress as damsels. Above us, a set of balcony doors opened and two little girls came out in red and white polka dot flamenco dresses as a group dressed as firemen paraded past waving flags. The Flintstones followed playing drums, saxophones and tubas. A sequined dance troupe shimmied along the street in red wigs, red bustiers and red tasselled trousers, all ladies this time, they garner the men's attention with ease. A witch cycles by with a full beard and fake chest, closely followed by a flamenco lady with perfect nails and a 5 o 'clock shadow, then a magician with gold bow tie, top hat and cape performed magic tricks as he walked to engage the audience. It was all so crazy, fantastic, bright, over the top and it went on for at least four hours, slowly weaving its way down the high street, stopping to perform so everyone could see the costumes and dancing. What a great community, driven to keep up tradition and enjoy themselves.

I wandered off to search for Bella, but it was like looking for a needle in a haystack as the street was packed with people. The sun was beaming down and it was 40 degrees. I could see people I knew but couldn't find her. I promptly bumped into Juan the builder who was a *camerero* for the night, waiting tables in a local bar. I tapped him on the shoulder and when he turned and realised who it was, I got a huge hug of welcome and a beaming smile before he hurried back to the job in hand and dashed off with drinks for the terrace. Bella grabbed me from behind, it was Mojito initiation time!

'Mucha agua, mucha agua, hey! Hey!

I'd been roped in to do the water run, an hour of adults having a water fight. How wet could you get?

Five of us wandered back to my place to change into something more suitable and I found a note on my windscreen. Having had too much to drink I really didn't pay it too much heed but fortunately Doug did and realised that the neighbour needed to get out at 6am to go to work. None of us were capable of driving so the kind neighbour drove it round to the car park whilst Doug guarded with his life, a space he had found. I imagined I had caused enough hassle with the neighbours with all the building work going on at all hours, so not moving it would have not been the best thing to do, so thank heavens for Doug. But in the sobering light of day it made me realise that my lack of Spanish was going to cause me problems. I really needed to buckle down and get the basics back into my head and then convert it to the local dialect as the neighbours all recognised me but I could do little more than say hello. It was not for them to struggle with English, it was for me to work on the Spanish.

I had been instructed on clothes to wear for this, so I changed into shorts and t shirts and shoes that wouldn't come off or be spoiled by a little water. We divested ourselves of wallets, watches and phones before we headed back out onto the main street as it approached midnight.

Lanjarón had swelled to about 20,000 people for that day and this was the main event. We headed up to the top of town amongst a throng of other revelers, charging up water pistols from the fountains. We got squirted occasionally, which is forbidden before the cannon goes and you can be fined! There was a lot of singing and shouting as we waited at the top of the high street. Then we saw headlights and three cars came round the corner, how they had been allowed through amazed us and the first car had his window down and was being very vocal about not being able to get through. Splat! A party goer had lined up his water pistol and fired, which gave the driver a rude awakening. Much to everyone's surprise the driver got out to berate the reveler then got back in to try to make his way out of town. I frowned a little as his car was rocked as I could only imagine myself in the same situation but then I would not have been so stupid as to try to leave town at this hour or berate someone in a water fight. Plus to lower your window at this point was asking to get wet!

The anticipation was like being at your first concert and waiting for the group you've eagerly awaited to come on stage. None of us had watches on so it was only when the fireman climbed the ladder to be on top of the tender that we knew we were close to the off.

The water canon was set off and we were

suddenly drowned in cold water. Even at the 20+ degrees at midnight, it was a cold, sobering wake up. More was to come. The noise intensified from people's cheers, songs and chants. It was almost hypnotic. Buckets of water and hoses linked to the kitchen tap rained water down on us then just as you had spluttered your way through that, water from the fire hydrants swept across the throngs and blasted you with icy cold water. Every time you caught your breath and got close to a cannon or a hose, there was much dancing and jumping up and down to the chants of 'mucha agua, mucha agua, hey! Hey!' before you were blitzed with the water and then slowly bounced your way down the street. Another hydrant and another set of hoses rained down on us. It was warm! A pleasant relief before we were zapped by more water cannons of cold water. I looked down at my squelching feet and I was walking in a river. A river at least an inch deep in the high street of Lanjarón, I couldn't get my head around it. The chanting continued and could be heard high into the mountains and we were having a great time. The next pause for *mucha agua* and I got blasted in a direct hit left then right; now I was starting to feel cold. Bella was feeling the same so as we were near my road we decided to divert for dry clean clothes and a much needed glass of wine. We squelched down the road, grinning broadly. We had been out there for an hour doing a walk that on a normal day would take about 15 minutes. It was an experience not to be missed.

After we had dried off and changed, we set off back into town. The street stalls were still selling food and drink and trinkets, and bands were still playing in the square as we partied on for another 2 hours in Bar Health. At 3am as I turned to leave I had to face my demon, Dom had come into the bar. This wasn't the person I fell for all those months ago, what had happened to him? he looked disheveled and unshaven. Even with all the troubles created, I'm not one to hold a grudge, life is too short and Lanjarón too small. I hesitantly went over to say hello, and received a glazed smile, before I left and weaved my way back through the throngs of people.

After the feverish highs of last night's water fight and the 3.30am bed time, it was time to face the other demon of the mule shed and those beams. Although Juan had made Bella jump up and down on the floor above the beams to prove the house was now safe, I felt like I was doing the walk of death as I really don't know what to expect. As I undid the catches and turned the big key in the door the sick feeling was back. I opened up to see firstly that the traditional oak doors were now in place and looked splendid apart from stripping and staining. I forced myself to look up and see six new *vigas* in place of the rotten chestnut beams. I cussed myself again for believing Dom was capable of doing the work and for being taken in by him when he said he had poked at them and that they were ok as they had been treated.

Rubble was all over the floor still but that could be cleared later with another skip or two and I had masses of tiles left over to use somewhere. The mosaic ones Dom splashed out on were lovely but these plain blue ones would have looked as good. The work that Juan has done was great and the place now stood proud once more, but what else would I uncover? Or was it because as yet, I hadn't put my own stamp on the place so was not feeling settled? I was starting to analyse every craze in the walls and every beam for holes. I was scared again that it would be a money pit. I had to lay down the logic. The house had the beams done so was nicely supported. The back wall now had the lintels in and was rendered against the weather. The lead pipes in the bathroom had been removed and copper ones in. If I could cope with that then I could keep coping until it is all sorted.

But I so desperately wanted this place to feel like me and it didn't. But that was down to impatience and logically there was no point in having lovely furnishings if I was going to get Juan to knock a few other bits and pieces about.

I set to on a cleaning mission and sweat was soon pouring down my face. I unpacked the towels, emergency escape ladder for the spare room [yes I know, hardly necessary when there is no one in there but something I thought of and bought] and other odds and sods I had lugged over. I cooled off for a little then cleaned the kitchen again. Then remembered that I needed to go and get a regulator for the gas bottle so that the cooker would link up again but the hardware store was shut until the following day. Not that it as a problem as in that heat eating hot food was not top of the list: drinking water was.

A siesta beckoned and I decided to recline on the lounger in the shade for a while and relax watching the house martins as they tumbled overhead. I was startled by '*buenos dias*' and I looked up to see my neighbour to the right, hanging out her washing. A perfect modern Spanish lady, hair highlighted a glorious shade of red, make up perfect and a beaming smile. There was me in an old summer dress sweating in the shade with my hair awry and my face like a beetroot. *"hola, me llama Charlotte"* a frown and I repeat myself, a smile, *"ah, me nombre es Adora, encantada"* and with a smile she went back to her washing. I dozed off and was woken by the music coming from the square; time to get the party head back on and go for the short walk into town.

As ever, it didn't seem to matter which bar I walked into Dom was there and whenever he saw me his face turned to thunder. Ah well, the worst was done and I acknowledged him politely and carried on into the bar for a drink with Bella. We left to wandered the streets listening to music. It was much more subdued and a lot of stalls had packed up, it was now time for the football, the European Championships. It was a time for people to come down from the mountain to watch it on the big screen in the bar, many I didn't know and others I only knew vaguely. It was the big match, the Final between Spain and Italy. Any excuse to be in town and watching the football with a few beers thrown in of course and Bar Health was rammed with a happy throng celebrating each goal with another round of drinks and what a match it turned out to be with Spain winning! That celebration went on well into the night, I doubted that any Spanish would be at work the next day.

I had a local journalist coming around to interview me for Living Spain magazine as she was doing an article on why people buy abroad and the properties on offer. She wasn't due for at least half an hour so I was surprised when I heard a tap on the door as I knew she would be late, especially as a mother of two lively young boys! With my stomach churning, I wandered downstairs in the hope it wasn't her or Dom and opened the door to a bearded hippy guy in shorts. I had never met this guy before so was a bit wary when he called me by name. "Hi Charlotte, I'm a friend of Dom and Bella's, I've done some work on your house." I'm puzzled at this, "and you are?"

"Tim."

I pondered, "Tiler Tim?"

"Oh, yes sorry, I forgot people know me by that name. I'm trying to sort out what has been going on with Dom as there are bills he hasn't paid and I wonder if you had paid them since you had been here?"

My heart sank and I felt very sick. "Hang on a minute.

Unpaid bills, to whom?" I was being cautious here as I'd heard about Tim and knew he was a friend of most people and had been here for 17 years. It was horrible to have to be so cautious but I didn't want to have more gossip spreading around town than there already was.

"Well, first of all there was a bar bill he hadn't paid"

I interjected, "Why the heck are you telling me this?"

"Well," Tim looked slightly awkward, "It's not your problem I'm sorry, then there is Almacen for the second skip."

"But I have receipts for 2 skips" I say puzzled.

"Ah but that could be for cement, as it probably came to the same amount."

I'm still confused and cautious, "Can you tell me how much money you gave him?"

"No! But let me tell you that it was more than enough to pay for the work done and the car." I was feeling angry and unsure where all this was leading so I tried to remain calm.

"So it was I'm guessing a four figure sum?"

My eyebrows raised, why was he fishing for that information if he already knew? "Oh yes, much more." I was starting to feel a bit upset and vulnerable as I was no way paying out on bills that I had been told were already paid.

"And there's me too" said Tim, "I worked here for the last two weeks before you got here and he hasn't paid me either."

I was speechless. I really didn't expect this. "I can't afford to pay out twice Tim, Dom told me he had paid you all and that you did two days work, that's all I know. I even had to pay Juan when I got here."
Tim shook his head, "It surprises me that he hadn't paid Juan but I believe what you have told me and I'm sorry that he has done this to you. I'm going to sort it out as best as I can. I want to retain Dom as a friend and am glad to have you as a new friend."

"Well, how are you going to get Dom to pay the bills if he hasn't got the money now?"
"He's going to work it off for the people he owes; that is the only way he can do it. I will also make sure he stays away from you and doesn't give you any hassle."
That was sounding more like a threat than a promise to me, I hadn't figured on him giving me any hassle. Wouldn't that be the dumbest thing he could do, apart from the fact he didn't look capable of doing anything if the last time I saw him was anything to go by.
"Don't worry Charlotte, I'll make it happen" and with that, Tim left me feeling bewildered and somewhat shocked. How much more detritus had Dom left in his wake, the carpet had once more been pulled from under my feet, had Dom manipulated Tim too?

I managed a quick shower before the bell rang and the journalist arrived. After a glass or two of wine and the declarations that all men were the bloody same, she took some pictures before we headed down to Bar Flower for some wine and tapas. I was beginning to feel like Bogart as we got near the bar 'in all the bars in the world you have to walk into mine' came into my head as I saw Dom seated outside. Ah well, polite greetings done once more, we went inside for vino blanco and tapas, then more vino blanco and more tapas before I decided I was ready for an early night [it was gone 11].

*

The rest of my days were filled on that trip with trying to promote myself as a business in transition. The logical thing for me to do was to promote the skills I already had so that when I moved to Spain I had at least a few clients within the surrounding areas. Hopefully this would make the big leap less daunting as far as work went. With many years of design and marketing know-how, I could offer advice on the coast and also to people like Bella who lived in the more rural areas and, despite being capable of what they were doing, had no idea how to market and develop it and increase their client base. So I was off to meet the editor of the Sentinella, a small English quarterly booklet, to talk about some advertising. I had built myself a web site specifically for the Spanish market, added a new company name of Business Ventures and produced leaflets and business cards. I knew I could do design and print services at a good price plus do them in small quantities that would suit local businesses. I wanted to explore the local areas and see if I could get any local companies on board for their promotional merchandise. As well as the piece in Living Spain, I had featured in an entrepreneurial piece in the Guardian. With the wide distribution of the Sentinella, it seemed the obvious first choice for marketing. I loved going down to Salobreña, a stroll along the beach and a seafood lunch at a beach front café with your toes scrunching the sand under foot. That day was different; a meeting in a café away from the beach, ideas exchanged with Kelly the editor, and the drive back up to town.

After a quick drink of water it was off to my second appointment of the day, reviewing the rooms of the Alcadima for the prospect of friends coming over for my 50th birthday later in the year. It was nice to see Amanda again as she was integral in my safety when I first came to the area 3 years ago after my fall when I was out walking.

My stroll there was a trip down memory lane and Amanda remembered me when I reminded her of the situation. She kindly showed me around the rooms I needed to see and offered a good rate for party bookings too. I loved this hotel and the gardens are so lush and tranquil with beautifully laid courtyards, I often wished I could buy a room there rather than a house!

It was a nice end to the day to meet up with

Mike and Jane who I had stayed in touch with. Although we couldn't always meet up in person, we often chatted over the internet. They came around to look at what developments had been made to my house and were amazed at the changes that I had made and were positive in their outlook for my future here. "We all have building issues," Mike said, "nothing here is easy but you will be fine, the work is done. Relax and enjoy it now." It was great to have their support and I was sure they were right: the worst was over.

Muy Calor and the Good Life

I must learn to shield the front window or cover the steering wheel! The steering wheel was so hot I could barely touch it so I started driving with finger and thumb while the air con did its thing; and then I was off to work. A day of work, yes work. Off up to Bella, not without some trepidation as it meant I had to drive the mountain track. Reason number 23 of why I wouldn't live up the mountain. This is a good track too, for a large extent it is concreted, but the way there is a sheer drop to one side is a little disconcerting to say the least! I had driven down twice but never up. The first hurdle is negotiating the correct back streets that lead you onto the track, that done you start the climb of around another 800m. I am a relatively confident driver, but even in this little Kia I was a bit nervous. I was not looking forward to meeting anyone coming the other way at all and, being alone, I didn't have a second set of eyes to spot dangers. Up I climbed, the car stalling twice on the tight bends [it was a nightmare hire car for that], past the landmarks I remember, various people's houses and parked camper vans. But the vegetation had grown so much in the last month or so that I was wondering if I would recognise Bella's track. Ah well, if I went too far and got to the end of the concrete I would know I had gone a few bends too far. You do feel like you are on a roller coaster that is dragging you slowly, slowly up to that first pause and tip where your stomach lurches. I came to a track I was pretty sure was Bella's and tucked the car into the shrubs, no way was I taking the little thing down there as I'd seen the ruts and knew one false move could give me a lot of explaining to do! I unloaded all my goodies, locked up and ambled down the track, still not sure that I had the right one so it was with relief to reach her gate and be greeted by an equally hot Bella. The haze across the Sierra Nevada today was heavy. At 11 am temperatures were already hitting 35'. How did anyone work in this?

After unloading goodies of fresh bread and lemon tart, Bella and I sat in typical British fashion, chatting over a cup of tea, then we had work to do. Bella's was a talented artist, sculpting things out of what seemed like fresh air to me! All manner of clay and metal pieces that sold well over the internet and through local garden centers. We caught up when I was over and discussed the next step for her business. Back in the UK I mentored start up businesses. So for the next few hours we were heads down discussing marketing and social networking for the business and how she could move it forward. A productive few hours and whilst we chatted away her daughter who was visiting prepared lunch for us. The woofers were called and we all sat around a big table in the shade to eat.

What's a woofer? Well it's not a dog! People travel the globe, staying on people's land in exchange for work. It allows them to see into the culture of the area, earn their keep before moving on to another country. It's also great to learn from them too and as Bella had terraces of olive and almond trees, help was needed to farm them when in season.

After the lovely lunch it was siesta time so we all split off to our own space, I opted for the shade of the sun house [contradiction in terms I know] and I was soon doing a nodding dog doze in the chair for 20 minutes. It was so relaxing being high above town, you couldn't hear a thing but nature. Sadly I needed to go back home so reluctantly said my goodbyes and did the nightmare journey down. If I'm honest, there was no rush, it was just playing on my mind that I had to drive down into town and my stomach was churning. With good reason! I started back off down with my hands clenching the steering wheel, you also have to bear in mind that I was still a novice at driving on the wrong side of the road and although a competent driver it's a default setting in the brain after thirty odd years. I got the worst two bends out of the way without a single car coming the other way and began to relax. On the next bend I could see across the distant track and it was clear. Around another sharp lefthander and that was clear too. I was glad as this was a narrow bit of track with no chance of pulling in only reversing for the brave hearted one. A right hand bend and damn, a Spanish car coming the other way that didn't belong to anyone I knew.

I stopped.

He stopped.

Hmmmm........ I looked left; sheer rock. I looked right; sheer drop. But a bit further back was a drive to a *cortijo*. Looks like I'm going to be the brave hearted one then.

Neutral.

Handbrake.

Reverse.....I was trembling.

I felt the clutch bite and started to manoeuvre backwards. Slowly does it. Oops, no, too close to the edge. Forward a bit and straighten up. Let's try the side mirror rather than the rear view...ah much better. I gingerly headed backwards and then turned into the drive..which was in itself a drop. I felt like I was purposely going to drive off a cliff. When your foot is trembling as much on the pedals as your hands are on the wheel, it's a weird experience. Handbrake firmly ON! The Spaniard waved and smiled as he drove past; yes, next time *amigo*, you can go back round the bend and let me past! Thankfully the rest of the journey down was uneventful and it was bliss to return to tarmac.

*

That evening I wandered down to the Health Bar for some food and to see who was about to chat to. I don't actually think that anything in Lanjarón is a taboo conversation subject over a *tubo* in the bar but

I tried to avoid getting caught up in any gossip. Life is different here, very different. Come here and pretend to be something you are not and you will only scratch the surface of life and its minutiae. Yes you can sit in bars and talk to the locals, get drunk, eat the great food on offer and go home with a tale to tell and the memory of great people. You will have only seen a small amount of what is on offer, but you will be sated and will have had a great time. Speak Spanish and you will peel back another layer, but you will still be a foreigner and the accent here is so guttural and the words shortened to something unrecognisable. But if you fit in, the town will choose you. It will lure you back like a mermaid does a fishing boat and drag you into its lifestyle, engulfing you in its daily routine and customs. You will take the bottle saying 'drink me' and spiral into another world that you didn't know existed. The mad hatter takes many guises and occasionally it will be you. You will learn about different people, cultures and religions; you'll accept others opinions that are not the same as you. You won't flinch at things that in your homeland would make you blow the dust off your soapbox, stand upon, and pontificate. You will accept the people who live here and more importantly, yourself. It’s a mind blowing experience without drugs. It can be a raw revelation that some people can't cope with but for most people it is the finding of nirvana and happiness. Don’t get me wrong, Lanjarón is not full of lazy cigar smoking millionaires, far from it. Most people here work hard for a living and that living is usually quite meagre but the quality of life is all important and if you can afford to live here, you have it by the bucket load

Sit outside a bar to see a ruddy group of Europeans settled in the sun in dusty trousers and walking boots discussing water is normal and I'd probably say a weekly occurrence. Don't expect this group to all be old greying men either, you'll have young pretty teachers, retired accountants, writers, aviation engineers and even an odd actor on occasions all discussing what is important, how to work with the land. What they all have in common is that they live out of town on the tracks so are all self - sufficient, it is something us townies didn't have to deal with at all.

Self- reliance for most of us was what we had seen on 'The Good Life' where Tom and Barbara turned their garden in suburbia into allotments and grazing for a pig and some hens. Toiling day in, day out, growing veg and having jolly japes with their neighbours in the posh bit of Surbiton.

Wrong. Self -reliance means much, much more than that.

As I said previously, the first time I went up the mountain for dinner with new friends [literally within 2 days of meeting them], I took along a cooked chicken wrapped in foil to keep the heat in. It was December 2011. There was little or no fencing or barriers unless it was the back of someone's property but laughingly, every so often there were stones painted white as markers to let you know that this was the edge and if you ventured any further, you were having flying lessons: minus the parachute. The second time I went up the track was when I was back to sort the house deal and I met Bella and somehow got myself invited up to hers for lunch. By now I had become slightly more familiar with village life [yes it's a town, but] and more relaxed in the company of locals who were in the main friendly and laid back. You could not expect to live like you would in a big town or city; this really was another form of lifestyle altogether. It also has the effect of making you question the use of resources at your fingertips. Do you wonder where water comes from when you leave a tap running whilst brushing your teeth? Do you ever wonder if that tap will run dry? Leave a light on when you are going upstairs for a shower or to work on the computer? How much will that drain your solar batteries? What will happen if there is no sun for a few days? How will you boil a kettle, blow dry your hair, make your toast? It is such a reality check that for days afterwards I was conscious of my usage of anything power related. Every time I went up to visit a friend in the *campo*, I would stand on their terrace and wonder at the work that has gone into creating this idyll and admire what everyone there created. It is truly inspiring and magical.

When you are in such magnificent scenery the

urge to walk and discover more beauty comes every day as you rise to see what the day holds. Rarely do I lie in bed past sunrise here, unless the shutters are firmly shut! I can't wait to get up and open the door onto the terrace and see what was going on. Paths, tracks and roads weave their way across the hillsides. Little curls of smoke that lead you back down to a *cortijo* or a *finca* nestled in the hillside. *Ermitas* sitting on little outcrops waiting for those that need them, a beacon of religious righteousness above towns and villages for anyone to feel peace in. Even on a cloudy day the view brings hope and beauty. But my boots have remained on their shelf in the bedroom unused much to my disappointment, other than the trips into the *campo*.

It was a pleasure to get up in the morning while it was still mild, well as mild as it gets in September which is..warm! To sit on the terrace with breakfast and watch the changing colours of the Sierra de Lujar as the sunrises above it from my left and the block of black starts to breathe into life. A watery ochre, then a warming red, to purples and then greens and grey of vegetation and stone emerge. *Cortijos* spring to life, vehicles moving along tracks of farmers who have already been working for an hour or more in the cool of the day. People going steadily about their life. I sat and watched the colours unfold in near total silence is a complete pleasure. I hope I will always marvel at the sunrises here, every day is different from the last and it is the most wonderful alarm clock. I am relaxed here, well, when things weren't going wrong, I sat and just watch what life had to offer. Not an easy life and it would certainly not suit a lot of people but for me, it was pretty perfect. Life in Lanjarón was looking positive again and I was back on track for working out future business ideas to keep me secure. Life was on the up!

My first Christmas

I was so happy. The house was now a home with structure and no building work needed for the time being at least. A two week visit for the festive season meant I could really settle in and put some trinkets around the place to make it feel more homely. It had been suggested that I take in a lodger for the time I wasn't there but after everything that had happened, I didn't think I could trust anyone and for what little income I could gain, was it really worth it? Maybe later on, who knows?

The real bonus was that the house wasn't full of dust. Cleaning didn't have to commence as soon as I walked in the door. I'd visited the supermarket on the way up so with the fridge and cupboards full I settled on the couch and flicked on the big old TV. I was at least glad to have inherited a massive dish on the roof terrace that could probably be seen from space. But there was rumour, not unusual in a small town but this time it turned out to be fact not fiction that the satellite supplying English channels was to be shut down. Still, for this Christmas, I could watch whatever I wanted. As the air chilled I threw on a pair of pjs, threw a fleecy blanket over my legs and relaxed in my cosy little house. It was so good to be home.

*

'Bong'

'Bong'

Half past something o'clock in the morning. I squinted at my phone...seven...groan, the work body clock still clicked in. The air was cold and a peek behind the shutters revealed darkness. Back under the duvet please.

By 9am it was light.

By 10am it was bright.

By 11am it was warm.

The first thing I wanted to do today was to visit the Chino Bazar one of two local shops that sold all manner of things that you didn't know you needed, time for a Christmas tree. Then to unpack the hand luggage for the decorations, that and a couple of presents was all that was in there. I was adept by now at cramming my life into 10kg of knick-knacks from one home to the other. Plus an endless stream of tea bags of course.

With limited space it had to be a small tree and I have to say the box was quite slim compared to how the tree looked on display even though the picture looked the same. Taking it out of the box it had plastic sleeves over the spruce branches which, once released sprang out into little green toilet brushes. All poked into the main trunk of the tree, it looked quite splendid. Within half an hour it was festooned with far too many trimmings, baubles and tinsel with enough left over to dot around the room from all the random hooks and nails. The few small gifts I had brought with me from close friends were popped underneath to finish things off. I was actually feeling festive! I had not spent Christmas in the UK for over ten years. Even when I was married there were no family celebrations to get embroiled in and, being self employed, it was the ideal time to take a decent holiday without worrying about missing any jobs. I've spent some lovely festive breaks in hotels and not worried about being alone at all and it was always lovely to see what the hotel was going to surprise you with. My favourite being a seven course meal which had included a six foot long Christmas pudding ablaze and being paraded around the dining hall by the chefs! That was also the night I shared a table with a lovely couple that I had struck up a friendship with. He didn't drink very much and for the first time in his life he went to bed in a very wobbly fashion and the next day had his first hangover and couldn't remember anything past the last course! He was 72. But this was my first Christmas in my new home. I had food in the fridge and had planned on getting some seafood for a treat, then feet up and enjoy the day like any other but I had been cajoled into going up the mountain to Bella's. I had no say in the matter; I was not spending Christmas day alone if she had anything to do with it, how could I argue?

With boots and Santa hat on I set off up the mountain along with her family and friends. Thankfully the drive up the mountain was uneventful and as I pulled into her gates the dogs bounded out to greet me. Inside, a single strand of tinsel showed Bella's rebellion for fancy frivolities in her house, but a roaring wood fire burned merrily in the corner. The champagne was opened on the terrace, the cork popping off into the compost heap and so, sipping champagne we wandered to the studio to view her latest sculptures before a succulent chicken dinner with home grown veg. Perfect.

With Bella snoring off the champagne in front of the fire I wandered out onto the terrace as the sun was sliding down behind the mountains leaving a light golden glow above the low clouds that were tucking themselves down into the folds of the peaks and troughs. Jack Frost was dancing across my shoulders as I enjoyed the changing view. I might not be in my house but the colour palette laid out before me as the clouds came in to shroud us for the night were a beautiful sight. Blackened peaks loomed out from the greyish yellow cloud that was tucking itself in with generosity. I really felt very lucky indeed.

Morning broke and I poked my nose from under the duck down quilt. Brrr. Thick socks and pjs on I entered the kitchen to be greeted with smoked salmon and eggs Benedict and a mug of builder's tea. Just what the doctor ordered after last night's drinking session in front of the fire. Monopoly must be accompanied by home brewed wine but too much and ouch!

"Eat up, we're off for a walk in a minute," Bella was already dressed and boots on. With breakfast plates added to the pile of yesterdays I quickly dressed and we were soon off and out along the *acequias* [water channels] and up to the head of the Rio. It was a truly beautiful morning and you could see for miles. Snow capped mountains in one direction, undulating farmland in another and in the distance, the feint outline of Morocco. What could be nicer? I genuinely could not think of anything better at that point in time.

Merry Christmas.

Moving On

It was March and I was back again. The rainy season appeared to be on hold as it had been the previous year and the sun was shining on the town. Big blue skies with hardly a cloud in them, so sitting outside a bar was feasible as long as you avoided the shade. Market day and the *guiris* [colloquial term for foreigners] all trekked down from their mountain hideaways to stock up on fresh fruit and gossip. Plus the group Spanish lesson of which I normally participated in via Skype. It was hysterical. I would be in the UK in a fleece with the heating on and my friends would be sitting in t shirts sipping beer! Working in pairs was even funnier, ask any of them. But this was a great way to integrate into the community too and for me, that's more of what it was about than anything. Today I joined in the lesson in person which was great fun. It's always great to catch up with friends you don't see from one visit to the next, but this is where the internet came in very handy. We were all in contact regularly; even if only to moan that the internet had gone down.

After Spanish class we moved downstairs onto the terrace to chat, Bella was sat in the corner of the usual Ambienza warming her hands on a coffee and chatting with Diego, it took me a minute to realise who it was as I had not seen him since my house warming. The waiter passed me a coffee and tilted his head towards them with a shrug of his shoulders.

Business or pleasure I wondered, I'd heard Diego to be both a powerful as well as attractive man but as I had not had time to chat with him before so I had not made any judgment myself. He owned a couple of restaurants both here and in Órgiva and a small hotel in the backstreets of Lanjarón. It was a common haunt for walkers who were only after the basics: a clean bed for the nights when they were not spending them under canvas up Mulhacén. He was rarely in town as his sister ran the place for him. Bella caught my eye, beckoned me over and introduced me.

"Join us"

"You are planning to move here yes" Diego's voice was rich and guttural like most of the men from this region, his eyes deep and dark and he wasted no time on pleasantries other than the standard kiss of greeting. Of stocky Gypsy build with an air of wealth, he held my gaze.

"Si."

"Your planning, how is it?"

"To move here? Slowly. I need work first."

"Can you not bring your English business here and work from home?"

"eso no es possible"

"*¿por que no*?"

My attempt at conversing in Spanish died at that point. Basics were fine but not an in-depth conversation of any kind.

"What I do in England I would struggle to do here. I don't speak the language well enough to build new clients. Also I am not sure I want to be doing the same thing. I would like to carry on designing yes but I can only see problems with the printing. I'd like to try something new."

At this point Bella excused herself "I must get home to feed the brood, I'll leave you two to chat." She gave me a hug, whispered, "call me later" and headed off to her car for the drive back up the tracks.

"You have known Bella a long time, you look like very good friends?"

"No, not long at all really. She has been my saviour in a number of ways if I'm honest."

"That is good, she is a capable woman, but a little strong willed if you know what I mean." He raised an eyebrow and smiled.

"Yes she certainly is" I laughed.

Diego signalled for more drinks, "Would you like to eat while we chat?"

"No I'm fine thank you. The tapas is good here and will do for me." He nodded and lit a cigarette. "So" There was a pause, "You need to work here, what have you got in mind to do?"

I sat back. I was not about to tell this man the extent of my ideas but I needed to test the water with a few of them at least to gauge his reaction.

"Well I'm thinking of offering a print and design service but mainly online to the English market. Also to build up an English speaking client base from down amongst the expats on the coast. Maybe offer business services and mentoring to them as I have done that for many years in the UK. I think some of the bars owners could do with a hand from good marketing and promotions." I really didn't want to say much more so I hoped this was enough.

"You have some good ideas but it sounds like a lot of hard work for a woman of your age."

"What?" no one had ever said that before!

He jumped in, "You English, you push yourselves too hard. You cannot work in Spain in the same way you do in England. It won't work. Apart from the heat, we Andalucían's do not work that way. If you work here, it is a much slower pace." I nodded, I couldn't argue with his logic at all. "Besides, aren't you coming here for a better quality of life and to enjoy yourself? What is the point of working so hard, you will have no time to enjoy this beautiful place." I took a sip of wine; he was making perfect sense.

"I have an idea." Over the next hour he explained the idea of setting up a business to promote the arts and culture of the area. With a foot in both the British and Spanish camps we could market goods and hopefully make some money from fairs. With Diego working to encourage contributors and organise the fairs in Spain, I would do the design, marketing literature and web presence from the UK. It sounded perfect and a low risk way of potentially getting a sustainable income so that I could make the leap to Spain if it worked. Plus there were many ways of expanding and increasing business. It seemed simple and overheads would be low to start with.

There are many crafts associated with the area and they were certainly not a dying art at all. But many of the tourists never went inland to see them, preferring to stay on the coast for the sun. We would not just be looking at selling to holiday makers either. The expat community is large in Spain with many settling quite happily on the Costas. So to be able to take them the traditional *jarapa* rugs and woven *esparto* baskets seemed a good idea. Along with these items there was of course the *jamons*, goat's cheese and home cured meats that were indicative of the area. It certainly sounded a plausible idea and Diego left me mulling things over.

* * *

I am naturally an ideas person and have been referred to as an entrepreneur: I called it survival! I saw entrepreneurs as wealthy risk takers and I am certainly not one of those. I needed to think through this opportunity and see what tangents my mind went off to. I fed off the creative process but I needed to let the initial idea swim around in the back of my mind for a while before I started looking at the pros and cons of the venture. The best thing that could happen would be that we all made money. The worst was that we would gamble a few hundred euros and walk away realising it wasn't going to work. Until you try, you never know.

Having put a roof over my own head since I was old enough to work without being employed by anyone else was I suppose quite unusual. Plus I had worked with the Chamber of Commerce as a small Business Advisor on a volunteer basis for many years. Seeing someone succeed with their dream job on their own merits was a wonderful thing to help with, so I was used to looking at the 'ifs and buts' of a situation. As an experienced designer and marketeer I was confident that we could create a brand that over time would develop and be synonymous with the area and its culture and hopefully bring wealth to the area as well as business for us.

Back at work in the UK the workload had been quiet since Christmas, but when this carried on into March and April it was very worrying. I was struggling making ends meet to pay the overheads on my unit and myself a wage. Time to clamp down on materials and stock and to not spend extravagantly in my personal life, [not that I usually was] just in case I needed to insert funds into the business. Any extra expenditure was out of the question until things picked up in any quarter of my life. I'd weathered every other recession over the last few years so I felt confident that I would be ok. I have to say I had been very lucky in that respect. I had seen many businesses around me fall apart during the last bout of recession. People amassing huge debts with suppliers and also allowing too much credit to their customers. All it takes is one client to default on payment and the walls start to cave in, I know as I've come close. It's a hard lesson to learn but one you don't forget. I had a big loss 10 years ago and learnt my lesson then, but you can't help feel sorry for people you have known for many years when they have to close the doors on a family business. As a small business, your work is also your life. I've never actually been employed by anyone so I don't know what I would do if I ceased to trade. I don't even know how to sign on for benefits! I had diversified over the years, originally I was a designer and screen printer. Then I moved into marketing before progressing into embroidered clothing. I was always trying to open another door before the last one swung shut. Screen printing was a dying craft. Technology had taken over for the most part and many of my old screen print jobs are printed using the digital format now plus the fact that it made my rheumatism flare up standing in one spot for hours. To be honest I am glad not to be doing so much of it. It's a hard profession to be in and as I specialised in printing onto metal, it was also physically demanding. A digital machine and embroidery were the way forward. I just hoped I could weather the current storm as well as I had weathered the previous ones. Currently I wasn't convinced.

So, as well as giving the project in Spain my attention I had to work on my own marketing in the

UK. I had no husband to offset the mortgage payments and no bank of mom and dad to borrow from should I have needed to. It was all on my shoulders which, after all the issues with the house in Spain was stressful but I wasn't admitting it. Once the marketing was implemented for the UK I could focus my attention on the ideas from Diego for Spain, but where did I start?

I had had a few chats with Diego via Skype and I had got a better feel for his personality as we chatted and I found that quite helpful. He was certainly an intelligent man and answered any questions I had regarding the produce we would sell, especially regarding perishables. Fortunately his contacts were all happy to do 'sale or return'. They could obviously see that it was good for them to be selling goods to a wider audience.

It was time to put pen to paper.

Money.

Research.

Target Market.

Profit and Loss projections.

Just a few of the things that needed consideration. With the goods we had decided to sell being sale or return, that saved us a huge amount of outlay and risk. Although Diego seemed convinced that a van load of local *jamons* would sell quickly, I wasn't so convinced. How many British people can be bothered to buy a whole *jamon* and would they know what to do with it? I certainly didn't know any! Plus, transporting large and heavy items would be a logistics nightmare.

Diego had already found our first venue down in Nerja so we had a date of two months ahead to plan and work towards should we do it. He would cover the cost of the stand and I would cover the cost of the marketing. Our target market would be the middle aged and older expats who had moved to Spain to live their new lives in luxury and warmth. I'd spoken to a number of people on the plane over and they were all under the impression that Lanjarón was a day's drive away and not just an hour or two. Some had even never heard of it which is rather ironic as they were usually holding a bottle of Lanjarón water. Very few had ventured inland at all, moving to Spain purely for the climate. It amazed me, so what better than taking a little of the *Alpujarra* to them, it would open up a whole new world. I also spent some time on social media asking questions of people living on the coast. Sadly they seemed to live in very English enclaves and eat an English diet other than the cheap Spanish wine and beer. As for the beautiful *jarapa* rugs, they had never heard of them and popped along to Ikea to get the same as they would in the UK!

Another avenue I thought would have been worth exploring was the tourist trade. In and around Lanjarón there were many beautiful hotels and a diverse range of activities from walking, climbing, horse riding to skiing and spa breaks. There really was something to suit everyone. But could we encourage people that it was worth coming inland and getting active or where they all too busy enjoying their sedentary lifestyle around the pool?

I was currently seeing as many negatives as positives. If we could encourage people to travel up to Lanjarón [it is after only a 30 minute drive from the coast] the local economy would benefit hugely. The hotels would enjoy the extra trade as much as the bars and restaurants. I know I was biased but the food in Lanjarón was very good across the board. If we could encourage people to come for the fiestas too, they would tell their friends and it would be ongoing.

It would be impossible to market this first event well, there was not enough time, but it would be a taster for the future and we could gain a lot of valuable information and start a database for emails and on line sales. It would be easy enough to set up a web page and a social media page but time consuming to add all the information and photographs. Technology is wonderful but loading data on web pages can seem painfully slow and tedious. We also needed promotional materials, handouts, brochures, price lists and business cards, plus of course, embroidered t shirts. Diego had already got local businesses on board for marketing but their contribution would cover the printing costs and I would be doing their artwork for free. It seemed I would getting more and more bogged down with stuff. 'Stuff' to produce, 'stuff' to research, 'stuff' to market; stuff, stuff and more stuff and I was no closer to making a decision than I had been at the start. That was not a good sign.

By way of a slight diversion I decided to look up the venue and see if that gave me any inspiration. Evidently the organizers had promised a 5000 footfall over the two days. A promise I found odd as it was their first event. I located the website for the venue and discovered it to be a modern building with two rooms for conferences and wedding receptions but it was away from the coast and on a modern industrial park. I emailed Diego and asked how many people had booked the show and what was the nature of their trade. A day or so later he emailed me the traders list; an insurance broker, a self published author, a garden centre, a beach bag lady and a mix of other unrelated businesses totalling twelve in all and nothing else was traditional Spanish. Nor was there anything significantly English that would be an incentive to spend a day indoors and away from the Spanish sunshine. What kind of people would be bothered to get in their car and travel to this show in this location, we needed to be in the expat community and have them drop in as they walked by.

I sat back and put my pen down. I really couldn't see this being the business opportunity it seemed to be at the start. If people on the coast were not interested in Spanish culture they wouldn't bother to travel to a show to see us or anyone else; it involved too much effort. I went back to my notes.

The marketing and promotion was a solid 6-8 weeks work. Time I would have to dedicate with no pay if we were to be ready on time. Time I could little afford with the way things were plus the added cost of the domain name and the printing. The cost of having a stand at the show was in the premium bracket but it seemed little more than a normal market but indoors. Then add in the logistics of getting all the goods there and set up. As Diego swanned around in a sports car we would have needed to hire a van. Factor in my flights and the accommodation in Nerja and costs were spiralling. I certainly felt like I would be doing the lion's share of the manual work and outlaying money that was more than expected. It was a lot to complete in a short space of time but 6-8 weeks of not earning any money in my normal business was not possible.

I'd made my decision but decided to sleep on it before letting Diego know. I couldn't do it. The investment of time and the research I had done did not seem a sound investment to me. I would email both him and Bella tomorrow and state the reasons why I could not be part of this set up and let them carry on without me.

But for now I was mentally drained. Whilst my mind had been in the Spanish project I had also had to continue working on the business. So for the last few weeks I had been working from dawn till dusk without a break in trying to remarket and get in new clients.

Add that to the stress of dealing with all the issues with the *mi casa* over the last two years and it had taken its toll on me. I realised I had pushed myself too far. Through all the building mess, the broken relationship, the loss of money, I had not once crumbled. I had battled on constantly. No tears, no tantrums and that had been a mistake.

I faced the doctor.

"Well, your Blood Pressure is a little high, any reason?"

"I...I think I need help." I began to cry. "I think I'm depressed. I need help." A box of tissues was slid across the desk towards me. He let me cry it out.

A sheet to fill in to clarify just how depressed. Suicidal? Does anyone ever answer yes even if they are? Medication prescribed and I was out the door to return in a few weeks. I sat looking at that prescription a long time before I handed it in at the chemist. Fluoxetine. I felt like I was admitting defeat. I had failed to stay strong and to cope. I was angry and annoyed with me. All I could think of was that I had failed. I'd failed to do enough research. I'd failed to see the signs that Dom was not who I thought. I'd failed to see my business being in trouble in the UK. And now here I was trying to decide if I was suicidal, maybe it would be better all around if I was, then the pain would go away and I wouldn't have to keep fighting.

Over the next few weeks I functioned in a haze. The only thing I forced myself to do was go to work, there was no choice. In reality I wanted to go to bed and hide. I didn't want to speak to anyone, I didn't want to go anywhere. The tablets kept me in this floating bubble, I functioned but felt like I was looking over my own shoulder. Very slowly I calmed down. My thought process was still awry. I took the blame for everything, despite the people I had spoken to telling me it wasn't my fault. My logic was telling me that it must be. There were dark days. So dark I was wondering my existence and why I must be so awful. In the evenings I tried to blot things out with wine and couldn't wait to take the little tablet that would float me away from everything. It was heaven to sleep without my mind still working, I'd never in my life slept like this before. I could sleep for ten hours at a stretch and it was peaceful. There was the odd night of nightmares where I woke sodden in sweat but for the most part the little tablets did their trick.

I was open with friends and close clients that I was taking tablets for depression and I had so much support it was humbling. I never knew so many of my friends had had these problems too and many find that medication is their saviour and remain on it. I could totally understand that. At some point you find an even keel and it's actually blissful to feel 'normal.' But I had to keep functioning and that really hacked me off. I couldn't be ill in an ill kind of way, I had to be ill in a well kind of way. The business was run by me alone and if I took time off for more than a week or two I would lose custom, then lose the ability to pay the mortgage and then what? It just added another pressure into the mix I could do without.

The tears slowly ceased and looking back at those days they are strangely black. I'm not sure if I had blocked them out on purpose or whether that's an effect of the medication. I don't know how I got through the rest of that year but I held on. Once more Julie was my saviour and I will never be able to thank her for her support. I would start to feel myself crumbling inside and pick up the phone

"Morning Julie, how are you?"

"Good ta, you?"

"Yeah fine"... I sobbed out the tension and Julie would just hang in there.

"I just feel so awful. My head is like this thick fog and I can't function. I wish I could have some time off from work."

"Can you manage just a few days at the end of the week?"

In between sniffs I thought about that. "No, not really. I have jobs promised for early next week and I may have to work late to get them done anyway."

"You can't keep working these hours, you've done it too long."

"What else can I do?" I began to sob again.

"You need to learn to say no."

"But people need stuff."

"But you aren't superwoman and they just play on your kind nature."

"I'm not sure I can go back to Lanjarón."

"Dom?"

"All of them. I feel such an idiot."

It was a vicious circle of self flagellation that the tablets only dumbed down. Only by speaking out loud were any of the pieces of this messy jigsaw ever going to fall back into place-if they ever would. Maybe there would always be something missing. For someone who always planned and researched any project, this one had left me in a mess and I needed more help to get me out of it. But Julie was always there. I would repeat myself day in day out and she never told me to shut up, she just let me get it out of my system. With her support I pushed to get CBT and managed to get seen quite quickly and over six weeks of treatment I learnt a set of skills to help me cope and evaluate situations. It was quite a traumatic time. I had to be open with the therapist for it to work. I had to accept that not everything was my fault: I had to let go. I learnt how to put me first and most of all to say no in a positive way. That took a lot of implementing but over time, I got used to it. Over time I got stronger again.

I set myself a date of the following January, almost a year after being on the tablets and after I had been to Lanjarón for Christmas, to come off the medication. I felt that the tablets had done their job and wanted to see if I could function without them. I had also told myself that if I wanted to stay on them then it was fine. In talking with those friends who had talked to me privately about being on antidepressants, I learnt it was nothing shameful and that they were a medicine like any other. I had come to terms, if not understood, what had happened and wanted to move forward. Apart for the wonderful restful sleep they gave me, they had done their work. They had forced me to slow down my work pace and to start to have 'me time,' not something I would normally have and something I continued to struggle with. I realised I was in danger of grinding myself into an early grave if I wasn't careful. If there was one good to come out of it all it was that it highlighted the need for me to change my breakneck pace at which I did everything and not to feel responsible for the world. I was allowed to take the world off my shoulders and let it deal with itself, it wasn't my problem and neither were other people's opinions and personality traits. Thankfully it also proved I needed the change of pace and lifestyle for my health and sanity. So for now I would keep my little bit of paradise.

I would continue with my plan to move to Spain... providing I felt ok over Christmas.

I had three weeks there to see how I felt and to 'live' there not just be on holiday: not that organising building work and starting businesses had been a holiday. If I didn't feel I belonged then I would reassess things and see what options I had.

*

The tree went up and the decorations hung around the house. The winter throws went on the couch and I felt happy again. Thankfully over the festive period the town was quiet. Those who lived up the mountain rarely came down and townsfolk were out by day in the winter sun, and in by their cosy wood fires by night. I too followed this routine, daily shopping for fresh fish and meat and lovely home grown misshapen vegetables with loads of flavour. Healthy soups and stir fries tempered with the unhealthy wine: what a lovely way to live. I had been calling Bella, but since I had declined the business offer, she hadn't responded to any emails or to any Skype or phone calls. I really didn't know why. Then I was blocked. What the heck? This made me wonder if I had just been brought in on the idea of hers and Diego's to do all the promotional stuff for free and would have then been cast aside. The corporate branding would have been no good to me but they would have a complete business set up at no cost to them. It seemed I had lost a friend who I held dear but more than that, that friend appeared to have a side to her that I wasn't aware of. Maybe I would see her over this Christmas and New Year period and see what had happened with the business.

Day by day a routine developed of shopping, cooking, cleaning, writing, and I felt so relaxed. I moved things around so that the living space worked better. I popped out for coffee, reading and writing in the local cafés. I felt free and at peace. No demons seemed to be following me.

The odd night I popped down to the bar, sometimes armed with my kindle to read. Banter with Fernando wasn't always necessary but a nice relaxed chat with Karen as she worked in the kitchen made a nice change as she was always so busy main season. I loved this bar as it had a mix of Spanish and English patrons and it was relaxing, I always felt at home and more to the point, I always felt genuinely welcome. Karen popped out of the kitchen, "What are you doing for Christmas?"

"Feet up watching TV; prawns in the freezer and wine in the fridge so I'm sorted." Christmas alone was not an issue, I had spent so many of them in that way now that I found it lovely to have the freedom to do as I please and of course, no sprouts: I hated sprouts.

"Alone?"

"Yes of course."

"No you're not, you can come to us and keep Dad company, you know he doesn't speak Spanish."

"But..."

"No, you are coming, you are not spending Christmas alone and that's final." Tears sprang to my eyes at their generosity. A Spanish family Christmas. I was too choked to speak.

Small Spanish town life was a wardrobe full of practical clothing. More often than not a complete mish-mash of colours with comfort and warmth/coolness the main reason for buying or hanging onto stuff for many years. Getting dressed up wasn't the norm. Thankfully I had an emergency dress and shoes in the wardrobe for such occasions, I just hoped it still fitted. I had no idea what to expect but thankfully I knew a number of the family by sight if not to speak to. The streets were quiet as I walked down the high street. Bright lights reflected of red tinsel on balconies. Lights on in windows beyond and I imagined families being together at this special time of year. A tight family led community with strong traditional values, it was what I loved about the place. I was actually nervous as I entered the bar and was pleased to see familiar faces and my oh my, what a difference all laid out for the family meal. It was lovely. As ever, Fernando was behind the bar and Karen was in the kitchen. I poked my head in with offers of help but was swiftly shooed off to enjoy myself. My oh my was that Basan dancing in the bar? And Paco, Paco in a suit. Carmen in a beautiful Spanish dress. All dancing, linking arms and drinking. Then Philippe and Anna, I didn't even know they were family. Before long we were all called to be seated, crackers pulled and plate upon plate of food began coming out of the kitchen, as ever Karen had excelled herself. Traditional Spanish dishes interspersed with three varieties of prawns, mussels and local fish. Stews and ribs and steaks. Rice and vegetables and pasta. It truly was a feast accompanied with some lovely wines and followed with party games.

As I wandered back to my house at some unearthly hour I savoured the evening, it had the true magic of Christmas past, a beautiful family occasion and one I will always remember and hold dear in my heart.

***

That Christmas meal was going to be the natural end. It seemed to tie up all the loose ends and end on a happy note of a new future. It certainly did for me. Leaving me a free spirit to come and go between my home in the UK and the one in Spain. I stopped taking the tablets and managed to continue with a better pace of life, no longer allowing work to run me ragged. The next month or so back in the UK was one of deciding on what I could do to once more make the dream of a full time move a reality. It really was time that I sold my business which was a noose around my neck. I did not love what I did any longer, my passion was just not in it even though I always gave 100% and more.

I put the business up for sale.

And it felt good. It was now a matter of time awaiting a buyer and who knows how long that would take? I couldn't afford the leap to Spain 100% after the sale but I hoped I could forge a new career working from home. Meanwhile I would carry on going off to Spain and start to relax and enjoy it, even going out on day trips to places I had yet to visit. Be a tourist! In the three years I had owned the house I had yet to just wander off in the car and see places for the hell of it, there had always been a reason to go here or there other than the odd trip to Granada.

I had also strengthened friendships with Richard and Kiersten from Spanish Highs who were mountain guides and lived on the edge of the village. For my next trip out I went with Kiersten bird watching. So good to get out and do something new and to a place I didn't know existed. Just our luck that there were no birds worth taking pictures of but it was nice to get out and be what I would call normal. I was driving back and asked the innocent question, "What's down that track?"

"Oh we can get to some fab photo points down there, go for it." So I turned onto the road pointing to a name I couldn't pronounce. Down past the lake [duly noted for a peaceful time when I needed one] and along the road....that was getting narrower.

"Turn left." I turned left. No tarmac. Oh gawd...a track. But it seemed ok. Twisting left and twisting right and up we climbed.

"Stop!"

"What?"

"Reverse back a bit I think we need to go right." Right? All I saw was a gorse bush! I slowly edged back and saw a little track weaving off uphill.

"Yup, that's it, go up there."

"Are you mad?'

Kiersten laughed, "Nope, I've only been up here a couple of times but I'm sure that's the one. Besides, if we carry on uphill there is nowhere to turn around."

By this time we had been driving up these tracks for about 20 minutes: I'd only asked what was along here! We approached a clearing and pulled over and scrambled over a grassy mound. Oh what a view! We were looking straight across to Mulhacén with snow on the higher peaks and possibly one of those little specs was Richard climbing! Our villages and various other villages were clinging to the side of the Sierra, it was a beautiful sight. Kiersten looked at the time, "Damn, I need to get back."

"Er...which way from here then?"

She was silent for a minute. "Carry on for a bit and I'll get us down." The track was getting rougher as we descended. It began to be like an all terrain 4WD course. My stomach was churning as we slowly made our way along. "STOP!"

I stopped with surprise, "What?"

"Ease to the left, you're on the really soft edge of track and if we don't get off it *we* will be off." Gulp.

I gently eased left and started to pay more attention to the edges. We stopped again. This time it was my decision.

"Erm..." I put the handbrake on and the car in neutral.

We both sat looking in front of us. The recent rains had made their own path along the track and had given us some huge potholes, plus a trench. At some point we would have to cross this trench. Where was the best point remained to be seen. Kiersten got out and walked down the track looking down then up. "Ok, we are going to go across here," pointing left, then stay here, then sharp across at this point," pointing at a dip in the trench. "You have to get your left wheel across there to deal with that pothole there."

"..........ok. Here we go!" I slowly moved the car forward, concentrating on the guidance that Kiersten was giving me. I was more than a little apprehensive about crossing the trench. A hard right and then straighten up. I could breathe. We had done it. I stopped and she got back in.

"Ok, let's go. Mind this hairpin though, adverse camber and loose gravel." Oops, there goes the stomach lurch again. We were round that smoothly, "There you go, easy down to the main road now." Oh Kiersten, why did you say that? Brakes on again.

Two little faces peering out of a Punto.
Two little faces working out where to go.

One little face relishing in the challenge.

One little face wondering what the heck she had got herself into but secretly enjoying it.

Out got Kiersten and, doing the pointy thing once more, I steered the Punto to her directions and we were back onto a pothole free track that stayed that way for the next half a mile before we popped out onto a road. Tarmac. I stopped the car and got out, happy to be standing on terra firma. Kiersten laughed. Did I mention it was a hire car?

It was a silly thing to be proud of maybe, but I was proud. I could have easily swapped over and let Kiersten drive as she loves the tracks but I felt like it was a good test for me, something for me to have achieved after all the problems of the last few years here. It was good for my confidence in me which was still lacking.

Friends to Stay

This was the year for friends to come and share my space. To get their heads around how others live and if I'm honest I was glad of the company. I was still somewhat under par as far as my confidence went so having a friend to stay was a pleasure; if a little unusual as I had lived alone for six years so sharing space was weird.

I am always nervous about friends from the UK coming into my home in Spain, it is so different from what we are used to. I remember how I first felt going into Dom's. I had no idea what lay behind the oak doors of these traditional Spanish houses and neither would they. So far everyone said they loved it and everyone loved the view and the whole ambiance of the town.

For Easter my friend Brian was coming over with me and he was no different; he fell in love, hook, line and sinker. Brian was a teacher but was unsettled. A few years older than me, he felt at a loss with his life, he needed to shake it up as he felt he was just existing. He popped in to see me at work a few days before I was due to fly out and as he was feeling so low I said why not come along with me to Spain, so he did! He loved the house, the town, the charming little side streets and he fell into my first night in town trap with ease. As you may have gathered by now, if I get to Lanjarón early enough I dump my bags and head to the bar for beer and with

Brian with me it was no different. Being a big guy, he felt uncomfortable with the *tubos* and requested a pint. Well the evening rolled on and many pints and many glasses of wine were consumed. He was fitting in well and as ever, various people came into the bar. He understood not one word of Spanish other than *cerveza* but after a few hours was listening intently to a little old Spanish chap telling him heaven knows what and he was nodding intently in what appeared to be all the right places. Seeing he was happily 'chatting' away I turned my back and carried on talking to Kiersten and Richard who we had met there. The next thing I knew, there was slow clapping going on. Victor a local Spaniard had challenged him to thumb wrestle! Two grown men standing there gripping hands with all their might trying to force the others thumb over to the side: well I think that was how it was done but as I was almost seeing double, I can't be sure! Getting Brian back up the road and into the house was a task, I'm sure we walked double the distance!

Easter is a time of great celebration for Spain with *Semana Santa* [Holy Week]. Every day there were parades from the church. The streets were lined with townsfolk as the massive doors to the church were opened to reveal the hallowed insides for all to see and out came the effigy of Christ to be parade down the street. Every day with a new set of followers in different coloured silk gowns and pointed hats that came over their faces too. I'm not religious so apologise for my lack of knowledge here but it was a pretty amazing site and I have great respect for the beliefs of these people keeping these traditions going.

*

The next trip out was with my friend Carole which was entertaining before we had even left England! Over the last few years I have witnessed the transformation and expansion at Birmingham Airport and also the more hi-tech security systems being put into operation. The first time I had my backpack swabbed I took mental notes for when I write a crime thriller, you just never know what comes in handy! So it's not always plain sailing these days. Carole got searched as we went through customs and I had both my handbag and my hand luggage dragged out for swabbing. It was the start of a political conference in Birmingham so security was extra tight. "You have powder in your bag madam, next to the camera." We opened the hand luggage. Ten packets of Cadburys Smash [cheese and chive] were there along with two tubs of curry powder [hot]. Thanks Penny; the curry powder had caused a security alert! Thankfully they were happy to let it pass but my handbag was also given a random explosives check. Out came another officer who emptied it completely and swabbed it in the most obscure places. Once the swab was cleared I had the job of repacking it all back in and trying to keep out of the way of the next guy who was being swabbed. Out of six people to come through security, only one passed without being checked bodily or hand luggage. I've never had security this tight before. Oh and why the Smash? Richard and Kiersten were off to Patagonia and it was a diet staple.

Check in.

Carole had hold luggage so this was a novelty.

"As you are priority ladies, you can check in your hand luggage at no cost." I wasn't really listening but declined anyway as I had expensive camera equipment with me. I had only printed off the boarding passes that morning as I was damned if I was going to pay extra for my seating [neither was Carole and as a northerner that was to be expected!]. Evidently Mr O'Leary, owner of Ryanair had given us priority boarding. Cheers! So we jumped the queue, well, that's what it felt like and were directed to our seats, 17A & 17B: Emergency Exit so extra legroom. Too late I tried to fake to my friend that I had treated her to extra leg room. Double bonus flight!

*

"Oh I'm sorry dear, I've been sick." I looked at Carole and we both wrinkled our noses as the plane rose higher. The stewardess appeared and provided a clean plastic bag; the lady behind us had been sick in her duty free.

Considering the storms that were coming over Andalucía at the time, it was a smooth flight. Damp tarmac greeted us on a pleasant warm evening. Knowing I had little wine in the house we grabbed a couple of bottles before we left the airport before finding the Marbesol rep. Once ticked off her list we headed out through the cigarette fog to the mini bus that would take us across the road to the car hire. We were lucky, within minutes the mini bus appeared. A couple in front of us put their cases in the back and we followed suit and headed for the side door and a seat. A previously unseen man in a tweed jacket was already on the front seat and winding forward the seat to allow access to the back row. How kind of him. The couple we followed hopped up and in and Carole my friend took the last seat. I reached for the winder to move the front seat back, "These seats are reserved." I heard as a protective arm came across the seat. I looked up to see Mr Tweed Jacket was hanging onto the seat I was trying to wind upright.

"Excuse me?"

"These seats are reserved." Out of the corner of my eye I saw golf clubs being loaded onto the back of the mini bus. Men with a plan, dangerous concept akin to German towel syndrome. Three seats, three men and me.

I think he thought I'd accept his 'reservation.'

I think he thought he was in the right.

Wrong.

My stuff was on before his mates: they could wait.

I continued to roll back the seats as another couple filled the two front seats next to the driver. Once rolled back I sat on it and forced him to move across to the far side spluttering at me the fact they were reserved. He wasn't happy. That left one seat and two men and tweed jacket insisting that I move. The driver just said we would squash up to fit us all on. I took great pleasure in sitting as close to him as I possibly could and I wasn't going to rush off either, I let the back row exit before I did. But of course they had another plan, clever beggars had thought ahead. Mr Grey Jacket was first off [reminiscent of Hugh Grant with a foppish hair style] and had the paperwork for the car so he headed up the stairs to join the queue, Mr Other Tweed Jacket would retrieve the clubs and cases with the help of first Mr Tweed. Smooth operation.

I smiled.

We got our bags from the bottom of the pile and I headed up the stairs to the office. Mr Tweed was in the open doorway with his buddies, "Excuse me Sir," I said as I gently laid a hand on his waist to access the office. Being British he automatically moved to let someone through not realising it was me. Being a regular client my booking details were already sorted and I could go to a different counter which was empty. In the matter of 15 minutes I had added the second driver, signed all the paperwork and got the keys. Tweedy was still in the same spot and sucking lemons as he let me back out through the door.

It was good to get on the road and once through the evening traffic surrounding Malaga we were soon on the darker stretch of motorway up to Lanjarón. Carole could not understand my excitement and the bonus of having the journey shortened as the new section of motorway was now open. This was great news to us regular travellers.

The weather forecast for the whole weekend was '*tormentas*' so I was glad that the drive was rain free. We pulled up at the house to drop off the luggage then weaved back down to drop the car in the car park and walk back to the house. It felt so good to be here.

I unlocked the front door and headed for the fuse board to switch on the electric... Nothing.

I turned it off then on again in a different order...still nothing.

Great. No lights, no power, no TV/wifi or fridge. Would I ever get my time in Lanjarón easy?

Thankfully I did have candles. Anyone living in rural Spain would be crazy not to have candles. Plus we had the wine from the airport and some nibbles in our bags so onto the terrace we went and made the most of it.

A new day dawned and the mountains were visible for a short while but we were soon covered in drizzly cloud. Thankful for having a gas hob at least we could boil water for the morning cuppa before heading for the deli and some breakfast of great coffee and traditional Spanish tostadas. A call to a friend who arranged for an electrician to pop down and have a look at the fuse board later in the day, so a day of pottering around and waiting. The electrician didn't come... he had to go into the mountains...argh. Hopefully tomorrow. Hopefully he could fix it.

Had I been cut off? It was feasible as anyone living in Spain will tell you; the electric company has a mind of its own. Plus I had been having issues with their billing since I bought the house. I was getting so many bills in different names that trying to work out which was mine was a nightmare. With the help of Alpujarra Conect we all thought it had been rectified over the last three years and that all bills were now in my name. Wrong. I was now getting bills for both meters downstairs not just my own. I went to check the meter and it looked fine. With the weather that had been going on we all assumed it was a blown fuse. If I had been cut off, it would take them more than a week to get them to reconnect, how do I explain that to a guest? 'Sorry, we are stuck with candlelight all week and no internet and charging your phone will have to be done in the car or one of the bars.' Ah well, would just mean we had to drink more wine and beer!

And then there was the gossip. I had not been back in town for 12 hours and I was being told gossip. Walking back from breakfast I saw a friend. A quick catch up and we were both on our way, but then I was called back. "Prepare yourself, your ex is in love."

The waiting game. Between 10 and 12 the electrician would arrive.

Dum de dum de dum.

TCC [two cups Carole as I had christened her as my mugs were not big enough for her caffeine dose in the morning] was fidgeting with her kindle. I was fiddling with my kindle and trying to enjoy reading 'The Bear That Ate My Pants' but I couldn't concentrate. I was clock watching tick tock, tick tock. Our minimal chat was centred around the cloud coming and going; the mountain range appearing then disappearing. Tick tock tick tock.

11.58 knock, knock, knock. "Electrician?" " Yeah". Stares at the fuse board....nothing...was it the storm maybe? No..out to the meter...open case, lifts off wires that were tucked up behind the meter not in it. I'd been cut off again. But why? With some swift work with the screwdriver power and harmony were restored. We could see to pee! But priorities must be sorted. Fridge on and beer and wine in! Now we could buy some fresh food, yeah!

Meanwhile a call to Alpujarra Conect about it all and then she called the electrician who had done a rewire for me not 6 months ago and had sorted all the paperwork with the electricity supplier. He called them again for them to say that I wasn't registered so they had cut me off!

At least now we had an afternoon to escape and have a run down to the sea and the supermarket. We hoped that the cloud on the Sierra was not down on the coast. But it got worse; thick low cloud shrouded the small villages at the coast, but at least TCC had got to experience the mountain road in daylight. A quick wander around the *playa* at Salobreña, a kebab [don't ask, I hadn't had one for years] and as the rain spots started to hit the pavement, we headed for the car and the short ride to the supermarket. I took the old road back up so TCC could see the vast rock faces and of course some more cloud. The rain followed us gently home but thankfully had stopped by the time we got there. The fridge was now groaning with goodies including real milk not UHT so a celebration cuppa was called for before a short siesta.

The new day dawned after a blissful sleep and with the greeting of a bright blue sky making a much needed appearance. A leisurely breakfast and off to the car for a drive up to the little white villages. Round the winding bends and up we went and as we did so the sky got bluer and bluer, it was going to be a lovely day. Obviously the nutters who overtake you on those roads have the ability to see around corners; they are *muy loco!* The sun in Pampaneira was glorious; it felt so good to be out and enjoy the warmth prickling your skin. As we wandered looking at the many coloured *jarapa* rugs my phone rang, it was Lisa. Good news, the electric company were sorted [again?] but the bad news was I needed to get it disconnected again before they found out or I could be liable to a 6k Euro fine! The old tummy summersaults were back again in an instant. I felt sick and sat on the nearest wall. "Can't it wait till I've gone home to the UK?" I asked "I've just got use to being able to see when I go to the loo or have a shower!"

"Sorry but they have been told of the situation and they will send a man around within two days to sort it out." But let me contact the electrician and see what he suggests, are you at home now?"

"No, up the mountain, I won't be home for a couple of hours at least."

"Ok, I will speak to him and get him to pop around later." I needed a drink. I explained to TCC what had happened and she was almost gobsmacked. "What? Sod 'em, let's have a drink." I couldn't agree more.

The phone rang again as we sat down, "Charlotte it is ok. I have spoken with Paco and as you have reconnected at the meter and not tried to bypass it, all is well." I sighed with relief. We could continue to see to pee. So the day had improved after the stomach churning moments. Oh and the reason I had been cut off? I had been confused with the empty house next door and I just needed to pop in and sign more papers. Three days here and I felt no nearer being on holiday than I had the week before I came.

I woke with raindrops bouncing off my head. What the...? *Tormenta*. The rain was hitting the ground then bouncing in through the window mesh and onto me. Bang and the door shut to the spare room, if TCC wasn't awake by her shutters rattling then that door would have done it! My house is well protected from the wind normally as it is mid terrace and settled back a little but this storm was gusting straight through. Laying there you could hear all manner of shutters, blinds and doors banging and rattling and patio chairs scudding across the terraces. Then as abruptly as it had started, it stopped. Complete silence. I drifted off to sleep only to be woken 'falling'. The dream where the house fell-in was back. Not a great start to the day plus an early start after too much wine doesn't always bode well. I was spending too much time running around on stuff and I wanted to get these papers signed and sorted and start to relax. Not fair on TCC either as she couldn't help and she was supposed to be on holiday! Off to the office in Órgiva we went, not without its complications as it was the local *feria* so streets were shut off in readiness and the car park full of fair rides. With a little help from TCC I managed to squeeze on the end of a row of cars by the big bins. It would do for now although I hated the drive away from this top road as the turns downhill were a bit tight! When we entered the office, my deeds were out on the desk with a naive copy of the plans printed off.

"So, this is your house here." Lisa pointed to a narrow strip in the plans.

"Err no. Mine is at the back. Remember ages ago about not having a front wall for the meter to go on as I had no front wall?"

"Ah yes. Communal hall and entrance. Hmmm. Well the Ayuntamiento has you down as owning both so hence you are having both bills. Also when they cut off your electric they cut off the wrong supply as the numbers were mixed up so we need to make changes which will have to be done through the courts in Granada." I sighed, I really was beginning to wonder if my dream location was trying to tell me something. But now we hoped we had discovered the root of the problems that had occurred since I had the house.

Maybe bills would now start to come in my name for the right meter?

*

Gossip, gossip, gossip. I'm really getting bored of gossip. But everyone seems to have something to tell someone about someone else. My past is my past, I don't need to know what 'he' is doing; why did people think I did? It was now 2 years on and I came to Lanjarón to relax and potter in my own house and see my friends but I was getting really upset that the locals were still gossiping about me and Dom and wouldn't let either of us get on with our lives. We were on speaking terms and had occasionally been in the same group of people and had a civilised drink. It wasn't fair that every time I set foot in town, there was one of a number of people who insisted on telling me something I did not give a damn about. I wondered if he was getting the same? Every time I started to relax, some nosey gossiping so called friend would fire a bullet in my direction. Did they really want me to relive the pain I'd suffered or did they not give a damn? They were really making me reconsider whether I wanted to be in this town at all, maybe I should just sell up and stay in the UK. On this trip the relaxing was taking some time in coming.

Granada!

Time for a little culture as I adore Granada. I was finding I was becoming a bit of a tour guide when friends visited but everyone did the same. Plus TCC and I were meeting with Penny and Perla who lived in Moraleda: Penny of the curry powder that got me pulled up at customs had been a friend of mine since I first came to Lanjarón, she had moved away to another town shortly after so our only contact was social media and our days shopping and Perla was her Spanish friend. As well as the curry powder there was a number of bags of 'Black Country Pork Scratchings' that she was hankering for. Five hours we tramped around Granada for a brief stop for food and a quick glass of wine. It was a glorious sunny day and I came back with sun-kissed cheeks and join-the-dots freckles on my arms. I was worn out and glad to be sat down in the car. We had a strange 30 second rain storm on the journey back and by the time we got home the sky had become a very ominous black. We had been dodging storms all week and had caught for the crazy one in the night but this looked like the heavens were just going to dump ten barrels of hell on us. Rumbles of thunder broke from the black clouds. The birds stopped singing and the wind picked up; whichever conductor had orchestrated this one was a master of mood and suspense. The light went an insipid yellow. It looked like we were definitely in for it. My phone buzzed, “Are you back from Granada OK?” from Kiersten.

“Yes why? We had a lovely day.” Then photos started to appear on social media. Hail stones almost the size of golf balls plus flooding. Cars were wedged across narrow side streets; some submerged in the flood water of the underpass. The whole of Granada city had caught for the storm moments after we had left and it was a mess. Thankfully, we had a peaceful night. Although it continued to threaten as we walked up town for dinner it passed overhead. No more effect than the strange light and gusty wind which died down by the time we went to bed. A peaceful night and a bright blue sky to wake us in the morning.

Time for TCC to do some souvenir shopping and experience the delights of the Friday market. Unusually, the leisurely saunter down the market did not end up in half a dozen people stopping to chat only the amusement of the mish-mash of fashion items for sale. Older, hippy ladies bartering for leopard print leggings and skimpy red knickers sold next to ones big enough to carry your chicken home in, not to mention winceyette nighties: in fact, was that dress crimpolene? The land that fashion forgot.

The shops were more fruitful as this area has so much that is locally made that it’s hard not to buy everything. Organic wines, delicious honey, olive wood products, olive oil, various witches [good luck in these parts], *jarapa* rugs, *esparto* baskets, even I succumbed to a small, 60mm high pestle and mortar carved from olive wood. Laden with goodies and the mathematics of how we were going to get this lot back to the UK [one *jarapa* rug for TCC] we headed back home.

My house is in a side street, a typical Spanish wiggly one so even though it is short, I cannot see my house until I have rounded the last bend. As we did so, there was a white van with ladders on the roof in front of my gates and the gates were open. My heart sank. The electricity company? What should I do? The fear of a €6000 fine for illegal connection was still ringing in my ears as my stomach began doing those knotty things again. Let's face it, my Spanish had improved somewhat but could I cope with a conversation about the electric and plead not to be cut off? Was I even too late, had I already been cut off again? The plan formed that we would walk around the front of the van and if he was there we would carry on down the rest of the street. Who am I kidding: who would purposely walk down a narrow street, squeeze between two cars to walk in front of a van with ladders on and casually look inside the communal porch and possibly into the eyes of the engineer and then carry on walking? Surely no one was that nosey even here?

Deep breath. I stepped over into the porchway and couldn't see the engineer. My meter box was closed. I breathed out and jumped out of my skin. He was around the corner on the top step working on the other meter for the empty house. His white helmet bobbed up to greet me. Gulp, what do I do now? A rather tentative "Buenos Dias."

A rattle of Spanish came back at me...I just gazed into lovely blue eyes... "er, *lo siento, mi habla espanol un poco"*

A smile. "Ok, are you Charlotte Jayne?"

"Si"

"I 'ave to turn electricity off. Sorry."

"Ok." This was going to be tough to explain. *"es no para mi casa."* I pointed at the meter he was in the middle of disembowelling.

"No?"

That worked then, time for hand signals with my left hand pointing at the empty house and my right at the right wall leading to my front door I continued, *"es no mi casa, aki es mi casa."* He scratched his head and looked at his electronic pad and repeated my name again.

"It says you live 'ere?"

"No, look." I pulled aside the beaded curtain across the neighbour's front door. The lounge was almost bare bar a chair and an oak dresser with a few trinkets. A layer of dust was easily seen on the furniture and the whole of the parquet flooring. He sat down on the steps looking at his electronic device. I had an idea. *"momento."* My paperwork. I could give him the electrician's phone number and show him the installation details for the new wiring I had to have done; he was totally confused. As I had only just found out that the *Ayuntamiento* had me down as owning both houses there had obviously not been time for this to filter through the system. Blue eyes looked at the paperwork once more.

"Ok, I disconnect this?"

"*Ok, no es mio*." He continued to disconnect the box then took a picture before being on his way and thanking me for the chat and explaining to him. Thankfully as I went into the house earlier I had flicked on my hall light so I knew he hadn't disconnected me again. As we finally got inside the house I was shaking. I'd dealt with the electricity man and we had understood each other, plus I still had electric. Had we finally got to the bottom of all the weird paperwork that came with my house? Only time would tell but first thing on Monday morning I was sending a meter reading and a picture of the engineer to Alpujarra Conect for the records. I knew one thing; I was going to get my fuse box switched on well before my next visit just to be on the safe side.

Andalucía day. February 28th

Unless you can get someone to get the basic shopping for you, be aware that ALL major stores are shut. Making the slip of not getting any wine at the airport, I arrived in Lanjarón in mid afternoon with the total of a packet of crisps and my hand luggage full of cream eggs and scratchings [again] for Penny . If the local mini markets weren't open later then I would be dining out.

I dropped my bag in the house and glanced at the mail, once more some paperwork from *endesa*, the electric company and a single sheet that had been put under the door. I assumed it was to do with the change of name and supply to me in the right house, on Monday I would scan it and send it over to Alpujarra Conect for them to tell me. I was a little puzzled as all paperwork was meant to go directly there whilst we continued to sort it out and had assumed that we had it sorted, ah well, time for some food.

It was lovely to be out in the sunshine, it really does make you feel more relaxed and healthier. There was a sharp chill in the air though so the jacket stayed on and the locals were all wrapped up in heavy winter coats and gloves. It was strange to wander past The

Health Bar and onwards to where Ambienza used to be to see Karen and Fernando as they had moved the business to the sunniest bar terrace in Lanjarón and created Bistro 31; a great location for Karen to cook some fabulous food.

It was busy with Spanish families having lunch in the sun as I wandered in to get myself a drink. Karen was still working hard in the kitchen so I popped my head around the corner to say hi, it was always nice to see her beaming smile of greeting. Grabbing a glass of wine I headed back out onto the terrace to enjoy the view and the warmth. Being at the far end of the main street and at the junction of the *variante* [bypass] there was a clear view from the bar and terrace across into the distance and the peaks and troughs of the Sierra de Lujar, I sighed, it was so beautiful whatever time of year. A speck in the sky up to the left caught my eye, a pair of booted eagles started to circle, I was home.

I mused about the last few years and what had gone on. It had all been incredibly painful but I had held my head high and gritted my teeth and carried on. What else could I do? Despite the set-backs my little house was turned into a home, a cosy little place that, when I looked back at the photographs of the journey I've been on, I started to realise I'm proud of and what I have achieved. I don't suppose there are too many women who would have done what I did, especially on the meagre budget that I had. But, things were niggling me. Nothing in particular really and I know my close friends in the UK had their concerns too. With all the issues I had had over the last few years and how it had affected my health, a few had said that maybe it might be best for me to sell the place and not go back. At first I disagreed immediately. I was not going to be driven out of a place that was so stunning it still took my breath away by some people who had no respect for others. But more recently I had wondered if I would be better off cutting my losses and selling my home even if it was at a loss. It had been an amazing part of my life and I had come through the other side, admitted with a certain amount of financial damage as well as mental and emotional scarring. But did I really want to be here anymore? Had all that had happened affected me more than I was ready to admit? Should I just hold my hands up and admit defeat, turn the key in the door and walk away or was there another way of looking at the whole thing that would even me out? Was I actually letting the gossips sway me? Was I expecting too much too soon from myself and what harm would it do to leave it nestled in place for another year until I could make a decision I was happy with?

It was four years now since I had bought my little bit of paradise and I was still having problems with all the paperwork and it was getting me down. We had unravelled and corrected so much over the previous years and it was all down to previous owners not changing over names on bills etc that was causing a lot of the problems. At least four of the Spanish names billed to my address were deceased, but they sent the bills anyway. Arriving and not knowing whether I would have electric was another stress I had to overcome. I loved Lanjarón and loved the friends that I had found I could truly trust, but was this house turning into a demon? With my health and the problems with the business in the UK, Lanjarón was supposed to be my getaway where I could relax. But every trip had me spending time running around sorting problems out and I wasn't sure I could cope with everything on my own anymore. I had lain in bed that night going through the house and deciding what I would take back to England if I decided to lock the door and walk away. In reality there was very little, I wouldn't want the reminders. Even writing this memoir had been shelved on occasions because it brought back so much pain.

Should I bother going?

I very nearly didn't get on the plane for that last trip. I wanted to be anywhere else but there, I was trying to think of any way to get out of going. I'd mentally hit a brick wall of fear for what was to come next, all the little things were nibbling away at me. I just wanted to go there and relax but I had hardly done that since I had bought the place. Every trip that I had there, there was always something. Meetings with friends rescheduled for electricians, days out cancelled because of having to do paperwork. Sit on a beach and forget my life for a day? It had never happened. Had I done the wrong thing and gone through all this for nothing?

But I went. I arrived late on a Sunday night. I bought wine at the duty free before heading out into the late night July heat. With windows wound down I relaxed into the steady drive along the coast and up to Lanjarón. I pulled into the car park to a chorus of cicadas heralding my arrival and as I walked along the path to my door the nearest water fountain was burbling away cool clear water. I filled my bottle and went to my house.

A light glowed in my porch, Aicha had ensured there was power and thoughtfully left a light glowing. Aicha was one of the few that I trusted. A quiet and lovely friend I had made through Kiersten. I haven't mentioned her much as she is one of those people who was always present but, with all the negatives going on, she was one of the positives. I entered the house and smelled something delightfully sweet in the air. As I headed upstairs it got stronger and there to greet me were a bunch of beautiful roses. Their fragrance had filled the whole house. They were all cut fresh from her own rose garden, how thoughtful.

I opened the door wide and gazed out at the Lujar as I had done many times before and a wonderful feeling of peace came over me. I was being dragged back here again, it wasn't going to let me go that easy.

Thank you for reading.

If you would like to know more about my experiences in Spain and see some helpful links, please subscribe to my website.

www.calamityspain.com

Also for website members there will be photographs of the area and some of the chaos that I went through.

Please remember to visit Amazon and leave a review, I would be very grateful

Charlotte

Printed in Poland
by Amazon Fulfillment
Poland Sp. z o.o., Wrocław

56191523R00121

Printed in Great Britain
by Amazon

14114780R00255

© Sarah Wilde 2022. All rights reserved. Sarah Wilde asserts the moral right to be identified as the author of this work.

This is a work of fiction. All of the characters, organizations, and events portrayed in this novel are either products of the author's imagination or are used fictitiously. Any resemblance to actual persons, living or dead (except for satirical purposes) is entirely coincidental.

No part of this publication may be reproduced, stored in a retrieval system, or transmitted, in any form or by any means without the prior written permission of Sarah Wilde, nor be otherwise circulated in any form of binding or cover other than that in which it is published and without a similar condition being imposed on the subsequent purchaser.

ACKNOWLEDGMENTS

Thank you to all those who leant their support throughout my writing journey. Some listened patiently to my wild ideas, some read my awful first draft whilst resisting the urge to advise me to look for a job. Other dear friends patiently allowed me to pick their brains on blurbs and cover designs, or gave me a hug when I thought I'd never make it to a publishable manuscript. You know who you are, and I love you for it.

This book is for my younger daughter, Maya, who kept a patient, and sometimes, enthralled look on her face as I read her excerpts. She never shied away from honest, constructive criticism.

For my recently departed father. I like to imagine he would have been proud to hold a copy in his hands.

For Kari, my book cover designer, who was patient, generous and brilliant.

For Emma, whose advice and support gave me the impetus to make the final improvements and made me believe I could legitimately call myself a writer.

For Ali, my muse; she knows what I'm talking about.

OTHER TITLES BY THE AUTHOR

The New World is the first book of The Completists trilogy. Please visit www.wildetales.com for details of the second book, *The Sacrifice*; the third book, *The Prize*; and the prequel, *Cara*.

If you would like to join Sarah Wilde's mailing list, and receive a free copy of *Behind The Shutters*, you will also find details on her website.

CW01647098

THE NEW WORLD

BOOK ONE OF

THE COMPLETISTS TRILOGY

SARAH WILDE

For Maya, the greatest warrior I know.

The time has come for all mankind
To leave the man and kind behind.
To take what's made by us alone
To take and mould it to our own.

Libretta Jones: Leader of the Completists

PROLOGUE

EXTRACT OF LIBRETTA JONES' DIARY - MONDAY 26 SEPTEMBER 2089

Each of us remember where we were when significant events happen. We remember how we felt, what we were doing, what we did next. My great grandmother vividly remembered what she was doing on 9 September 2001 when she saw footage of the first plane ploughing into one of the towers of the World Trade Centre. She was 21, the same age as I am now, and she'd just given birth to my grandmother whom she gathered to her, wondering what kind of world she had bought her child into. For me, it was two weeks ago, Sunday 11 September, when I settled down in my favourite armchair and started reading Cara's diary, the diary that had been hidden from us by the government. Yet another example of the attempts by men to eradicate women's history. Mum had told me about a spate of horrific murders in 2022. She was too young to remember them herself, but my

grandmother told her about the murder of four men who had each abused and exploited women. They never caught the woman responsible and she became part of folklore, talked about in hushed awe whenever women gathered together without their men. I didn't get out of that chair until I had finished the last page, and when I did, I had changed forever. It was like a smouldering match landing on parched grass. A rage spread through me like a wildfire. The first thing I did was to ring the girls and arrange to meet, and today was the culmination of that meeting and the five previous years of talking and planning. Today the world heard about The Completists.

As I volunteered to be the voice of the Movement, it was my face that appeared on all the publicity we put out, inviting women to lead a life free from the judgment and control of men. 'Fight with your Feet' is our slogan, and the response from the men has been as predicted. Within hours of our publicity hitting every media channel available I was contacted by God knows how many men, and they all asked the same question. Why? I was also contacted by several female journalists and funnily enough their question was, why now?

Naturally I had my official answer ready, but I wanted to scream at them, how can you even ask that question? Do you know how many women are raped or sexually assaulted every day, who suffer physical or mental abuse at the hands of the men

that are supposed to love them, who still don't get paid the same as their male counterparts, and are denied the economic opportunities their men enjoy. Who, in other supposedly progressive democracies don't even have autonomy over their own bodies! And do they get justice, do they get support, do they fuck. They get side-lined, put to the back of the queue, or what really enrages me, they get silenced. Told to sign Settlement Agreements so that the boss who put his hand up some girl's skirt won't have his career prospects compromised, whilst she has to leave with some money in her pocket, but without her dignity. And if she refuses to sign, then, it is made clear that her career prospects will be compromised. Funny how the other term for these "Agreements" is Gagging Orders. And let's not forget all the incredible women who've been written out of history. BUT, what I actually said was how 'frustrated' we were with the interminably slow progress being made to make this country into a place where all people are treated in the same way, regardless of whether they have a vagina or a penis. The Completists' aim is to speed things up by offering an environment where women will be supported to be the best they can be, a safe environment, a caring environment, free from the worst of male behaviour (from any male behaviour, actually, given it will be male-free). It went down like a cup of cold sick! I bet tomorrow the papers will be full of derision. They

will say what we are proposing to do is impossible, ridiculous, but more importantly UNNECESSARY. It's like the police at the scene of a car crash telling the public to move on, there's nothing to see here, but our eyes are wide open. Cara opened mine so wide they can never fall shut again. And what they don't realise is that, for the first time, there are four young women who have the power, and the wealth to actually carry this through.

Mum is being very supportive. I can tell she's proud. She's fought for equality in the boardroom all her life, as have all our mothers, but I know she's worried. We're trying to keep the identities of everyone but me hidden. I know the risks. I know there is a strong possibility I might be attacked or killed. I will put contingency plans in place, but I'm not scared. I'm prepared to die rather than let the Movement fail. It's time! We can't sit around waiting for men to bring about change. Why would they? It's to their disadvantage. Well, look out boys, because we're taking control over our own destinies. It's about time we helped ourselves. We're going to create The New World. I can feel it in my bones!

PART ONE
26 YEARS LATER

CHAPTER 1

Kate sat in the dingy GYNE waiting room watching a parade of stomachs pass her eyeline. Some of the women didn't look at all pregnant and she assumed they were visiting the fertility clinic. It was unfair they had to use the same waiting room as the women who were on their way to having what these flat-stomached women so desperately desired. The male fertility clinic was in a separate new wing which had recently been opened by the Prime Minister. It was the first state-of-the art facility of its kind and within its pristine walls vasectomies were now achieved by taking a pill. They were reversible, with no known side effects. The men were monitored for 24 hours in private suites, tested to ensure the "operation" had been successful, and then released back into the wild, rested and temporarily infertile. It had been hailed as a significant scientific breakthrough.

Another stomach passed which looked as though it was about to pop, and she gave the owner a sympathetic smile. That had been her less than six weeks ago, and she remembered her discomfort and impatience for it to end. Kate was experiencing a similar set of emotions now. An hour had already ticked past her appointment time and she begrudged

waiting for some man to peer at her nether regions simply to tell her what she already knew. Kate did not need Dr Sylvester to confirm her vagina had healed nicely, she was sitting on these hard plastic chairs without wincing; and this morning, the reflection in the mirror she held between her legs, showed a vagina that resembled the one she had before Cara had made her dramatic exit.

'Mrs Kildare?'

Kate looked up at the nurse standing in the doorway and smiled. She hurried over to her with an apologetic look on her face. 'I'm so sorry, Mrs Kildare,' she whispered, 'but Dr Sylvester has been called to an emergency caesarean and there's no-one else free to see you. We thought he'd be out by now. Can you come back at the same time next week please. I've made the appointment for you, and written it down. Again, so sorry about this.'

Kate managed a forgiving smile as she took the flimsy piece of card from her hand, and before she had closed her fingers around it, the nurse was calling the name of the next patient. Kate wandered back down the bland, pale green corridors to the exit. She was about to call Sophie, to warn her of her imminent arrival, when she changed her mind. David was working from home this afternoon and an hour alone together might really help things. She knew he was keen to resume "marital relations" and he hadn't laid a violent finger on her since she fell pregnant. Perhaps he had changed, perhaps she should make this last-ditch effort to see if they could have a future together. Sophie wouldn't mind. She loved playing mum, and Cara slept most of the time anyway. Kate felt ready to feel David's hands run over her skin. Her slender figure had already returned, much to Sophie's annoyance. Kate had always been the prettier one, and she knew her sister envied her long blonde hair, clear skin and blue eyes. Sophie constantly moaned about getting the shorter straw on the

genes front, but Sophie did not realise what a blessing that was.

Fifteen minutes later she turned into her road and was annoyed to see a red mini parked in her spot. She didn't recognise the car and crawled past it, scanning the street for an alternative. She started as a car beeped its horn. Was there someone behind her? Then she looked to her left and saw Jane from number 5 waving frantically. Kate lowered her window. 'I'm just leaving, Kate. Take my space, I'll be gone for hours.' Kate smiled at her, noticing her lurid pink top. She wasn't convinced it complemented her neighbour's skin tone.

'Thanks, Jane. Perfect timing.' Jane's blue estate pulled out and she instructed her car to parallel park itself.

She wanted to creep up to David's study and surprise him so she decided to go through the lounge French windows at the back of the house, rather than use the front door. She slid through the doors then froze.

'Shouldn't I be going soon?' a woman's voice asked from upstairs.

'Not yet. She should be gone for at least another hour, and if you think I'm not about to take full advantage of that gorgeous body of yours, you are very much mistaken. Come here!'

She heard the woman laugh and imagined her naked body being pulled back under the fresh duvet cover she had put on their bed that morning. Kate didn't want to go up the stairs, she was drawn up them by some internal force over which she had no control. The bedroom door was ajar and she watched the curly brown hair of her husband in between the legs of a now moaning woman. Kate's eyes followed the slender legs up to a gently rounded stomach, past full, pert breasts, to rest on her face. Her eyes were closed and her lips parted as she strained her neck back in ecstasy against Kate's pillow. It's strange how people can sense when someone is watching them. She wasn't

sure how long it took before the young woman's eyes opened and saw her there, but it took only seconds before she jerked her hips away from David and he turned his head in Kate's direction. Kate turned her back on them and went downstairs, walking into their kitchen, her legs shaking as she grasped the worksurface for support. Hurried steps scurried down the stairs, the front door slammed and David burst into the room.

'I'm so sorry, Kate. She's nothing to me, nothing. Just a bit of fun.' He spoke quickly, combing his thick mop of hair with frantic fingers, his brow as creased as her bed sheets.

She refused to look into his wild eyes and was unsure her voice would work. 'You did look like you were both having fun,' she said, surprised at her choice of words and her tone. There was no evident anger, nor bitterness, there was nothing. She felt nothing. She turned to face him. He could have wiped his face, she thought, noticing his top lip still glistening.

'I've got to pick up Cara now,' she stated as she picked up her bag and left him standing, speechless in his boxers.

As her car drove her to her sister's house, the idea that had been lurking in the back of her mind for so long, came out of the shadows and invaded her mind. She realised most women would feel anguish at what she had just witnessed, but all Kate felt was a sense of relief. She now knew what she had to do. She had thought about how she could escape her marriage, her past, her pain, so many times before, and now she would put those plans into motion. She knew she would have to act quickly. She couldn't risk Sophie sensing that something was off. If she found out what David had done there would be drama and complications, and Kate couldn't risk being persuaded to change her mind. Not now she had Cara to protect. She ached to tell her sister, to share her pain, but she

was practised at hiding her inner turmoil from her, she was a Pro in that department.

Outside Sophie's house, she looked in the rear-view mirror to check that her face was with her. She couldn't afford to show any emotion that might spark a question of concern from her twin. Her face was playing ball, dead eyes, fixed smile. Satisfied, she headed for the door. Before she had raised her arm to knock, it opened.

'Great timing, Sis. She's just gone down. I put her in her car seat just in case you showed before she woke up.' Sophie raised her hand as if quietening down an adoring audience. 'I know, I'm a natural. No need for thanks.' Kate laughed at her easy confidence. 'So how did it go. All good down below? Undercarriage secured and ready for take-off?'

'My consultant was called into an emergency caesarean. I have to go back tomorrow morning. Any chance you could flex those super mum muscles again?' Kate was genuinely pleading. She needed at least a few hours of peace and quiet to do what she had to do.

'For you, my dear sister, I will clear my hectic domestic schedule, but it will cost you.' Kate raised her eyebrows quizzically. 'An evening out this weekend. Just the two of us. We haven't been out without the boys in ages.'

'It's a high price, Sophie, I'm not sure...' Kate teased. 'Saturday night at around 8? Although David may kick up a fuss. I'm not entirely sure he knows which end to insert her bottle.'

Sophie laughed, 'Just make sure you stock up the fridge. She finished that bottle you gave me in minutes. How long does it take to get one bottle of breast milk anyway?'

'You don't want to know,' Kate said. 'So, I can drop her off just after 9.00?'

'Sure can. Looking forward to it. I'll just go and get Sleeping Beauty.' Her sister disappeared into the house. Kate was happy to stay on the threshold today. Happy to keep

things simple and straight forward. The rest of the week was going to be anything but.

As she placed her baby on the seat beside her, checking the automatic securing mechanism had done its job, she congratulated herself on her performance. 'I'm not sure why I was so worried about your aunt noticing anything was wrong,' she whispered to Cara, 'she's so wrapped up in her own world, she wouldn't notice that mine was falling apart, she never has.'

When she got home the house was silent. No strangers, no husband, no moans of desire. She placed her sleeping daughter in the lounge and wandered into the kitchen. There was a note on the polished wooden counter top written in David's scrawl. "I've gone away for the night, BY MYSELF. You need some time to think. It was a shock for both of us. I do love you and Cara. Please forgive me. David." 'Coward,' Kate growled as she screwed his note up and deposited it in the bin. She continued to address the balled-up paper. 'Cara deserves to have a better future than you can offer her. I was having a little wobble about leaving you, but now I know exactly what I'm going to do and your absence has just given me a head start, so cheers for that.' She laughed and let the bin lid close and slide itself back under the work surface. She went to grab her phone to begin dictating a letter then changed direction, striding towards their antique dresser and rummaging around in a drawer until she found an old notebook. She would do this old-style; she didn't want any digital record of what she was about to do, there was too much at stake. Kate sat down at the kitchen table and started to write.

CHAPTER 2

Cara broke into a smile as she was handed over to Sophie. 'Pleased to see your favourite aunt, are we?' Sophie cooed at her.

'Her only aunt,' Kate said, laughing. She felt lighter than she had in years; floating on the euphoric feeling of being back in control of her own destiny. Kate had felt that way once before, the day she had left home after her father died.

'You seem happy. Did someone put that undercarriage to good use last night?' Sophie asked playfully.

Kate was momentarily startled by the question and stammered over her reply, 'Might have, not saying.'

'Oh my God. My sister, getting all coy over sex. It must have been a very long abstinence!' Sophie laughed, oblivious to her sister's discomfort. 'Well, good luck at the hospital this morning. I hope you don't get told off for jumping the gun!'

Kate shook her head despairingly at Sophie, which made her laugh even louder. Cara squealed in excitement and bashed her tiny fists against her car seat. 'I hope you both have a lovely morning discussing my sex life or lack of it,' she said, blowing them both a kiss and walking to her car.

'Love you!' Sophie shouted. Kate raised her hand in the air, and gave her sister the middle finger.

'Love you more!' Sophie shouted in response.

She opened the car door and turned to wave goodbye, but Sophie had already taken Cara inside. She sighed, every glimpse of her sister was now a precious gift. She got in and told the car where she wanted to go. Her stomach felt like she was going on a first date.

There was one space left in the station car park. Kate sighed with relief. She was on a tight schedule and time wasted searching the streets for a car parking space would have been frustrating. As she sat on the train into central London, she reread a copy of the letter that was signed and sealed in a pristine white envelope. She gazed at the blur of the green countryside they were passing through, and let her mind wander. Is it enough? Have I got the tone right? Will there even be a suitable vacancy? Stop it, Kate, the tone's fine. Not too desperate. It just makes my predicament crystal clear. They'll help me if they can. That's why the Movement started. To help women like me.

The sound of the train doors opening snapped her out of her reverie. She looked up and watched several women in black trouser suits get on. Completists. She saw them acknowledge one another but then look straight ahead, avoiding any eye contact with the other passengers. Kate noticed some of the men give them contemptuous glances. Could she cope with their hatred? She hoped she'd find out.

She left the train at the next stop and made her way to the exit. The escalators were full of sombrely dressed women. They looked like crows perched on a tree. She had never seen so many Completists in one place before, but then again, she had never visited one of the largest, and certainly the most prominent, Completist company in the country.

As she emerged onto the pavement, it was as if her world had been flipped. The skyline was dominated by a vast build-

ing. It's opaque walls of grey glass looked ominous and powerful. Femmeur plc was no shrinking violet. The Chosen Ones in their brightly coloured clothes were now in the minority. Dots of colour in a dark sea of women. The atmosphere had changed. The Completists were the ones who looked comfortable on this street; their domain, their rules. The Chosen Ones scurried to other destinations, heads down. Kate had chosen an outfit to reflect her status, a woman in transition. She wore black trousers, but had chosen her palest pink top, which peeked out from beneath a charcoal grey jacket she had kept hidden from Sophie. She'd swept back her long hair into a tidy bun, but some of her waves had escaped their bonds and were now caressing her cheeks. She took a deep breath, pushed her shoulders back, held her head up and stepped into the revolving door.

The interior of the building was a different world. The foyer was flooded with light and full of fresh flowers, and the previously mute women were now chatting and laughing with their colleagues as they made their way to the lifts. A group of women sat in easy chairs to the left of the reception area, drinking coffee and munching on breakfast pastries, relaxed and happy to be at work. Kate thought of her own office and smiled to herself. Their reception was all business, no play. Visitors talked in hushed voices and the only women were either behind the reception desk or secretaries scurrying through on errands. She approached a young woman who gave her a warm smile as she arrived at the curved glass counter. A gold 'C' made entirely of paper butterflies hung on the wall behind her like a golden halo. 'Good morning,' the woman said, 'Welcome to Femmeur. How can I help you?'

'I have an urgent letter for Angela Stephens and I wondered if you'd be kind enough to arrange for it to be delivered to her now, if that's possible? I'd be grateful if I could wait to see if she has time to see me this morning. I appreciate it's a big ask. She must have a very full diary...' Kate handed

the girl the letter and stood, holding her breath for her response.

'Let me give her assistant a call. One moment.' The woman touched the auricom in her ear and spoke a name. She looked encouragingly at Kate. 'What's your name?' she asked as she waited for a response.

'Kate Kildare,' Kate replied, returning her smile.

'Hi Beth, I have a Kate Kildare in reception with an urgent letter for Angela. What's her diary like this morning? Could she read the letter and possibly give Kate a response? She's happy to wait.' Beth obviously asked her a question, as she replied to it in the affirmative, then touching her ear again, she smiled at Kate. 'You're in luck. Beth will come and get the letter now. Angela has an hour before her first meeting, so if you want to wait, she may be able to see you.'

'Thank you so much. That's amazing. Really kind of you. Where should I wait?'

'Take a seat over there,' she said pointing to a waiting area in front of the reception desk. 'Can I get you something to drink? We have delicious hot chocolate!'

'A water would be great. Thank you,' Kate replied, thinking the hot chocolate would be too much for her summ-ersaulting stomach to cope with. She selected a very comfort-able red velvet chair and admired the flower arrangement on a low glass table in front of her. As she reached for her glass to take a tentative sip of water, a middle-aged woman approached the reception desk, took her letter and glanced over at her, smiling. Then she strode towards the lifts, carrying Kate's future in her hands.

It was precisely 32 minutes later when Beth approached, telling her Angela would see her. She followed the short, slightly overweight figure towards the lifts. She had been watching women come and go in the foyer, and had noted that no-one wore heels, and Beth was no exception.

As the doors sealed them together, Kate smiled nervously

at her companion. 'Don't be nervous, Kate. Whatever you said in your letter had a very positive effect on Angela. She doesn't normally upset her routine, especially first thing in the morning.' Kate smiled gratefully as the lift reached the sixth floor and released them. The open plan office spread before her was light and airy and the carpet they walked on absorbed the sound of their footsteps. Beth led her to the only office, tucked away in the corner; the glass opaque walls ensuring Kate's first glimpse of the woman she needed to impress was when she stood up to greet her. She had silver grey hair loose to her shoulders, cut in a layered bob. Her skin was pallid but flawless. Kate looked directly into her pale blue eyes, shook her hand and smiled.

'Kate, please take a seat. Thank you for coming in this morning. I've read your letter and the C.V. you enclosed and I'm pleased to say that we're in a position to help. We have an opening that you're ideally qualified for. It hasn't even been advertised yet, which is our normal procedure with every vacancy. But I've spoken to our CEO about your particular circumstances and she has given me the green light to offer it to you, *if* we both decide it's a good fit.'

This was more than Kate had dared to hope for, and she listened carefully to every word Angela uttered as she described the role. 'So, what do you think?' she finally asked.

'I'd love to be considered for the role of HR Manager, and it would be a pleasure to work for you.'

'Well, I'm not sure you're qualified to make that assumption just yet,' Angela said smiling, 'but I'm glad you feel ready to take on a larger role than you currently have. And we don't work *for* anyone at Femmeur we work *with* them. Whilst we have our chain of command, like anywhere else, that just signifies varying degrees of decision-making responsibility rather than status. Everyone who works here does so because they have a particular set of skills we need, and everyone is valued equally for those skills. We also use first names, so please call

me Angela.' Kate nodded and Angela continued. 'Tell me what you enjoyed about your last role.' Kate responded to each and every question she was asked with honesty and her inquisitor appeared satisfied with her responses. Finally, Angela leaned back in her chair and looked her in the eye. 'I do need to ask whether you're sure you wish to become a Completist. Whilst other Completist companies employ Chosen Ones, Femmeur does not. In our experience the cultures are not compatible, and any Chosen One who would fit in here is more likely to be a Completist in her heart. We want women to feel truly free to develop their talents without judgment from men or CO's, because their judgment is rarely limited to job performance.' Angela looked at Kate waiting for her response.

'That's exactly what I want and need, both for myself and my daughter. I didn't give you a full personal history in my letter, my current situation is difficult enough, but please believe me when I tell you that men have given me very little and taken far too much. The only good thing that ever came from a relationship with a man is Cara.'

'On that note, Femmeur has a free crèche for all working mothers which is open during normal office hours. We also have an excellent subsidised canteen, a free first-rate health centre and a gym. We don't encourage overtime unless absolutely necessary. Beth will give you the address of your nearest Completist Reception Centre and a letter of your job offer from us. But the offer is contingent on you turning up there within the next week. We can't hold the job open for you any longer than that. The Centre will inform us of your attendance. Is that clear?'

'I think you've just offered me my dream job?' Kate said, smiling.

'I did. Glad you see it that way. But you do understand that you only have a week to become a Completist.'

'I do, and it can't come soon enough as far as I'm

concerned. I'm so grateful. Thank you.' Sophie's face suddenly loomed large in her mind and she swallowed hard.

'Don't be. You're qualified. I believe we'll work well together and helping women escape from the control and judgment of men is why the Movement was formed, so naturally, if a woman in your situation approaches us, we're going to help them if we can. Thank you for coming in, Kate, and I very much hope to get that call from the Centre in the next few days. They will explain all the other arrangements for your transfer, unless you have any further questions?'

'No. Thank you, Angela. I've taken up more than enough of your morning. I very much look forward to working *with* you.'

'As I do with you,' she replied, standing up and offering Kate her hand to seal the deal. She walked her to the door. 'Beth, would you be kind enough to show Kate to the foyer. Hopefully she will be joining us very soon as the new HR Manager.'

'That's wonderful news,' Beth responded. 'Many congratulations. Do you have time for a quick tour? You'll probably want to see the crèche, Angela explained you had a baby.'

Kate glanced at the time. 'I'd really like that, but my sister is looking after Cara and she will be expecting me back very soon. She doesn't know I'm here.' Kate looked at Beth for understanding.

'No problem. Rest assured it's a lovely space. It's run by a group of working mothers who volunteer to take on the role, obviously earning the same salary as before, and they do a wonderful job. They're backed up by a small team of professionals. Cara will be in excellent hands.'

'Thanks Beth, and thank you for taking my letter to Angela. You can't begin to imagine what it means to me.'

'Oh, I think I can. We all have our stories to tell, Kate, but one tip, if I may?' Kate nodded. 'Never ask, wait for people to share.'

'Got it. Thanks again, Beth.'

'You're welcome. I'm so happy things have worked out. See you soon, I hope.' And, giving her a cheerful wave good-bye, Beth headed back to the lifts and Kate stood, once again, in the sweet-smelling foyer and felt her world shift on its axis. She was both elated and frightened, but there would be no turning back. She just hoped she could make the transition without revealing the truth about their father.

CHAPTER 3

The next morning rain was forecast. David had returned home, and Kate made him believe she could forgive him, given time. He'd even tried to kiss her as he left for work. She had contemplated returning his embrace, a final goodbye kiss, but it felt unnecessary. As Cara began her mid-morning nap, she quickly gathered the essentials and loaded the car. It was time. Kate shuddered as she leant into the car, hands shaking as she attempted to secure her belongings in the back seat so they wouldn't shift and wake her daughter. Cara looked so peaceful, undisturbed by her fumbling. As she straightened herself, she caught a glimpse of her face in the rear-view mirror and recoiled as the pain in her eyes punched through the glass.

What she was about to do made perfect sense, yet no sense at all. She said her mother's address in a slow, clear voice, then put the car into manual. She needed the distraction. As she started to pull out, another car flashed by, horn screaming. Her shoulders felt tight, and her head was throbbing. She shouldn't have to be doing this. This was bullshit. She checked again and pulled out. The wrongs that had been done to her

would now be paid for by the one person in the world she truly loved, besides her daughter: her twin sister, Sophie.

As she paused at the junction with the main road, she recalled their childhood night-time ritual before their father insisted on separate bedrooms. She smiled. Three goodnights, three air kisses, and hands held out in the dark distance between them, to be silently squeezed, three times. She could hear again their sniggering giggles as they spied on two teenagers, entangled in their first embrace. How was she going to live without Sophie? Kate glanced over at Cara, who had been soothed into an even deeper sleep by the motion of the car. Everything had changed now. She couldn't allow her daughter to feel or experience what she had. Cara needed to be protected, and this was the only way to do it. She might not be mother of the year – God knows she hadn't had the best role model – but she could at least do this for her. Her breath became jagged as she imagined Sophie's reaction to her news. Her sister had spent her adolescence cocooned in a cosy bubble of endless praise and admiration, whilst she had been suspended in a dark, inky ocean of self-loathing, fear and rage. Sophie grew up believing the universe was organised to meet her every wish and desire, and when this was challenged, she threw a tantrum. Kate didn't blame her for her flaws, she blamed their parents. Her twin had sailed through life relatively unscathed, save for a job that forced her to travel around the south of the country selling the latest laser filing software to dull people in even duller jobs. She had even managed to catch the one man who was the object of desire for many of her peers, despite being the plainer one. But Sophie had always known how to flirt and she exuded confidence, unlike herself, who kept her head down and her guard up. Kate straightened her back, turned on the wipers and blinked away her tears.

As she opened the front door to her mother's house, she kicked herself for not sending Sophie a message warning them Cara was asleep; her mother was yelling at her from the

kitchen to check it was her. Who else was it going to be? She glanced nervously at Cara for any signs of wakefulness as she placed her car seat in the front room and hurried down the hall towards the kitchen. God how she hated that kitchen. So many unhappy mealtimes spent avoiding eating, whilst listening to the three of them chat happily together in a state of constant mutual admiration. Even the décor seemed to mock her; olive-green worktops that sat uncomfortably on the Mediterranean blue kitchen cupboards, which in turn clashed with the terracotta walls and the sunshine yellow of the "feature" wall. Her mother's kitchen looked like a taverna run by an annoyingly optimistic Greek family. She had nagged their father into the new kitchen after informing him that "if a Mediterranean kitchen was good enough for Jennifer la-di-da Hinchley at number 6, it was good enough for her". The only problem being that Jennifer had taste and their mother didn't.

Kate rushed into the kitchen, putting her finger to her lips. 'Cara's asleep,' she said. 'I've put her in the front room.'

'Excuse me! How was I to know?' her mother replied, shooting her sister a triumphant look. Their mother had obviously been bitching about her behind her back. 'So, here we both are, as summoned. Are you going to tell us what this is all about?'

'Blimey, Mum. Let her catch her breath! Fancy a cuppa, Kate?' Sophie looked worried. 'Are you alright? You look like you haven't slept in a week.'

'Thanks, Sis. You look lovely too. And no to tea, thanks, I've just had one.' Kate sat down at the kitchen table. Their mother sighed impatiently.

'I'm leaving David,' Kate said quietly, looking at her lap.

'What?' their mother said, over-plucked eyebrows shooting up her forehead.

'Why?' Sophie asked, her hand reaching for hers. 'What's happened?'

'I found him in our bed with another woman. Last week.

The day of my hospital appointment. When you looked after Cara.'

'Oh God. How awful!' The colour drained from her sister's face.

'Is he having an affair then?' their mother asked, joining them at the kitchen table. She placed the tea tray in the middle of them. It was laid with three cups.

'He says not, Mum. He says it was a one-off. That he still loves me.' Kate tentatively raised her head.

'There you are then. I'm sure this is a blip. Men find the transition to fatherhood difficult sometimes, they can behave oddly. You can sort this out.' She gave her a tight-lipped smile. 'And don't forget, you've only just had Cara. Your hormones are all over the place. You're not thinking straight.' She patted her hand as though Kate was an elderly woman with dementia. Kate glanced over at Sophie and they exchanged a wry smile. 'A child needs both parents to feel properly secure, and a marriage isn't only about being *nice* to one another.'

Kate flinched; her mother had never been able to talk about sex. 'It's not just about his inability to keep his dick in his trousers,' she snapped, rolling her eyes heavenwards.

'There's no need to be crude,' their mother retorted. 'What else is your husband guilty of then?' Sarcasm dripped from her mouth like honey from a spoon.

'He beats me, Mum. At least he did before I was pregnant. And now I think it's going to start again, and I won't put myself through that.' Kate's voice was monotone, controlled, she couldn't afford to let her emotions get the better of her, not in front of her mother.

'Oh, Kate!' Sophie stared at her and reached for her hand again. 'Why didn't you tell me?' Kate detected a hint of annoyance in Sophie's tone. She knew her sister would be hurt that she hadn't confided in her, any minute now her bottom lip would start to tremble.

'I'm not sure. I guess I was ashamed. It didn't happen that

often, and he was always so sorry afterwards. He kept promising it would never happen again, and I kept giving him another chance. I suppose that's what you do when you love someone.'

'Precisely my point,' their mother said, breaking their connection. 'I'm not condoning a man hitting a woman. Of course, I'm not. Your dear father never laid a finger on me. He was the gentlest man I ever met. But surely, David wouldn't start again, not with Cara around? I can't believe he would do such a thing.'

Kate clasped her hands together. Her knuckles turned white. Sophie leapt to her defence.

'Look, Mum. I'm sure we don't know the half of it. If Kate thinks her marriage is over, then we have to trust that she knows best and is making the right decision.' Sophie faced her. 'Where are you going to live? You can move in with us if you want, until things are sorted.' Kate tried to smile, but she could feel salty tears pricking her eyes. She swallowed hard.

'Sophie, this is the hardest thing I've ever had to say in my entire life... I'm going to become a Completist. I've got my qualifications now, and Femmeur have offered me a really good job in their HR department.' The words tumbled from her mouth, her eyes pleading with Sophie for understanding. 'I'll be able to afford a place of my own and they have childcare facilities for Cara.'

'Hold on. What the fuck? But that means you'll never be able to see me again, doesn't it?' And there it was, the beginnings of a tantrum. Out of nowhere Kate had a perverse urge to laugh. She watched as her twin's bottom lip started to wobble and clouds of indignant anger formed in her eyes. She couldn't blame her. Sophie wouldn't be able to take this in, she would see it as a betrayal.

'I don't get it. I don't understand why you'd want to join those women. They hate men. They hate us!' Sophie's hands

fell onto her lap. Kate reached out to hold them, but Sophie snatched them away.

'Sophie, they don't hate men. They just want to live their best lives, free from male bullshit.'

'You see, Sophie, she's already been brainwashed by that filthy cult.' Their mother had a look of sheer disgust on her face. They both ignored her.

'Kate, how could you? I may never see you again, and even if I do, we won't be able to talk. You might as well be dead, except you won't be, will you? You'll be alive, living a life I'll know nothing about, living your life without me. Jesus, Kate! Peter and I are trying for a baby. How can I take pleasure in that, knowing you'll never hold him? Don't you care that Cara will never know me? Please don't do this, please!'

Their mother stood up. 'This is quite ridiculous!' She was shouting. 'So, your husband hit you and cheated. You're not the first woman to have suffered that and you won't be the last. It doesn't mean you get up and leave your life, your family. You try again. You make it work!' Her face was contorted with contempt. 'You're such a selfish girl. I wish you'd had a boy, then you'd have to make it work, wouldn't you? Those witches don't allow sons, do they? And no matter what else you are, even you couldn't abandon your child!'

Kate glared at their mother. The warmth and regret she had shown Sophie, drained from her eyes as they narrowed, fixing her unblinking gaze on the woman looming over her.

'You mean like you abandoned me to your husband.' Kate spoke calmly, but her voice was icy, her face ashen.

Their mother looked confused. 'Are you mad? What are you talking about?' She turned to Sophie for confirmation that Kate had completely lost her mind; but Sophie was frozen.

'The reason I'm joining those "witches", is because I refuse to suffer anymore at the hands of men who are supposed to care, love and protect me. Your precious husband,

my father, started creeping into my bedroom when I was eight years old. He wasn't getting what he needed from you, so he came and took it from me. I didn't even understand what was happening, but I felt the pain. Every Wednesday while you were searching your numbers for a full house at bingo, he was in my bedroom, crushing me, his beery breath filling my nostrils. Have you any idea what rape feels like? I was just a little girl.' Kate's voice fractured, her eyes once again, threatening tears, but then she shook herself, like a dog shaking off water. 'So, forgive me if I haven't got the will to keep trying with these bastards, but I'm done!'

Kate reeled as their mother slapped her hard across the face. 'You pathetic, little whore. How could you say that? Tell such filthy lies about your father? He wasn't capable of doing such a thing.' Her voice started to break. 'He was a gentle soul.' Sophie rushed to her side. Her twin glared at her as she cradled their mother's head to her chest. Kate could take no more. She was the outsider once more. Her sister had reverted to her adolescent self, siding with her mother, making her the enemy.

Kate stood up, looking down at the two of them, and pushed her shoulders back. Then she saw her sister's loyalty falter and sensed her panic.

'Don't go, Kate,' she begged. 'Please! Not now. You're in such a bad way. You've probably got postnatal depression. You don't know what you're saying, what you're doing.' She grabbed her arm. Kate turned towards her and held her shoulders, twisting her body away from their mother's, so they were head-to-head.

'Sophie, listen to me! Please try to understand. I'm not lying about Dad. He told me he'd kill you if I told anyone, and I believed him. I put up with it, to protect you. And I've put up with every other piece of shit that's been flung at me since.'

'But you grew up, Kate. Dad died. If this is true, surely you would've told me then?'

'Really? When you were grieving, devastated. You adored him. You were his little princess. What he did to me drove a wedge between us when we were growing up. It changed me. Didn't you ever wonder why I stopped smiling, stopped eating? I was raging, Sophie, and my anger had nowhere to go. It was eating me up inside.'

'Even if what you're saying is true, it's not my fault! Why are you punishing me? I don't understand!' She looked like a lost and forlorn four-year-old. Then their mother was pulling her away from her, like she'd done for so many years. Trying to break their bond, to keep Sophie for herself. Kate felt her emotions shutting down. She refused to be a part of this eternal tug of war.

'I'm not punishing you, Sophie. Everything changed when I had Cara. I can't let men hurt her like they've hurt me. You'll understand when you have your own baby. Do you think I want to lose you? You mean everything to me! But I have to protect Cara. And this is the only way I can do it. It's killing me knowing I'll never hold you again, laugh with you, cry with you. We've grown so close again since Dad died, we're stronger than we've ever been. Please, please know I love you so, so much and, if there was any other way, I would take it. You have to believe me.'

Sophie started to sob. 'This can't be happening, it can't. Kate, please don't go. I can't bear it.'

'Let the bitch go, Sophie.' Their mother's voice was granite. 'She's not worth your tears. Don't forget, she's done it before. Remember when she was 16? She left us, less than a year after your dad died, without a second's thought.' She turned her twisted face towards Kate. 'You were always a cold child, and now you've grown up into a lying little slut. I bet David never even laid a finger on you! You've caused me endless trouble, and now this. Just go! I never want to see your face again!'

Sophie looked from her to their mother, and in that

instant, Kate could see she had lost her sister for a second time. Sophie's pain had morphed into hatred. She started stroking their mother's hair and turned her back on her. *She doesn't believe me. I shouldn't have said anything about her precious father. It's all broken, gone to dust. I have nothing here to lose.* Kate shuddered as she walked back down the hall to her sleeping child, away from the only family she had known and towards, what she hoped would be, her new one.

CHAPTER 4

Kate sobbed, chest heaving, as she drove away from her mother's home. Cara had slept through everything. The car was crammed with her most precious possessions, and the further she drove, the more certain she was she could never go back. Not now, not after everything that had been said. Would she ever see her sister again? Sophie was right. Even if their paths were to cross, she would not be able to risk speaking to her. There were far too many people who would love nothing more than to report a Completist for breach of the Segregation Rules. The stakes were too high. Life imprisonment. Then who would protect Cara?

She wouldn't even be able to find Sophie on social media. Browser access was controlled via retina recognition, and both factions had developed closed systems. The security used to shield Completist data was the most advanced in the world. As soon as Kate joined, she would only ever be able to find information on other Completists and it would be the inverse for Sophie. Kate would know nothing more about her sister. She would never know Sophie's children and, if her sister became ill, she wouldn't be able to help. When one of them died, there would be no last goodbye, no deathbed reconciliation.

The memory of Sophie's expression, as she turned her face from hers, was fuelling her tears. She had anticipated her mother's reaction. She knew she would dismiss anything that might shatter her naïve world view; while her words had split her skin like a knife point on a ripe plum, it was Sophie's rejection that had ripped her apart. She thought she had prepared herself, but how can you prepare yourself for the annihilation of the other half of your soul?

As she pulled into the car park of the local Completist Reception Centre, she glanced at her sleeping daughter. 'It's you and me now, my lovely girl.'

She unbuckled Cara from her car seat and carefully transferred her into her baby sling. Cara didn't stir. Was she ill? Kate touched her baby's forehead to check her temperature. Satisfied all was well, she grabbed her bulging backpack and headed for the door.

There was a short queue in the clean, bright reception area, and she waited, gently stroking the soft hair on Cara's head, trying to steady her own breathing and still her mind. She focused on the gold 'C' emblazoned on the glass reception desk. The frosted glass was backlit which made its edges shimmer, solid yet fractured. She was conscious of her pale pink jumper, which marked her out as a rookie, a newcomer who didn't know the rules. Kate knew Completists only wore neutral colours, but she hadn't wanted to signal her plans to her sister and mother. No, that wasn't strictly true; she had wanted to keep one foot in their world for a little longer. She had done her research. Colourful clothes were not the only things about to be eradicated from her life. They would wipe all trace of her from the Chosen Ones' records and create a new digital profile of their own. When she walked back to her car, any record of her previous life would be gone; she would only have her memories, and the colour pink.

When she reached the reception desk she was greeted with a warm smile and directed towards a circular waiting room to

her right. As she sat on one of the comfortable chairs, she noticed three doors leading to interview rooms. Which door would lead her into her new future? A future where she would be alone. A blank canvas wiped clean of her messy and sordid past upon which she could draw her own plans and dreams for them both. She thought of David coming home to an empty house. He had been so quick to step into the role of protector, shielding her from the unwanted advances of the other young men in their office. He seemed to sense her vulnerability. What a great game he had played. He took things very slowly with her. First a lunch together in the staff canteen and then a drink after work. It was months before he suggested a dinner date and by then she liked having him around. She trusted him. He had drawn her into his net and closed it tightly around her. She hoped the Completists would not betray her trust as her husband had.

A young, smiling woman came out of the middle door and called her name. Kate took a deep breath and followed her into the small, bright room. It contained a desk with a computer screen on it, and a vase stuffed full of yellow mimosa. 'Take a seat, Kate. I'm Sarah and I'm pleased to meet you. This will take a little time. I assume you have all the necessary paperwork?' Kate gestured towards the stuffed backpack and nodded. 'Great, then let's begin. Let's start with your birth certificate.' Kate reached into the backpack, hauling out a large pink folder and handing it across the desk. 'Thanks, Kate. Just before we get going, are you absolutely sure about this? Once I've inputted all your details into our system, I'll be activating a programme that will wipe you off the Chosen Ones' systems. You won't exist in their world. The only way you can have contact with any of your previous friends or family members is if you choose to seek them out, and if you're caught making contact, it's life imprisonment. There are no exceptions to that. None. Do you understand?'

‘I’ve done my research. I understand about the severity of The Segregation Act, but thanks for checking.’

‘Of course. Some women still think that leniency will be granted for exceptional family circumstances, but that’s just not the case. It’s a cruel and pointless piece of legislation which we are constantly lobbying the government to repeal, but for the moment, it exists, and there are over 400 women sitting in prison cells who will never see the outside world again. But the rules only apply to previous friends and family members. You’re free to interact with complete strangers. Completists do business with men and COs every day. God forbid the government would put any unnecessary obstacles in the way of making money.’

Kate laughed, and Cara stirred against her chest, then settled back into her slumber.

Two hours later, Sarah looked up from inputting the last piece of Kate’s life history into their system. ‘This is it, Kate. I’m about to push the button. After this you will be a Completist.’

Kate felt as if she was holding a gun to her sister’s head and was about to pull the trigger. She pushed the image away and nodded at Sarah.

Kate was given the address of a Transition House, where she would go through the Assimilation Programme, covering the history and culture of the Movement and learning about the norms of behaviour when mixing with COs and men. They would also find her a new home in a Completist house, where she could take her time to settle into her new life, while she looked for a permanent home of her own. Cara was now awake; she gurgled in response to her mother’s voice as Kate told the on-board computer where she wanted to go. As she took her first journey as a Completist she watched the world

pass her by. She saw a new housing estate, the sun glinting off the hundreds of glass roofs and watched the clusters of wind turbines silently turn their blades, slicing through the atmosphere like hot knifes through warm butter. It was the same world, but she had altered her place within it.

The woman who ran the Transition House welcomed her warmly, introducing herself as Christine. She had already been briefed by the Reception Centre and showed Kate to a simple, clean room. The bed had been made up with fresh, crisp, white cotton bedding and a Completist pin had been laid on the pillow, a yellow rose placed next to it.

'I'll give you a few moments to get used to your new surroundings,' Christine said, smiling gently. 'When you're ready, come on down and we'll have some tea and cake.'

Kate sat on her bed. The mattress gave under her, it felt firm, yet welcoming. She gazed out of the window at the late spring trees, their bright green leaves hungry for sunlight. Everything was so normal. There were no heavy-framed pictures of the founding members looming over her. Apart from the pin and the rose, this could be any room in any guest house. She picked up the pin and followed the curve of the 'C' with her fingers, it was engraved with the Completists' slogan; 'To Divide is to Conquer'. A solid gold-coloured teardrop hung inside the letter, attached at its point, with the infamous blood red enamelled Y chromosome at its centre.

The creamy white walls and the crisp white bed linen, made her feel like a postulant, preparing to take her vows of celibacy; but she would not be giving up her life to serve a god or care for the poor. Her decision was far less selfless. She was taking a new life for herself and her daughter. If she did some good for others along the way, all the better. She was exchanging fear for optimism, and would have the protection of the Movement. They were strong now, and getting stronger all the time. One day they would take over and make new laws, then it would be the men who would have to watch their step.

Kate heard the kettle coming to the boil and stood up. 'Shall we go and have some lovely cake?' she asked Cara, who beamed at her and thumped her hands against her carrier with excitement.

'Can I hold her?' Christine asked, as Kate entered the kitchen. 'It's been ages since I held a baby. Don't worry, I haven't forgotten how to do it! Now help yourself to tea and cake. I've put a folder of useful information for you on the table, but I'll take you through the main points.'

Kate poured them both a cup of tea and served herself a large slice of chocolate cake; feeding Cara gave her a healthy appetite. She looked over at the middle-aged woman gently bouncing her daughter on her knee. She had a kind face and strong eyes. She looked capable, trustworthy. Perhaps it was her short hair and the dark grey jumper and trousers, perhaps it was the way she held her daughter, whatever it was giving her that impression, Kate felt she was in safe hands. She asked Christine if she could serve her a slice of cake, but she shook her head and, dragging her gaze from Cara's engaging smile, turned to look at her, suddenly serious.

'The most important thing you can do is give yourself time to get used to your new world. It's very different. You'll feel like a stranger.' Kate stopped chewing at Christine's tone.

'What do you mean? It's still the UK, it's still filled with men and women.'

'But you're a Completist now. People will treat you differently. Men and the COs will, at best, ignore you. At worst they will insult and shame you. You're their enemy now. Be on your guard, and don't takc it personally!' Christine laughed.

'Any other advice on how to handle it?' Kate wasn't laughing.

'Keep your head up and look straight ahead. Ignore them. Keep to the main streets, stay among people when travelling.' Kate nodded. 'Don't be scared, be vigilant. Violence towards Completists has drastically reduced since the Uprising began.

If you ever feel in danger, call a Completist taxi firm. They're extremely quick to respond, and they're subsidised by the Movement. They'll get to you faster than the police and they're combat trained.'

'Jesus! Now you are scaring me.'

'Sorry, Kate. That was meant to reassure you! The Movement doesn't advocate violence, unless it's necessary to preserve life, needless violence is the prerogative of men. We do something far more subversive, we withdraw our vaginas.' Christine winked at Kate. She responded with a schoolgirl snigger. 'Listen, it's not really dangerous out there anymore, but don't take unnecessary risks, develop a thick skin, and you'll be fine.'

Kate took another mouthful of cake. The memory of a Completist woman being kicked and punched as she lay defenceless on the ground assaulted her thoughts. She had wanted to help, but David had gripped her arm and made her walk the other way. It had happened on the way home from their little wedding reception. She should have known then what kind of man he would turn out to be.

'You know about The Segregation Rules?' Kate nodded.

'I actually remember the day they were announced. It was on the same day the government passed The Self Determination Act. I was five. My parents were furious with the government.'

'They had no choice. We weren't going away and Completists were creating economic and social instability. They wanted us to disappear in plain sight. They were haemorrhaging women and saw the Movement as a serious political threat. The Segregation Rules made it look like they still had the upper hand.'

'The lady at the Reception Centre told me there were over 400 Completists in prison.'

'That doesn't surprise me. There were quite a few in the first five years. There seemed to be a new forlorn face staring

out of your mobile every couple of weeks. But once people got used to us living alongside them, minding our own business, reporting became less frequent, thank God. Do you have any other burning questions, I think Cara's getting bored!'

'Here, give her to me. She's due a feed.' Christine handed her squirming daughter back and she nestled her into the crook of her arm, licking her knuckle before offering it to Cara to suckle. She felt the soft warmth of her baby's mouth, and was also comforted. 'How long do you think it'll take to find us a place in a Completist house? Not that I'm in a hurry to leave you!'

Christine smiled. 'No offence taken. You need somewhere more permanent while you find your feet. It normally takes between one and two weeks. They'll want to find you a place near your new job, and with other women of a similar background. We can't always guarantee a perfect fit, but we try our hardest to get as close as possible. Most women don't stay long. You'll find an information sheet on the Completists' Homebuyer Assistance Scheme in your folder.'

'That sounds great. Thank you, Christine. I feel in safe hands.'

Christine stood up and started to clear the table. 'Once you've fed Cara, I'll help you unload your things. I noticed you had quite a car full. If there's anything else you want to know, anything at all, just ask. Everything will be fine. I haven't had a chance to explain all the benefits of being a Completist, but believe me, there are so many. I don't know why you joined, but most people never look back. It's an incredible way of life. A joyous one. You've joined the most functional family in the world!'

Kate grinned at this kind, wise woman who had welcomed her into her home. 'That's good to know, Christine, really good.' She walked back to her room, soothing Cara. She would feed her, then get on with unpacking once she was down. As she nursed her baby she thought of her sister and felt

Sophie's pain. A tear dropped onto Cara's cheek. 'I'm sorry, my darling girl,' she said wiping it away with her sleeve. 'Have I made the right choice for us?' Cara stared at her with her clear blue eyes, and reached out both chubby arms, as if she wanted to cradle her mother's face.

CHAPTER 5

Sophie couldn't stop crying. Peter had tried his best to console her when he got home, but he was clearly out of his comfort zone. He stood awkwardly in front of her in their spotless, cream kitchen.

'It's like she's died!' she said, in between sobs that racked her chest. 'But worse! And I'll never see Cara again.'

'I can't believe what she's done. That Movement, it's poison. And what she said about your dad, it's insane!' Peter handed her a tissue.

Sophie wanted him to hold her instead, to tell her everything was going to be alright. That she was his world and he would never leave her.

'Mum's hysterical. It took me ages to calm her down. I had to call her doctor in the end. He gave her a sleeping pill. I wish I'd asked for one.'

'I can call our medical firm. They can arrange to have some sent over.'

Sophie looked at her husband. He didn't have a clue. Nothing like this had ever happened to him. He had a charmed life. He had never known loss like this. She was suffering and he was incapable of making her feel better. She

wished her father was still alive. His hugs always made her feel safe, but as she remembered his strong arms and the smell of him, she heard her sister's accusations and cursed her, as her fond memories turned sour. Sophie shuddered, she would never accept Kate's version of events. She would just have to pull herself together. She turned her back to him and blew her nose. Straightening her back, she tucked her light brown hair behind her ears, smoothed down her jumper and turned to face him again.

'Don't worry. I'll be alright. If she can live without me, then I can live without her. She obviously doesn't love me, or she wouldn't have done what she's done. I even offered to put her up while she sorted things out with David.' As she heard her own words they rang in her head like a tuneless bell.

'He was on the phone to me earlier, asking if I knew where she was. Apparently, she just packed a few things and left without saying goodbye. I tell you, there's a cold, unforgiving heart inside that girl. I feel really sorry for him.'

'I don't! If he'd been nicer to my sister, this might not have happened!'

'Do you honestly believe what she said about him? I've never seen David as the violent type. Have you seen how he plays football? He tackles like a girl!'

Sophie swallowed a sigh. How had he managed to mention football at a time like this?

'I'll make us some supper,' she said, barely hiding the contempt in her voice.

'Thanks, love. I'm starving!' Peter said, oblivious to his failings and obviously thankful that things were back on track.

As she prepared the food, the pain swelled again in her chest. She saw her sister's face, but blinked it away, along with the tears that kept blurring her vision. She would have to be brave and find a way to fix herself. Her love for her sister crawled, bleeding and crippled, into the darkest corner of her mind.

CHAPTER 6

The day after she arrived at the Transition House, Kate decided to go clothes shopping. Christine gave her directions for the nearest Completist Shopping Centre and, over breakfast, showed her a style book the Movement had put together, to give an idea of what her fellow Completists wore.

'I don't understand why there's a dress code. Shouldn't the Movement encourage members to dress how they want?' Kate asked, looking up from the glossy pages.

'I can see why you'd think that,' Christine responded with rehearsed diplomacy, 'but the Founders believe women predominantly dress to attract men. We might tell ourselves otherwise, but we're hard-wired to do it, and then society exploits that instinct to make money. They also believe that women use clothes to compete with other women. How many times have you been put off a new item of clothing by some negative comment from a friend? How did it make you feel?'

Kate laughed as her mind went back to the time Sophie ruined her favourite new top, claiming it was an accident. Kate was sure she had done it deliberately. It was just before she decided to leave home. They had gone to a friend's party

together and she had received numerous compliments from their male friends. She was so angry with Sophie. She had only recently put on sufficient weight to develop small breasts, having delayed adolescence by starving herself and covering her emaciated body in baggy, dirty tracksuits and hoodies. Kate had done this in the misguided belief that her body would revolt her father; but after talking to other survivors of incest, she understood she had actually prolonged the body her father craved, that of a child.

'That's why they decided on classic cuts and neutral colours,' Christine continued, 'to create an even playing field, relieve the pressure of appearance as much as they could. Completists leave playing dress-up to the Chosen Ones.'

'I suppose that makes sense,' Kate said, leafing through the guide. She actually liked the look they had gone for: elegant and understated. Assured.

The Shopping Centre was a revelation. Christine had insisted she take a Completist taxi to get there and had offered to babysit Cara. Kate had never seen so many women in one place. The atmosphere surprised her. Everyone was so relaxed. The cafés were overflowing with women, laughing and talking together. The pace was slower. There were no men sitting glumly outside shops, tapping their feet impatiently, or scrolling dejectedly through their phones in search of entertainment. No arguments in the department stores and furniture shops. Something was missing. Kate laughed out loud. That was it, what was missing was compromise. Everyone was so happy because they could buy whatever they damn well liked. This was going to be fun! As she pulled on some grey, tailored trousers that skimmed her figure without clinging to it, she remembered how David insisted he accompany her whenever she needed a new outfit. He always wanted her to buy the clothes that hugged her frame, accentuating the feminine. He dismissed neutral colours and complimented her whenever she tried on pale pinks and blues, telling her how

"pretty" she looked. Kate had never wanted to encourage men to stare at her, but she did want to please David, so she went with it. Now Kate didn't have to, and she could buy what made her feel good. Looking at herself in the mirror, she realised she was grinning from ear to ear. Kate even bought Cara some new clothes, far plainer than the pretty outfits she was used to dressing her in, thinking her daughter might as well get used to the world she would grow up in.

A week later Kate was standing at the front door of a large Victorian townhouse, looking like a Completist in a light grey jumper, black leggings and calf length black, flat boots. She rang the bell and Karen, who looked like she was in her early thirties, opened the door and smiled at her. Kate noticed a sprinkle of freckles on each of her cheeks, and her thick auburn hair was tied back in a low ponytail.

'Good morning, Kate. And how are you, Cara?' Cara gave her a huge grin. 'She's a little cutie, isn't she? Come on in. As I'm sure Christine explained to you, I'm the housekeeper. It's my job to make sure you have everything you need. I also keep the communal areas tidy and pay the bills on time!'

'Hi, Karen. Yes, she explained the set up. Good to meet you.'

'You've got the large bedroom on the ground floor with an en-suite. We thought it would make things easier with the baby. It's the first door on your left.'

Kate opened the door and was relieved to see a clean, spacious, bright room. The bed was already made and there was plenty of space for Cara's cot. 'This looks perfect.'

'I'm glad you like it. I'll give you a guided tour of the rest of the house and then I'll help you unload your things.'

Karen showed her the lounge and the kitchen. She had been allocated a cupboard for her food and half of a spotless

fridge. There was a large kitchen table with six chairs and a highchair.

'There are three other women living here, one of whom also has a daughter, a little older than Cara. She's started crawling, hence the safety catches on all the low-level cupboards! I'll introduce you to everyone at dinner. We usually eat together at 6.30, but if you'd prefer to cook your own food, that's not a problem.'

'No, I'd like to join you. It all looks great. The place looks spotless. Thank you so much.'

Karen gave her a broad grin. 'I think we'll get along. Now, let's get all your stuff unloaded so you can start to get yourself organised, and don't hesitate to ask me if you need anything. I'll be in the garden, weeding!'

Half an hour later, Kate sat on the bed surrounded by all her worldly possessions. She'd left everything else with David. Her divorce lawyer could sort out the division of the furniture. She was in no hurry for it; it was only stuff. She had the two most important things, Cara and her freedom.

CHAPTER 7

Sophie turned her face away from Peter as he came into the kitchen, sniffing out his breakfast, but he still noticed her swollen eyes. He sighed as he approached her, turning her to face him, gently holding her arms.

'Sweetheart, I know this is difficult for you, but it's been over two weeks now, you've got to move on. There's nothing you can do to change things. She made her decision. You can either let it ruin our lives or learn to live with it. I hate seeing you like this.'

Sophie pushed herself away from him and reached for a tissue to wipe her nose. 'Is that how long I'm allowed to grieve for my sister, my twin, the person I have been closest to my entire life? Two weeks?'

'Come on, Sophie. That's not fair. You know I didn't mean it like that. I know you guys were close, but even you admitted you grew apart as teenagers. It was only after she left home that you got tight again.'

'What are you trying to say?'

'I'm saying that you've lived your life without her in it before, and you can do it again.'

'I was a child then, Peter. And anyway, there was apparently a good reason why that happened...'

'If you believe what she said about your father. Let's not argue, it's the weekend. Let's try to enjoy ourselves.'

'You off to play football?'

Peter sighed again. He knew a loaded question when he heard one. 'You know I am.'

'Have a lovely time. Stopping for some breakfast before you go?' Sophie's voice was flat, monotone.

'No, I've lost my appetite. I'll get something down at the clubhouse.'

Sophie slumped in her chair as she heard the front door close. The house was now an echo chamber for her sense of emptiness. Her mother would not say Kate's name and Peter's sympathy was clearly spent. She didn't want to speak about it to her girlfriends; losing a family member to the Completists was shameful. No Chosen One wanted to be tainted by a desertion. For all his callousness, Peter had a point. She couldn't go on the way she was. She almost wished she'd kept her job after they were married, but David had insisted she stay at home; she had too much time on her hands, too much time to think.

For the last two weeks she had noticed every Completist who crossed her path. She had grown up with these sombre women. At first, they had been a novelty, but she soon learned they were to be despised and spurned. Her mother made sure of that. She would tug on her daughters' hands, pulling them away, crossing the street to make a point. 'Arrogant, that's what they are. Have you seen the way they look ahead, walk so upright, so proud? They think they're better than us, but they're not girls, they're traitors to their sex.' This speech was repeated so often that her mother's words no longer registered, and she began to ignore these women moving among them but separate. Grey spectres living in a parallel universe.

But now she saw them everywhere. They loomed large,

and she hated them. They had taken her sister from her and she searched among them every time she went out, looking for Kate; her heart quickening when one of them shared Kate's hair colour, her profile, or anything that might mean she was about to see her sister again. She knew Kate was still in the area, because she worked at Femmeur's headquarters; but London was a thousand villages, so the chances were still slim.

She heaved herself up to make a coffee. As the brown liquid spluttered into her cup, her sadness evolved into the familiar anger which had been growing in intensity over the last fortnight. If their paths did cross, she wasn't sure if she would hug her or slap her face. How could her sister have done this to her? Kate had thrown the jigsaw of her life, so nearly complete and perfect, into the air to land in a thousand pieces, and she had been left to put it together again, knowing that, when she did, she would be presented with a completely different picture. Had she ever known who her twin truly was? Nothing made sense and Kate was the only one who could provide her with answers to the thousands of questions crashing around in her skull. She had to let her go, it was her only way to survive.

CHAPTER 8

Kate folded the last of Cara's clothes and placed the neat pile into the last empty drawer of the sturdy chest of drawers sitting next to the voluminous wardrobe, a throwback to the Victorian era. The house was quiet, waiting for its occupants to return from work. Cara stirred from her afternoon nap and Kate walked towards her cot. 'Hello you,' she said softly, stroking her cheek. 'Good sleep?' Cara's eyes focused on her face; still and trusting. 'That was good timing, little lady, I was beginning to think of your aunt and it was making me sad. Let's get you fed and changed, then how about some fresh air?' She lifted her from her cot and felt the warmth of her body fill her own. 'I've been thinking,' she continued, 'in another week, I'm going to have to start my new job, and you're going to have to give up this,' she said, looking at the breast she was offering to her baby. 'It's been long enough, you've got all the antibodies you need now, and I'm not sure I'll have the time to express enough milk to keep you going all day.' Cara's eyes never left her own as she spoke to her whilst she fed. Kate had introduced the bottle to her baby a couple of weeks ago. She would be glad to get her freedom back. She had never related to the women who raved

about the precious connection they felt whilst breastfeeding. She didn't need to stick her nipple in Cara's mouth to feel connected to her, and the whole process made her feel more like a cow than a person. 'Had enough?' Cara fed quickly, and appeared to inflate as her breast deflated. 'You look like you're about to explode,' she said, chuckling at her plumpness. 'Right, let's get out of here, have a little wander around and see where we've ended up.'

As she pushed the stroller in front of her, she felt as if she were on a film set run entirely by women. It was one thing to be told that Completist neighbourhoods had become ghettos but quite another to wander through one. Every woman she passed smiled at her, most of them wished her a good afternoon. Was she in central London or had she passed through some portal into a parallel universe? Kate saw a small shop at the end of the street and decided to buy herself a snack. She did her usual reverse entry, pushing the door open with her back, but before she was over the threshold the door gave way behind her. 'Here, let me get that for you,' a woman's voice said.

'Thanks,' Kate said, turning to face the voice. It was owned by a young woman with the greenest, most sparkling eyes, Kate had ever seen.

'How are you doing?" she continued, as if greeting an old friend.

'I'm fine, thank you,' Kate said and then to her surprise, added, 'actually I'm a bit freaked out.'

The woman laughed. 'And why would that be?'

'I've only just become a Completist and this is my first walk around a Completist neighbourhood, and well, it's weird. I'm not used to the lack of men, and people are so open, so friendly. As I said, it's weird.'

'It must be strange for you. These neighbourhoods are no-go areas for COs and their men. They left as we moved in. My mum and I were one of the first to settle here. I was only six

when we arrived. I can tell you, it's much better now. Now it's safe to walk around at night. Before the COs left us to it my mum refused to leave the house after dark.'

'I hadn't thought of that. Freedom of movement. Wow.' The woman laughed again at Kate's expression.

'Welcome to your new world. What can I get for you?'

'Oh, I just popped in to grab a snack, I'm not sure I can last until the communal tea at 6.30 p.m.'

'You staying with Karen?'

It was Kate's turn to laugh. 'I see, everyone knows everyone around here. Amazing. This is a village in the middle of the biggest city in the country. And yes, I'm staying with Karen.'

'She's a lovely lady, and a great cook. I wouldn't buy anything too substantial, you'll want to save room for supper, believe me.'

'I'll just take these then,' Kate said, handing over a small packet of peanuts. She offered the woman her middle index finger, which she scanned. 'Well, it was a pleasure to meet you,' the woman said, her eyes twinkling, 'I'm Oonagh, by the way, and feel free to pop in anytime whilst you're here. I'm happy to answer any questions you might have, or just chat. I hope you settle in. Karen loves house hunting, by the way. She'll help you when you're ready to move on.'

'Thanks, Oonagh. I'm Kate and this is Cara.'

'A warm welcome to you as well, little Cara. You're going to love your new life. Your mum's a wise and clever woman.'

Kate laughed, 'The jury's out on that one.'

'It'll all come good, you'll see.'

When Kate reached her house she was greeted by voices and laughter coming from the kitchen. She stowed away the pram in her room, and after checking Cara's nappy, she headed nervously towards the noise. As she entered the kitchen, a host of smiling faces turned towards her. Karen leapt to her feet. 'This is Kate and Cara, our new arrivals.

Come and sit here, Kate,' she said gesturing to an empty seat next to hers.

'What a beautiful baby,' said a buxom woman, with a smile as broad as her hips. 'I'm Bridgette and that's my little girl, Sabrina, whose face is covered in strawberry jam, and is doing a great job of covering the floor with it too by the looks of things.' The woman jumped up and started assaulting her daughter's face with a wet cloth which she then used to clean the floor, whilst apologising to Karen over her shoulder.

'Let me finish off the introductions,' Karen said, eyeing the cloth in Bridgette's hands. 'This is Annie.' A diminutive woman with soft grey eyes gave her a welcoming nod. 'And these two are the Sim sisters, Jane and Claire.' They both gave her an identical smile. Then the elder of the two asked her how she liked the neighbourhood.

'I've just got back from my first walk and it was surreal. I didn't see a single man.'

'I know. I felt the same way when I first went out with Sabrina. I hadn't realised how much I scanned my environment for them, if that makes sense?'

'Risk assessment,' Annie said quietly.

'Maybe, or perhaps validation?' Jane suggested. 'Perhaps we don't really exist until a man has noticed us.'

'God, I hope that's not the case,' Annie added, almost under her breath. Kate looked around her, she was evidently not the only one who was struggling to make the transition, but she was too hungry to ponder philosophical questions, and the smells coming from the oven made her stomach gurgle loudly with anticipation.

'Sorry about that,' Kate said, blushing.

'Don't be ridiculous,' Bridgette said laughing. 'We're all human, you don't have to disguise your bodily functions here. No-one is going to think you're less attractive if you fart in this house!'

'Good to know,' said Kate, thinking that she would still

try and keep her internal organs in check, simply out of consideration for her other housemates. Bridgette made her feel self-conscious. Her easy nature, highlighted how tightly sprung Kate felt. She still carried the knot of her anger deep within, nurturing it with a sprinkle of bitterness and a soupçon of resentment.

CHAPTER 9

Kate reached over and stopped her alarm. It was her first day at her new job; the honeymoon was over. As she came to, she heard noises from the kitchen. Every housemate worked, and she was obviously not the only early riser. Cara had slept through the alarm, and she padded past her cot to the en-suite, checking her chest was rising and falling, hoping to grab a shower before she woke.

She liked her housemates. They had made her feel welcome, cooing over Cara, and giving her tips on how to negotiate her new world. They had all advised her to take a taxi on her first day, but she was ready to go out into the world as a Completist. This would be the first time she had submerged herself into the non-Completist world since her transfer. Whenever she had taken Cara for a walk, she had kept to the streets surrounding her house.

Kate studied her reflection. She saw a well presented Completist wearing a smart pair of black trousers and a charcoal grey blouse. She didn't recognise herself, but was excited by the person standing in front of her. She could sense a change happening inside her. The first trickle of confidence squeezing through the arid cracks of her psyche.

Annie was eating breakfast when she emerged from her bedroom.

'You look great,' she said, as Kate entered the kitchen.

'Thanks. I was going to have some cereal, but I'm not sure my stomach is up to it.'

'You'll be fine. When's your taxi coming?'

'I've decided to take the bus.'

'You sure? You've got enough to cope with today. Do you really want this to be the first time you mingle with men and the COs?'

'Blimey, Annie. I've been doing that my entire life, I'll be fine. I know it'll be different, but I'll keep my head up and eyes ahead. How difficult can it be?' Annie ignored her question.

'Good luck and I hope you enjoy your first day. Can't wait to hear all about it at dinner.'

Kate slipped her jacket on, checking her gold pin was safely attached to the lapel, and walked out of the front door towards the main road and the bus stop, Cara safely cradled to her in her sling. As she left the familiar back streets where she had walked with Cara over the last few days, the crowds grew denser and there they were: the first men she had seen in over a fortnight. Kate couldn't help herself, she glanced sideways, wanting to see how they reacted to her. She wished she hadn't. Their eyes were on her as she walked, judging, dissecting. She could feel their thoughts tickling her skin. *Fail to satiate us and we'll take you. Make us the centre of your universe or we'll forsake you. Voice your opinions too fiercely and we will render you powerless until you learn to keep quiet. You pass by untouched because we have decided you can; but transgress and you'll see how thin the veneer of civility is.* Kate checked herself. Now she understood. Pushing her shoulders back, she held her head high and looked straight ahead. Nothing had changed. She was still afraid. If anything, it was worse. As a CO she had had her defences. A gesture or an expression could smooth out a crackle in the unspoken communication

between the sexes. A submissive bow of her head to dissolve any rash assertiveness; wide-eyed wonder to bolster a weaker intellect; and her pretty, innocent smile to banish the sexual predator back to his cave. A buffet of deflection. But as a Completist she overtly, if silently, snubbed men every time she stepped into their realm; and neither they nor their women liked it. Kate's heart raced, and she stroked Cara's back through the material of her sling, to comfort them both.

The bus was packed. No-one offered her a seat, not even with Cara bound to her chest. Why hadn't she listened to the advice she had been offered? This world looked the same; yet it was completely alien to her. This was going to take some getting used to.

CHAPTER 10

Kate took a Completist taxi home that evening. She was happy but exhausted.

'Busy day?' the driver asked her, perhaps noticing her weary expression in her rear-view mirror.

'First day in a new job,' she explained to the eyes assessing her.

'Give it six months and you'll be laughing,' the driver said, the laughter lines around her eyes deepening. Kate smiled and the blonde bob in front of her straightened to face the road ahead.

Kate unlocked the front door and went straight to her bedroom. She removed Cara from her sling and lay her on the bed, cuddling up next to her. Cara started to do limb gymnastics, checking everything still worked after her short confinement. Kate stared up at the ceiling, thinking this would be one of those rare times she would have liked David around; to hand Cara over to his care whilst she took a hot shower and had a nap. She glanced at the time, twenty minutes before supper, she could just close her eyes for a few seconds. Cara threw up all over her blouse.

'So how was it?' Annie asked, as Kate took her seat at the

dinner table dressed in a hoodie and leggings, placing Cara's baby carrier at the end of the table so she could join in. Everyone was waiting for her response.

'The job was great, the journey there, not so much.' Her audience waited. 'I was naïve. I felt crushed, suffocated.'

'It's rough the first time. But it gets easier,' Annie said softly.

Bridgette laughed: 'If it's any consolation, I didn't listen either.' She turned her unflinching gaze to rest on Kate, who was, once again, struck by the strength and confidence of this dark-skinned woman. 'Thought I could sail on through unscathed. I'm no stranger to prejudice. White is still might, and men are still dicks. You'll sort out the safest route from Completist point A to Completist point B.'

'Yes, it's only when you're in transit that you have to put up with the shit. When you got to your destination the world changed, didn't it?' Karen asked.

'It sure did. And it made up for every hateful glance, every dismissive gesture. It reminded me of the Shopping Centre. Such a sense of freedom, of safety.'

'Are Femmeur's offices as plush as everyone says?' asked Annie.

'They're spectacular. They've got a staff canteen on the ninth floor with a huge wall of sliding glass doors leading to a rooftop terrace. The views are breath-taking. You can sit on the terrace and have lunch in the summer, and the food was excellent. Almost as good as Karen's!'

'Not possible,' Karen said, and everyone laughed.

'On that note, could you pass the bread please, Kate. I want to soak up this delicious dressing,' Annie said.

Kate smiled and reached for the bread-basket. She liked Annie. They shared an inner turmoil that they sensed in one another.

'Anyone else want some?' Annie asked the group of women, waving the bread- basket in the air.

'Please,' Bridgette said. She gave her daughter a crust, more for gum relief than nutrition, then paused, looking at the faces that surrounded her.

'OK. I have a question. I don't want to put you off your food, but is anyone going to use a Facilitator? Or maybe someone already has?'

Everyone stopped eating, forks halfway to mouths, and all eyes turned towards Bridgette, who roared with laughter. 'I'll take that as a no!'

Karen spoke up. 'I've used one, more than once.'

All eyes switched to Karen, who put her fork down, preparing to share her wisdom with her captive audience. Kate looked at her empty plate. Annie shifted in her seat.

'You guys are newbies, but I've been in the Movement for six years now, and we all have needs. That's why these men exist. No demand, no service required.'

'Is it frowned on?' asked Bridgette.

'Not frowned on exactly, more like a necessary evil. Did you know that women have a stronger libido than men? But they make us ashamed of ours.'

'Probably so they have a chance of keeping up,' Bridgette said, laughing loudly again.

'So how does it work then?' Annie asked quietly, looking up from the remains of her salad.

'There are several agencies, all offering slightly different services, satisfying different appetites, shall we say. Search for Facilitator, select an agency and browse the men on offer. Click on the man you like and place your order. The agency contacts you to make the arrangements.' Kate felt sure there would be no Facilitators who would cater for her.

'Take-away sex. I like it!' Bridgette said, as she recommenced her meal with gusto. 'Is he delivered to your door, or do you have to meet discreetly in some dark, seedy hotel?'

'Whatever suits you,' Karen replied.

‘Is it safe?’ Kate asked, and Annie flashed her a grateful look. Kate’s eyes smiled back.

‘Totally. These men are meticulously vetted by the Movement. I can’t stress that enough.’

‘I bet the Movement keeps records of all the members that use them,’ Claire chimed in. ‘Everything you do online can be monitored. And while no-one really bothers now advertising on social media is illegal, I don’t believe they wouldn’t be interested in what we’re up to.’

‘The Movement are quite transparent about the data they capture. All I can tell you is they insist that any data is anonymous, and I’ve never heard any evidence to the contrary.’

‘How much does it cost?’ asked Bridgette, sitting back in her chair, plate wiped clean.

‘It’s very reasonable compared with the rates for CO prostitutes because it’s subsidised by the Movement,’ Karen replied.

‘No way!’ Bridgette said, slapping the table with her palm and grinning broadly. ‘I love being a Completist!’

Kate looked at Annie and their eyes flickered with mutual discomfort. She wondered if either of them could ever type the word ‘Facilitator’ into their search engine, and what Annie had experienced at the hands of men.

CHAPTER 11

It was Kate's second day. This morning a taxi was waiting. She wasn't scared, she was late. Kate had woken with a start; her natural body clock kicking in when her manual one failed. Its failure was inevitable because it had not been set. The exhaustion of her first day had sent her to bed at the same time as Cara. It must have slipped her mind.

She just made it to her desk on time, and sat with her coffee, breathing in the rich aroma wafting up from her mug. She hated having to say a hurried goodbye to Cara, but one of the mothers in the office crèche had scooped Cara up and distracted her, realising Kate was in a panic.

Kate's floor was open plan, save for one office, which belonged to the HR Director. It was one of only two offices in the building where the glass walls were opaque. The only other person with a private office was Libretta Jones, the Head of Femmeur and the leader of the Movement. Kate was scheduled to meet her today at 11.00. She was going to meet a Completist icon, and she hadn't had time for a shower.

Her seat faced the glass wall overlooking the City's rooftops. Kate was the only one looking at the view. Everyone

else was staring at their screens. She thought again of the day she had joined her first company as a trainee, the day she had met David, the day she had fallen in love. A nervous 16-year-old, intimidated by the men in the department who had been far too keen to introduce themselves.

Once she started to gain weight after her father died and to take care of her appearance, she caught glimpses of the look she had seen in her father's eyes every Wednesday night. She naturally lowered her eyes, unwilling to be continually reminded of men's desire for youth, the younger the better. She thought David saw beyond her appearance, saw her. He became her shield, deflecting inappropriate comments and sly advances. There were no men here. Here, she had no need for a shield. Everyone saw her, no-one was seduced by her beauty; her only power was her brain.

'Are you OK?'

'I'm fine,' Kate replied, turning to her right to address her neighbour. She wished she remembered her name. 'Just taking a moment.'

'Of course, I still remember what my first week was like. It's pretty intense here, isn't it? If there's anything you need, let me know. I'm Beth, by the way. In case you're as bad at remembering names as I am!'

'Thanks, Beth.' Kate laughed. 'One more question. Do you have children?'

'I do. She's three.'

'Is she upstairs?'

'No, my mum looks after her for me.'

'How?'

Beth laughed. 'She's a Completist, one of the first. I was raised a Completist.'

'Oh, right. Wow. I'm sorry, I didn't think... '

'Don't worry. Why do you ask?'

'I got the distinct impression that the women in the crèche

preferred mothers not to visit their children during the day. I was wondering if that was the norm.'

'I have friends with children in the crèche and you're right. It's not encouraged. It unsettles the children. You know you can download the crèche app on your mobile? The place is crawling with cameras. You can see how she's doing whenever you like. I'll ping you the link.'

'Thanks. I'm sure they did tell me, but I was too busy saying goodbye to take it in. Right, I better be getting on. Thanks again, Beth.'

Kate set a reminder 15 minutes before her 11 o'clock meeting. She didn't want to be late.

Libretta's office was on the penultimate floor. Kate stepped out of the glass lift into a floor flooded with daylight. All the walls were glass and London stretched out around her. Beth had told her to turn right and head straight on until she couldn't go any further. A woman looked up as Kate approached her enormous desk.

'Hello,' she said. Her voice sounded like a bell. 'You must be Kate, Libretta is looking forward to meeting you. Follow me, I'm Sally, Libretta's Assistant.'

Sally knocked on a solid wooden door then opened it. Libretta stood up, smiling, her hand extended. She was dressed in an immaculate black suit which was draped effortlessly over her slim frame. Her hair was white blonde and cut into a bob, each strand cut with precision and care. Kate took her hand. Her grip was firm. 'I'm very pleased to meet you,' Kate said.

'Likewise. Please take a seat. Can I offer you a coffee? Or tea?'

'No, thank you.'

'How are you finding leaving Cara? It must be tough.'

Kate was taken aback. 'It is tough, but the app helps, and

most of the time I'm too absorbed in my work to think about it.'

Libretta laughed. 'And what do you think about your role so far? Do you think you'll enjoy it?'

'Very much. The office is so friendly. Intense but relaxed. I couldn't put my finger on why at first,' Libretta was watching her closely, 'but then I realised. No male gaze. Brilliant!'

Libretta laughed again. 'Makes quite a difference, doesn't it?'

'It makes *all* the difference.'

'And you're getting all the help and support you need?'

'I am, thank you.'

'How do you find Angela Stephens?'

Kate paused, searching for the right word. 'Intimidating!'

'I'm sure she would be delighted to hear it. Every HR Director should have an edge to her, like a good headmistress. Firm but fair. She plays bad cop, so I don't have to.'

'Your reputation doesn't support that statement, Miss Jones,' Kate said, immediately grimacing at the use of her surname.

'Call me Libretta. You've been listening to too many COs. I'm just not prepared to play the victim. A woman is a victim until she decides not to be.'

'You're right. Only, I wish it was easier to make that decision.'

'I'm delighted you did, Kate. I predict a bright future for you here. I'll be watching your progress with interest.' Libretta stood.

'Thank you, Libretta. It was a pleasure to meet you.'

'Remember, I have an open-door policy, if you can get past Sally!'

Kate laughed and shook her hand again, returning the pressure of her grip.

As she walked back to the lift, she suddenly craved a cigarette. Had Sophie started smoking again too? Kate could

have one now, having bought a packet from Oonagh the day before she was starting work, her nerves getting the better of her. She could spare herself a few minutes and pressed the lift button to take her to the top floor. There was one other woman standing outside on the rooftop terrace, her slender frame supported by the brick wall she was leaning against, the smoke from her lungs rising in a cloud above her. Kate stood a few feet to her left and lit up. The woman turned to her and smiled.

'It's a beautiful morning for some fresh air.' Her voice was deep, with the beginnings of a rasp caused by inhaling too much of it.

'It certainly is. I've just met Libretta.'

'Ah, that explains your craving. How did you find our great leader?'

'I liked her. She's such a presence, if that makes sense?'

'It does, and she is. The woman is a powerhouse. I'm Fran.'

'Kate. Second day in, and very pleased to be here.'

'Which department?'

'H.R. You?'

'P.R.'

'Exciting!'

'Challenging. Libretta likes to speak her mind.'

'How long have you been here?'

'Just over a year now.' Fran stubbed her cigarette in the ashtray, grinding the end into the metal. 'Do you fancy having lunch with me?'

Kate had taken an instant liking to this woman, she reminded her of a black panther, without the ability to maul her to death. 'I do. Thanks. I wasn't looking forward to being the new girl, sitting on her own, pretending not to care.'

'Exactly. Why do you think I asked? It's not because I like you.'

Kate laughed. 'It's always great to be pitied. See you at 1.00?'

'See you at 1.00 by the lifts.'

She watched her new friend leave, her gait was almost feline, and took a final, long drag, blowing the smoke into the clear blue skies of London.

CHAPTER 12

When Kate returned to her desk, Beth also asked her to lunch. Kate explained the situation and invited Beth to join her the following day. Beth had been kind to her and Kate was not one to forget a kindness.

Fran was already waiting when she stepped out of the lift.

'Good to know you're the punctual type. Can't stand people who act like your time isn't precious.'

Kate laughed. She liked Fran's directness. She couldn't stand bullshitters. Neither could she stand tardiness.

'Shall we see what's on offer?' Fran said.

Trays laden, they sat near the terrace doors, in readiness for their post-meal nicotine. They chose a blue topped table. The restaurant was decorated with tables in an array of colours, it made it look like a field littered with wild flowers.

'So, how long have you been a Completist, Kate?' Fran asked in between mouthfuls of a perfectly prepared kale salad.

'Nearly a fortnight.'

'Still feel like you're in the twilight zone?'

'I do, although the sun's appearing on the horizon.'

'I remember feeling like I was standing in front of a

mirror. I could see the world I knew reflected in it, but I couldn't seem to touch it.'

'Alice, unable to go through the looking glass?'

'Exactly. It took a good few months before I was able to orientate myself and walk comfortably alongside my old parallel universe, knowing I would never be able to connect with the people I had left behind.'

Kate started to speak, but hesitated.

'Why did I become a Completist?' Fran said. 'That's what you want to know, isn't it? The question we dare not ask. I get why they don't encourage prying. Forget the old, live the new, but the past moulds us, doesn't it. It makes us who we are. You can shed your outer skin, but the core remains. I became a Completist because I was married to a very violent man. I knew he would kill me one day, and my family wouldn't help.'

'I'm sorry, Fran. That's one of the reasons I left. My father's dead and my mother, well, the least said about her the better. The hardest thing was leaving my twin sister.' Kate stopped eating.

'That's tough. I've heard some twins are so close they can feel the things their twin feels even though they're miles apart. I left behind my six-year-old son.'

'Shit.' Kate stared at her new friend, overawed by her sacrifice.

'Yep, it is shit. I still see him. Actually, I spy on him, when he gets dropped off at school. To make sure he's still alive and kicking.' They looked at one another. There was nothing more to be said.

'What do you like most about being a Completist?' Kate asked, moving away from their pain.

'The space in my head. Space where hopes and dreams are taking root. Wait. It will happen to you too.'

'I think it's already beginning. In the moments when I forget the pain I've caused my sister, the overwhelming feeling

is one of relief. I don't regret my decision. I had to protect my daughter.'

'How old?'

'Ten weeks.'

'Her name?'

'Cara.' Fran laughed. 'I know. Named after the woman who was the catalyst for the Movement. I think I'd already made up my mind when I was pregnant, don't you?'

'Looks that way. At least now she has a chance to be her best self.'

'I hope so, Fran. I really do.'

They both pushed their plates to the side at the same time and nodded towards the terrace. They laughed at their synchronicity.

'Great minds think alike?' Fran asked, smiling.

'Precisely. Time for some fresh air!'

CHAPTER 13

Kate only stayed in the Transition House for about four months. She liked her housemates, but she was about moving forward, staying in the main current of life, and that house was shallow water, where you could happily float around forgetting you needed to get downstream. The Completists Homebuyer Assistance Scheme was generous and nimble. If you had a secure job, they had your back, and she was working in one of the most prestigious and successful Completist companies in the country.

The choice of which area to live in was made simple. Completists could, in theory, live anywhere, but why move into a neighbourhood where you were not wanted when you could move into one surrounded by like-minded people? There was another big advantage about belonging to a movement that was shunned by the majority, you could still find a bargain; and the more Completists moved into an area and drove the house prices down, the bigger the bargain to be had. Kate thought this was hilarious. Completists were an affluent, successful minority who transformed the areas they lived in, renovating houses and encouraging Completist entrepreneurs to open cafés and shops. It was no wonder their estate agents

had taken over. They were the only ones who could explain why a house in a well-maintained street, in a well-serviced area was selling for far less money than the equivalent home in a non-Completist area without offending prospective buyers.

Kate had settled on a run-down Victorian townhouse, the only nod to modernity being the obligatory solar panels on the roof. She had fallen for the boarded-up fireplaces, their colourful ceramic tile surrounds peeping through the cracks in the wood. She loved the tiled hallway, partly obscured by the cheap lino favoured by the previous occupant, who had lived there her entire life. Kate sensed she had been a kind woman. There was a gentleness about the place, a sweetness in the stale air.

Moving day soon arrived. She had been unloading the car for less than five minutes when the first of her neighbours came out of the house opposite hers; a tiny woman, scurrying towards her with a cake tin.

'Welcome to Wandsworth, and our dear road. My name's Jenny and I've been here for three years now. You'll love it! I've bought you a chocolate cake; most people like chocolate, don't they?' She searched Kate's face for reassurance that her assumption was not misplaced.

'We love chocolate, don't we Cara, thank you so much!'

'You're very welcome. She's lovely. How old?'

'She's nearly six months old now. I'm Kate, I'm really pleased to meet you.' Kate held out her hand and her diminutive neighbour shook it with a strength that took her by surprise.

'Look, I'll leave you to it. But please, don't hesitate to call on me, day or night, if you or little Cara need anything.' With that, she scurried back to her house, turning and giving Kate a cheery wave as she went. Jenny Wren, thought Kate as she carried the cake tin into her new kitchen.

It wasn't long before Kate closed her very own front door and walked back to the dilapidated kitchen, catching her toe

on a rogue piece of lino. 'First job on the list, rip up the lino before it kills us both,' she said to her daughter who had started mithering and squirming in her sling. Cara was getting hungry and could no longer be ignored. Kate freed her from her restraints and placed her in the highchair she had set up, anticipating this moment.

'It's been quite the year, Cara, hasn't it?' Kate said in a sing-song voice, as her daughter enthusiastically bashed the plastic tray with her tiny metal spoon while Kate tried to get food into her mouth. 'What do you think of the new place then? Do you like it?' Cara gurgled back at her, intently watching her mother's mouth; her own tiny lips copying the shapes in an attempt to emulate Kate's sounds. 'How do you think I'm doing? Are you proud of the way I'm handling all this? I think I've settled into my job and I'm very proud of the way you've settled into nursery.' Cara bashed her tray again as if delighted at her mother's praise. Kate laughed, 'Well I am, really proud.' Kate noticed the framed poster of the painting by Klimt of twins being lovingly held by their mother. Sophie had given it to her when she left home, not realising the irony of the image. Kate had thought about throwing it out, but it represented how a mother should feel about her children, and when she had come across it again whilst unpacking, she'd hung it on a random nail sticking out of the kitchen wall for safe-keeping. She looked back at Cara. 'I wonder if you have a cousin on the way? Do you miss Sophie, I do. She'd laugh at this place. Her house is all eco efficient, streamlined and sanitised. Sometimes I wonder at how different we are.' Cara let out a shrill squeal, and Kate realised she had been talking to the air above her daughter's head. Cara was letting her know she didn't appreciate her lack of focus.

'Right, young lady, I think you've had enough. Time for bath and bed. Once again you've managed to get more of your dinner on yourself than in your mouth.' She lifted Cara into her arms and headed upstairs. She didn't make it to the first

floor before her doorbell rang. It made her jump. Who knew she had a doorbell! When she opened the door the first thing she saw was a smile.

'Hello. I'm your next-door neighbour, thataway,' the woman said, beckoning to the left with her head. 'I'm Jackie.'

'I'm Kate. Please, come in.' Jackie hesitated, looking at Cara, whose head was resting on her mother's chest.

'I've bought you a bottle of my favourite relaxant. I thought you could probably use a glass, but I can see that won't happen until your charming child has fallen dormant. Shouldn't take long by the look of her, I bet it's been an exhausting day for you both. So, I'll leave you to it. But how about tomorrow? There's a lot to tell you about the neighbourhood. We're an active bunch and I know everyone will be dying to meet you. I personally favour the Book Club. It's been running for over a year now and we've successfully read and reviewed zero books, but I can safely say we have reviewed numerous grape varieties. All the best people are in the Book Club. No pressure!' Her neighbour gave her another glimpse of her impressive teeth and thrust the bottle at her.

'Why don't you come around at 8, Cara's normally down by then.'

'It's a date, Kate, until tomorrow.'

'Until then.'

Kate closed the door. 'Jackie the mouth', she said to Cara, mentally fixing her neighbours name in her mind. She looked at her sleepy daughter. 'Look what I've got, Mummy medicine! Let's get you bathed, young lady.'

When she re-entered the kitchen an hour later, Kate headed for the fridge to pour herself a very large glass of wine.

This year had been filled with months, weeks, days and hours of work, mothering and moving, and Kate was exhausted. She sat down at her kitchen table, its surface battered and bruised by years of constant use, and took a large gulp of the delicious wine her new neighbour had gifted her.

It was strange to be alone. No colleagues or housemates to share her thoughts with. This was her space, her home, and it would be decorated as she pleased. There would be no compromising done here. If Kate wanted to cover the sofa with a sequin infested throw, she'd bloody well do it. An unlikely scenario as Kate considered sequins to be the spawn of the devil; but the point was she could. Just like making a date without having to check if it would interfere with someone else's life, a life more important than her own.

It was so quiet. Kate listened. She could just detect the odd passing car, a reminder of the outside world. She wondered how many other women were sitting in their kitchens, alone. Parallel parked up this road, separated by walls, quiet and still. But perhaps not, perhaps friends were visiting friends, laughing and sharing their days, their aspirations, their dreams. Kate topped up her glass. The road was peaceful, but not oppressive, and she felt optimistic about the future, after all, it had taken less than two hours to be provided with wine and cake. She remembered the first night in the house she had bought with David. A spare bedroom for the family they were contemplating. Not a single person had knocked on their door that night. They hadn't given it a second thought. They had had each other. He was still her kind, thoughtful protector back then, his darker counterpart still hidden from view. The bed was the first thing they made.

She reached for her mobile on the table beside her. Kate hadn't thought about sex since the conversation around the kitchen table in the Transition House. It had been a long time since she had felt a man's hands exploring her skin. Did she miss it? That feeling of submission, of being powerless. She shouldn't, but she did.

Kate entered the word Facilitator into the search engine. Several agencies appeared, but she was drawn to the dark colours of a site called 'No Boundaries'. Kate knew what she was looking for, even though she could never voice those needs

to another soul. And she never would. Her tastes had emerged from dark origins, a sexuality crawling from a diseased pupa, an ugly moth, always aiming for the light, but existing in the darkness.

She clicked on John. He looked strong, brutal. There was no joy emanating from his eyes, only a dark promise of control, of orders given, and being silently obeyed. Her eyes scanned his sales pitch, and her body twitched. She shut down the site. Life was good. That was her past. She had her future to think of and it didn't include John.

CHAPTER 14

When Kate woke up the next morning, her libido had tucked itself away. After breakfast, she dropped Cara off at Femmeur. A mountain of packing boxes awaited her and she could plough through it much quicker without Cara's demands on her attention. Her possessions had grown exponentially from her original car load. Kate had been gathering items whilst at the Transition House, enjoying shopping expeditions with her housemates. David had also released all of Cara's nursery furniture, having finally accepted she was never coming back. He refused to release any of her possessions. It was going to be a long divorce, and it was being negotiated through a Completist lawyer to avoid direct contact with him, but that seemed to make things easier.

She picked Cara up at 5.00 p.m. tired but exhilarated by all she had achieved. Cara went down easily, worn out by whatever she had got up to at Femmeur. Kate was grateful her daughter had welcomed sleep so easily as her neighbour was prompt. The doorbell rang at precisely 8.00 p.m.

'Come in, come in,' Kate said holding the door wide open. 'Welcome to 'work-in-progress.'

‘Fear not, I will not judge. I’m in the same state, well, not quite this bad!’ Jackie said, eyeing the lino floor.

Kate laughed. ‘Come on through to the lounge, your relaxant awaits.’

‘Your place is a mirror image of my own, except I’ve knocked that wall down.’ Jackie said, pointing to the wall that divided the kitchen from the lounge.

‘You personally?’

‘No, although I wish I could’ve. Would’ve saved me a fortune.’

‘Do they have Completist building companies?’

‘Sure do. And they’re as good as the men, and probably a little better at tidying up after themselves.’

‘I still can’t get over how little I knew about this world when I was a Chosen One. I had no idea about the size and extent of it. It really is like living in a parallel universe.’ Kate passed Jackie a full glass of white and nodded in the direction of an armchair, which Kate had recently unearthed from a mountain of clothes.

‘The government doesn’t exactly want to share the story about how we’re flourishing with the rest of the population, but people will soon start putting the pieces together for themselves.’

‘Maybe, but humans are pretty good at ignoring what’s right in front of them, especially if it makes them uncomfortable. Anyway, tell me about the neighbourhood.’ Kate gave Jackie an encouraging look and sat back on her new sofa.

‘Where to start! There’s a lot going on. But here’s the lowdown on your immediate neighbours. Your other next-door neighbour is Anne. She’s about 65 and a retired school teacher. She was one of the first, and has fascinating stories to tell of the Uprising, especially after a few of these.’ Her eyes flickered towards her glass. ‘Then opposite there’s Jenny.’

‘I’ve already met her. She’s lovely. She bought me - ‘

‘A chocolate cake?’

'Yes!'

'She bought me one too. She is lovely. We call her The Wren. Not very original, but it kind of suits her, I think. She'll do anything for anybody. You have a ready-made babysitter there, I'm sure of it, and she doesn't drink, so no clash with the Book Club!'

'So, who's in this 'Book Club'?'

'An elite group of women with impeccable taste. Apart from my good self and Anne, we have the lovely lady whose brainchild it was, Rowena. She's an architect and a great source of gossip from the dark-side.'

'The dark-side?'

'The dark-side, your old team. The majority of her private clients are CO's. She's very high end, and the super-rich are unfortunately still comprised of rich heterosexual couples who compete with other rich heterosexual couples. We call her our double agent. Rowena is brilliant and cunning. She gains their confidence by dropping in the odd derogatory comment about Completists, and now she has a reputation as a charming anomaly, an exotic the oligarchs like to employ to show their friends how liberal they are. You'd be amazed at the information they share with her. There's been a few husbands who run large corporates with rather too much influence within the government; it's fascinating stuff. We all reckon Rowena is a Guardian, but their identities are secret, and she will neither confirm nor deny our suspicions, even when she's off her head. Very annoying!'

'The Guardians basically run the Movement, don't they?'

'Correct, they support the four Founders and the woman who heads up the lot is Libretta Jones. She's our spokesperson, and the only one whose identity is in the public domain. But she makes up for the others anonymity. Our Libretta is no shrinking violet.'

'She's my boss, I work for Femmeur. Anyone else?'

'Two others, Helen and Mandy. Helen of Troy, as we like

to call her, is stunning. She's like that gay guy all the straight women lust over. I'm sure every man looks at her and thinks, what a waste. She told us she joined because she was fed up with being prized for her skin and not for what her skin contained and now feels liberated from her beauty. I get it, but I can't resist teasing her about what a terrible shame it is that she's so irresistible!' Jackie laughed, flicking her hair back and raising her eyes to the heavens.

Kate smiled, but she had a great deal of sympathy for Helen, she knew how dangerous beauty could be. It was a curse, not a gift.

'Last, but not least, Mandy. Mother of three girls who always looks like a train wreck. She has a wicked sense of humour. Give her a chance. She can come across as a little aggressive at first, because she's naturally suspicious of people, but you'll see, she's one of the most loyal and consistent people I've ever had the pleasure of meeting. I don't think you'll have a problem. You seem like a tough enough cookie.'

'They sound a fascinating group, but they might not want another member.'

'I've already spoken to them. They're up for it. So have a chat with The Wren and get her over next Tuesday night. I'll pick you up at eight. We're meeting at Rowena's next week. Her house is a five-minute walk from here. You're in.'

'Right, great. What book are we reading?'

Jackie looked at her quizzically for a second. 'Ha fucking ha. We're reading Sauvignon Blanc by Anne Hadaday.'

CHAPTER 15

Kate couldn't believe what she was seeing. Gothic towers clad in lead rose to greet the evening summer sky. Jackie laughed at her expression.

'I know, pretty impressive stuff. Haven't you ever seen The Royal Victoria Patriotic Building?'

'No, I had no idea it existed. It's incredible. Rowena lives *here*?'

'Not only does she live in this glorious building but wait until you see her apartment. It used to be owned by some rock star, way back, when this place was first converted into flats, and it's stunning. I told you, she's brilliant, and she's doing very well.'

They were the last to arrive. Everyone was already seated in the vaulted lounge, glasses charged, chattering among themselves. The mullioned windows were flung wide open, an invitation to the evening breeze. A curved staircase invited you to explore the mezzanine above, under which nestled a pristine kitchen of polished wood, gleaming chrome and hand-made tiles. The opposite wall of the vast room featured an impressive stone arch surrounding a heavy oak door, which Kate

imagined led into a light-filled master bedroom with a spacious en-suite bathroom.

'You have a very beautiful home, Rowena. Thank you for inviting me.' Kate handed her a decent bottle of white, wishing she had bought the more expensive Chablis. All eyes were on her, but they were smiling eyes, save perhaps those of Mandy. At least, Kate guessed it was Mandy; it wasn't a difficult deduction. Anne was significantly older than the rest of the group, and you couldn't miss Helen; that only left the dark-haired woman who had scraped her unruly curls into a messy bun, tendrils escaping like a crazed octopus.

'I'd like to introduce Kate to you all,' Jackie said, addressing the group.

Everyone raised their glasses, smiling broadly. Kate returned the gesture, with the glass Rowena had thrust into her hand moments before, and took a sip of some delicious white wine she couldn't identify.

'You can't avoid the inevitable,' Mandy said turning to her. 'You may as well get on with giving us your potted history to satisfy our curiosity.'

'Right,' Kate said, remembering Beth's words after her interview. Mandy obviously hadn't read the memo about prying into people's former lives. She perched on the end of the voluminous and spotless white sofa, feeling exposed. 'Not much to tell. I have a twin sister, Sophie, who I'll never see again, which causes me great pain. And a ghastly mother who I'll never see again, which is a huge relief!' An encouraging group chuckle coaxed her on. 'My father died when I was 16, and I moved out shortly after. Nearly divorced from my not so gentle, kind and thoughtful husband David, and I joined you lot in May. Moved into my new house a mere week ago and find myself here, in this glorious building, surrounded by fucking Completists.' The group joined in with her own laughter and the ice was broken. Even Mandy managed a grin.

'And you are very welcome,' Mandy said, the rest of them

nodding in agreement. 'We were talking about Simon. Have you had the pleasure yet?'

'No, not yet.'

'You will. He'll sniff out fresh meat and he lives at the end of your road. One of the very few men who live among us, and believe you me, the ones we attract are scumbags. The ones who really loathed us moved on, once they realised they couldn't get to us in our safe little ghetto, leaving behind a handful of narcissists who believe they're so irresistible they could bed a Completist. He's a pest. We were trying to devise a cunning plan to encourage him to move into a new neighbourhood.'

'Not all the men are pests,' Helen said, her soft voice a sharp contrast to Mandy's strident tones. Her golden hair flowed effortlessly over her shoulders in relaxed ringlets. 'Old Sam's a sweetie,' she said to Kate. 'He's a widower, lived in Wandsworth all his life. He always says he doesn't blame us for wanting to live without men. Calls his sex a bunch of spoilt, lust-filled heathens. He's hilarious. We all make sure he's looked after. We know he'd never turn against us.'

'How about setting a honey trap, luring Simon into one of our houses, drugging him with Rohypnol, then taking photos of him in degrading sexual situations and threatening to post them on social media, with the caption, "Simon gets a taste of his own medicine" if he doesn't move?' The words popped out of Kate's mouth before she could stop them. The room fell silent. 'I'm not serious, it was meant to be a joke!'

'That's a relief,' Rowena said, 'I thought a man had infiltrated the group. Although sometimes I wish we could fight fire with fire. That kind of thing happens to women, yet still we're expected to be better than them. Even if we wanted to do it, we'd never get away with it. The police would believe him over us, and we'd end up in jail. And can you imagine how damaging the publicity would be for the Movement if the story got out.' Rowena shuddered.

'As I said, it was meant as a joke. I have a dark humour, and I keep forgetting what it's like for you.' Kate stopped and then corrected herself. 'For us.'

'Nothing wrong with a twisted mind,' Mandy said, giving her a reassuring smile, 'but it's true that Completists are treated like all women were before the second wave of feminism hit in the 2030's. Men have far more protection against violence than we do, which is ironic given they are more able to protect themselves. It'd be worth a lifetime behind bars to see his face though!' Mandy said, winking at Kate. Kate rather liked Mandy.

CHAPTER 16

When Sophie discovered she was expecting, the first person she wanted to tell was her sister. As she looked at the test in her hands, the loss hit her with the force of sledgehammer. She had no compunction about withholding the news from their mother. Sophie was in no hurry to start being told how to be pregnant. Now, ten weeks later, here she was, sitting in the hospital waiting for her second scan, her reluctant husband by her side.

Peter had been delighted by the news; and had spent the following Saturday night celebrating his fertility with his mates down the football club. They were both throwing up the next morning, but for very different reasons. Since then, he'd shown little interest in how his baby was developing and how she was feeling about growing someone inside of her, which frankly wasn't great. The midwife reassured her that her morning sickness should ease after the first trimester and she was counting down the days. Sophie already despised the roundness of her belly and the fullness of her breasts. She had always struggled with her weight, unlike her sister who had inherited their mother's slender frame. Sophie had starved herself to get into her wedding dress, but her body had stub-

bornly reverted to its natural weight as soon as she started eating normally again. Peter's disparaging glances at her increasing waistline over the last month had not gone unnoticed, and he was only here with her now out of a sense of duty, but perhaps when he saw his baby on the monitor, he would begin to start making a fuss of her.

'I wish we could know the sex,' he said as he flicked impatiently through his social feed, looking for something to absorb time. 'Your sister's lot put a stop to all that, didn't they? If they didn't use genetic engineering to control the sex of their children, we'd be able to know if we're having a boy or a girl. I don't get why Parliament passed that law. Wanting to know the sex of a baby once it's been created is completely different from choosing the sex from the get-go.'

'I know, it's really frustrating, but we'll know soon enough.' Sophie hated the way he now referred to Completists as "her sister's lot".

'Soon enough for you, perhaps, but not for me.'

They both jumped at the sound of their names being called and followed the nurse into a small room. Within minutes their baby was on the screen in front of them. They both gasped as they saw their large-headed offspring floating peacefully before their eyes with its tiny hands and feet and even tinier fingers and toes. Sophie turned to Peter. He was spellbound. Finally, she thought, finally he'll be with me in this. She reached out and squeezed his arm.

Peter left the hospital a different man. He held Sophie's hand as they walked to the car. 'I reckon it's a boy,' he said, giving her hand a squeeze. 'Did you see him kick?'

Sophie squeezed back. 'I think so too,' she said, smiling up at his happy face. She didn't, but if the thought of having a son made him happy, she'd go along with it. What harm could it do? And if it meant she would finally be treated with the care and respect she was due, then everyone was a winner.

CHAPTER 17

Emmeline was born a year and ten days after Cara on the 28 March 2116. Sophie's pregnancy had been the distraction she needed. She had even enjoyed spending time with her mother, who loved shopping for baby things as much as she did, and far more than Peter. Her mother had also made a huge fuss of her, unlike her husband, whose enthusiasm for his pregnant wife had waned shortly after their second scan. His main contribution to the process was talking to her stomach about what position the baby could play on the pitch. He was evidently hoping for a centre forward. As her due date approached, she fretted more about how Peter would react if it was a girl.

The birth was quick and relatively easy. As Emmeline finally slithered from her body, Sophie's first instinct was not to look at the baby on her chest, but at Peter's face. There was no doubt about it, he was upset. Sophie wrapped her daughter in her arms, shielding her against his disappointment.

'Look at her tiny hands, Peter. She's perfect, isn't she?'

'She's lovely, Sophie. Well done. What are we going to call her?' She could hear the strain in his voice as he made a valiant

attempt to sound happy. Unlike Peter, Sophie had always had a feeling she was having a girl. She was ready with her answer.

'I think she looks like an Emmeline. Do you like that? It means peaceful home or industrious.'

Peter laughed. 'Emmeline sounds fine, and I'm all for a peaceful home!' He leant over and kissed her forehead, ignoring his daughter. 'I'm going to ring everyone with the news. See you in a minute or two.'

Sophie looked at the little face staring up at her, her blue eyes were a stark contrast to her fine, dark hair. She stroked her cheek and felt her daughter lean into her finger, relishing the connection. This tiny creature was a wonder she couldn't quite believe existed.

'Did he want a boy?' the midwife asked.

Sophie tore her gaze away from her baby. 'You picked up on his disappointment too, did you?'

'I've seen it a hundred times. Men, especially the alpha male types, always want a boy. I think they're afraid of little girls. People are often afraid of things they don't understand!' The midwife chuckled as she tidied up. 'Don't worry, his protective instincts will kick in soon enough. She'll melt his heart, I'm sure. Such a pretty baby. Well done Mrs Ferguson. You did really well.'

'Thank you, so did you.'

'It's all about teamwork. I'm going to have to take Emmeline for her checks, but I'll have her back in no time. You lie back and relax. You must be exhausted.'

Sophie stared at the ceiling. She hoped Peter had protective instincts, she really did. Her sister's face popped into her head. She was smiling. Sophie started to cry bitter tears. Why wasn't she here beside her, sharing this, not God knows where doing God knows what.

CHAPTER 18

Kate looked out of the kitchen window. The sun was behaving as promised, but it was windier than predicted. 'I think we're going to need our coats today, Cara.'

'We walk with Fran and Lucky!' Cara squealed excitedly.

'We do, we do. So, we need to hurry up and finish breakfast!'

Kate relished Sundays. The one day she allowed her mind to shut down from work. She loved her job, but everyone needs a break. Her hard work was reaping dividends. Libretta had taken a shine to her, and she had recently been promoted to Assistant HR Director eighteen months after she'd started. She was going to make damn sure she was considered for the top job when Angela retired in a couple of years' time.

They arrived at the designated meeting spot a few minutes early. Cara ran around in circles, her arms spread wide, trying to catch the wind. Kate gazed at the field next to their lay-by. A million blades of wheat rippled like waves, as the breeze ruffled their soft heads with its gentle caress.

'Fran!' Cara shouted, and Kate turned back towards her

car to see her friend pulling up beside it. She waved and smiled.

'Watch out Cara, the beast is released,' Fran said, as the passenger door slid open. A large, black Lab jumped out, her rear end wagging with joy as she rushed towards Cara, who threw her arms around her neck. After ensuring every trace of breakfast had been removed from Cara's face, Lucky bounded towards Kate, who bent down to make a fuss of her.

'How are we all?' Fran asked. 'Ready to hike the good hike?'

'We certainly are,' Kate replied, fastening Cara's carrier onto her back, for the inevitable moment when Cara's little legs would give up and her arms would stretch up towards her.

'I thought we'd do that lovely circular walk past the quarries today,' Fran said.

'Sounds perfect.'

They each took one of Cara's hands and set off, swinging her high in the air, whenever they encountered a particularly deep rut in the tractor tracks' they were following. Lucky stayed a little way ahead, sniffing the scent trails of dogs and animals that had recently passed that way. She regularly looked back to check her pack was alright, then her nose returned to the earth.

It always took a few miles of small talk before their bodies relaxed into a steady rhythm which allowed the meatier subjects to rise to the surface. Today was no exception. Cara's little legs had already given up and she was stowed away on Kate's back.

'I hear you're making a success of your new role, under the doting eye of our leader,' Fran teased.

Kate gave her a withering look. 'I can't help it if Libretta recognises brilliance when she sees it.'

'And dedication. You've earned it, my friend.'

'I'm not sure about that. It's easy to work hard when you love what you do. And when you don't have a man to look

after. I have so much more time! No supper to cook, no dishes to do, unless I want to do them, no picking up dirty laundry and making sure David has a clean shirt for the next day. I hadn't realised how much time and head space men took up. Half my brain power was spent figuring out what he needed. I thought it would be really tough being a single working mum, and I'm not saying it's a breeze, but with help from neighbours and friends, and the crèche, it's been much easier than I'd imagined.'

'Would you contemplate having another?'

'I'm not sure, would you?'

'Lucky's enough for me, and if fate hadn't intervened, I wouldn't have got a dog. Not because I didn't want one, I didn't deserve one, not after giving up Simon. I just feel blessed that I was the one to find her.'

'Every time I think of how she was dumped in that skip it makes my blood boil. Look at her. How could anyone turn their back on such a loving, beautiful animal.'

'I know, I'm very lucky to have her.'

Kate pointedly ignored her weak pun. 'You're not lucky, you deserve one another. I wish you didn't feel so guilty about leaving Simon. You have to stop beating yourself up. You had no choice. If you hadn't left him by joining the Movement, you would have left that house in a coffin!'

'I know. But the trouble is, he doesn't. And I'll never be able to explain it to him because of the sodding Segregation Rules. I'd feel better if I knew that one day, he could seek me out, but will things ever change? Then I'd be able to tell him how much I love him and how it tore me apart to leave him with his dad. Sometimes, when I spy on him, I will him to turn and catch my eye, so I can connect with him for a second. It never happens. Talking about eyes, Cara's are shut. She's fast asleep.'

'I know. I'm carrying a bag of sand!'

They stopped to look at the quarries below them. The sun

scattered handfuls of tiny crystals across the water's surface. They were silent for a moment. An elderly couple approached from the opposite direction and Lucky greeted them warmly. They smiled as they patted her head.

'Beautiful day, isn't it?' the man said as they passed.

'Amazing. Enjoy your walk,' Kate replied.

'Thanks. Same to you.'

Kate turned and smiled at Fran. It was one of those rare times their separate worlds rubbed shoulders. They were in normal walking gear; and on a Sunday, in the middle of the countryside, a child and dog in tow, they were two girlfriends spending time together, their partners off doing their own thing; probably reuniting for a pub roast. At least that was what the couple who had just passed them were thinking.

CHAPTER 19

‘I’m pregnant!’ The room fell silent. Kate’s eyes scanned Helen’s belly.

‘I knew it!’ exclaimed Mandy. ‘It was either that or you’d got breast implants.’

‘As if, Mandy!’ Rowena exclaimed. ‘Helen, that’s amazing news, congratulations! I have an urgent need to give you a hug.’ Helen laughed.

‘That’s why you’re all drinking a delicious mocktail.’

‘What!’ exclaimed Jackie, examining her glass with suspicion. ‘Are you serious?’

‘About the pregnancy, or the lack of alcohol?’ Helen said.

‘No alcohol?’ Jackie pouted.

‘Don’t worry, my little alcofrolic, there is white wine chilling in the fridge, and red breathing on the counter-top.’

‘In that case, cheers!’ Jackie said. ‘I predict Kate will be next, after all, Cara will start school this autumn, won’t she? Ideal time to crack out another.’

‘Not me, I’m focussing on my career,’ Kate lied. She had already made an appointment to attend a Generation Centre in a fortnight’s time and this was a golden opportunity to understand what she was about to go through.

‘How’s the new job going?’ Helen asked, ‘HR Director in less than 4 years, that’s a stellar performance, Kate, you should be very proud. I know we all are.’

‘Excuse me. Now is not the time to discuss my new job. I want to know all about Helen’s news. Who’s the father?’

‘Don’t answer!’ Anne interjected. ‘I’m just going to nip to the kitchen and recharge my glass, and I don’t want to miss this.’

‘Bring the white through, will you?’ Jackie shouted after her.

Anne came through with the red and the white. When everyone had been served, they sat looking at Helen expectantly.

‘Are we all sitting comfortably? Then I’ll begin. He’s tall, blonde and ugly.’

‘Ugly?’ Rowena asked.

‘I lied about that bit. But I did give an ugly man serious consideration. I wanted my daughter to be safe.’

‘But she’ll be raised as a Completist. That should drastically minimise any risks,’ Anne said.

‘Exactly, Anne. I’ve already done the best thing I could to protect her, so I chose a handsome Swiss mountaineer.’

‘Does he yodel as well?’ Jackie asked, laughing.

‘That particular attribute wasn’t listed in his profile, but you never know!’

‘Sorry for being dumb, but could you tell me how Completists get pregnant, I’ve only heard vague rumours,’ Kate asked, starting her fact-finding mission.

‘Of course, Kate. Why would you know?’ Helen turned her kind eyes on their newest member. ‘It’s quite simple. You go to a Generation Centre and look through their database of donors. After you’ve chosen the one you want, it’s a simple procedure of placing his female sperm into your uterus using an instrument called a Viedonne. It takes about ten minutes.’

‘OK, back up. You didn’t have to take any fertility meds?’

'Nope.'

'And you fell pregnant immediately?'

'Yep. First time. But that's not unusual. Completists have spent a fortune on developing the science in this area. We're eons ahead of the CO's. Most women get pregnant after one attempt. I've never heard of it taking more than two.'

'Do they ever get the gender wrong?' Kate couldn't believe how easy this all sounded.

'You mean some rogue male sperm gets in the sample?'

'Exactly. What happens then?'

'I've never heard about any mistakes, has anyone else?' Helen looked at the others. Everyone shook their heads.

'It must be a possibility, because you have to visit a Gender Verification Clinic when you're 6 weeks pregnant, just to make sure it's a girl, don't you,' Anne said.

'That's true, so I guess there must be a small risk, but as far as I'm aware, it's 100% reliable. The appointment seemed to be more about checking the health and progress of the foetus,' Helen continued.

'What would happen if they did get it wrong and you were carrying a boy? Would the Movement make you have an abortion?' Kate was getting quite excited about her upcoming appointment, but she was still finding it hard to accept things could be as simple as Helen was describing.

'They would never do that,' Rowena said emphatically. 'I'm certain you would be given the choice of whether to keep the baby.'

'But you'd have to leave the Movement if you did, wouldn't you?' Kate continued.

'You would,' said Anne solemnly. 'No sons allowed.'

'I'm not sure I agree with that policy,' Mandy said, staring at her glass. 'I think the Movement should allow members to raise sons.'

Kate sensed the mood in the room changing, and she didn't want to ruin Helen's celebration. 'Well, here you are,

Helen. Sitting pretty – as always – brewing a beautiful baby girl. The whole procedure sounds incredible. I had no idea!' Her comment gently shook each of them out of their contemplation.

'As I told you before, my friend,' Jackie said, 'Completist triumphs are hidden from the dark side. Why would the government want to give COs another reason to transfer? There's already so many!'

'Come on, Jackie. Don't be mean. Men give their COs so much!' Jackie looked at Helen quizzically. 'Cystitis, thrush, extra housework, heartache, heartburn, heart-felt appreciation and recognition...' Helen's words were drowned out by her friends' laughter.

A happy group of women left Helen's house that night, merrily wending their way through the streets of their neighbourhood to their respective front doors. They shouted their goodbyes, a little too heartily for a Tuesday night, as each one peeled off from the group.

When Kate opened her lounge door, she found The Wren fast asleep on the sofa. She gently placed her hand on her shoulder and Jenny woke with a start.

'I've only just dozed off, you know,' she said, guiltily.

'I'm sorry, Jenny, I'm later than anticipated." Kate was concentrating on not slurring her words. "There was a bit of a celebration tonight, Helen's pregnant.'

'What wonderful news! She'll have a beautiful daughter.'

'I think that's a fair bet. Do you want a cup of tea before you go?'

'Go on then, I do love hearing about what you girls get up to.'

CHAPTER 20

Kate decided to walk to the Generation Centre. It was only twenty-minutes from the office and the weather was glorious. The Spring sky was blue and cloudless and the hundreds of trees that lined every street in central London were coming into leaf. Kate had thought long and hard about having another child. She had been raised to believe that a child should have a mother and a father; and despite her father being a force for evil, there was a part of her that still questioned the morality of choosing to raise a child without one. It angered her to acknowledge the hold her conditioning had over rational thought. Cara was evidence enough that you could raise a happy, healthy child in a male free environment. The deciding factor had been Sophie. She wanted Cara to have a relationship with this new child like the one she had experienced with her sister. She still missed her, but her mind always turned to the moment when Sophie chose her mother over her at that final meeting, and that abandonment left a kernel of pain deep at her centre which she rarely acknowledged and seldom tapped into. It was too difficult.

Kate took a deep breath when she arrived at the white

front door of a smart townhouse, the discreet name plaque confirming her destination had been reached. The white theme continued inside. Walking down the completely white hallway and entering the pulsing white of the reception, Kate felt as though she had died and gone to heaven. Every piece of furniture, every surface, and even the receptionists dress was white. The lack of any other colour was a distraction, and Kate's eyes flicked around the room searching for an inconsistency. She was the only one there.

'Can I help you?' a friendly voice asked, drawing Kate's attention back to the youthful woman behind the reception desk.

Kate looked at her young face, and suddenly wondered whether she was past her reproductive peak. She was only 30, but this fresh-faced beauty was making her feel ten years older. 'I have an appointment to discuss having a baby, with a Miss Sanderson,' Kate replied.

'Of course. Please take a seat. Would you like to start looking through the Father Album whilst you wait?'

Kate nodded, and the girl picked up a lap monitor and handed it to her. 'Take a seat, Miss Ingleton. You're Jean's first appointment. I'll let her know you're here.'

As soon as she sat down, Kate tapped the screen and, following the instructions that appeared, chose her filters. She had already decided to find someone who looked like David, to increase the chances of some kind of family resemblance between Cara and her new daughter. She doubted pure-bred Completists would even think about this aspect. It was the Movement's policy not to allow their donors to father more than one child with the same woman. She entered the characteristics to bring up look-a-likes and tapped search. Kate's pulse was racing as the first face appeared on her screen. She'd heard a dubious story that the Movement originally wanted the selection of father's to be based solely on character traits and background information, to reflect the ethos of not being

valued for beauty alone, but there was an outcry from members. Kate doubted the truth: the founders were intelligent women who would never expect members to make a blind choice. It was a tall order to choose a father without allowing all the senses a chance to make their evaluation, but then again, that was not a luxury afforded to women whose culture dictated that their parents select their husband. They had to rely on another's assessment of what was in their best interests, just as Kate now had to rely on the Movements judgment of what men would even make it into the Fathers Album. But at least there were still some choices to make.

Kate instantly dismissed the first man simply because his nose was too prominent. Swiping right again, a more promising face greeted her. She was immediately drawn to his kind eyes; but kindness could vanish as quickly as rain after a summer storm, nevertheless she read the information supplied to the right of his photo. He had a high IQ and taught English Literature at a university. The next paragraph confirmed he had never had a major illness and there was no evidence of any in his genetic makeup. She looked more closely at his picture gallery and noted his slender frame; but he looked strong. Kate checked his height. He was a little shorter than her ideal. Just as her finger was poised to swipe right, a woman's voice addressed her.

'Miss Ingleton.' Kate looked up. 'I'm Jean Sanderson. Pleased to meet you.' Kate stood up and took her outstretched hand. She had a firm handshake. 'If you'd like to follow me.'

Kate was led into a spacious office, which to her relief, had pale ochre walls and soft orange cushions on a voluminous sofa. She was about to head for the chair by the desk when she realised Jean was sitting herself on the sofa and beckoned Kate to join her.

'I see you've already started to have a look at your options,' Jean said, gesturing to the lap monitor, now at rest beside Kate. 'What do you think? Found someone you like?'

'I've only looked at two profiles, but I quite liked the second one,' Kate said, suddenly feeling like a teenager.

'You were raised as a CO, weren't you. This must all seem rather strange.'

'It does, but I can see the advantages,' Kate replied, straightening her back.

'Tell me,' Jean said, folding her hands on her lap. She looked about the same age as Kate, but she had a freshness about her which made Kate doubt she had any children of her own.

'I guess the main advantage has to be that Completist babies are planned for and wanted. The second one is that the men are carefully vetted and you choose them when you're sober!' Kate looked at Jean hoping she would smile at her last comment and relaxed as she saw a smile spread across her face.

'Well put, Kate. May I call you Kate?'

'I think as we may have an intimate relationship in the near future, that would be appropriate.' Jean smiled again and Kate felt at ease. She could do business with Jean Sanderson.

'Let me explain the procedure and then we can discuss timings.'

'Aren't you going to ask me all sorts of probing questions to decide whether I'm a fit person to have a child?'

'I don't think that's necessary. What is a 'fit' person anyway? I already know you have a daughter, and I already know you appear to be doing a great job at raising her according to her nursery reports which you granted us access to. That's a better start than a lot of children get, isn't it. We check what we can, Kate, and that's quite a lot, but no one knows what goes on within our homes, so no screening is going to be perfect. I am, however, interested to know if you have any health concerns which might affect the pregnancy.'

'I sailed through my last pregnancy, but the birth was difficult. I'd like to know how often I'll be monitored and what my birthing options are. I have a friend who's just gone through

the impregnation process so I think I know what to expect, but I don't know much about what happens in between getting pregnant and holding the baby in my arms for the first time.'

'You choose the frequency of your scans. And if you have any concerns in between your scheduled appointments, we'll see you straight away. Our hospitals are the best in the country. The maternity suites offer all the options you would expect and perhaps a few you won't know about.'

Kate looked at Jean quizzically, how many ways could you give birth, she wondered.

'The Movement is in the vanguard of research in this area. One of our innovations is a new method of what the COs would term a caesarean, but which we call a natal extraction. If the final scans show that the baby is unlikely to be in the best position for a natural birth, or is too large, we have developed a new way of removing the baby that doesn't leave a scar, and more importantly speeds up the healing process so that you'll be back on your feet and able to do anything you want to do within three days.'

Kate looked at Jean suspiciously, hardly able to believe what she was hearing.

'I know, it's amazing, isn't it. Whilst most members have great support networks, we are still single parents, so the Movement made it a priority to develop a process which would have the minimum impact on the health and mobility of its members. You can even elect to go down this route from the get-go, but we do encourage natural childbirth, when it looks safe to do so.'

Kate immediately knew she would be opting for a natal extraction. She had no desire to have her nether regions torn apart again.

'Can I take the Father Album home with me, or do I have to make a choice here.'

'We prefer you to choose here. There's a great lounge with

drink and snacks available and we're on hand to answer any questions you might have. You can pop in and use the lounge at any time. You don't need an appointment. It's open and staffed from 6.00 a.m. until 11.00 p.m. You don't have to rush, you can take your time. When were you hoping to give birth?'

'I'd like to aim for the beginning of April.'

'So, we'll schedule the impregnation for the beginning of August. That's good, that gives you a good eight weeks to pick a father. Do you have any other questions?'

'So that can happen, can it? No delays, no waiting lists, just book me in and off we go.'

'Kate, this is the most important decision our members make in their lifetimes. It's the one decision you can't undo. The Movement haven't and wouldn't skimp on resources in this area.'

'Amazing. Thank you.' Kate didn't know what else to say. She felt happy. Happy to be a Completist, to be part of a society where her needs were being met. As she left the Centre, she imagined holding her new baby in her arms, raising her in a secure and calm home. Enjoying every moment.

CHAPTER 21

Kate hurried to catch her bus. She hoped it would stop. If it was the bearded bastard, she might not be lucky; he was not fond of Completists. She watched it approach, gliding silently along the empty road like a silver phantom. Her luck was in. It was the bald-headed guy. She hopped aboard and her stomach lurched. Her daughter was making her presence felt, although none of her fellow passengers would ever have known it; she had chosen her beautifully cut suit with care.

Her search for a seat became more desperate with the first wave of nausea. She had seen men give up their seats for the Chosen Ones before, but the sky would turn green before a man would give up his seat for a Completist. Normally, it wouldn't have bothered her. She had chosen her life and The Chosen Ones theirs. There were consequences for both.

She spotted an empty seat towards the front of the bus. Could she make it without vomiting on someone? Shakily she threaded her way down the bus, grabbing each seat she passed for support. Her hands were clammy. Almost there, head up, eyes straight ahead. She paused, studying the back of the woman she was about to sit next to. Then she noticed the light

brown, wavy hair held loosely with her sister's favourite clip. Her stomach lurched, she almost reached out her hand to touch her shoulder, then snapped it back as if she'd touched a burning coal. What was she thinking! Her sister hated her. She'd made that clear. Shit! Why this morning, why did Sophie have to be on her bus this morning? Five years without ever running into her twin and here she was, waiting to be her bus buddy. Bitter bile scorched her throat, she felt faint. Her mind told her to turn back, to escape; but her body was having none of it. She was sitting down, whether she liked it or not.

Could she avoid a scene? She didn't have the energy for it this morning. Kate sat gingerly, keeping as near to the aisle as she could, shifting her body, so her back was pointed towards her sister, who was engrossed in a book. Keep reading, Sophie. Only a few stops to go. Then she could disappear into her world, without disrupting her sister's.

Perhaps she was too still, her breathing shallow and silent; perhaps it was her smell, a smell only subconsciously recognised by the same tribe; perhaps her sister simply chose to look up at that moment. Whatever it was, Kate could sense the hatred pound into her like a wave, crashing against her body with the force of a tsunami. Tiny pin pricks of sweat developed on her forehead, but she refused to acknowledge the malevolent force beside her, praying Sophie would do the same.

She could feel her sisters' eyes drilling into her, and the images she had tried so hard to suppress flashed across her mind.

Her sister grabbing at her clothing, pleading with her not to leave her life.

Her mother's harsh words, goading her barked response, dragged from the deepest part of her, backed by the fury and pain of years of deceit and distance she had never wished for, but was forced to endure. The shocked seconds of slack-jawed

silence. Sophie's watery stare, and her mother's wild eyes. Sophie cradling her mother's head to her chest.

Kate shuddered. This was too risky. She got up and walked unsteadily to the back of the bus. She waited for her stop, her back to her twin who had turned her back on her, all those years ago: uniting with her mother against her.

She clung to the metal pole by the door for support, praying Sophie's stop was after hers. The bus slowed and a man pushed past her, shoving her aside with his elbow. He stopped to let a pretty blonde Chosen One get off the bus before him. As he did, he looked back at Kate and smirked. It was going to be one of those days. She sighed as the bus started silently moving again. These small acts of retribution were easy to handle in comparison to the violence the first Completists had had to endure, but she still wished the Movement hadn't issued guidelines on how to dress; it made them stand out, becoming easy targets. The muted colours, the high necklines and the fact that nearly all members wore trousers, turned them into drab, androgynous sparrows in a sea of flamingos. The Chosen Ones had begun to dress in ever more colourful, flamboyant clothes, once the Movement became established; anxious not to be mistaken for 'one of them'.

The bus slowed once more and Kate moved unsteadily towards the exit, leaving her sister behind for the second time in her life.

CHAPTER 22

The next day, Kate forced the encounter with her sister out of her mind. Today her focus was firmly on her daughter.

'Wake up, my lovely girl,' she said as she sat on Cara's bed, stroking her daughter's hair. 'It's an exciting day today. Your first day at big school!'

Cara stretched her arms above her head and looked at her. 'I'm not ready to go to big school yet.'

Kate laughed. 'You'll love it. You'll learn some amazing things and make lots of new friends.' Cara stared at her, unconvinced.

'Let's get you dressed in your new uniform. It's all on the chair, ready for you.' Kate reached for the black trousers and white polo shirt.

'Mum, I can dress myself. I'm not a baby anymore.'

She stood back and watched her daughter. As Cara picked up her grey sweatshirt, she looked at the words embroidered in red. 'What does *Succisa virescit* mean, Mum?'

'Every Completist school has the same motto, "Cut us down, we grow back stronger".' Cara looked unimpressed. She

pulled her sweatshirt over her head and stood staring at her, a petulant look on her face.

'Right. Now for your hair? You can choose what ribbons to wear.' Cara smiled for the first time that morning and asked her to plait her hair; but not too tightly. Her daughter carefully selected two tiny pink bows and handed them to her.

'There. You look lovely. Really smart. Now let's go downstairs and make some breakfast.'

Cara toyed with her cereal, watching it turn into brown sludge.

'What are you worried about, Cara?' Kate asked, forcing the impatience from her voice. Her new offspring was making her feel particularly nauseous this morning.

'What if nobody likes me?' Cara replied.

'That's not going to happen. You made plenty of friends at nursery school, didn't you? And you'll do the same at your new school. I promise. Everybody will be feeling like you. They'll all be nervous. Now come on, let's get going. We don't want to be late on your first day.'

When they opened the front door, the conversation stopped. Kate took her daughter's hand and they walked together, heads up, looking straight ahead. Kate could feel Cara's hand gripping hers and she glanced down at her daughter to give her a reassuring smile. Cara's hand relaxed a little.

As they crossed the last main road separating them from her new school, they passed another little girl being led by the hand in the opposite direction. She looked the same age as Cara and was also dressed in a school uniform; but hers was the colour of spring grass. She was skipping next to her mother who was smiling down at her, swinging her arm in unison with her daughter's. As their paths crossed, both pairs averted their eyes and fell silent. As soon as they had passed, the mother resumed her friendly chatter, as if Cara and her mother had been a momentary ripple in their lives, a heat

shimmer on summer tarmac. Kate checked her daughter. It hadn't fazed her. She had seen this a thousand times in her short life and, unlike Kate, accepted this was how life was.

When they reached the school gates they were greeted by a storm of ribbons, flapping in the autumn wind like the wings of startled sparrows. Cara stopped, and looked anxiously up at her.

'Look. There's a little girl over there who looks like she needs a friend.' Kate pointed towards a small girl, standing motionless at the edge of the crowd. Her hair was plaited in tight, blonde, unadorned pigtails. She wore large round glasses, which magnified the fear in her eyes. Kate watched as Cara smiled at her and the little girl smiled back.

'Off you go now, Cara. I love you, and I'll be here to pick you up after school.' Kate put her hands on Cara's shoulders, propelling her forward towards the noisy, dark throng and turned to go. She didn't look back. She didn't want Cara to see any sign of the distress she was feeling. Teary goodbyes were not going to help her daughter get on with her day.

CHAPTER 23

The War Memorial Hospital for Women suited its name. It dominated the street, looming over the other buildings; a futuristic warrior, crouched, ready for action. It was both threatening and comforting. Dark opaque glass slid up against sleek cream marble walls, which embraced the building as they curved around it.

Inside its curved walls, in the ward next to its state-of-the-art birthing suite, Kate was sitting up in bed, scrutinising her reflection in the small mirror she had taken from the drawer of her pristine, white bedside cabinet. Not bad for a woman who gave birth less than five hours ago, she thought: perhaps a little tired around the eyes. The glow of achievement still radiated from her face. She had done it, and all by herself. Perhaps that wasn't entirely true. Anne had given her a lift to the hospital, but the entire book club had been on stand-by. Mandy had been a tower of strength and support, taking Cara whenever she was overwhelmed with fatigue; but it was Fran who was now caring for her daughter. Fran was the one she trusted with her darkest secrets, and Fran was the one Cara knew the best.

The contrast of this birth to Cara's couldn't have been greater. She remembered asking David to shoot her at one

point, the pain was so bad. When her contractions started this time, she wasn't concerned. She'd stuck to her guns and requested a natal extraction. She would not have history repeating itself. She glanced over at the Perspex crib beside her and smiled at her little winter baby. It was 5 February 2121 and there was a thick blanket of snow on the streets outside. She hoped Fran would not be delayed by the weather. They should be here soon. She pushed her fingers up through her blonde hair, trying to add some volume, then smoothed down the white duvet cover.

The other women in her ward were already surrounded by various mothers, sisters and aunts; all listening intently to birthing tales as they took turns to coo over the new arrivals. She shook off the frisson of sadness rippling over her skin and sat upright, waiting for *her* family to arrive. She heard the ward door swish open and there they were. Cara was holding Fran's hand, her eyes scanning the room, seeking her out. She waved at them. Cara released her friend's hand and ran over to her bed, resting her head on her lap and wrapping her arms tightly around her waist.

'What a lovely hug!' Kate said, stroking her daughter's hair and smiling at Fran. 'Come with me,' she said, lifting Cara's head and getting out of bed. 'Cara, I'd like you to meet Gemma. Gemma, this is your big sister, Cara.' She motioned to the chair and Cara took the cue and sat down expectantly. Kate lifted the white bundle and placed Gemma into Cara's arms. Gemma squirmed against her sister, her tiny hands pushing against her dress.

'Let her hold your finger, Cara,' she encouraged. Cara slipped her little finger into Gemma's palm and her tiny fingers curled around it; a seahorse tail coiled tightly around a shaft of seaweed. Cara looked at her mother's face, her eyes wide with wonder and delight.

'She's funny, isn't she, Mum? Can I help you look after

her? I'm a big girl now, aren't I? I wouldn't hurt her or drop her.'

'Of course you can, my darling girl. You're her big sister. It's your job to make sure she's safe and cared for. The same as it's my job to make sure you're safe and cared for. We can help each other.' Kate turned and smiled at Fran. They both looked at Cara, who was completely entranced by her baby sister. Cara was nuzzling Gemma's head, then she looked into her tiny sister's eyes. They listened as she solemnly promised never to hurt her or make her cry. Fran and Kate exchanged teary glances.

'So, what do you think, Cara? Will she do?' Kate asked.

'We love each other already,' Cara replied.

'I think you're going to be the best sister ever,' Fran said. 'But I think we should be going soon. Your mum and baby Gemma need to rest. And we need to go home for some tea.'

Cara looked at her mother. 'I'm glad you got Gemma put into your tummy. I know she cost a lot, but I think she's definitely worth it.'

Fran laughed. 'I'm glad you feel that way, Cara. And I think you're absolutely right.'

Cara was reluctant to give Gemma up, but the promise of her favourite pizza allowed Kate to ease Gemma out of Cara's arms.

'Why don't you give her a kiss goodbye then give me another big hug.' Kate said. She watched Cara lean in and place the softest of kisses on her sister's forehead, then Kate laid Gemma in her crib. She was surprised at how attached Cara already seemed to be. It reminded her of how she had been with Sophie, before everything changed.

'When will you be coming home?' Cara asked.

'Very, very soon, I promise. Probably tomorrow.'

'Can Gemma come and pick me up from school?'

'I'll be picking you up from school for a little while longer,' replied Fran. 'Your mum and Gemma need to stay in

the warm for a few days. Now, what extra toppings do you want on your pizza?'

Kate smiled at Fran's cunning, and waved her goodbye as she guided Cara towards the door. Fran winked at her and, with a swish, they were gone.

She walked over to the crib. 'I think you and your big sister are going to be good friends,' she whispered to her daughter as she lifted her into her arms and carried her to her bed.

CHAPTER 24

Exactly a year later it was Sophie's turn.

'You can push now; but remember pushing doesn't mean screaming. I want you to put all that energy into the push.' The midwife's voice was cold and firm.

Sophie didn't want to start pushing. She didn't want the pain of childbirth, the feeling of being out of control, the mess, the aftermath, the baby. She didn't want a second child; it was her sodding husband who had wanted to 'complete' their family. She hadn't co-operated, only pretending to give up the pill, yet the frigging universe, or whatever greater power controlled their fate, had other plans. She had got drunk, thrown up the tequila and her pill, and promptly fallen pregnant. She couldn't even remember the conception.

She had considered an abortion and had even visited a backstreet Gender Testing Clinic in secret; but when she got the results back, she couldn't get rid of the son her husband yearned for, even though she no longer yearned for her husband.

'Come on, you can do better than that! What goes in, must come out. Now let's have a really good effort for this next contraction.'

Sophie wanted to punch the patronising bitch so hard, what had gone in had been significantly smaller than what was trying to come out; but she balled up her anger and put it into the push, imagining a huge hand pushing the baby down her birth canal. The hand wasn't gentle.

'That's much better. Well done! We'll have more of those please.'

That's it. I'm going to punch her, she thought. She must be a Completist who has infiltrated the hospital to torture Chosen Ones in their darkest hour. Perhaps I should suggest we call security, or perhaps the drugs are scrambling my brain.

She looked at Peter's anxious face. He was squeezing her hand in a futile attempt to help her through this steaming pile of crap.

'He better grow up to be a millionaire football player after all this fucking pain,' she snarled at him in between contractions.

'So, you think it's a boy this time?' Peter beamed at her. 'You're doing brilliantly, Sophie, really brilliantly. Not long now, my beautiful angel.'

'Don't you beautiful angel me, you steaming piece of shit, this is all your fault...' Her tirade was interrupted by her most powerful contraction yet, and it took her breath away. She went into herself and put every ounce of the hatred she was feeling towards the bitch, Peter and the creature who was tearing up her insides, into one silent, massive push.

Charlie was born at 11.55 p.m. in the crumbling Highgate Hospital. After he was placed in her arms, and after several seconds of careful consideration, she decided he was worth all the effort and beamed at Peter. He was grinning like a Cheshire cat. Charlie was perfect. Even Peter was alright. But she still hated the midwife standing at the foot of the bed with a smug look on her face.

CHAPTER 25

When Emmeline came to the hospital to meet her little brother for the first time, Sophie's mother was already sitting by her bed, partly obscured by the flowers and cards covering the scratched, grubby melamine of her bedside cupboard. Sophie watched her daughter approach, holding her father's hand, a big blue balloon trailing behind her. She was exhausted, her mother had been there for over an hour and she hadn't stopped talking, but Emmeline's reluctance to let go of the balloon made her smile. What would she make of her brother?

'Hello, you. Come and give me a big kiss.' Emmeline wandered over and allowed herself to be hugged.

'Daddy said you'd *had* my brother,' she said, staring at her stomach. 'Is there another one waiting to come out?' She looked distinctly unimpressed at the prospect and Sophie laughed for the first time since the birth.

'Don't worry, Trouble. It will take a little while for my stomach to go back to normal. It's what happens when you have a baby. Do you want to meet Charlie? He's over there in his crib. You can hold him if you like.'

Emmeline approached the crib, peering through the see-

through sides at the tiny face moving back and forth beneath the blue woollen cap that was too big for his head.

'Isn't he going to be too hot in all those clothes?' she asked, curious but unconcerned.

'He's not very good at keeping himself warm at present, so we have to snuggle him up in lots of clothes until he gets a little fatter. Do you want to hold him?'

Emmeline looked at her father.

'It's alright, Emmeline, he won't bite.' Peter looked bemused at her reluctance. 'You sit over there, next to grandma, and I'll bring him and put him on your lap.' Emmeline walked dutifully towards the empty seat. Sophie's mother lifted her onto the chair and, with her empty arms, demonstrated how Emmeline should hold him.

Sophie watched her daughter's face as she sat holding Charlie. He squirmed against her, his head nuzzling her cardigan. Emmeline looked awkward and uncomfortable.

'So, what do you think of Charlie? He's adorable, isn't he?' Sophie heard her mother say as she leant over and placed her little finger in Charlie's hand. 'Look, Emmeline, he's holding my finger. I wish your granddad could have been here to see him. I always thought he secretly wanted a boy.' Sophie glanced at Peter, rolling her eyes.

'Can we go home now?' Emmeline asked. Peter laughed, taking Charlie from her and cradling him in his arms. Sophie's gaze transferred from her daughter's face to her husband's. The contrast was significant. Sophie realised Emmeline would have been more excited if her brother had been a new book to read, but Peter looked like all his Christmas's had come at once. The sun shone from his eyes as he gazed at his son. Sophie noticed Emmeline's expression had turned from boredom to anger. She was looking at the floor, her arms crossed in front of her. Sophie sighed. There was trouble ahead.

CHAPTER 26

Kate hated organising her children's birthday parties. Her own children were fantastic, but other peoples were noisy and annoying. At least the 18th March 2125 would be the last time she would have to invite Cara's entire class. Cara hadn't kicked up a fuss at her arbitrary cut off point. She hadn't asked why, after ten, she was no longer allowed large parties. It was about the only thing she didn't question these days. The little girl who had wandered through life, accepting the two different worlds surrounding her, had gone. These days, Cara asked a hundred questions a day. Why do none of my friends have fathers or brothers? Why do we never shop in the same stores they do? Why do we never listen to music played by men?

That had been the latest one. Cara had wanted a boy band that her classmate Abby had been going on about for the party playlist. Kate had never warned to Abby's mother. She told her daughter more about the Chosen Ones than she was meant to.

At least the mothers didn't all hang around now. The children were old enough to be left unsupervised, so she and Fran were running the show.

'Is that the last plate of pink crap to go on the tables?' Fran

asked her, eyeing up the enormous pile of every pink sweet available to womankind.

'Yep, that's it, my friend. We can stop and have a coffee and take stock of the pink wonderland we've artfully created.'

'I'm surprised you've encouraged such obvious and outdated gender stereotypes,' Fran said laughing as they looked around the village hall. It was festooned with different shades of pink bunting valiantly competing with the strings of a hundred pink helium balloons, swaying gently, like a bloom of ethereal jellyfish.

'Believe you me, this isn't my doing. Cara is such a girly girl. I don't know where she gets it from. Perhaps her father's side of the family?'

Fran laughed. 'From what you've told me about him, I doubt it! Where are the little darlings, anyway?'

'Hopefully outside where I left them, mooching around the playground.'

'Shall I call them in and see what Cara thinks?'

'Why not. The first guests will be arriving soon.'

Kate watched her daughter's face as she entered the hall. Her expression was one of sheer delight.

'Mum, it's amazing! Thank you so, so much. I wish Caroline was coming. She would've loved this.'

'I know. I wish she was too. It's tough having a birthday party without your best friend, isn't it? Never mind, we'll save her a piece of cake, for when she's feeling better.'

Gemma was trying to jump up and catch a balloon string when the door opened, and the procession of girls began.

Kate and Fran were rushed off their feet ensuring every child had plates brimming with pink additives, but finally the disco began, and they stood on the sidelines, watching the girls swirl and sway in front of them.

'I bet this isn't so different from a CO's daughter's party,' Fran shouted at her. 'If my memory serves me correctly, the

girls used to be the only ones dancing anyway, while the boys hugged the walls, or hit one another.'

Kate laughed. 'You have a point, but at least Cara won't end up with lemonade thrown over her. I remember refusing to dance with a boy at a school disco, and he ended up drenching my favourite pink dungarees.'

'Hah! Mystery solved. Pink dungarees! I always knew there was a softer side to you!'

'I didn't choose them. My mother picked them out!'

'Ah, but they were your favourite.'

Kate hit her friend on her arm and searched the room for Cara. She spotted her exchanging angry words with Abby, then running towards the toilets.

'Keep an eye on things for me, will you? I'm going to see if Cara's alright.'

She weaved her way through the dancing girls and opened the door to the toilets. Her heels clacked across the tiled floor as she searched for her daughter.

'Cara, are you in there?' she said, addressing the only closed cubicle door. There was no answer.

'Did Abby say something to upset you?'

The cubicle door opened to reveal a red-eyed Cara. 'Mum, why don't you ever explain things properly to me?' she asked, crossing her arms in front of her chest. 'Abby's mum tells her everything about why we live differently from the Chosen Ones. She made me feel like an idiot, at my own birthday party.'

'Abby's mum shouldn't be doing that. You'll have all your questions answered at the end of this year by the school. It's better that way, because you can make up your own mind about things, without being influenced by my experiences and beliefs. Remember, I was brought up as a Chosen One, you have been brought up as a Completist. I look at the world differently because of my history. Does that make sense?'

'I get it, Mum. But I'd like to know how you feel about things too.'

'I promise you that, once you've heard what the school have to say, we'll sit down together and have a good chat about everything. I'm not trying to hide anything from you, or make you look stupid!'

She looked at her daughter, struggling to make sense of her world and knew she had told her a white lie. She *was* trying to hide things from her. She didn't want her daughter to be tarnished by her own childhood; there would be no history repeating itself under her roof. She stepped towards her daughter and opened her arms. Cara rushed into them and hugged her.

CHAPTER 27

Sophie watched her daughter's relationship with her brother develop with utter dismay. Having never had a brother, she was shocked by the different dynamic that existed between them: it was alien territory. Her hopes of ever seeing them playing happily together had vanished.

Emmeline wanted to create things; Charlie wanted to destroy things. She wanted to walk, he wanted to run. She always talked in a normal voice, he shouted at the top of his. Emmeline helped her whenever she could, Charlie created more work; but Peter thought Charlie was great. Every time he knocked something over, he would roar with delight and scoop him up in his arms, calling him his 'little destroyer' or other stupid phrases. His obvious preference for Charlie had not helped matters. Charlie was three now, and it was apparent to Sophie that Emmeline had all but lost interest in him.

She knew her daughter sloped off to hide in corners of the house and garden where Charlie would not think to look. All the girl wanted to do was read. She was currently reading *The Lion, The Witch and The Wardrobe*, a book her English

teacher thought she would enjoy. Mr Brown was the only man she appeared to like.

Sophie was angry with Peter for not spending more time with Emmeline. These days she was angry with him most of the time. Ever since Charlie had been born, he would swoop in for his tea after work, give Charlie a bath and swoop out again; either to train with his mates down the football club or meet a friend down the pub. She barely saw the man. Sophie sometimes wondered whether he was up to his old pre-marital tricks. Kate had said to her on her wedding day, 'You're about to marry the man of your dreams. You're the woman who pinned down the *Player* of the Year,' and she hadn't been referring to his football skills. Everyone knew Peter Ferguson played as hard off the pitch as he did on it, but all that had changed when he had met her, hadn't it? But would she really be so shocked if he had succumbed to temptation? She knew their marriage was disintegrating. She had gone up a dress size and they hardly touched one another anymore. She lashed out at him, and he didn't hold back either. The majority of their conversation was long range warfare, sniping at one another at every opportunity with belittling comments and acidic put downs. When he actually stayed around long enough, their evenings would often end in full blown rows; their angry, ugly faces snapping at one another like street dogs fighting over a bone. Sophie tried to avoid arguing in front of the children, but she was sure Emmeline had overheard them on occasion.

She reached for the potato peeler. How had she got here? Her life was supposed to be perfect. Her wedding day had been wonderful. Everyone had said how beautiful she looked, and Kate had been so kind, so supportive. She'd even kept quiet about being pregnant with Cara to avoid taking away any attention from her on her special day.

Sophie shook Kate from her head. She didn't want to be reminded of the good times; it was too hard. The bitch had ignored her on the bus, turning her back on her, refusing to

take the opportunity to say sorry. She dragged images of her father's kind face into her mind so she could hate her sister once more for telling those awful lies about him. She attacked the vegetable in her hand, wondering if Peter would be on time. He was getting home later and later. The previous week, she had heard his car pull up, and had peered out of the lounge window to see him sitting there, as if he couldn't bear to come in. This evening she would make a real effort to be nice, even if he was late. Placing the pan on the hob, she went upstairs to tidy herself up and apply some make-up.

Tea was nearly ready when he got home. He came into the kitchen, ruffled Charlie's hair and sat down at the table.

'Good day at work?' Sophie asked.

'Not bad. You?' he asked, without looking at her.

'I had a nice day, thanks. Did the shopping, sorted out the kids' bedrooms and generally had a good old tidy up.'

'Oh, sorry. Yes, the place looks great.' He still didn't look at her. 'How's my little lad. Did you help Mum tidy your room?'

'I didn't say it was a day filled with miracles, Peter!'

Peter laughed half-heartedly and she started to dish up the meal. 'Emmeline! Teatime!' she shouted into the hallway.

'That girl is never around when you want her. She's in a world of her own, that one. Away with the fairies. Girls, eh? Charlie. If only we knew what was going on inside their heads, life would be so much easier!'

Sophie sighed as she sat down. 'Peter, love, don't say things like that to Charlie, he takes little enough notice of me as it is.'

'Don't start, Sophie. Let me have my tea in peace.' He pushed back his chair and shouted into the hallway, 'Emmeline! Come down here at once, your tea's getting cold.'

She tried to keep the conversation going while they ate, but Peter seemed intent on finishing his food as soon as possible and taking Charlie for his bath. He didn't comment on her appearance.

'I'll get this lad ready for bed while you girls finish up. See you in about half an hour, if the little scamp behaves himself.' He lifted Charlie from his seat and carried him over his shoulder. Charlie chuckled and kicked his legs with joy.

Emmeline looked at her.

'What's on your mind, Trouble?'

'Do you like Charlie better than me too?' her daughter asked, quietly.

'Don't be silly. I love you both the same.'

'Do you love Daddy the best?'

Sophie didn't know what to say. She got up and started stacking the plates. Finally, she said, 'There are all kinds of love in this world. Sometimes love can even look like hate, but it's still a kind of love.'

Emmeline nodded quietly and left the room.

Sophie was stacking the dishwasher when Peter came back into the kitchen.

'Sophie, I've told you not to stack it like that. It won't clean the saucepans properly if you put them that way round.'

Sophie forgot to close the kitchen door before she lost her temper.

'I'm serious, Peter. I can't take this anymore. My life has completely changed, but you still get to do exactly what you want. Every bloody Saturday afternoon you play football with your mates and leave me here with the kids. You come back later and later because you don't want to come back to a moody wife. But did it ever cross your tiny mind to let me have an afternoon off to do what I want to do with my friends? No, because you never think of anyone but yourself. You're an egocentric, selfish human being and I don't want to live with you anymore!

Oh, don't look so shocked, if you've got the nerve to tell me you didn't see this coming, I'll throw this incorrectly stacked saucepan at your thick skull. If you haven't noticed

how unhappy I've been since Charlie was born, you really are an insensitive bastard!'

Sophie heard the lounge door slam and glared at Peter. She ran down the hallway.

'I'm sorry, Emmeline,' she said. 'You shouldn't have heard that.'

She sat down beside her on the sofa and took her hand. 'Are you alright?'

'Not really. Why can't it just be you and me? I know there are other families who don't have fathers or brothers. Why can't we be like them? I wish Charlie had never been born!'

Sophie didn't have a chance to reply. Emmeline rushed out of the room, slamming the door behind her.

CHAPTER 28

It was the day of the tri-decade celebrations, the 30th anniversary of The Self-Determination Act, which had given women the right to live without men. Kate took several deep breaths, inhaling and exhaling to the count of ten. Everything will be fine, she told herself repeatedly. Her heart started to slow down and her stomach quietened. Her daughters had been more excited about opening the first door of their advent calendars.

'Girls, where are you? Don't forget we're going to leave earlier for school this morning.'

Cara hurried down the stairs, munching on a piece of toast and marmalade, with Gemma trailing behind her.

'Have you cleaned your teeth?' Cara nodded. 'Do you have your swimming kit?' Cara nodded again. 'Homework on the Uprising?'

'Mum, I'm not a baby anymore, I've got everything I need. You should be asking Gemma those questions, not me.' Cara smiled fondly at Gemma who raised her eyebrows in complicity and giggled.

'OK girls, let's get going. It's a big day today and I don't want any trouble, just smiles and laughter, as it should be.'

'What do you mean by trouble, Mum?' Cara asked.

Kate froze for a second.

'It's nothing to worry about girls. Some men aren't very happy we've chosen to live without them, and our celebration reminds them of that. So, they can sometimes be a bit mean to Completists on these special days. That's why we're catching an earlier bus today, less men around means less likelihood of any trouble.'

She looked at her daughters' faces. Her breezy tones did not seem to be reassuring them.

'What do these men do then?' Cara was standing rooted to the spot. She was clearly not going to leave the house without a satisfactory answer.

'Lovely girl, it's nothing to worry about, honestly it isn't. They won't hurt us, they can be mean, that's all. They might say something nasty to us, or spit at us.' Cara looked at Gemma and they both stared at her in horror. 'But that's very unlikely. Things are much better now. It's been 30 years since the Act was passed and people are getting used to us. Don't get upset. I'm sure the school will explain why this day is so special, then you'll understand things a little better.'

As Kate locked the front door behind her, she glanced at her daughters. She was pleased they looked like sisters; she'd done a good job of selecting a man who resembled David. The only notable difference was Gemma's hair; whereas Cara had her waves, Gemma had ringlets, loose corkscrews that crowded around her face and gently bounced around her features whenever she moved her head. They were huddled together on the pavement, hand in hand, waiting for her. She gave them a reassuring smile and took her place in front of them, holding her head up, eyes forward, knowing they would follow suit. Why couldn't she keep her big mouth shut? They must be shitting themselves. But they'd be fine. It was too early for trouble.

They were approaching Church Street when she saw the

man. He was walking on the other side of the road, the collar of his cashmere coat pulled up against the wind, his stone eyes monitoring their every move. Her heart began to pound. Don't make eye contact. Look straight ahead. Jesus, calm yourself. He's not going to attack a mother with two young girls, he's a businessman on his way to work.

Oh God, I'm wrong, he's crossing the road, shit.

Before she could shout a warning, he was on them. She swung around to see him wrench Gemma from Cara's grip; within seconds he was holding her, little feet dangling inches from the ground his hand clamped against her mouth to muffle her screams.

Cara had frozen. Kate stared at this stranger threatening her family. Her mind raced. She wanted to rush at him like a bull, knock him to the ground, but she held back, sniffing the cold air between them, animal instincts assessing the situation.

'What a pretty daughter you have, but no handsome son. I suppose little boys grow into big, bad men, don't they and that would never do,' he sneered. 'But you still paid for a man's sperm to get her, didn't you? You still need our seed don't you, you stupid bitch? Not really complete without us, are you.'

She continued to stare at him, rage rampaging through her head, thoughts bubbling like a cauldron. Rip his fucking head off. No, don't. Pander to his bruised ego, apologise, bow head, because he's got your little Gemma. The freak. She saw a dark stain spreading down Gemma's trouser leg. Her insides buckled.

'You're right, Sir. We're not complete without you and I'm sorry if that angers you, but *please* don't take it out on my daughter, she's an innocent in this. Please let her go. If you want to hurt someone, hurt me, not them.' She saw Cara looking at her, disbelief on her face, as she watched her bow her head to this man. Kate was ashamed, but she would do whatever it took to make Gemma safe.

Her words seemed to deflate him, and he let Gemma go. She staggered towards her. Gemma's action released Cara, and she came to her too. He stood staring at them; his anger transformed into contempt. Kate wrapped her arms around their shoulders. They buried their faces in her coat, wetting the fabric with their tears.

'You lot are living a lie, and you're teaching your children the same lie. You should be ashamed of yourself, we're not the enemy!' The man spat his words at her; then, shaking his head, started to walk away.

'I think you've just shown them you are, you piece of shit,' she muttered.

Kate stood silently, watching him as he disappeared around a corner.

When she was certain he had gone, she knelt down in front of her little girls and held their chins, forcing them to turn their heads and look at her.

'It's alright. We're alright,' she said, her tone commanding them to believe her. 'He's gone, we're safe and I'm going to call our taxi firm and get them to take us to school. I think we've all had enough of men for one day, don't you?' She reached into her coat pocket and took out a tissue, gently wiping the tears from their cheeks. 'Stop crying now. That's it, deep breaths. Everything's fine.' She handed each of them a dry tissue. 'Blow your noses whilst I call the taxi. I love you both, and we've got nothing to be ashamed of.'

They nodded their heads in unison and she released their chins. Cara straightened her back, gripping Gemma's hand. They were both trembling, heads held up, watching her make the call. The taxi was with them in minutes. As she bundled the girls in the car, she thanked the driver.

'No problem, 'she replied. 'Every Completist taxi firm is on high alert on days like this. We double up the staff, just in case.' She gave Kate a reassuring smile in the rear-view mirror and pulled out.

Kate walked her children through the school gates and told them to wait together while she looked for the teacher on early morning duty. Kate hurried off, looking back to see Cara wrapping her arms around her sister who was watching her intently. She found Miss Brown in the school office and explained the situation. They both went out into the playground to retrieve the girls.

'I'll be here to pick you up after school. We'll go home in a taxi. Now please don't worry anymore. Miss Brown has said you can stay together for the entire day, if that's what you want to do. I love you, and I'll see you later.'

She started to walk away but glanced back as she reached the gates. Miss Brown was holding their hands, leading them inside to find some dry trousers and pants for Gemma.

Cara looked over her shoulder and their eyes met. It was clear her daughter wanted to be with her, but Kate gave her a cheery wave, turned away and hurried towards the waiting taxi, her heart breaking.

CHAPTER 29

The mood in the office couldn't have been more of a contrast. The reception was full of flowers, and a champagne breakfast had been laid out in every conference room on each of the nine floors. Although it was early, most of the employees had obviously had the same idea as her and were milling around smiling at one another. Some were no doubt wondering whether it was still too early to drink champagne; others had no such qualms. Today they were not here to work, they were here to celebrate the Movement's achievements over the last three decades and decide together how they were going to shape the next one. Libretta Jones, their CEO, was due to kick things off at 9.30 a.m.

Kate was not in the mood to make small talk. She went to her office and hung up her coat. She slumped in her chair and put her head in her hands, regretting leaving the children at school. Should she have taken a family day and gone home with them, or would that have sent the wrong message? Wasn't it now more important than ever they heard about the Uprising, so they could put this morning's events into some kind of context? She sat up straight and rang the school. Juliette Flanagan, the school's secretary, answered.

'Hi Juliette, it's Kate Ingleton, Gemma and Cara's mum. I wanted to know how the girls were doing, especially Gemma. Are they OK?' She heard her own voice breaking; her breathing faltered as she tried to keep herself together.

'Hi Kate, they're fine. Gemma's been washed and changed, and they're together in Cara's class. The Head is talking to the whole class as we speak. She felt the girls should share their experience, talk it out. If it's any consolation, another pupil also had a difficult journey to school this morning. A man slapped her mother across the face on the bus.'

'Oh God, that's awful. But yes, I guess they won't feel so alone.' Her voice was steadier now.

'Please don't worry, Kate. They're in safe hands. As you know, there are no formal classes today. We'll keep them together for as long as we can, but, as you know Cara will be taught about the Uprising in far more detail than is appropriate for Gemma, so we'll have to separate them at that point, but we've got some fantastic party games organised for the younger ones and I'm sure Gemma will be fine by then.'

'Thank you, Juliette, I appreciate it.'

'Please feel free to call us at any point for an update. Naturally, if we feel the girls need to be with you, we'll let you know. I hope you can enjoy the celebrations.'

'You too. Thanks again.'

Kate heard the click of the line being disconnected. She removed the tiny bud from her ear and placed it carefully in its holder. She should really try to put this out of her mind. After all, if it had happened to another family, she would have been momentarily shocked, but would soon have dismissed it as one of those things that can happen on Celebration Days. She needed to toughen up. It was only because it had happened to her family that she was continuing to dwell on it. She stood up and went to join her colleagues.

She scanned the boardroom for a friendly face, her eyes soon picking out Fran. Fran had noticed her too and was

weaving between groups of women, making her way towards her.

'Hey, Girl! Your face doesn't appear to know it's a Celebration Day. What's up?' Fran touched Kate's arm.

'We were attacked this morning on the way to school. This man grabbed Gemma and proceeded to tell me I wasn't complete without men because I still needed their jizz to make my children.'

'Oh shit, Kate. Are the kids alright? He didn't hurt them, did he? Sorry, stupid question, you're here. It must've been horrible.'

'It wasn't the greatest start. Poor little Gemma wet herself she was so scared.' Her voice was trembling again. 'I mean, what gives him the right to terrorise a five-year-old? I had to be all subservient to placate the bastard when I wanted to charge at him and rip his head off!' The box in the attic of her mind started to shake, as the anger she was so afraid of tried to escape its bindings. She could see Fran's mouth move, but she couldn't hear her words. Then Fran touched her arm and she refocused.

'Breathe, Kate. That's right. And again. Better. Look, I know it will take Gemma a long time to recover from this, but you're one of the strongest people I know. She'll be fine. You'll be fine.' Fran handed her the glass of champagne she was holding. 'Get this down your neck, and that's an order not a request. I'll grab myself another in a minute.' Kate did what she was told.

'I'll go grab us both another,' she said, managing a weak smile. 'Shit Fran, it is a Celebration Day after all, and this morning was a little reminder of why the Movement is so necessary.'

'That's more like it. Oh, and if you could manage a couple of those egg tartlet thingies, they're delicious.'

Kate was on her way back to Fran, arms full of champagne

and tartlet thingies when the request to gather in the auditorium came over the loudspeakers.

They made their way down to the first floor, swilling down the pastries as they went. Kate was looking forward to Libretta's address; she respected and liked the woman.

They settled themselves into their third-row seats, placing their glasses in the armrest holders. The seats were plush and voluminous. They reminded Kate of a cinema she had visited as a child, with each seat as comfortable as an armchair. She felt the same excitement and anticipation when the music began and the lights went down. The room hushed.

Libretta strode on to the stage, her ash blonde hair shining in the spotlight. It was beautifully cut, as was her black suit. Her jacket was undone, revealing a soft cream open-necked shirt. On her feet she had her signature pair of flat, crepe-soled, patent leather loafers. They glinted in the spotlight she was bathed in. Libretta had made it known she had never worn heels again once the Uprising started, because she had to be prepared to run at any moment.

The huge screen lit up. The Completist logo looked like a Viking shield looming large behind her. The room broke into a cacophony of clapping and cheering. Libretta beamed.

'Thank you, my friends, thank you. And welcome to the tri-decade celebrations.' The cheering became louder. Libretta smiled again and waited for the noise to abate.

'We have much to celebrate today. It's been an incredible decade for us. But before I share with you the amazing progress we've made, let's take a moment to remember why we are here.' She turned to look at the screen behind her. It showed the faces of four men.

'In 2019, Cara Williams brutally murdered four men who had exploited, controlled and abused women in the worst possible ways. These murders really shook the male population, perhaps because she was the first female serial killer to execute men using methods that reflected their particular

vices. Or perhaps it was because she was never caught. The result was a radical reduction in overt violence and abuse toward women. However, what did not change was our economic exploitation by men.'

New words and graphs replaced the men's faces. 'In 2019, less than 25% of every company's board of directors were women, despite 75% of women being economically active. There was not a single business sector in the UK where women were paid better, on average, than men. In addition, while half of all university degrees were undertaken by women, over 70% more men achieved first-class degrees. Not because women were less able, but due to unconscious biases held by the men assessing the students. In 2019 a first-class degree raised the holder's earnings by between 9 and 13% six years after graduation. When the Uprising started in 2089, I could have shown you virtually the same slides. Because in 70 years, nothing had really changed, nothing!'

Four pictures of women rose up behind her, one of whom was Libretta's mother. 'But perhaps that wasn't entirely true. Some women, including these four, tried to effect change. These ladies where all members of a gender diversity campaign group called the 30% Club. Their aim was to get more women into senior positions in the FTSE 300 companies and smash the glass ceiling stopping women's career progression in managerial and professional labour markets in the UK. Despite being some of the brightest and best brains in business, this group failed to achieve its objectives. Enraged by the constant barriers and prejudices that thwarted them, they made a pact. They would run their own firms, generate their own wealth and power, and demonstrate to men that business is better when it is run by women. As they put their plan into action, things did start to change.

I took over Femmeur plc from my mother the year Cara's diaries were found in The Bank of London Gold Vault. The year was 2089 and the disclosure that the government had

evidently hidden these documents from the public, was the biggest scandal of the decade. Speculation was rife this had been done, not to cover The Mets failure to make headway in the case at the time, but to keep the thoughts and fears of Cara a secret from the female population, who had come to regard the unknown perpetrator of those murders as a freedom fighter, rather than a terrorist. Nobody knows how those diaries had landed in the government's hands, but many believe Cara had arranged for them to be sent to The Prime Minister shortly after her death. For those of you who have recently joined us, I would urge you to read them. I regard Cara as the most influential woman of the second millennium. I believe she was the catalyst that changed our world.

I read those diaries in 2089 and the new generation of daughters who inherited the 30% Club's businesses decided enough was enough!' A new set of women's faces appeared behind her to a rapturous round of applause. This time, Libretta's face replaced her mother's.

'We had grown up together. Listened endlessly to our mothers and their friends discuss the difficulties they were facing. And at the root of every obstacle was a man. We began to talk about how we would eradicate these obstacles, and five years before we each took over our mother's companies and started the Uprising, we created the Completist Movement.

It started as a joke when one of us reappropriated the phrase 'Women; can't live with them; can't live without them.' It was at one of our weekly meetings when Rebecca Manning said, 'Men: can't live with them; *can* live without them,' and there it was. We spent the next five years planning how women could live without men. By the time we had the wealth and power our mothers had entrusted to us, we had a detailed plan of how we were going to finally free women from the constraints men put on them.'

A massive cheer rose from the audience and Libretta beamed again. She raised her right hand.

’Thank you for your acknowledgement of the work and planning that made our world possible. But what really made it possible was the courage and conviction of those women who believed in the Movement and risked everything to become part of it. As soon as we took over our mothers’ companies, we fired the few remaining men and started introducing our idea to our workforces. Word spread like wildfire. It was as if we were offering a product guaranteed to make you look 20 years younger.’ Libretta laughed and her colleagues laughed with her. ‘We soon realised this was a world women wanted to inhabit, and we started our campaign in earnest, opening hundreds of safe houses. But our vision had a huge price tag. We knew it wouldn’t be an easy ride, but everyone was shocked at the wave of murders of the first brave women who decided to join us.’ The faces of ten women filled the screen behind her and the mood in the room shifted.

‘These women were among the first to attempt to divorce their husbands and leave behind their sons to join the Movement. They were all motivated by the violence they had experienced, violence hidden behind their own front doors. The first husband to exact revenge on his wife, Eileen McDonald, made headline news. She was going to leave him to join us. She never made it through her own front door. At the time, UK reported cases of violence against women were at an all-time low, so his retribution was all the more shocking. He inadvertently kick-started the Uprising. Women who refused to be oppressed started their own divorce proceedings. In the first fortnight after Eileen lost her life, 4,230 divorce petitions were instigated. The men, whose egos could not accept their wives’ audacity, fought back, and within the same month, the other nine women behind me had been killed by their husbands. We all know their names.’ Libretta paused for a moment, the room was silent.

‘Other men spoke out, urging us to reconsider. They told us to stop the Movement, while decrying the violence against

us. The murders finally stopped, to be replaced by assaults and derision against any woman who openly wore the Completist symbol on the streets. Completists lost their jobs and were thrown out of their homes. Fortunately, most men confined their anger to words. The media was flooded with articles against the Movement, and every day brought another prominent man calling Completists a bunch of hysterical women who had lost their minds. Then the women's counter movement started, the Chosen Ones. Their rhetoric was even fiercer than the men's, as we anticipated it would be. Suddenly mothers were against mothers, sisters against sisters and families were torn apart. Our society divided itself in two.

Every woman here has their own story. Each of you has paid a high price to live the life you want; some of you are still paying it. I can do nothing but applaud the courage it takes, every single day, to go out in the world with your heads held high, teaching your daughters to do the same. But understand this. All the loss, pain and hardship we all continue to suffer has resulted in a real choice for women. And 30 years ago, on this day, that choice became our right! Any woman now born in the UK can live a life without men determining who she will become and what she will be able to achieve. And you have yourselves to thank for this!'

The audience rose to their feet, stomping in unison, and the room shook with their power. Libretta shouted above the thunder. 'So, let's celebrate!' and the stomping women roared their approval.

It took a full ten minutes before Libretta could leave the stage. The screen behind her told her employees to reconvene in the auditorium in one hour's time for an update on the Movement and goal setting for the next decade. The women filtered out of the room back to their respective boardrooms to recharge their glasses.

'I'll say one thing for our Libretta, she sure knows how to

work a crowd,' Fran said, her face glowing from the joy of being part of something. Kate turned to her friend and smiled.

'She sure does. And it still feels good, doesn't it? Despite what happened this morning, it still feels worth it. You don't have any regrets do you, Fran?'

'While I'll never be able to put into words what it feels like to want to hold someone so much it makes every cell of your body ache; yes, it has been worth it. But I still hope, one day, Completists will be able to raise sons as well as daughters.'

Kate reached out and touched her friend's arm. 'Let's raise a glass to that, Fran. Come on, last one to eat a tartlet thingie is a man lover!'

CHAPTER 30

'I can't believe you named me after a murderer!' Cara exclaimed as Kate arrived at the school to pick her daughters up.

'I prefer the term "freedom fighter",' Kate replied, laughing at her daughter's outrage.

'No wonder there's over five Cara's in my class! But I still don't really understand why she murdered those men.'

'I think that'll be explained to you in more detail when you're in the Upper Form. Now don't forget, don't discuss anything you've learned today in front of Gemma. Explaining the world and why the Movement came about is a difficult, complex and potentially frightening thing if not handled in the right way, Cara. We've all been scared enough for one day, haven't we. Your sister's still too young to be able to handle the information you've been given today. Remember that.' Kate paused. 'Look, my lovely girl, I know you're desperate to understand everything right now, but it's important that it's explained by people who have no agenda. Completists believe that joining the Movement is a matter of free will. If you're presented with the facts in an unbiased way, you can make up

your own mind about whether being a Completist is a good idea or not. That's why I don't want to be the one to tell you. My own experiences shouldn't influence your decision. Do you understand what I'm trying to say?'

'I think so. What's happened to you might make you think being a Completist is a good thing, when perhaps it isn't. I need to make my own mind up.'

'Precisely. And once you have all the facts, you'll be able to do that.' Cara nodded. 'Now let's go and find your sister.' They made their way to Gemma's classroom. She was standing outside the classroom door, by herself, looking forlorn. 'How are you feeling, Gemma? Did you manage to enjoy the Celebrations?'

'Not really. My tummy still hurts. I can't stop feeling frightened.' Gemma stared up at her, her big blue eyes imploring her to make everything better. Kate gathered her daughter into her arms and carried her to the waiting taxi. Gemma put her arms around her neck and buried her head in her coat. The anger she had managed to suppress at the office started to course through her veins.

'Don't cry, little one. Not all men are horrible. There are lots of good, kind men in the world. We were just very unlucky this morning. Things will settle down now, I promise.'

The taxi driver opened the door for her and gave Kate a knowing smile. 'Do you want to sit in the front with me?' she said to Cara.

'Yes, please!' Cara replied.

'Are you going somewhere nice for dinner?' she asked her young passenger.

Gemma tensed. Kate quickly answered the taxi driver's question on Cara's behalf. 'We're going to stay in tonight with a takeaway. Whatever you fancy, girls. And I've bought your favourite pudding.'

'Raspberry pavlova?' Gemma said, smiling for the first time since she had picked them up.

'Bingo!' Kate replied, ruffling Gemma's hair. 'So, you'd better tell that tummy of yours to get better!'

But Kate knew it was going to take her daughter a long time before she felt safe again; perhaps she never would.

CHAPTER 31

Sophie hated these days and was grateful they only happened once a decade. Peter had left early for work, but at least he had dressed Charlie. She knew the days when he had tried to jolly her out of the black mood that descended on her whenever the Movement was shoved down her throat by the media had long gone, and he knew today's Celebrations would be all over the news. He'd never been much of a fan of her sister anyway, and when she had joined the Movement his opinion of her had hit rock bottom. Sophie was convinced he had even shifted the blame for the disintegration of their marriage onto Kate.

She attempted to smother her rising anger as she prepared breakfast, but she couldn't resist turning the radio on. Charles Petard, one of her favourite presenters, was in the process of announcing he would be interviewing Libretta Jones at 10.30 a.m. that morning on Channel Five, when Emmeline wandered into the kitchen.

'What is he talking about? What are the tri-decade celebrations, Mum?' Emmeline asked, as yet unaware of her mother's mood.

'For goodness sake, Emmeline. I would've thought you

would've known by now that Completists are women who have chosen to live their lives without men. Today is the day they celebrate 30 years of the UK government recognising their right to live in this, frankly, bizarre way. It's a big day for them, but it's not for us. We largely choose to ignore these days as we don't think living without men is something to celebrate. It's a little weird, don't you think?' Then Sophie remembered her daughter's conversation the night she had heard her arguing with Peter, and she stopped talking.

Emmeline didn't bother to answer her question; she had another of her own. 'But why do they all want to live without men? That's what I'd like to know. What made them make this choice in the first place?'

'That's a difficult question to answer. There are lots of different reasons. But these women all have one thing in common, they blame men for all the bad things which happen in their lives, especially if they don't have very successful careers. They think men are not giving them better jobs on purpose, because they're women. This is ridiculous. It was already against the law to discriminate in this way when their campaign began.' She really didn't appreciate her daughter's inquisitive mind this morning. She shoved a bowl of cereal in front of her, hoping it would shut her up. It didn't.

'But, Mum. If it was ridiculous, why did the government agree to let them live like this?'

'Emmeline, we live in a democracy, and if there are enough people who want something, no matter how misguided they are, then the politicians will let them do it. In the UK we have freedom of speech and freedom of choice, unlike other countries with dictatorships. In those countries leaders make the people live in a way that pleases *them*, rather than the people. Now hurry up and eat your toast, we're going to be late. Charlie, come down here at once, your porridge is ready!'

Charlie ran down the stairs, plonked himself in his chair and wolfed down his porridge. Sophie turned away; he might

only be five, but she made a note to be stricter with him about his table manners in future.

When Sophie returned from the school drop off, she tidied up the kitchen and settled down with a coffee in the lounge. It was nearly 10.30 a.m. She turned on Channel 5.

The handsome face of Charles Petard appeared on the wall monitor, his hair freshly cut and in its usual slick style, showcasing his strong, square jawline.

'Good morning, Libretta, on this auspicious day for the Completists.' Sophie scowled at the woman who had taken her sister from her.

'Good morning, Charles. I hope you're in equally good spirits?'

'It's always a special day when you're celebrating 30 years of a divided society, Libretta,' Charles said sarcastically.

Libretta appeared to let the remark slide off her skin and fall to the floor at her feet, discarded and forgotten.

'Perhaps you'd be good enough to share with us what *you* perceive to be the major achievements of the last decade.' He sat back in his chair, clearly waiting to be amused by her response.

'With pleasure, Charles. I'd like to start with this. The last ten years have been the most peaceful decade of the Movement's existence to date, for which we are very grateful. The number of reported incidents against our members has dropped to under 500 a year, compared to over 20,000 in the first decade and 6,000 in the second. We hope, with all our hearts, this is an indication that our society is less divided than before and that a new era of cooperation and tolerance is upon us.'

'That does indeed *appear* to be good news, Libretta. But isn't it more likely the rest of us have simply learnt to adapt our behaviour on the outside, while still harbouring anger for what the Movement has done to our communities within?'

'Damn right, Charles!' Sophie shouted in support.

‘The latest government survey wouldn’t support your view, Charles. But who knows what’s really going on in the minds and hearts of us all?’

‘The findings of the survey, I believe you’re referring to, concluded that only 56% of those outside the Movement stated they accepted the Movement’s right to exist. Hardly a ringing endorsement.’ He looked pleased with his observation.

‘We’ll probably have to wait a few more decades for a ringing endorsement, Charles. But at least things are moving in the right direction,’ Libretta replied politely, giving him a beaming smile.

‘I think a number of us would have a problem with your use of the word “right”, Libretta. I’m not sure that acceptance of the Movement’s *right* to exist, means this is the *right* direction for society to be going. Surely a united country is preferable to a divided one?’ Again, he sat back in his chair with a satisfied smirk.

‘Of that, there is no doubt, Charles. But for a people to be united, they must share the same basic beliefs. And until we do, Completists will stand by our beliefs and you will stand by yours. I continue to hope each side can keep a useful dialogue going so eventually we might have a meeting of minds.’

‘How can there be a meeting of minds when you are against 50% of the population, Libretta?’

‘You tell her, Charles,’ Sophie said ramming her biscuit into her mug of coffee.

‘Are you referring to men, Charles?’ Libretta asked evenly.

‘I am.’

‘Then I must disagree with your statement. Completists are not against men per se, we are against men limiting women by controlling their behaviour and the economic infrastructure which enables this control to continue.’ Charles seemed agitated at her response, shifting in his seat.

‘So, all we need to do is to run society in the way *you* want to see it run and everything will be fine, will it?’

Libretta delivered her response straight into the camera, rather than at Charles. 'Exactly, Charles. Start basing economic reward on merit rather than gender. Start sharing the job of raising the next generation equally, and start seeing women as men see themselves. Then we can unite to create a more fulfilling existence for everyone who lives in our country.'

'How do you hope to achieve this when thousands of your members have abandoned their sons? Hardly conducive to raising a generation of men well-disposed towards Completists!' Charles was becoming aggravated, and his anger was now plain to see.

'I would hope these boys will come to understand it was their fathers' actions that led their mothers to take such a painful decision, and work to ensure women will never again be forced into making a virtually impossible choice merely to enable them to live as men do.'

'And there, I believe, we have the crux of the matter.' Charles turned his head towards another camera so he too could speak directly to his viewers. 'The Completists continue to lay the blame for our divided society squarely at the feet of men. Taking no responsibility for the harm and damage they are inflicting on every woman, man and child in this country by continuing to believe every failed career, every failed relationship and every failed life a woman has experienced has nothing to do with her own shortcomings but is the sole result of men's prejudice against them.' He turned to look at Libretta again. 'How can this be the case when the majority of women still choose to live with men, and appear to be doing fine, Libretta? Doesn't your Movement make a mockery of these women's choices?' Sophie could see from his face that he believed he had struck his killer blow; however, Libretta just smiled and continued to speak in the same measured tone.

'When the Movement began, Charles, we had 100,000 members, just 0.3% of the female population. Thirty years on,

we now have over 30% of the female population, that's 9.9 million Completists. At the current rate of growth, in the year 2148, 23 years from now, there won't be a single female left for a man to marry. I wonder what that says about how *real* the choice to be a Chosen One is, Charles? I would suggest men need to stop and think about how they need to change in order to reverse this trend and create a society in which women can play an equal role. When you are haemorrhaging, you try and repair the damage, not open the wound even further.'

'Thank you for speaking to us this morning, Libretta. Unfortunately, we've run out of time. And if Libretta's prediction of the future is correct, I suggest everyone involved in the wedding business starts looking for alternative employment.' Charles was directly addressing his audience again; and finished the broadcast with a cheeky wink.

Sophie turned off the monitor, sat back and stared into space. Libretta had got the better of Charles; in fact, she had made some good points. Who knew there were now nearly ten million Completists? Was she the one burying her head in the sand?

CHAPTER 32

Three weeks after the Celebrations, Sophie was in the lounge putting up the Christmas decorations. Carols were playing and she felt decidedly chirpy. The Christmas tree was ready to be decorated by the children and she couldn't wait to turn all the fairy lights on. It was Saturday, and Peter, having taken heed of her last outburst, had already taken Charlie out for the morning. She was waiting for Emmeline to appear. Her daughter had a habit of lying-in until mid-morning, with her nose in a book, and Sophie was happy to have a little time to herself.

As she stepped back to admire her handiwork, Emmeline padded into the room, still in her pyjamas.

'You're up early?'

'My stomach was rumbling. I think I need my breakfast. But I can get it, Mum. You carry on. It looks lovely.'

'Thanks, Trouble. But don't be silly. I'll take a break and make you some toast.'

As she prepared Emmeline's breakfast, she asked her daughter about the end-of-term festivities. She was unusually brief with her replies.

'Is there something on your mind, Emmeline?'

‘I wondered if I could ask you a question, but I don’t want to make you cross.’

‘I won’t know how I’ll react until you ask it, will I? Go on. I’m ready for anything this morning.’ She smiled reassuringly at her daughter, who was fiddling with the tablecloth.

‘If any woman can choose to live as a Completist, why did you decide to live as a Chosen One? Please don’t be angry, I’m curious, that’s all.’

Sophie froze for a second, dishcloth hanging limply by her side. Then she turned and continued to wipe down the sink, playing for time. Finally, aware that her pause was making her daughter nervous, she straightened her back and looked directly at her. ‘Why are you asking?’

‘Sometimes, I think Dad and Charlie make you sad. I know they make me sad. Would life be better if they weren’t in it? I’m sorry, Mum. I really don’t want to upset you. You don’t have to answer.’

Sophie swallowed. She hadn’t expected to be so upset by her daughter’s question. Emmeline looked like she could burst into tears at any moment. Her daughter tried so hard to make her happy. She always offered to help her and instinctively knew when to stay out of the way, and Sophie suddenly understood why. She sat down beside her and held her hand.

‘I’m so sorry you feel this way. I had no idea you could sense my unhappiness. It’s complicated, Emmeline. You’re right, I get frustrated with your father, but it’s not his fault really, it’s the way life is, and sometimes, life is a little unfair. Things are improving for women, but your dad seems stuck in the dark ages. He still seems to think women were put on this earth to serve men, and sometimes it makes me so cross. He hates Completists. He hates the way they have turned their backs on men. He dismisses them all as being against his kind, yet he can’t see how it’s his behaviour, and men like him that started their campaign in the first place.’

‘Do you hate Completists, Mum?’ Emmeline was looking

at her intently, as if she was afraid Sophie would stop speaking if she broke eye contact.

'I used to hate them. But now I just feel angry because they're not trying to change my world. Instead, they've turned their back on it, which is cowardly. Yes, that's it. I think Completists are cowards.'

Emmeline looked confused. 'Why is it their job to change your world?'

Sophie couldn't think of a satisfactory answer. She stared out into the lifeless December garden. 'I guess it isn't really, is it?' she said more to herself than her daughter. Emmeline touched her shoulder.

'Thanks, Mum. Thanks for listening to me. I'll go upstairs now and give you some peace.'

CHAPTER 33

Kate was looking forward to dinner. She had an announcement to make which would make Cara very happy. She was growing up so fast. A teenager! She had decided to mark the occasion.

The pasta was ready. 'Cara! Gemma! Tea's ready.' She heard them gallop down the stairs.

'Yey! It's pasta!' Gemma said, smiling at the steaming bowl in front of her.

It was good to see Gemma happy. It had been over three years since that bastard had grabbed her, and it had left its mark. Every time they had to leave the house her anxiety was palpable.

'Cara, my pretty girl. You're growing up so fast, and I think it's high time you started to choose your own clothes'. Cara sprang to her feet and smothered her in kisses.

'Whoa, slow down!' Kate said, grinning broadly. 'There are going to be a few rules.' Cara sat down and eyed her suspiciously. Kate noted the anxious look on Gemma's face.

'You'll have a budget to stick to, and they must be clothes you can wear every day. No party dresses or things you'll wear only once. It's the same rules for shoes. I'm afraid I'm not

going to let you spend your money on a high heeled pair of party shoes. But if you want to buy an expensive pair of trainers, then that's your choice. OK?' She looked at Cara, her expression making it very clear she would be unwise to contradict her.

'OK, Mum,' Cara agreed. 'How much do I have to spend?'

'£2,000. I reckon that should be enough for a couple of pairs of trousers, a couple of tops and a pair of decent trainers.' Kate realised it wasn't a fortune, but it was a decent amount for a first spending spree.

'Thanks, Mum, so much! Can we go to The Circle Shopping Centre?'

'I was thinking the same thing,' her mother replied, winking at Gemma. 'And Gemma, please don't worry. We'll be as safe as houses. No men are allowed in The Circle.'

Cara woke her up the following morning, bringing her a tea. Gemma padded in a few seconds later, rubbing her eyes.

'My, my, this is a first,' Kate said sarcastically, pushing herself up on her elbows to take the drink from Cara's hand. 'Thank you, darling girl. Look at you, dressed already. You look really nice. Gemma why don't you get dressed and we'll have breakfast together before we set off.'

'I'll go downstairs and put some toast on,' Cara said as she sped out of the room. She was in a rush to get out of the house, but Kate could sense Gemma was feeling anxious.

'Good idea. But if the bread gets jammed, don't get it out with a knife, call me, alright?' she shouted. Cara was already halfway down the stairs. She turned to Gemma, 'Are you alright, little one? Come here.' Gemma wandered over and sat down on her bed.

'It's alright, Gemma. You don't have to worry. Everything will be fine. Now let's both get dressed before your sister electrocutes herself or burns the house down!'

She swung her legs out of bed and sat cupping her mug in

her hands. She patted Gemma on the bottom, and watched her daughter pad back to her bedroom. Kate had wanted to scoop her up in her arms and hug her, but that wouldn't have helped ease her nervousness.

The Circle was already busy, even though the shops had only been open for ten minutes. As they headed out of the underground car park towards the entrance, Gemma froze at the sound of men shouting.

'Daughters need fathers too! Only mothers just won't do!' Gemma's grip tightened around Kate's hand. She knelt in front of her, holding her daughter's arms firmly.

'Listen, Gemma. This is nothing to be afraid of, I promise. This happens sometimes. It's only a group of men protesting. They will shout a bit and wave their banners, but they won't hurt you.'

Gemma looked into her eyes, searching for any trace of fear, then nodded and tried to smile.

'Don't worry, Mum, I'm OK. Come on Cara, let's go. Which shop do you want to visit first?' Cara took her sister's free hand and they walked forward as one. As they turned the corner, the protesters' chants grew louder. They all tried to look straight ahead, heads held high, but none of them could resist a sideways glance. Kate stopped walking. She felt faint. Her eyes had briefly locked with the curly-haired, well-built man standing in the middle of the group. Oh God, it's him. He recognised her too and she saw his eyes scan the group, finally resting on Cara. Cara met his gaze, proud and defiant; then she saw her daughter's expression change.

'Mum, why is he looking at me like that?' she whispered.

'He's your father, Cara. He's your father.' What else could she say? Cara turned to look at the man again, her mouth open, her body still. Kate was also studying him. His hair was the same mop of loose curls, but his face was lined, the twinkle in his eyes extinguished.

Gemma started to cry.

Kate swept her into her arms and, grabbing Cara's hand, marched past the group of men, into the female-only haven within. She didn't stop walking until they reached Cara's favourite café. 'We're going to have a drink and a cake. We need something sweet after that shock,' and sitting Gemma down on a chair, she handed both the girls a menu.

'Right, what's it to be? I am personally going to have the biggest piece of chocolate cake they have, because I need it!' she said in an overly cheerful voice.

'Me too, Mum, I need it too.' Cara was clearly trying to sound as cheerful as her mother.

'I'm going to have to have two slices.' Gemma said, making them both laugh. They reached for each other's hands.

They ate the cake in silence, until Cara gently said, 'Mum, why did you leave my father? He looked like he might be a good dad.' Kate put her fork down. Gemma stopped eating.

'How people look on the outside is not always the same as how they are on the inside. Take a handsome man, like your father, and say this man owned a dog. The man might pass you in the street as he walks his dog, and smile at you. The dog may be wagging its tail, pleased to be out sniffing the world. But when they get home, the dog does something the man doesn't like. It's not the dog's fault, it doesn't realise it's doing anything wrong. Instead of gently telling the dog not to do it, the man kicks the dog, hurting it, thinking the dog will realise he has to stop the behaviour to avoid being beaten. But the dog is afraid now, and when an animal feels fear, it cannot learn. The dog is no longer sure it trusts the man so, the next time the dog does the same thing, and the man goes to kick it, the dog bares its teeth at the man and growls. This makes the man even angrier. How dare the dog try to attack him. He is the master of the dog. He is better than the dog. The dog must know its place. The man fetches a belt and beats the dog, until

it is whimpering, rolling over onto its back to submit to the man, to tell him he can stop, he has won. The man stops. What do you think happens when the dog next misbehaves, Cara?' Cara paused for a moment, then smiled.

'I think the dog must hate the man now, so when the man goes to hit him, the dog will bite the man. And he should, because he doesn't know how to treat his dog, he shouldn't be allowed to have one.' Cara looked pleased with herself.

'That is what the dog should do. Well done. Unfortunately, it's not what the dog actually does. The dog is now so scared of the man that, as soon as it sees the man is about to beat him, it retreats under the kitchen table, trying to protect itself from his blows, rather than fighting back.' Cara looked puzzled.

'But why should the dog be afraid? He has sharp teeth and is probably as strong as the man.'

Kate smiled.

'You're right, it doesn't make sense, unless you understand the dog has been raised to see the man as his master, and a dog should know better than to attack his master. In a good dog's mind, if he submits to his master, then the master will give him protection, food and warmth. And that may be true if you have a good master. But a bad master, like this man, will beat his dog to death. Your father was like this man, Cara. I couldn't stay with a man like that now, could I?' She reached over and gave Cara's hand a squeeze.

Cara's eyes filled with tears. 'Did you used to have a pet dog, Mum? Did he beat him?'

'He did, Cara. But our dog was cleverer than most, he didn't stick around to be continually beaten. One day he ran away from home and we never saw him again. Now let's finish our cake and put this sadness behind us. I see a kind, brave girl sitting opposite me who needs some new clothes. And I have another one sitting beside me, who wants to help her choose them.'

Gemma pulled Kate towards her, wrapped her arms around her neck, and kissed her cheek. Kate instantly knew she understood what she had really been saying. She wished she wasn't so bright. She was too young, and already too afraid of men.

FOUNDERS MEETING

Libretta swept silently away from Chester College seated in the back of her black Bentley. She had an annual commitment to present a select group of students with their degrees, and Chester was the best Completist University in the country. She always enjoyed the occasion, but today the graduation ceremony had overrun, and she was in danger of being late for the Founders' Meeting. She hoped the traffic would be on their side. As they left the ancient city behind and headed through open countryside, Libretta noticed the first leaves emerging from the trees, the weak afternoon sunlight creating vivid sparks of green as they sped past. She loved this part of the country but she couldn't afford to waste time staring out of the window. Reluctantly she turned her head away from the spring landscape and back to the leather interior of the car.

For a second, she panicked, unable to immediately spot her bag. Had she left it at the college in her haste to leave? Her eyes scanned the back seat and then she noticed one leather handle. She leaned over and heaved her bag up from the floor. It must have slid off when they had to swerve suddenly in the City Centre to avoid hitting a student that had been accidently pushed off the pavement by an over

exuberant friend. She opened her leather bag and took out the policy discussion document. The meeting could be a possible turning point in the Movement, so she had to be fully prepared.

As the Bentley turned into the tree-lined avenue that led to the house, Libretta looked up from her papers, gathered them together, and slipped them back into her bag. After several minutes she could see the chimney stacks of the house appear above the trees, then seconds later the front façade appeared wrapped around a rectangular courtyard with an oval lawn of emerald green in its centre. The car pulled up outside the ancient sand stone walls crawling with ivy, and she noticed, with some annoyance, she was the last to arrive. She opened the car door and felt the gravel beneath her feet crunch satisfyingly as she made her way to the arched stone entrance. The heavy oak door was opened by Marilynn, which surprised Libretta; she had been expecting her assistant. Marilynn was incredibly glamorous and had the mannerisms and looks of her namesake.

'Libretta, how lovely to see you again. Come in, come in. Everyone else is already in the library. There's quite a buzz in the air. Everything has been set up as you requested. We're all looking forward to your opening presentation.' Marilynn always spoke quickly. It gave her the air of someone who would endlessly fuss over you, finally driving you to distraction.

She continued talking as the two of them walked briskly towards the library; a beautiful, high-ceilinged room, flooded with light from the six tall windows, framing a garden which reflected Marilynn's fastidious nature. The room's oak-panelled walls were lined with books standing on shelves covered with intricate wood carvings of acorns and oak leaves, a forest forever fossilised by the carpenter's chisel. As they entered, ten heads turned and smiled at them in welcome. Teacups and plates of cakes and sandwiches littered the

polished tabletop; Libretta noticed a few slices were already being tucked into.

She took her place at the head of the table. Marilynn poured her a cup of tea and took her seat to the right of Libretta's.

'Ladies, here we all are, safely gathered together, without a journalist in sight! Congratulations one and all!' The women smiled warmly at their host. Libretta was also very fond of Marilynn who, despite her appearance and incessant jabbering, was as sharp as a pin, and a voracious defender of the Movement. 'Our Chair has arrived, directly from Chester, having met the next intake of gifted young women who will soon, no doubt, be gracing our companies' corridors. We're here today to discuss the shape of these young women's futures. This could be one of the most important meetings we'll ever attend in our lifetimes as Founders and Guardians of the Movement. On that note, I'll hand over to Libretta, who will outline the two key issues we're here to discuss.' Marilynn sat down, smoothing her pleated silk skirt into order.

Curtains slid effortlessly across the windows, and the wall behind Libretta's chair lit up in unison with the small reading lights embedded in the tabletop. It made the table look like a strange UFO hovering silently above a forest floor.

'Good afternoon everyone. I trust you have all read and digested the briefing documents, so you know why we're here. But I'd like to begin by summarising the current situation.' Libretta swivelled her chair around to face the wall behind her where key facts and figures were now visible.

'Over the first three decades of the Movement we experienced an average conversion rate of 3.3 million women per decade, with the last decade accounting for 6.9 million conversions. Had this trend continued, every woman in the UK would have become a Completist by 2148. However, here we are in 2128 with only 35% of the female population having joined our ranks. Over the last nine years our conversion rate

has steadily declined. Today we find ourselves only converting around 158,000 women a year. We are assuming this is because our commercial activities are affecting the whole of the UK economy. In other words, COs are benefitting economically from the Movement without having to become part of it.

Our main aim was to achieve economic parity for women, so men started to regard us as their equals, not their inferiors. We believed we could run businesses better than they could, and bring something new and unique to the corporate world. The first question for us today is, have we achieved our aim? If we have, what does this mean for the future of our Movement?

The second question is this. The birth rate of males in the UK has dropped significantly. We now have a country made up of two halves. The CO half has a shortage of women, and we do not! We have genetic selection to ensure members give birth solely to daughters. It seems perverse that the government still refuses to use genetic screening to control the gender of the COs' offspring, given the situation. Instead, last year, they introduced a policy to encourage the abortion of male embryos. Why not control the sex of the child from the outset, rather than put a woman through what is still a traumatic and risky procedure?'

'Seriously, Libretta. That surprises you?' Marilynn said, raising her eyebrows. 'The government are more concerned with politics than the wellbeing of their women, and to allow pre-selection of female offspring, as we do, would have been political suicide. Whereas a quick abortion, while unpalatable, is a slightly easier pill for the population to swallow.'

'Fair point, well made.' Libretta acknowledged. 'They would have done better to allow women to have more than one husband.'

'Now that *would* have been a truly cruel piece of legislation!' Marilynn exclaimed. When the laughter died down, Libretta continued.

'As I was saying, the last decade saw the birth rate for males drop from 55% of live births to 38%, and still there won't be enough CO women to go around. Naturally, the future trend of live male births is inextricably linked with the future trend of converts, and the continuation of the COs' policy of encouraging aborting males. It's a virtuous circle for us. The more women they lose to the Movement, the more urgent their need to increase the proportion of their female population at the expense of a new generation of men. If we can revive our conversion rates, their policy will simply produce more potential Completists. We must decide whether we believe our conversion rates have flat-lined because we have achieved our aim, and hence the gender ratio of births will also settle down to this new norm, or whether we have more to achieve, more women to convert, which will further reduce the male birth rate. Ultimately, we could have a society where women might choose to give birth to boys purely to ensure the continuation of women in the UK.

I'm looking forward to a lively debate, so let's start with the question of whether we have achieved our aim of economic parity. Marilynn, would you like to kick things off?' The host of the meeting was always deferred to first and then the other founders would take their turn before opening up the debate to the Guardians.

'Thank you, Libretta. My view is very clear. Looking at all the facts and figures regarding the economic success of all Completist companies and their impact on the UK economy, I think we have clearly shown companies run solely by women are contributing to the economic prosperity of this country. I also note that, even the companies run by men, now have far more women sitting on their Board of Directors than before the Movement started. In this respect, we've certainly made ourselves redundant as leaders of a movement founded to achieve economic parity. However, and this is my key point. If we were to disband the Movement, can we be sure there would

not be a slow regression to how things were before the Uprising? It might take centuries to unravel what we've achieved, and our members may be sufficiently committed and robust to ensure this never happens. But I'm not convinced. I believe we still have a role to play, even if it is more of a policing role, to ensure what has been achieved cannot be undone.'

There was a general nodding of heads, then Sylvia Gerry spoke. Sylvia had short hair and had worn horn-rimmed round spectacles since she was an infant. She was considered to be highly intelligent among her peers, with a refreshingly forthright way of expressing herself. She also had a gorgeous red-headed partner, which often caused a little jealousy. Completists generally acknowledged their lesbian members had it made. No prejudices, no discrimination *and* free sex. They had it all.

'I'm with Marilynn, but I'll go one step further. The majority of the women in the country still live with men, and they do that because they believe in romance. This is quite bizarre, considering the plethora of evidence clearly showing women are more successful, more fulfilled and live longer and happier lives when they live without a man. This message is still not getting through because of government propaganda, which smothers our success stories, but never fails to show every small difficulty or problem we encounter as a failure and a weakness in our ideology. While our economic lobbying can no longer be ignored, we still have a fundamentally patriarchal society, because the Chosen Ones still believe falling in love and raising children is better than running the bloody country! I would strongly advocate we redefine our key objective as political equality, design new policies around that, and back it up with policing the economic framework we've created. After all, our ultimate aim is surely to bring about true equality between men and women, and we are still a way away from achieving it.'

Kerry Greer, the owner of one of the largest Completist

companies, shouted 'Here, here!' She faced Libretta and continued. 'To even suggest we're done is preposterous in my view. Every action of the most powerful men in the country shows us, without a shadow of doubt, that they still firmly believe men should dominate women.' Kerry's pearl necklace swung against her cashmere jumper as she emphasised her points by thumping the table. 'Despite everything we have demonstrated, despite the very real possibility their inability to adapt and embrace change could mean the end of their species living freely in this country, they *still* desperately cling on to power, as if sharing it would negate them as people! This feeds directly into Project Manhood, which has been going on covertly for over twenty years. Wrestling with the question of whether men's thirst for control and power is inherent or learned. We've been struggling with this. Wanting to believe it is a learned response so we could allow our members to have sons who could be raised to truly view women as their equals, with the end result of unifying our society once more. But the empirical evidence seems to indicate this may be something which can, sadly, never be achieved.' She sat back in her chair, her pearls once more at rest.

As the debate unfolded, it was clear the Movement was far from over. There was only one Guardian who believed their job had been done: Hermione Honeyfelt, who headed up Project Manhood. She believed there were enough powerful and influential women to take matters forward without the backing of the Movement, emphasising it was time for these women to act autonomously. This, she had muttered, would be true freedom. The group politely but decisively dismissed her views, while tucking into their cake as she addressed them. Hermione was now bristling at being so easily ignored.

Libretta tapped her teacup with her spoon. 'I believe everyone who wishes to speak has now spoken?' There was a general nodding of heads. 'I think we're in a position to vote.

All those in favour of the Movement continuing, albeit with a new aim, please raise your hands.'

'Excuse me, ladies.' The door of the room opened, and Marilynn's assistant stood at the entrance.

'Margaret, what is it?' Marilynn asked, unsuccessfully attempting to hide her annoyance at being interrupted.

'The cameras have picked up an intruder in the grounds, currently heading in this direction. He's either a journalist, or a lost tourist who, from the size of the telescopic lens on his camera, feels rather inadequate in the trouser department.'

There was a gentle ripple of laughter from everyone except Marilynn and Sylvia.

'Good God, Margaret. Did he definitely break into the grounds? Are we absolutely sure no side gate was left unlocked?'

'I checked everything myself, Marilynn. The perimeter was absolutely secure at 7.00 a.m. this morning.'

'Right, screw him. I've had enough of this constant harassment. Release the dogs.'

Libretta stared at her old friend.

'Are you sure that's wise Marilynn? They'll rip him to shreds.'

'I understand your concern, Libretta, I really do, but I doubt anyone knows he's here. You know what these people are like. They get much more money for exclusives. It's more than likely he hasn't told a soul where he was heading. He's probably a freelance anyway, trying to make enough money from intruding on this private meeting to buy himself a yacht in the Med. Imagine the kudos of unveiling, for the first time, the identity of every Founder and Guardian.'

'I understand your frustration, but I don't think this is a decision you should take alone. Would you abide by the decision of all of us on this one, Marilynn? You know we never advocate violence. It's been a founding principle from the start of the Uprising. Imagine the headlines if they discovered we

had purposefully released vicious dogs to deal with a trespasser. It could do untold damage to our credibility.'

Marilynn scowled at Libretta. 'But what about the danger to us if our identities are revealed?' she huffed, but then resentfully capitulated. 'Fine. Let's put it to the vote. Hands up those of you who feel I have a right to protect my own property from trespassers?'

'I believe that's what's known as a leading question, Marilynn.' Libretta smiled at her friend. 'Allow me to suggest another. Hands up all those who agree this trespasser deserves to be ripped limb from limb for his transgression?'

Libretta stared in amazement as over half the women in the room raised their hands.

'Libretta, the room has spoken. Off you go, Margaret, and please advise us of the outcome.' Marilynn smiled at her assistant and reached across the table for another piece of carrot cake.

PART TWO

CHAPTER 34

Cara wished with all her heart she was at home instead of sitting in a toilet cubicle looking at her blood-stained knickers. She didn't know what to do. The pain was excruciating, and she was revolted and frightened at the blood coming out of her body. She knew what was happening. Her mother had given her everything she needed months ago; but should she tell someone, or keep it a secret until she got home? This was a big deal. Apparently, she was now a woman, at the grand old age of 14. Her childhood was officially over. She wasn't entirely sure this was something to celebrate. Adulthood seemed a rather serious business, all career planning and financial management. However, she did rather like the thought of being able to have a baby.

Cara wasn't inclined to dwell on her future, her mind was occupied with far more important matters. What captured her imagination were boys. She couldn't seem to stop thinking about them.

It was difficult to get a proper look at them when she was out with her family. Her eyes were always straight ahead; and in the places they frequented, there weren't many of them anyway. Occasionally some got on the bus as she travelled to

school, and she could cast them the odd sideways glance without being spotted by Gemma, who she suspected might tell her mum if she openly ogled them. Unsurprisingly, she realised she was most attracted to the boys with dark curly hair, like her father's. The image of him was as sharp today as it had been four years ago. She had tried to picture him as a bad man, to put the longing she had seen in his eyes out of her mind, but whenever she thought of him, there he was, in every tiny detail. He had only ever been an outline in black and white until the day they had seen each other, and now he was coloured in.

Her mother beamed at her when she announced her news at supper.

'Does it hurt?' asked Gemma, looking rather perturbed at this turn of events.

'A little bit at first,' she lied, 'but all the pain went away when I took one of the pills Mum had given me.'

'You're lucky,' their mother said, addressing them both. 'They didn't have such effective medicine when my mum was a girl. Some women had to take to their beds for the first day because the pain was so bad.'

'Why do we have them?' Gemma asked.

'They let us have babies, if we want them.' Cara replied, trying to keep things as simple as possible. Gemma glared at her.

Her mother then proceeded to set out, in detail, the plain scientific facts regarding the reproductive cycle.

'Got it,' said Gemma, looking defiantly at Cara. 'Thanks, Mum. One last question though, how does the sperm get inside to fertilise our eggs?'

Cara giggled, and waited to see which answer her mother would choose.

'When we want to be pregnant, we go to a specialist doctor, choose a father from a catalogue, and the doctor places the sperm inside us with a special instrument called a

Viedonne. A Completist invented it and it has a 90% success rate, so you often only need to go through the procedure once. I got pregnant with you after one visit.'

So, this was how she was going to play it, Cara thought. She was now torn between respecting her mother's wishes and fully educating her inquisitive sister. She would have to tread carefully.

'That's not the only way women get pregnant though, is it, Mum? That's not how you got pregnant with me.'

Her mother raised her eyebrows, a weary expression on her face.

'Sorry, Mum, but the school do teach us about the alternative way of getting pregnant. And now we're on the subject, she may as well hear it from you as from her teachers. After all, you have at least experienced it. Miss Cunningham, Gemma's biology teacher, doesn't have any children.'

Her mother sighed. 'Fine. Thank you, Cara,' she said, failing to keep the sarcasm from her voice. 'There is another method, only practised by the Chosen Ones. They sleep with their husbands, who put their penis inside their wife's vagina and the sperm travels from the man's penis into his wife's womb. It is a much less reliable method. Some COs want children but can't get pregnant, and other COs don't want children and get pregnant by accident. I much prefer our method. We are totally in control and every child we bring into the world is very much planned and wanted.'

'But you wanted me, didn't you?' Cara asked, suddenly unnerved by her mother's answer.

'Of course, I did, Cara!' But there was something in the way her mother hesitated for a split second before replying which placed a seed of doubt in Cara's brain.

'Okeydokey, all clear about everything now, Gemma?' her mother said as she stood up and started to clear the plates away. 'Who wants homemade apple pie and ice cream?'

Cara declined the offer and asked to get down from the

table. She went to her room and sat on her bed. She couldn't bear it if her mother hadn't really wanted her and had then taken her away from a father who, despite what she had said about him, evidently did. Cara closed her eyes and pictured his face. She recalled his sad brown eyes searching her own, longing for a spark of connection. Was it time to pay him a visit? How was she going to find him; she didn't even know his surname? She was sure there were other girls in her situation. There was bound to be an organisation out there which helped trace fathers. She reached for her mobile and touched the screen.

Cara's assumption was correct. Within five minutes she had composed an email to 'Reunite', an organisation promising to "heal the pain of a fatherless existence". Cara wasn't sure she was in pain, but she was sad and more than a little curious about her father. She paused over the send button. Her mother was going to be so angry with her, she would feel betrayed, wouldn't she? And what if her father didn't want to see her? How would that make her feel? But how could she live her entire life without understanding why her mother had left him to become a Completist? She pressed send. She stared at the screen, a rush of nausea and excitement surging through her. That night she barely slept. When she did drift off, her dreams played out different scenarios of their meeting. In some, her father would hold her in his arms, tears of joy filling his big brown eyes, but, in others, he was brooding and angry and she woke herself up feeling frightened of what he might do to her.

By the next day she had a reply. By the end of the week, they had traced her father, contacted him, and established he would very much like to see her. Their messages were reassuring and kind, encouraging her to agree to meet him. As the days passed, she grew accustomed to the idea, and she finally agreed to a meeting at the café, a few minutes' walk from the school gates. Cara had a study period she could skip, so she

could see him and still be back in time to catch the bus home with Gemma. She was surprised at how easy the whole process had been, how willing the organisation was to help her. They had never asked for her mother's contact details to make sure she was happy, but then the organisation was run by men in the same situation as her father, so perhaps she wasn't that surprised her mother's opinion meant nothing to them. While Cara was anxious to see him again, guilt began to nag at her. She shouldn't be doing this behind her mother's back. It was wrong. When she woke on the day they were due to meet, she was sick with nerves and shame. What if he *was* a bad man? What if he tried to hurt her, or even worse, kidnap her, to punish her mother for what she had done to him? She wouldn't know where she was or be able to find her.

By breakfast time, she had decided to leave a note for her mother on her bedside table, in case the worst happened. If it did, she knew her mother would never forgive her.

'Cara, you haven't touched your cereal, are you feeling alright? You're as white as a sheet.' Her mother touched her forehead. 'You don't seem to have a temperature.'

'I'm fine, Mum, stop fussing.' Cara had wanted to sound reassuring, but her guilt had made her sound snappy and irritable.

Her mother gave her one of her sideways glances. Cara was sure she could sense she was hiding something, but Cara had chosen this day with care. She knew her mother had an important work presentation. She wouldn't have the time or the inclination to fuss over either of them.

'OK, Cara. But if you feel any worse during the day, make sure the school phones me and I'll arrange to have you picked up and brought to the office. You know we have a sick room for children there. You can lie down until I finish work.' Cara didn't respond. It was her mother's turn to sound irritated: 'Cara, did you hear me?'

'Yep, sorry, Mum.' Cara replied.

'Let's get this show on the road then. Upstairs for teeth cleaning, and back down here in 15 minutes, ready to go.'

Cara rushed upstairs, grabbing a pen and some paper from her school bag. She couldn't find the words and time was ticking by. All she managed was, 'Dear Mum, I'm so sorry.' She screwed up the paper, threw it on the floor, and hurried to the bathroom to clean her teeth.

She could barely concentrate on her lessons and the day dragged its heels, time itself chastising her for her selfishness. Finally, 4.00 p.m. arrived. As she walked out of the side gate towards the café, she began to wonder if she really was ill. She felt faint and was finding it difficult to breathe. It wasn't far to the café and her hands trembled as she pushed the door handle down and pulled the door towards her. She saw him immediately. He had chosen a table at the back of the café and had looked up as soon as he heard the door open.

Everything went quiet and she stood still, afraid her legs would give way if she took another step. He got up and strode towards her. He was dressed casually; nonetheless, Cara could tell he had chosen his outfit with care. The muted colour of his linen shirt blended seamlessly with his faded jeans; she even liked his suede shoes. Cara was pleased to have such a good-looking father.

'Cara, are you alright?' His voice was soft and lilting.

She nodded at him as he linked his arm with hers. It felt strong and steady. She could smell his skin. He smelt like a summer pine forest. She leant on him and they walked together to the table. He pulled out her chair and guided her into it.

'Don't worry, Cara. I'm as nervous as you are. Apart from the shopping centre, this is the first time I've met you since you were a baby. You can't imagine what this means to me. I can't believe you're actually here. It's all a bit surreal.'

They sat for a second, staring at one another, then they

both laughed; it was the same laugh, which made them laugh again.

'That's better. It was all getting a bit overwhelming, wasn't it?' he said, smiling. 'What would you like to drink? Do you want anything to eat?'

'What I would like is to know your surname. That's the one detail the men who arranged this forgot to tell me.' Her voice was quiet, almost a whisper.

He looked shocked. A flash of anger lit up his eyes, forked lightening in a summer sky. 'She never told you my name?' he said quietly, playing with the words, allowing them time to sink in.

Cara felt she had betrayed her mother.

'Cara,' he said, regaining his composure and smiling at her. 'My name is David, David Kildare. Very pleased to meet you.' He reached out his hand and Cara shook it.

'Pleased to meet you, David Kildare,' Cara said, her voice growing a little louder; but was she? Her mother wasn't a stupid woman. If she had decided to leave this man, she must have had a good reason. Cara needed to be careful. Her eyes wandered around the café. It was a relief to see quite a few tables were taken.

'Tell me something about yourself, Cara. What do you like doing? What's your favourite subject at school?'

Before Cara could answer, the waitress came over to take their order. Cara asked for an orange juice and her father ordered a coffee. So, my father, David Kildare, drinks his coffee black.

'Cara, cat got your tongue?'

'I like sport best, especially swimming,' she answered awkwardly.

'What a coincidence! That's my favourite thing to do. Your mum and I used to go swimming every Saturday morning, when we were first married.'

'What age was Mum when she married you?'

‘She was four years older than you, Cara.’ It was Cara’s turn to look shocked. She knew her mum had her when she was 25, but she didn’t know she had been married for seven years by then.

‘Has your mum told you anything about her life with me?’ her father asked, seeing her expression.

Cara didn’t want to answer. She didn’t want to say anything that would put her mother in a bad light. She didn’t want to say anything about her mother, or Gemma, or her life. She suddenly realised where her loyalties lay and stood up, as the waitress approached with their drinks.

‘I’m really sorry, but I think this was a bad idea. I’d like to go now. I’m so sorry,’ and she turned and walked out of the café, pushing the door and gasping in the fresh air as she stepped outside. She ran back towards school and the only family she needed.

When they got home her mother was sitting at the kitchen table; the crumpled piece of paper she had thrown on the floor lay smoothed out in front of her.

‘What are you sorry for, Cara?’ her mother asked in a stern tone. Cara panicked. She stared at her mother, then at Gemma, then back at her mother.

‘Gemma, darling, would you mind popping upstairs to your room for a few minutes. Cara and I need to have a private chat.’ Gemma looked confused, but she had heard her mother use this tone before, and she wasn’t about to argue with her.

‘Sit down, Cara. What’s going on?’ Then her mother’s voice softened. ‘You do know you can tell me anything, don’t you? Whatever you’ve done, it’s nothing which can’t be forgiven or put right, if needs be.’ Cara wasn’t sure either of those things could be applied to that afternoon’s events.

‘Come on now. It can’t be so bad, surely?’ Cara noticed how anxious her mother had started to look.

‘Oh, but it is bad,’ Cara said, barely able to look her in the eye.

‘Please, Cara, tell me. You’re starting to make me really worried.’ Her mother reached over and put her hand on hers.

Cara looked into her mother’s eyes and told her what she had done. She was waiting for her expression to switch from concern to anger, but she sat quietly, listening to her.

‘I’m so sorry, Mum. I know it was wrong to go behind your back, but you never talk about the time before you became a Completist, and I guess I wanted to make sense of things, to know who I was and where I came from. To know if I was wanted, or part of an awful mistake.’

‘Oh Cara, I always wanted a child, I just didn’t want one with your father. We had been trying for a number of years and nothing had happened. Unfortunately, by the time I fell pregnant with you, I had discovered he was not fit to be a husband, let alone a dad.’

‘I don’t understand. How did you know that?’

‘Remember the day you met him, and I told you the story about the man who beat his dog? It was your father who beat me, and I wasn’t about to let him beat you too.’

Cara didn’t know what to say, she reached over and held her mother’s hands. ‘I’m so sorry, for everything.’

‘Come here. Let me give you a hug. You don’t need to apologise. It was difficult to tell you bad things so I chose to tell you nothing. I’m the one who should be apologising.’ They stood together. The tightness of her mother’s arms reassured Cara that all was forgiven.

CHAPTER 35

After she met her father, Cara tried to put boys out of her mind, but over the next few years she saw them everywhere. She couldn't really understand her continued fascination with them. None of her classmates seemed to share it. They were too busy discussing which university to go to. The majority favoured the ones founded by the Movement, which were entirely female campuses. Cara was currently having a recurring argument with her mother, who, predictably wanted her to attend a Completist University, stating Completist employers favoured candidates from these universities over mixed Unis. Cara's argument was that she should broaden her horizons before starting a career which would narrow them again. Her mother was having none of it. It was a Friday night when things came to a head.

'Cara, admit it, your choice of University is being driven by your desire to mix with men, rather than selecting the one which can offer you the best prospects of success. I've seen you looking at boys, you can't keep your eyes straight ahead when they're around.'

'Mum, you're wrong. Brighton's Graphic Design Course is one of the best in the country.'

‘One of the best, Cara, but not *the* best. That accolade belongs to Chester Uni, which happens to be run by Completists. So, tell me again. What it is about Brighton that trumps Chester?’

‘Mum, honestly! It’s obviously not *only* about the course. Have you ever wondered why your generation do so well in business?’

‘I *know* why we do. We are focussed and determined individuals.’

‘Naturally. But dare I suggest there is another reason? Your generation has mixed with men, so you can handle them when you have to deal with them. Which does occasionally happen, despite the Completist mission to monopolise the entire economy! They still run some of the most powerful and successful businesses in the UK, whether you like it or not. Don’t you think it would be advantageous if I became confident and comfortable around them? You know, in case I actually have to have a professional conversation with one.’ Cara knew her point was valid, and she couldn’t resist delivering it in a slightly triumphant and patronising way, knowing that would get under her mother’s skin.

‘Cara, say this *is* about your libido. You know I can organise for you to have a man, don’t you?’

‘What on earth are you talking about?’

‘Completists are not naïve fools, Cara. We do understand human biology. The drive to reproduce is a powerful force. Women are hardwired to want to attract a mate. Unfortunately for us, this urge is difficult to satisfy without unnecessary complications. So, we found a work-around. There are Completist businesses which provide men of all ages, shapes and sizes, who will come to a hotel room, or your home, and have sex with you for money. The Chosen Ones call them prostitutes. We call them Facilitators.’

Cara started to feel her cheeks grow hot.

‘I know you might find it difficult to talk to me about

these things, but having these urges is nothing to be ashamed of. Lots of my friends use Facilitators.'

'Have you used a Facilitator, Mum?'

'I did once. But while their fees are subsidised by the Central Fund, they're still quite expensive. And I found the experience a little disappointing. I have other ways of dealing with those urges.' Cara thought she was going to throw up.

'How about this, Cara. Why don't I spare your blushes and set up an appointment for you? I'll make all the arrangements. You just have to turn up. If you decide you don't want to go through with it, then fine. I would rather you had this opportunity and *then* decided where you want to go to university. How does that sound?'

Cara bit her lip. 'Fine. If you think it will help, I'll give it a go,' she responded, in a tone which indicated she was doing her mother a favour, then turned away to avoid witnessing her satisfied expression. When she was safely in her room, she turned on her mobile and distracted herself with her favourite programme. Within five minutes it was interrupted by the ping of a message notification. Her mother had sent her the link to the Facilitator website. She shook her head in disbelief but couldn't resist opening it.

The next hour was spent scanning profiles of men until her eyes rested on Sam's. His eyes were kind, and he was smiling mischievously. He stood, bear-chested, his taut stomach muscles drawing her in. She clicked on his profile. He was 22 and had been a Facilitator for two years. 'I'm gentle and considerate. All I want to do is to put a woman at ease and give her pleasure.' Her stomach flipped. She stared at him again; his wavy chestnut hair fell softly around his beautiful face. He was the one. Begrudgingly, she pinged the link to his profile back to her mother.

Kate smiled at her daughter's choice. Sam reminded her of David, although he was in much better physical shape than her ex-husband had been when they met. She called the number.

'Good evening. I'd like to book number 502 for next Saturday night please. I would like him for the entire evening. He will be meeting my daughter, Cara Ingleton. She's 17 and a virgin. Please give him explicit instructions to, how can I put this, give an underwhelming performance.'

The booking agent laughed. 'I understand completely. Leave it with me. I'll email you with all the arrangements.'

Kate went to the fridge and took out a bottle of wine. She poured herself a generous glass and sat down, holding it in her hands, feeling the cool liquid on her skin. She wondered whether she had done the right thing. Perhaps she should have simply insisted Cara attended Chester; but she knew her daughter. She knew how obstinate she could be. She took a large mouthful of wine and swilled the coldness around her mouth. No, she was her mother. She had to protect Cara. Men were dangerous and destructive. She'd done what every good Completist mother should.

CHAPTER 36

Cara had never been so nervous. All the sex websites were blocked on her mobile, and her entire sexual knowledge was based on her school biology lessons.

She arrived at the hotel two hours before the appointed time. The thought of getting ready in front of her mother was intolerable. Cara wanted to look glamorous and sexy, and her mother would surely ridicule her efforts.

She looked at her reflection in the large full-length mirror. Her light brown hair fell in soft curls, skimming her shoulders. The recent cut and blow-dry, paid for by her mother, made her look five years older; and her smoky eyes and pale lips were the result of online tutorials. She had obliterated the 17-year-old virgin and created an experienced 22-year-old.

She examined her body. While she was very slim, she now had the breasts she remembered coveting when the DJ had come strolling into the Community Centre on her tenth birthday. Cara's stomach was flat, but her belly had a gentleness to it which made her want to run her hand over its surface. She turned her back to the mirror and strained her head to catch a glimpse of her bottom. She was pleased with

what she saw. The carefully selected G-string fitted her perfectly and she hoped it would please Sam.

She reached for the pale blue slip dress she had bought from a CO shop with her allowance and slid it over her head. It flowed over her skin like liquid mercury, skimming her breasts, buttocks and belly. She pulled on the slingback sandals and looked at herself again: satisfied she had done all she could to look attractive. She really wanted him to want her. The only advise her mother had offered had been to lie on a towel in case she bled and order a bottle of wine from room service and have a glass before he arrived, advice she was now taking. She was about to pour herself a second when she heard a gentle knock on the door. She froze momentarily, then, checking her reflection for a final time, she opened the door of Room 231 and there he was, as handsome as his photos, beaming at her.

'Can I come in?' he asked, after a few seconds.

Cara nodded, and stood aside. A flood of unfamiliar emotions surged through her, lighting up her insides. He smiled again and a warmth spread across her skin, burning between her thighs. She saw his lips move but wasn't sure what he was saying. He shut the door, took her face in his hands and tilted it gently upwards. He kissed her, almost imperceptibly on her lips, then her cheeks, and then her eyelids; his lips caressing her skin with a tenderness she hadn't expected. She could feel the back of his fingers stroking her neck and cheek; then he gently tucked her hair behind her ears.

'Hello, Cara,' he breathed in her ear. 'I'm Sam, and I'm very pleased to meet you.'

She opened her eyes. He was still smiling. His features had softened and his eyes glowed. He scooped her up in his arms and carried her to the bed, laying her down. Then he was beside her. Everything was happening so quickly, but somehow it felt right. He propped himself up on his elbow, his free hand stroking her shoulder, nudging the spaghetti straps of her dress down her arm

as he started to kiss the crook of her neck. Up until that point, Cara had been passive, immersed in the wonderful sensations flooding her body. Now she turned towards him, wanting to feel his lips on hers again. He leant in to kiss her, and this time his kisses were harder, and she returned the pressure. Their intensity grew, until their hands were entangled in each other's hair and their faces flowed effortlessly together. It was difficult to remember to breathe and she tore her mouth from his for a second to catch a breath of air before returning to his lips. She didn't want to stop. Her focus was broken momentarily as his hand rested on her belly. It wandered towards her knickers. She inhaled sharply.

'It's alright, Cara. There's no hurry. If you don't like anything I do, touch my shoulder and I'll stop immediately. And don't worry, you have me for the entire evening, so there's no pressure. Although I have to admit I want you so much it hurts.' Cara didn't care if he said this to all his clients. Here, in this room, with his soft hands caressing her, she believed him. As she relaxed, his hand slid her knickers down and started their exploration.

An hour later, they lay quietly, breathing in unison. Cara felt liberated. She looked around the room, a place she had completely forgotten while his flesh had been touching hers. Then she remembered her mother's advice and glanced at the sheets. They were still white and pristine. She breathed out and relaxed. She was at ease here, with Sam by her side. All was right with the world and within herself.

Cara didn't want him to leave, and Sam didn't seem to want to go.

'Are you OK?' he asked, turning to face her.

'I'm better than OK,' she replied, the embers of her desire shining in her eyes. 'Do you mind me asking how you became a Facilitator?' she asked shyly, then added 'because I'm very glad you did,' lest he thought she was judging him.

Sam laughed and stroked her cheek with the back of his

fingers. 'It just happened. I was working in The City, in a job I didn't much like, and one lunch time, a friend of mine confessed he had started to offer his services and was loving it. I knew women liked me and I liked women, so I thought I'd give it a go. That's it.'

'Is it ...' Cara hesitated, her face flushing with embarrassment.

'I think I know what you want to ask. Is it like this with all my clients?'

Cara nodded, staring into his eyes, willing him to give her the answer she wanted to hear. He turned his head away from her and stared up at the ceiling.

'Cara, this isn't bullshit. I think you're the most incredible girl I've ever met. I really want to see you again. Not as a client, but on a date. Could you bear to go out with a man who does what I do for a living?' If Cara could have seen his expression, she would never have doubted his sincerity.

'But you don't know anything about me.' He turned his face back towards hers and met her gaze.

'When you have the kind of connection with someone we have, you know you'll like that person, no matter what you find out about them.' His eyes were devoid of deceit. She stared into them, feeling her longing stir again.

She pushed her desire to one side and considered his statement. Cara wasn't sure it was true and, in any case, she already knew it couldn't work. 'I'm going away to Uni after the summer,' she said quietly.

'Let's make it a summer neither of us will ever forget then, shall we?'

Cara wanted to say yes, but she knew it was pointless; her mother would see to that.

'It's not possible, Sam. You must know that. We need to be realistic.' She hated herself for saying those words. They jarred, here in their own fantastical universe. She tried to stroke his

arm, but he scowled, then rolled over and got up, pulling on his clothes.

'Jesus. You lot have had the romance squeezed from your hearts. I really do feel sorry for you. Anyway, you know where I am if you want to see me again, and your mother's credit card is up to it. By the way, tell her you were disappointed. It will make all our lives easier.'

As he slammed the door behind him, Cara felt wretched. She lay, motionless, staring at the now empty space beside her, noticing the dent on the pillow where his beautiful head had been minutes before. She breathed in his scent and wondered at this new, strange feeling of emptiness that was seeping into her body. Sam had unlocked a secret part of her. A part she knew was inside, but had refused to acknowledge. She really liked him. She wanted to carry on exploring these new emotions. They felt good. Her mind had become one with her body, and every cell had vibrated to the same frequency. She needed to see Sam again. No, she had to see him again, to fill the void in her that he had created. This feeling wasn't emptiness, it was the feeling of being incomplete. She didn't care that he had acted like a jerk when he didn't get what he wanted. He gave her what she wanted. Why couldn't she date him? Life was a bitch.

CHAPTER 37

Kate was on tenterhooks. She tried to look nonchalant as she washed up the breakfast dishes. Cara hadn't come down for breakfast, and she didn't want to wake her. It wasn't every day you paid someone to take your daughter's virginity. She was aching to know how Cara was feeling. Gemma was mooching around the kitchen, getting under her feet.

'Gemma, is your swimming bag ready? Mandy will be here in ten minutes and I don't want to keep her waiting.'

'I packed it last night, Mum. I'm ready to go. Could I have another piece of toast and honey? I'm still hungry, and I'm going to need all my strength today. I'm taking my gold exam.'

Kate had completely forgotten what a big day it was for her younger daughter. 'Oh, Gemma, I'm so sorry. I've been a bit distracted with work over the last few days. Of course, you can.' She popped some bread in the toaster and gave Gemma a hug. 'Do you feel ready for it?'

'I think so. I'm a bit nervous about the life-saving bit. I just hope I don't have to save Sally's life. She's huge. It would be like trying to beach a whale.'

Kate laughed. Gemma was so straightforward and funny.

She was very easy to love. She was about to give Gemma her toast when the doorbell rang.

'Here, take this cloth for your sticky fingers. You'll have to finish it in the car.'

Gemma grabbed her toast and picked up her swimming bag from the coat rack. 'See you in a couple of hours, Mum.'

'See you, my lovely. And best of luck!'

The front door slammed and Kate sat down at the kitchen table to fret in peace.

Cara *must* have heard the door slam. She was surprised she hadn't come down to wish her little sister good luck; she always knew what was going on in Gemma's life. Kate started to wonder whether her daughter had been traumatised by the whole experience and was up in her room, sobbing. She couldn't tolerate the uncertainty any longer.

'Cara!' she shouted. 'Do you want some breakfast?' She heard her daughter get out of bed. She appeared at the top of the stairs in her pyjamas, blue hoodie being pulled over her head.

'Hi, lovely girl. You hungry?' She wanted to ask if everything was alright, to hold her in her arms, but she sensed she needed to tread carefully.

'Morning, Mum. Yeh, some toast and honey would be great. Was Gemma OK?'

They were both politely dancing around one another. She put some bread in the toaster. Then she stopped. Cara was standing, hands shoved into her pockets. She could bear it no longer.

'Dare I ask how it went last night? Are you alright?'

'It was fine, Mum. It wasn't what I expected, although I didn't really know what to expect. You were hardly forthcoming with the pointers.'

Kate winced. 'Oh God, I'm sorry, Cara. I thought you'd know all about the mechanics from school.' Cara looked at her and smiled.

‘I did. But it’s more than mechanics, isn’t it? It’s emotion too.’

‘How did you feel then?’ she asked, perhaps a little too dutifully.

‘Let me ask you how you felt when you were with my father, in the early days, when I assume you loved one another.’

Kate blushed. She hadn’t anticipated discussing her intimate feelings with her daughter, and she could feel Cara’s antagonism growing. She wasn’t sure what was going on.

‘Yes, I guess you’re right. It’s more about feelings than anything else. But it was different for your father and me. We had known each other for a few months before we did anything, so there was already an emotional connection between us.’

‘How nice for you. That’s an impossible scenario for me, isn’t it? I get to see a picture and read a profile on my mobile.’ This time her daughter did not hold back her sarcasm. Cara seemed to deeply resent her previous life as a Chosen One. She bristled. Was Cara attacking the Movement?

‘Cara, this is how things are, and for good reason. I don’t know why we’re arguing. All I wanted to know is whether you’re alright and whether it helped in your Uni choice.’

Cara was raging now. ‘It’s not that simple though, is it, Mum? He was a human being, not a commodity to be used and discarded. He was a lovely human being. I don’t get our way of life sometimes. It seems we’re throwing the good out with the bad.’

‘Cara, you know why we choose to live without men. They have more of a negative influence on a woman’s life than a positive one. And unfortunately, you can’t have your cake and eat it!’ Kate was shouting now. She couldn’t understand where this was coming from. Had Sam not followed her explicit instructions, or was Cara feeling guilty about paying someone to service her needs? She took a deep breath and

calmed herself down. 'I guess that answers both my questions. You'll be going to Brighton, and you're fine. In fact, you're rather taken with men. Or at least this particular one, *and* his performance between the sheets. Well Cara, I suggest you get yourself a summer job, then you can save up for Sam as a "going away to Uni present" to yourself.' Damn, that was a low blow.

'You're wrong, actually. I can already see mixing with men as a Completist is asking for trouble, so I'm going to Chester. Thanks for Sam, he really helped clarify things for me. But I will look for a summer job, as it would be nice not to have to hang around here!' Her daughter stormed out of the kitchen and stomped up the stairs.

Kate slumped in a chair and stared out at the garden. She wished she could explain all the reasons she had joined the Movement, to make her daughter see men for what they really were. She didn't really understand what had just happened. This Sam chap had evidently deviated from her brief.

Her mind wandered back to the evenings with David after they were first married. They had been her favourite times with him. They would chat about this and that, touching fingers, stroking arms. Then, as they laughed at a funny story, or were complicit in their dislike of a work colleague, their mutual stroking became more intimate, their touches more urgent, until they would roll towards one another and kiss: long, hard, deep kisses. He, holding the back of her neck, directing the angle of her head; she, fingers locked in his mass of curly brown hair, willingly arching her neck so his mouth could wander where it chose across the landscape of her face. She had loved those times. As she played out the nights they spent together, her hand meandered towards her thighs, and her fingers lingered between them.

CHAPTER 38

Making a dramatic exit was all very well, but she hadn't even grabbed a piece of toast. She would dress and go to Caroline's house. Her mum would give her breakfast. Cara was like a second daughter to her, and she had a lot to discuss with her best friend.

Cara had met Caroline on the first day of school and they had been inseparable ever since. She had appeared shy at first; but when Cara had got to know her, she discovered a fire-cracker beneath the surface. Few people made the effort, because Caroline was odd looking. Her eyes were too big for her face, and her head was too large for her body. She looked like an emaciated owl. Cara loved her dry sense of humour and her willingness to question everything. She could ask her any question, as long as she was prepared for an honest answer. Caroline was not easily indoctrinated. She would listen, consider and then make up her own mind.

Cara didn't bother to say goodbye to her mother. She was an adult now. She should be able to come and go as she pleased.

Less than 20 minutes later, she was sitting in front of a plate of toast and marmalade, with a hot mug of tea. 'Thank

you, Suzanne,' she said, giving Caroline's mum a beaming smile. 'This looks delicious. The toast is exactly how I like it.'

'I know, Cara. I've been making you toast for quite a while now! I'm going to get on with the housework. I'll leave you girls to catch up.'

Caroline pounced on Cara the minute her mum had shut the kitchen door. 'So, old friend, what's it like to be a *real* woman? Feel different now you've had a bit of *real* man inside you?'

'You know I don't believe fucking makes you a real woman, Caroline. Don't be a dick.'

'Nice choice of insult! Come on, spill the beans. I can see the truth flickering behind those not so innocent eyes.'

Cara looked at Caroline. Could she trust her? This was a big one. Caroline might be open-minded, but she was a true Completist. She had looked at all the evidence independently and was not a fan of 'the penised ones', as she liked to call men. 'All I'm prepared to say is, I think you should try it. You might be surprised. It's much more than you would expect.'

'I take it Madame was entirely satisfied by the service, or should I say "servicing" she received.'

'Don't say it like that. It's not like that. It's not a cold thing. You feel emotions you've never experienced before, and they're good emotions.'

'I've heard of this syndrome, Cara. It's called SPD, Sexocentric Personality Disorder. It's more common in Completists than people let on. Some Completists use Facilitators twice a week or more, if their salary allows. These women seem to be addicted to whatever these emotions are. They can't get enough. The powerful ones consider it a real threat to the Movement. They've even set up support groups to see if they can help them overcome their addiction. Perhaps you should go to one. You know, nip it in the bud.' Cara expected her friend to follow her statement with laughter, or at the very least, a wry smile; but she was deadly serious.

‘Are you kidding me, Caroline? What’s actually wrong with having a positive emotional response to sex?’

‘Am *I* kidding! I can’t believe what you’re saying. The romanticisation of sex is the single biggest factor, after economics, that contributes to the enslavement of women by men. That’s one of the founding beliefs of the Movement! You know this; or has sex already addled your brain?’

‘Jesus, Caroline. Maybe you’re right. But this morning you feel wrong, everything feels wrong.’ She picked up a slice of toast and took a bite. It stuck in her throat. She grabbed her tea and tried to swill it down.

CHAPTER 39

Emmeline slapped her alarm off and moaned. At least her stomach wasn't hurting. She checked her night pad and breathed a sigh of relief. It was over for another month. She hated being on her period. It was messy and inconvenient, and she had already decided she would never have children, so what was the point. Emmeline got dressed and wandered down to the kitchen. Her mother was pottering around, as usual, waiting to feed her family, as and when they each made an entrance.

'Is it possible to have my womb removed?' she asked breezily, as she reached for the kettle. Her mother laughed at her.

'No doctor is going to perform a hysterectomy on a healthy 17-year-old woman, Emmeline. How you feel about having children may change dramatically once you've fallen in love and settled down.' Emmeline raised her eyes to the sky in exasperation, offering up a silent prayer to give her the patience to deal with the annoying woman in front of her.

'Mother dearest, I have no interest in men. So, falling in love with one is going to be a little tricky, isn't it? Anyway, I'm 18 soon, so I'll be making my own decisions about my body

and shall be seeking out a doctor to perform the operation.' She stared at her mother defiantly, kettle poised under the tap.

'Emmeline, drop the attitude. What are you trying to tell me? Do you prefer women?' Emmeline snorted with laughter.

'No Mum. Just because you don't want to have sex with a man, doesn't mean you want to have sex with a woman. Jesus, its 2133, Mother. Some women want to get on with their jobs, using their free time to do other things they enjoy, instead of caring for husbands and children. Some women find this to be a fulfilling life. Imagine that, Mother. A fulfilling life.'

'I wish I had recorded this conversation. I would love to play it back to you on your wedding day.'

Emmeline sighed, went over to her mum and gave her a hug. 'You and Dad are complete dinosaurs, but you're my dinosaurs. And I do love you, not so much Dad, but I do love *you*.'

Her mother laughed and gave her daughter a squeeze. 'You're a funny one, Trouble. But you're my funny one. I love you too.'

'On that joyous note of family harmony, is it OK if I go and meet Tess? We're going to study together. After we've made out, of course.' She winked at her mother who raised her eyebrows and shook her head in despair.

'What time will you be back?'

'What time will you have prepared the family dinner, my little domestic goddess?'

'We'll eat at seven.'

'Then I shall see you at 6.55 p.m. Toodle pip, or whatever it is you dinosaurs use as a cheery goodbye.'

Emmeline slung her school rucksack over her shoulder and headed towards Tess's house. She adored Tess. She was pretty much the only other girl in her year who didn't sit around discussing future wedding plans, make-up or boys. Tess wanted to be a doctor and go abroad to help children in poverty. Emmeline admired her ambition, despite the children

bit. Emmeline had decided on a career as an engineer. She wanted to design and build things. She wasn't entirely sure what things, but preferably big things, things that got things done. They both had their sights set on Cambridge, and were library buddies; hiding away from the pretty gigglers who were banking on rich men to pay their bills. Emmeline was under particular pressure because she had chosen to pursue English, as well as the obligatory maths and physics. She needed top grades in the latter two, to convince Cambridge she was an engineer, not a frustrated poet.

She knocked on Tess's front door. The door opened, revealing her friend, looking sad and saggy in her pyjamas.

'I'm so sorry, Emms,' she said. 'I've thrown up three times already, so you're on your own. I would have sent you a message to let you know, but I was too busy watching my guts coming out of my mouth.'

'OK, Tess, enough details, I get the picture. Sorry, you're feeling shit. Hope to see you Monday. If not, let me know if there's any work you need picking up from your teachers and I'll bring it over. But only if you promise not to vomit on me.'

'Thanks, Emms. Now I would get going if I were you, otherwise I might be adding to your delightful outfit, and not in a good way.'

'I'm gone,' Emmeline said, backing away from her friend. 'This is me going. Catch you later, you disgusting specimen of humanity.' She turned her back on her friend, raised her arm in farewell and headed for the school library.

The library was quiet; it was Saturday, and most of her peers were out, doing whatever it was that normal 17-year-olds do on a cold weekend in January. She stood searching for a quiet corner. As she walked towards a vacant desk, she saw her English teacher browsing the bookshelves. He was a tall heavily built man. He'd probably played rugby in his younger, fitter years. There was still some muscle tone, but his waistline had softened with the start of a beer belly. Emmeline wasn't

sure about Mr Edwards. There was no doubt he was a great teacher, and he did have an easy charm; nevertheless, there was something off about him that Emmeline couldn't pinpoint. She gave him the benefit of the doubt as he was always very attentive and helpful, and willingly gave up his free time to go through her essays with her or discuss any issues she was having with the texts they were studying, but he was no Mr Brown. He glanced her way and gave her a warm smile. Emmeline smiled back and dropped her rucksack on the desk, settling down to a spot of quantum physics, a subject she found particularly challenging, given her predisposition to all things large.

After about half an hour she sensed someone approaching. She raised her head. Mr Edwards was standing in front of the desk, smiling down at her, his dishevelled jumper and jeans blurring the usual line between student and teacher.

'I'm sorry to disturb your studies, Emmeline. But I was about to have a coffee break and wondered if you would care to join me?'

'The canteen isn't open on a Saturday, Mr Edwards. And I seriously wouldn't recommend the vending machine's attempt at a latte.' Mr Edwards laughed.

'I know, Emmeline. I tried it once and never again. No, I was going to suggest my study. I have a coffee machine hidden away in the corner. It's the only reason I'm so popular with the other teachers! We could discuss the latest assignment if it would make you feel less guilty about taking a little time to share a hot drink.'

His last comment was a little slippery, but she actually did have a question about the assignment he had set; so, she wouldn't entirely be wasting her time.

'Deal, I will steal your coffee *and* your expertise. Sounds like a splendidly one-sided bargain to me.'

Mr Edwards laughed again and led the way. She had never been to his study before, or any other study. The teachers

tended to regard them as sacred student-free areas, preferring to hold any one-on-ones in the many private study rooms dotted around the school. She was curious to see what it was like, to get some further clues as to the inner workings of Mr Edward's mind.

When he opened the door, she saw a cliché. Beaten up brown leather armchairs, frayed cushions, and wall-to-wall shelving stacked with books. He even had essays stacked in uneven piles, surrounding the edges of his desk like dilapidated Roman ramparts. The only surprise was the smell of stale smoke and the overflowing ashtray on his desk. Mr Edwards didn't look like a smoker and she had never smelt cigarettes on him.

'Please, take a pew,' he said, gesturing to one of the shabby chairs. I see you've noted my filthy habit. You don't smoke do you?'

'I don't. My father does, so it doesn't bother me. And I know how you nicotine addicts like to top yourself up when caffeine is involved.'

'Why thank you, Emmeline, don't mind if I do.' He handed her a coffee mug and perched on the edge of his desk, taking a sip of his coffee and lighting a cigarette.

'So, what can I help you with?'

'I was wondering whether you were after a full character analysis of Catherine, or whether we should focus more on the plot arc to demonstrate why she falls for Alex. Although frankly, I can't see his attraction.'

'Goodness. What's wrong with Alex? Is it the age difference which bothers you?' Mr Edwards shifted his body.

'No, it's not that. I understand why some younger women are attracted to older men. It's his arrogance. He really thinks he's something special, and she doesn't seem to mind his self-indulgent eulogising.'

'That's certainly one interpretation. May I ask you a question?' Mr Edwards shifted his body again.

Emmeline studied him, waiting.

'Do *you* find older men more attractive than younger men? Forgive my prying, but I have never seen you hanging around with any of the boys in your class.'

Emmeline started to feel uncomfortable. Jeans and a baggy jumper were one thing, but prying into a student's sexual preferences was definitely more than blurring the line between student and teacher, it was erasing it.

'I'm too focussed on my studies to waste time on flirting, Mr Edwards.'

'I would have to disagree with you there, Emmeline. You flirt with me.'

Emmeline was horrified. 'I wasn't aware I was flirting with you. I was merely passing the time of day.'

'Oh, come on. You're here, alone with me now, aren't you? I've seen the way you study me sometimes. Are you wondering what it would be like to kiss me, to feel my hands caressing your body?'

Emmeline couldn't find any of her words. How could he have misread her so fundamentally? Mr Edwards apparently took her hesitation as confirmation his assumptions were correct. Before she could utter a sound, he had her head in his hands and was kissing her. His lips pressed hard against hers, his tongue trying to part them, to explore her mouth.

She pushed him off, the armchair scraping across the wooden floor, as she attempted to create some distance between them.

He stood up straight, advancing towards her.

'Don't be a tease. You know you want this, so relax and let it happen. I promise I'll make you feel amazing.'

Emmeline tried to get up from the armchair, but he was on her, pushing her back. He gripped her hair, arching her neck towards his mouth, wet lips kissing her taut skin; his knee pinning her thigh against the worn leather. Raising her arms, she pushed at his body and pain shot through her as he twisted

her hair, wrenching it from her scalp, until every follicle was screaming in protest. She was overwhelmed with panic. He's ripping my hair out. I can't breathe, I can't move. Then his other hand pushed up inside her T-shirt, yanking her bra down to paw at her breast. 'Please stop, I don't want this.' Her words choked her as they battled against her strained vocal cords, his grunts drowning out her pleas. In one movement he pulled her out of the armchair and onto the floor, a ragdoll being slammed against the hard wood.

'That's better, now I've got you where I want you. That's it, open those legs a little wider. There. Oh my God, you feel delicious.' He was touching the flesh beneath her knickers. His fingers entered her and he moaned. 'You're wet, I knew you wanted me. Now stop struggling and let me take you.'

Emmeline was crying now. How could her body have betrayed her like this?

She let herself go limp and, thinking he had won the battle, Mr Edwards removed his hand from her hair and crouched over her, looking down into her face. 'That's better, now we can really have some fun.'

Emmeline took her chance and raised her knee up with all her might, pushing him off her as soon as her knee had reached its target. He rolled over, groaning, clutching his crotch. She was up and out of the door, yanking her torn tights up as she ran.

She didn't stop running until she was outside her own front door. All she could think of was being in her mother's arms. She had left her rucksack by her chair in the library, so she didn't have her keys. She rang the doorbell over and over again, thumping her fist against the wood. She could hear her mother's footsteps as she scurried up the hall. When the door opened Emmeline launched herself at her, and the tears and anguish she had been holding in since she left Mr Edwards' study spewed out of her in powerful, wrenching sobs. Her mother wrapped her body around her daughter's and held her.

When Emmeline had stopped heaving out her pain, her sobs replaced by jagged breaths; her mother held her snotty, wet face at arm's length, looked into her eyes and asked, 'What happened to you, Emmeline?'

'It was Mr Edwards,' she stuttered, 'my English Teacher. He invited me into his study for a coffee, then he attacked me.' Emmeline couldn't take her eyes off her mother's.

'Did he hurt you badly, Emmeline?'

'Oh, Mum, it was awful. He put his fingers inside me...' Emmeline started to sob again, but her mother continued.

'Emmeline, did he rape you?' Emmeline saw the fear in her eyes.

'No. I managed to fight him off by pretending I was giving in.' Her mother released her face and gathered her back into her arms.

'My poor baby. My poor, sweet, baby girl,' and she rocked her daughter as if she was five again and had fallen over and bloodied her knee.

When Emmeline had calmed down, her mother sat her at the kitchen table with a hot, sweet tea.

'I'm calling the police now, Emmeline. That bastard is going to end up rotting in jail for this, career and life over.'

Emmeline didn't argue. Mr Edwards was scum. She had sensed it, a faint odour which made the air grow stale in her nostrils. She should have trusted her instincts.

Emmeline never saw Mr Edwards again. She was determined to put him behind her. She tried as hard as she could to concentrate on her studies, keeping a tight hold of her dream of attending Cambridge with her best friend.

CHAPTER 40

Sophie was worried. She wondered whether she should broach the subject of a therapist for the hundredth time with her daughter. She reached for the salt and absent-mindedly added a pinch to the vegetable stew she was making. Since Emmeline had received her exam results, and realised she wasn't going with Tess to Cambridge, she had gone downhill. Sophie had thought she might cheer up when Imperial College confirmed their offer, but Emmeline continued to stay in her room, barely eating or speaking to anyone.

Peter was going to be absent, again. He had sent her a message saying he was going to have to work late. It happened so often these days, she barely batted an eyelid. She skewered a potato to see if it was done then shouted up the stairs.

'Emmeline, it's teatime!' Charlie was already at the table raring to go, as she placed a mountain of food in front of him.

'I'm not hungry!' Emmeline shouted from her bedroom.

'Charlie, do you mind if I leave you to eat alone for a moment? I need to go upstairs and speak to your sister.' Charlie raised his eyebrows, but smiled at his mum as he lifted his knife and fork to get stuck in.

Sophie knocked on Emmeline's bedroom door.

'Can I come in?'

'If you must.'

She was lying on her bed, reading as usual.

'You know I love you, right?' she began. Emmeline eyed her suspiciously, not gracing her question with a response. Sophie ignored her silence and continued. 'When a person loves someone, they care about their wellbeing, they worry about them.' Again, Emmeline's expression remained taciturn. Sophie sighed.

'I'm really worried about you, Emmeline. You haven't been yourself for the entire summer. And since the exam results, you've disappeared inside yourself. I mean you haven't been cheeky to me for weeks!' Sophie smiled at her daughter and patted her shin. Emmeline had not moved when she came in, leaving Sophie to perch awkwardly on the end of her bed. She looked at her daughter, and Emmeline stared at her. So, this was to become a battle of wills, was it? Sophie wished she could have had this conversation with Peter around the kitchen table; but as he was hardly here these days, she was obliged to tackle her daughter alone. Charlie saw more of him than she did. He spent every Saturday with him down at the local football club, while Peter trained the under-16s.

Sophie realised this was likely to go on for a while; her daughter was a stubborn as she was. She would have to play her ace, something she kept in reserve for the seminal moments of her life. Sophie was surprised how easily her tears came; what had started as a strategy soon became a genuine release of the fear simmering inside her.

She saw her daughter staring at her in horror. Emmeline had only ever seen her cry once before, after the assault. Within seconds she had wrapped her arms around her.

'Mum, please don't. I'll see a therapist if you want me to.' She gently pushed her mother away, holding her at arm's length. She looked into her eyes, demanding an acknowledge-

ment of her offer; but Sophie could no longer speak. Her sobs got louder as she nodded at her daughter like a child. Emmeline pulled her close once more and gently rocked her to and fro until her sobs subsided; then reached over to her bedside table and handed her a tissue. Sophie blew her nose, and Emmeline reached for another. She wiped her eyes and gave her daughter a weak smile.

'I'm sorry, love. I hadn't realised how worried I was. How sad your sadness makes me.'

'Don't be silly, Mum. It's made me realise this impacts the whole family...' she paused as Charlie shouted up the stairs that he had finished his tea and was off to play football with one of his mates. Then she smiled mischievously for the first time in months. 'Actually, that's a lie, it doesn't seem to be impacting Charlie at all!' They both laughed.

'Like father, like son!' Sophie said, shaking her head, and laughing again.

'Come on,' said Emmeline. 'Now we have the house to ourselves, let's go downstairs and have some tea together. I'm starving.'

CHAPTER 41

Emmeline had chosen the only female therapist who didn't look like one. She had scrolled through the options, glancing at faces who stared sympathetically back at her, making her want to slap them hard. Francesca Roberts looked like she should be in a boardroom, not in an armchair opposite some nutter. Her expression told Emmeline she didn't take any shit and, when she rang to arrange an appointment, her voice confirmed that impression.

Emmeline had found the place easily enough. Her mother had offered to accompany her, but she wanted to do this by herself. She pressed the buzzer of the smart townhouse, standing shoulder to shoulder with the other houses, like sentries, endlessly guarding their private square of trees and grass. The door lock released, and she let herself in. Sitting in the artfully designed waiting area, Emmeline hoped she had made the right choice. This was costing her parents a month's worth of take-aways, so she was obliged to give it a shot.

She searched for the source of the weird noise, it sounded like wind blowing through trees. It was coming from a small speaker on the bookcase behind her. She wondered whether its purpose was to stop her from hearing any of the conversation

which was being held behind the door facing her. If it was, then Francesca's money had been well spent. Occasionally she could hear muffled snippets of conversation, but none of the words were actually recognisable.

After a few minutes the door opened, and a bespectacled young man emerged. He stared at the floor as he exited, avoiding eye contact. Then Francesca came out. She was wearing smart, flared dark grey trousers, and a round-necked, light grey, silk blouse. Her hair was tied up in a loose bun, a few ringlets artfully teased out, softly caressing her defined cheekbones. Her appearance was effortlessly elegant. Emmeline was impressed.

'Please come in, Emmeline,' she said, her voice calm but commanding.

How could she possibly refuse? She stood up and stepped into the room. She surveyed her surroundings. The room was calm and welcoming. There were two soft cream armchairs, gathered around a low, bleached wooden table which proffered the obligatory box of tissues. It was housed in a cream silk-covered box which complemented the fabric of the armchairs. A console, to the side of Francesca's armchair, offered rows of designer water, labels facing forwards, with plain glass tumblers arranged neatly in front of them.

'Would you like some water?' Francesca asked matter-of-factly.

'Yes please...' she replied, unsure as to whether she should address this creature as Francesca or Mrs Roberts.

'Please call me Francesca,' she said, smiling at her.

'Yes please, Francesca,' Emmeline said, smiling back.

Francesca placed a glass and a bottle of water in front of each of them and settled down in her chair, placing her black leather-bound notebook on her lap. It had a smart pen attached to it, housed in a leather loop.

'Firstly, I'd like to explain how I conduct my sessions, as not everyone has the same approach. I adhere to the Mirror

Method of therapy which started to gain popularity in 2025. The practice is based on sessions being a conversation, although the views and opinions I express will be selected on the basis of your beliefs. The aim is to help you decide who you really are, by reflecting your beliefs back at you, in order to identify any areas causing anxiety or concern. Once these have been identified, we can then work on strategies and solutions to address them. The ultimate objective is for you to emerge at the end of the therapy, knowing who you are and what you stand for. Also, to have the insight to recognise triggers which could tap into any areas of weakness, so you can minimise any damage those triggers might have, if left unchecked.' Francesca was watching Emmeline closely as she spoke, apparently looking for signs that she was following what she was saying. She appeared satisfied and continued.

'It was an approach which evolved in response to the needs of the first generation who grew up during the early days of the social media explosion. They became adults who didn't know who they were, as their focus was to be liked and approved of in the digital world, not the real one. Their key fear was being judged by others and they crumpled beneath that judgment, as they didn't know how to defend themselves. Firstly, because their beliefs were often based on whichever online groups they had joined. And, secondly, because this generation learnt not to stand out from the crowd. They were exposed to relentless criticism if they expressed a single opinion which displeased those they shared their digital lives with. They adopted popular beliefs, stuck within the groups which supported those beliefs, and were automatically and unthinkingly against anyone who challenged their group's view. Mental health and suicides rose to unprecedented levels among this generation, who became known as the "Lost Boys".'

'After the Lost Boys in *Peter Pan*?'

'Exactly, Emmeline. Do you enjoy reading the classics?'

‘I do, reading is my raison d'être, Francesca.’

‘Why?’ Francesca asked, seeming genuinely interested.

‘Why inhabit one world when you can explore hundreds of others?’

‘Why be one person, when you can be anyone you want to be?’ Francesca added, raising an eyebrow in query.

‘Maybe that too. But it’s more about being limitless rather than limited. I don’t enjoy boundaries, either physical or metaphysical.’

Francesca smiled. ‘Could you explain in a little more detail, Emmeline?’

‘Children are limited due to their age, inexperience and economic dependence. Women, and men, are limited due to their sex, their gender, their circumstances, and access to natural resources. And so, it goes on. Restraints abound. We’re all living in narrow lanes defined by the social constructs and the natural resources of our particular area of the globe. Pretty tedious if you ask me.’

‘You appear to have given this considerable thought.’

‘It doesn’t strike me as a matter of considerable thought, more a matter of keeping your eyes and mind open to the world around you.’

‘What about restraints which are imposed on you by an individual?’

Emmeline looked at Francesca and smiled. How to get to the nub of any deep-seated anxiety: step back from the global view and examine the minutiae of a person’s life. She shifted in her chair and reached for her water.

‘Can anyone impose a restraint on you that you choose not to acknowledge?’ Emmeline asked Francesca.

‘It depends how honest that choice is, doesn’t it?’ Francesca replied.

‘What do you mean?’ Emmeline watched her intently.

‘I mean, we can make a logical choice not to be restrained, but still be restrained on an emotional level. If that restraint

threatens something we only know subconsciously, we may not even be aware of why we still feel at odds with the logical choice we've made. The subconscious is where our secrets live, secrets which make us vulnerable in the conscious world. But we still know they're there. Even if we're too frightened to bring them out into the light to examine them, know them and neutralise the threats they pose.'

So, is this the real aim of these sessions, to neutralise those dark hidden secrets that lurk in the subconscious.'

'That depends on whether you have any, Emmeline.'

'Oh, Francesca. I think we both know I do.'

'Then, with your permission, I'd like to help you.'

'I'll think about it and let you know next time. Some secrets are best left as secrets, don't you think?'

'Alcoholics Anonymous, whom I'm assuming you're aware of, have a saying: "You're only as sick as your secrets". But it's a big topic. Let's revisit it in the next session, and you can tell me your answer. For the rest of our time, I'd like to ask you some questions about your life to date. Is that alright?'

'Fire away. But I'm not sure it'll take long. It's been a relatively unremarkable one.' Emmeline settled back in her chair.

'What is your earliest memory, Emmeline?'

She had never been asked this question, and it took her by surprise. She started sifting through past events, rapidly sorting them into chronological order. 'I'm not sure whether this is the earliest thing I can remember, without spending more time thinking about it, but it's certainly the memory that pops into my head.' Francesca nodded at her, encouraging her to go ahead. 'I remember my mother telling me I was going to have a baby brother or sister and holding my hand on her stomach. I didn't understand what her stomach had to do with anything, so I remember her having to explain about babies growing inside a mother's body until they were ready to come out. What I remember most is the feeling of horror about having been inside my mother. I remember being quite

upset and my mother giving me a hug and laughing at my reaction. But I also remember sensing her disappointment. I'm not sure she knew how to handle it. I think she hoped it would be a Disney moment. Her little girl feeling her sibling kicking and moving and looking up in wonder into her eyes, excited to meet the new life within.' Emmeline raised her eyebrows and rolled her eyes as she spoke the last sentence.

'You're obviously not a fan of Disney!' Francesca laughed.

'I'm not a fan of sugar-coated sentimentality. It encourages unrealistic expectations, fostering disappointment.'

'Would you say you were disappointed or enchanted by your life thus far?'

Emmeline paused. She resented the pertinent question. She resented being drawn back to something she was in the process of burying. She was not ready.

'I'd have to say enchanted to that one, Francesca. Overall, my life has been a blessed one.' They both knew she was lying, but Francesca merely made a note on her pad and segued seamlessly into her next question.

'How would you describe your brother, Charlie?'

Emmeline smiled to herself. 'The human equivalent of a wasp. Persistently annoying, seemingly pointless, and something you can never seem to bat away, no matter how hard you try.'

'So, you would say you have a close relationship?'

They both laughed. Emmeline was warming to this woman.

'I just don't *get* him, or my father. At least my father helps to pay for things. But the pair of them seem to be parasites, feeding off my mother. And there's no symbiosis. As far as I can see she gets very little back from these relationships.'

'You seem a little angry.'

'I am. Because, growing up, I was always responsible for my mother's wellbeing. Always having to think about her, her needs, her feelings. And I really resent it. I was constantly

having to mitigate their destruction!' Emmeline started to cry tears of frustration and she snatched at a tissue and wiped her eyes. 'Shit, I wasn't expecting that.' She laughed awkwardly, searching Francesca's face for a reaction to her outburst.

'I think we may have unearthed one of those secrets. It's always an overwhelming feeling when it happens.' She smiled tenderly at her. Emmeline blew her nose.

Francesca continued to explore Emmeline's childhood, teasing out her recollections with delicate, well-placed questions. Emmeline was surprised when Francesca called time.

'Will I see you next week?' she asked.

Emmeline nodded, taking another tissue to replace the sodden one she was still holding. Francesca stood up and walked towards the door. Emmeline found herself mimicking the client before her, bowing her head as she left the room and hoping the weird noise machine was still working.

CHAPTER 42

Francesca beckoned Emmeline to sit down. She gestured to the console behind her and Emmeline nodded and she handed her a bottle of water and a glass.

'Emmeline, last week, you said you'd think about whether to allow me to help you uncover the secrets which inhabit your subconscious and potentially limit your conscious life. Have you made a decision?'

'I have. I'd like to give it a shot. After all, I'm at liberty to stop the sessions whenever I choose, so it's hardly a big commitment, is it?'

'That's, of course, correct. But I would be reluctant to dedicate my time and effort to someone who wasn't willing to put the work in themselves. Self-discovery is not an easy path. As I said last time we met, we keep certain things hidden inside ourselves because we believe they threaten our very survival. In order to know ourselves, we must not only face our secrets, but we must also relook at our world. Are our secrets threats because we live in an unhealthy world which doesn't nurture us? Sometimes, we don't need to change the secrets, we need

to change our world. This is no easy task and it can only be done if we are committed to going through the, often painful, process of making fundamental changes to either our secrets or our world, or indeed both. A person needs to be committed to even have a chance of achieving this.'

'I hadn't adjudicated for the fact you might care deeply about the outcomes for your clients. I thought, obviously unfairly, that your motivation might be financial.'

Francesca laughed. 'I love your honesty, Emmeline, so let me be honest with you. My financial success stems from my sincere desire to help my clients. I appear to be quite good at my job and the lovely repercussions are the material things you see around you. Plus, I get a warm fuzzy feeling inside.' She smiled playfully. 'It's win, win. Another big plus for me is that my success means I have a waiting list. So, if I don't think someone shares my commitment to achieving a good outcome, I can politely show them the door.' Francesca smiled at Emmeline, apparently waiting to be convinced of her desire to work with her.

Emmeline's mind was racing. This was too frightening, too intense, too hard. Her mind was a sinkhole filled with the rubbish of her life. Could she drag it all out into the fresh air?

'I'm not sure you should waste your time on me. I'm fine and I'm functioning, and my parents can't really afford this self-indulgence. Let's call it a day.'

Francesca stood up. 'No problem. But I do hope you're not letting your fear of what you might uncover affect your judgement. I get the sense I'm dealing with a very courageous, intelligent young woman, and I think you'll be able to handle the journey. However, I respect your decision, and you know where I am if you change your mind. You won't go to the bottom of the waiting list. I'll make something work.' She put out her right hand and Emmeline shook it.

Leaving the room, she noticed the empty seat by the book-

case. She hurried to the front door and opened it. Emmeline saw a woman, looking straight ahead, head held high, followed by two young girls holding hands. She burst into tears.

CHAPTER 43

Sophie drew the car up outside Emmeline's digs in Brixton. It was the final week of her daughter's first year at Imperial College, but today marked the end of her university career. Emmeline had been called by the Head of the Faculty of Mechanical Engineering yesterday, who had told her she would not be allowed to continue her studies due to her poor attendance at lectures. His voice had been laden with regret. He had made it abundantly clear that the decision had not been taken lightly and only after the several warnings he had given her, had gone unheeded.

Sophie was nervous. Over this last year, her daughter had become a virtual stranger. Since the divorce, she had barely stepped across the threshold of Sophie's new home, preferring to stay in Brixton for the holidays. Sophie was finding it hard to deal with. It was bad enough being an 'Outsider' without being rejected by the one person who had always had her back since Kate had walked out of her life.

She called Emmeline to let her know she was outside and waited, constantly checking her rear-view mirror, hoping she would be able to stay in the one parking space allocated to the house which had miraculously been vacant. The gentrification

of Brixton, which had started over a century ago, was now complete; in fact, the area was going downhill again. Sophie considered the renovated houses and flats which surrounded her. Some had pretty front gardens, but others were clearly owned by people whose idea of gardening was buying a house plant. Emmeline's house belonged in the latter group. The windows were in need of a repaint and she noticed the front door had some dents in it, perhaps inflicted after being purposefully closed on someone who had wanted it to remain open.

Emmeline wasn't living in the best part of Brixton, but it was all her daughter could afford. One small, rented room in a house converted into eight bedrooms, three shared bathrooms, and a communal kitchen and lounge. Sophie was not anxious to re-enter the house after seeing the state of the kitchen when Emmeline moved in. She was pretty sure her daughter would become ill within weeks. The place needed drenching in disinfectant. She checked her watch and the rear-view mirror for the umpteenth time, tapping her hand on the steering wheel, as she waited impatiently for her daughter to emerge. She had warned her last night she would be arriving at the crack of dawn. She didn't like driving around London, and she wanted to avoid the extortionate entry fees they charged all private vehicle owners who came into the city after 9.00 a.m. London traffic was practically non-existent now, apart from the silent electric buses, the licenced taxi firms and the chauffeur-driven cars of the very rich or the country's politicians, most of whom fell into both categories.

The front door opened and Emmeline staggered out, with one huge rucksack on her back and dragging an enormous suitcase. Sophie leapt out of the car.

'Let me help you with those,' she said as she approached her daughter, who looked awful. Her face had several angry spots on it, and the bags under her watery eyes seemed as large as the suitcase she was dragging behind her.

'Don't worry, Mum. I've got it. Just open the boot.'

Sophie did what she was told and helped her daughter lift her luggage into the car. They both got in and fastened their seatbelts in silence. Sophie turned on the engine. She glanced at her daughter and squeezed her leg. 'Are you alright?'

'I'm fine, Mum. Please, let's get out of here.' Emmeline tried to give her a reassuring smile, but Sophie saw a crushed spirit and her heart ached for her daughter.

They were home in under an hour. She helped Emmeline lift her luggage out of the boot, then went to unlock her tiny house. Despite the fresh lemon paint on the windowless walls of the hallway, chosen specifically to raise the spirits, Sophie wanted to cry. She turned left into the open plan room that served as her kitchen, dining room and lounge, and moved towards the kettle.

Emmeline came up behind her and looked around. 'I like what you've done with the place, Mum. It looks cheerful, but cosy. Much better than when I was last here.'

'Thanks. Do you want a cup of tea and some breakfast?' She turned to look at her daughter. Their eyes met, then they stepped towards one another and hugged. Neither wanted to let the other go. After a few minutes, they both relaxed their arms and stepped back from one another. Sophie laughed at her daughter's tears through her own, and reached for a tissue, handing a second one to Emmeline.

'What a pair, eh, Mum? How the hell did it come to this?'

A few minutes later they were sitting at Sophie's tiny kitchen table, munching toast and marmalade and slurping their tea.

'Have you seen or heard anything from Dad or Charlie?' Emmeline asked her gently.

'Nope, nothing. Once the final settlement was in my bank account, that was it. I don't even know where they're living now. You do know Outsiders aren't allowed to make contact with their spouses or male children after they're divorced,

don't you? I have to wait for them to make contact with me. There's no way of tracking them down, unless you hire a Private Investigator, and their rates are extortionate.'

'I didn't realise. I'm so sorry, Mum. You obviously considered contacting them then? I would be allowed to see them, wouldn't I? Why didn't you ask me for help?'

'Oh, Emmeline, I assumed you'd know about all this. You used to be so clued up on this kind of stuff. If a woman instigates a divorce from her husband, she's automatically responsible for any daughters and the father gets custody of any sons. I may as well have joined the sodding Completists. You're treated in the same way. It's pretty disgusting. I would never join that Movement, turn my back on my whole way of life, but there you are. I'm no longer eligible for any state benefits, including healthcare, and I lost my job. And *you* never get to see your father or brother again, unless they choose to contact you. I guess that's why we're called "Outsiders"!' Sophie laughed dryly.

'Shit, that's harsh. So, your entire society choose to turn their back on you. Even when you're not turning your back on them?'

'Our society, Emmeline. And, yes. Their view is, if you're not completely with us, you're against us. At least they still allow daughters of divorced parents access to state benefits. I guess they don't want to encourage you to join the dark side.'

'But this is bollocks! You're not turning your back on the way the COs live; you were just unhappy in your marriage.'

'You're preaching to the converted, my love. The only way I get back in is to remarry. But the idea of dating again is too much for me at the moment. Mind you, I've been inundated with offers! There are plenty of men of my age out there who've never managed to find a wife. Remember, it was your grandmother's generation who were the first to leave their husbands, taking their daughters with them and leaving behind their sons. By the time their sons were old enough to

marry, there weren't enough eligible women. Your father was lucky to get me. You would have thought he would have worked harder to keep me.'

Her daughter seemed to be struggling to make sense of what she was saying.

'So, basically, the government have arranged things to pressurise you into remarrying, if you want to re-join society?'

'Rather like the Completists force women to abandon their sons if they want to be part of the Movement. At least we have equality in this respect. Both factions present women with difficult choices.'

'Seems like a shitty equality to me.' Emmeline said, as she got up to make some more toast. Sophie watched her slim frame walk across the room. Her daughter appeared frail, weakened. When had she last eaten a decent meal?

'You're taking the fact that you're potentially never going to see your father or brother again very much in your stride, Emmeline. Especially considering you've only just found out!' Her mother laughed.

Emmeline turned to look at her, the butter knife loosely waving in the air, like a drunk trying to wield a sword.

'Is it really surprising, Mum? Charlie and I tolerated one another, and that was on a good day. As far as my darling father is concerned, he wasn't interested in me, he was too engrossed in his little man. Dad's inability to cope with anyone's emotions, other than his own, is legendary. I've never met a man less capable of seeing what a selfish little cunt he is, and that's saying something. I'm assuming this was the underlying reason you finally jumped ship. Am I right?' Emmeline turned her back to spread the butter on her toast; and somehow, the distance this gesture created, enabled Sophie to talk freely.

'I was 23 when I married your father. It was difficult at home. My father had died when I was 15 and his death aged

my mother. She became set in her ways. When your father came along, I'd had enough.'

'But if women were in short supply, you must have had other offers, so why him?' Emmeline asked, continuing to prepare her toast.

'Your father was a very handsome man. He was captain of his football team, and all his friends loved him. It's very flattering to be pursued by a man who's the centre of everyone's attention, at least down the football club. Your father wasn't only a good player on the football pitch, you know. He had quite a few girlfriends before me, which also raised his standing among his mates. He had actually gone out with numerous women and cast them aside. Quite the cocky Casanova. He made me feel truly desired. And I've always had a thing for the bad lads.' Emmeline had quietly sat back down at the kitchen table. Sophie could tell she was trying to be nonchalant, but she knew her daughter well enough to see she was listening intently.

'So, I get why you said "yes" to his proposal. But what was it that finally made you say enough was enough?'

'I discovered he was a narcissistic, selfish, little cunt, like you said earlier!' They both laughed. Sophie hadn't used those particular facial muscles for months, and watching Emmeline's face light up filled her with joy.

'Oh, Emmeline,' Sophie said as the final gusts of their mirth ebbed away, 'it's so good to see you again, to talk. I thought I might have lost you for good at one point. I get the feeling things have been far from easy for you at Imperial, but you never opened up to me...' Emmeline interrupted her, her good humour appearing to take a rapid nosedive.

'Mum, how could I open up to you? You were neck deep in your own shit. You didn't have time to wade through mine.'

'I'm so sorry, Emmeline. You're right. You've been on your own this last year. I know I've let you down. I think I was lulled into a false sense of security when you decided you

didn't need therapy. But I didn't bother asking why you made that decision because I was too busy coping with the breakdown of my marriage. I sent you off to Imperial, hoping everything was going to be alright, but it hasn't been, has it, love?'

She slid her hand over her daughter's and looked into her eyes. She tried to convey her regret, wanting to tell her she understood why she saw anger and hurt in the eyes looking back at her. She reached out and stroked Emmeline's hair. 'You know I love you. I always have.' Emmeline's eyes filled with tears, which became sobs and then howls. Sophie wrapped her tightly in her arms, trying to stem the flow of her daughter's anger and frustration.

'Stay with me, Sophie. We can take our time and fix each other.'

CHAPTER 44

The auditorium was packed with mothers, siblings and friends of the girls they were here to see graduate. There was a happy buzz among the crowd of smartly dressed women; and the emotion infecting them all, was pride. They were gathered together to celebrate achievement and excellence; to launch the careers of the brightest and the best. They all knew the future of the Movement would be in these young women's hands.

'I can't believe my big sister has done this,' Gemma whispered, as the crowd fell silent. Kate squeezed her hand, her own eyes bright with excitement.

The crowd broke into applause as the Mistress of Chester College came onto the stage. Kate was surprised at her appearance. She reminded her of a kindly maiden aunt, rather than the ruthless educator she had imagined.

'Thank you. Thank you all so much for coming here today to celebrate the achievements of your daughters and friends. And what a beautiful, early summer's day it is. It's been a tough three years for all our students. They've dedicated themselves to their studies, albeit occasionally taking the odd break to down a glass or two at The Dog and Duck! As you know,

the girls who will be joining us on this stage to receive their degrees are those who have achieved the highest of standards. Many have left, realising they were better suited to other careers, which are equally as valid, leaving only those capable of gaining firsts to complete their courses. While we aim to get as many of our students onto this stage as possible, we're proud to have never lowered our standards. And each year, on average, we lose 70% of our girls. So, today we should all be extremely proud of the 300 women who will stand before you. I'm now delighted to hand over to our guest speaker, Libretta Jones, CEO of Femmeur and one of the founding members of the Completist Movement.'

There was a standing ovation as Libretta came onto the stage, her ash blonde hair as finally cut as the suit she was wearing.

'Mum, look. She's wearing her patent leather loafers!' Kate had forgotten this was the first time Gemma had laid eyes on her boss, and how much of a celebrity she was to millions of women.

'Good morning, and welcome to Chester University. The first University founded by the Movement for the education of our daughters. Enabling them to learn without distraction and interference from the fathers and sons of the COs. This institution has become a beacon of excellence and now ranks as the third most revered educational institution in the country after Oxford and Cambridge, an incredible achievement in 35 years.' The clapping resumed.

'Anyone who graduates from Chester is guaranteed a job in one of the Movement's companies. My own company will take over 10% of these graduates and we are only one of over 40 Completist companies who are ranked in the FTSE 100 Index.

Completists now make up around 50% of the population of women in this country. We employ the brightest and the best and we pay the same salary to women as men earn for the

same job. The effect of this has been to raise salaries throughout the UK for women as, in order to even attempt to poach our talent from us, male-run companies have had to make their remuneration packages much more attractive. Naturally, the Completist Effect, or the CE, as I like to call it, is never acknowledged in the media. They would rather report this as their achievement in finally honouring the Equal Pay Act. Not much of an achievement given it was enacted over 166 years ago.' There was a ripple of laughter from the audience. 'For the first time in over 170 years, there is no longer any need for Equal Pay Day. A day which marked the point in the year when women effectively worked for free for the remainder of the year due to the gender pay gap. Another significant indicator of the CE is the number of women on the boards of UK companies. My mother was a member of a group of women whose aim was to get 30% of every board of every FTSE 350 company to be comprised of women. Where they failed, we have succeeded. Fifty percent of every FTSE 350 company boards are now female. Women now have an equal say in the running of every major company in this country!'

A massive cheer erupted. Libretta smiled at the audience and held her hands up to request some calm.

'Every young woman I'm about to meet will enable this trend to continue, and help us maintain the original aim of the Movement. The eradication of the economic exploitation of women! So, let us thank them, and all those who have gone before!'

The audience stood up and started to stamp their feet, a tradition started at the first Completist Conference, when the moto had been, 'Fight with your feet,' a slogan designed to inspire women to walk away from their old life and become a Completist. Kate realised it was the first time Gemma had ever taken part in the tradition, and she watched her laugh as she stomped; filled with joy at contributing to the deafening noise of defiance and power.

'My legs are beginning to ache!' she shouted, as the stomping continued.

'But it feels good, doesn't it!' Kate shouted back. At a signal from Libretta, the laughing crowd resumed their seats and the award ceremony began.

They both cried when Cara appeared. Kate was so proud. She had always known her daughter was bright, but it took more than intellect to be on that stage; it took determination. She had sometimes doubted whether her daughter had the necessary steel in her backbone to make it through. Today she had been proved wrong; yet she couldn't help noticing Cara only smiled, her lips sealed; unlike her peers whose grins exposed both their teeth and their joy. Cara's eyes were not shining as brightly as theirs. Kate put it down to exhaustion. She knew Cara had buried her head in her books over the last three years, and her efforts had obviously taken their toll. She soothed her anxiety with the thought that her daughter would now have three weeks to rest and relax before she started her job at Femmeur. She was looking forward to having her at home again, and to travelling to and from work together.

After the ceremony, they waited impatiently for Cara to join them. She finally pushed her way through the crowd, smiling and waving, and was instantly leapt on by Gemma.

'You clever little shit! Well done, Big Sis. I didn't think you had it in you!' Kate smiled at her pair of beautiful girls.

'Thanks, Little Sis. I think. Talk about a back-handed compliment!' Cara broke free from Gemma's embrace and turned towards her mother.

'My lovely girl. I'm so proud of you. I can't wait to take you home and spoil you rotten. You look exhausted.'

'You're such a mum, Mum. I'm fine.' Her daughter kissed her tenderly on her cheek, and they made their way to the exit and then home.

CHAPTER 45

Cara got out of the car and looked at their well-tended house. It was odd to think this was her home again, at least until she could afford a place of her own. Gemma hadn't stopped talking, catching her up with every minute detail of her life over the last three months. Cara had put herself in solitary confinement during this period: the final push before her final exams. She had drifted off into her thoughts during the journey, Gemma's relentless chatter a soothing mantra, taking her into a meditative state. She was glad uni was over. Glad she had pleased her mother and made her proud. She wasn't particularly proud of herself. Her studies had simply been a distraction rather than a passion. The college, a monastic retreat from life. She wore her studies like a hair shirt, enjoying how one pain smothered another far worse one, which relentlessly gnawed away at her insides; sublimated by the reality she had chosen to absorb herself in. How would she distract herself in the three weeks before she started work?

'I had to choose my upper study subjects last week, Cara,' Gemma said, helping her lift her trunk from the boot. 'I think I'm going to do Art like you, and also English and History. I'm

wondering if I might be a good enough writer to pursue a career in journalism. What do you think?' They had reached the front door and plonked the heavy trunk down for a minute to catch their breath.

'I think you should do whatever will make you happiest, Gemma. You should follow your heart. I wish I had.' Cara could see her response had puzzled her sister. 'What I meant to say, Gemma, was Fine Art, rather than Graphic Design, was where my heart lay. But I didn't think I was talented enough to do it. Don't make the same mistake. Believe in your abilities and give it a shot. Trust me, you've nothing to lose.' Gemma nodded, and they bent their knees and picked up the trunk, turning it sideways to ease it through the front door.

'Are you alright, Cara?' Gemma said. 'You seem a little sad to be home.'

'Oh, Gemma. You've always been so sensitive to my moods. I've missed you so much. Come here and give me a hug.' Gemma stepped over the trunk and put her arms around her; they squeezed each other so hard they almost stopped breathing.

They let go of one another and laughed. 'Now that was a bear hug and a half!' Cara said. 'I hope that's the kettle I can hear you filling, Mother,' Cara shouted down the hallway. 'Gemma, I'm really glad to be home, and especially glad to see you, now let's get ourselves a cuppa shall we, I'm parched.'

They wandered towards the kitchen, leaving the trunk in the hallway. Three mugs were set out on the table. They all sat down in their usual spots.

'So, Cara. What are your plans for your three weeks off? You certainly deserve some R&R after the work you've put in over the last three years.' Her mother beamed at her over her tea. 'I know I've said it several times already, but you can't imagine how proud I am of you. And not only because of your results. You obviously impressed them at the Femmeur interview. Marketing only take on the very best designers.'

‘Thanks, Mum. It felt good to get the job. The people seem nice and the package is great. I’m not sure what I’m going to do with myself to be honest. I’ve forgotten what to do with free time.’

‘How about I kick things off by booking you into a spa for a couple of days? There’s a lovely one, not far from here. It’s my treat. A graduation present. Have any treatments you like.’

‘Thank you. I might book myself in for a new haircut too. I feel like I’ve let myself go a little these last three years. I could do with a bit of a makeover before I start work.’ Cara could see the relief in her mum’s eyes. She knew she wanted to walk into Femmeur with a presentable daughter on her first day, as well as a supposedly brilliant one.

Gemma grabbed her mobile. ‘Let’s look at some styles now! What length do you want it, long, medium or short?’

‘Slow down, Gemma. I only decided to have it done a minute ago! I need to think about it. But now I’m going to unpack, then we can reconvene for the make-over chat.’

The mattress sagged as she sat down and examined her bedroom. It was exactly how she had left it three years ago. She hadn’t had the time or the inclination to do anything to it during the holidays, she had been too buried in her books; but looking at it now, she realised she wasn’t the only one in need of a makeover. She had changed. The pink walls were too frivolous, too carefree. Pale greys and white bed linen were now more her style. Something simple and soothing. She opened her wardrobe doors and surveyed the clothes she hadn’t bothered to take with her; having chosen to dress solely in comfortable sports leggings and hoodies. The pretty dresses belonged to a stranger. Then she saw the blue dress. She reached out her hand to touch the silky fabric.

CHAPTER 46

A week later, Cara emerged from the Covent Garden hairdressers feeling more alive than she had felt in years. She was now as groomed as she was ever going to be. The spa had sorted out her skin, the hair on her skin, and her nails; and now she had a wonderful new haircut. She noticed men glancing at her appreciatively, despite her gait giving her away as a Completist. I must be looking damn hot, she thought, as she wandered down the street, glancing at the clothes in the shop windows. She had already treated herself to one new outfit, which she was currently wearing. Her mother had not approved of the hip-hugging black skirt and the fine wool burgundy top with its scooped neck.

Her eyes rested on a pale blue slip dress, very similar to the one she had worn the night she met Sam. She wished he could see her now. She wished she could feel his skin sliding over hers. But why couldn't she? This was the ideal moment. Opportunities like this would soon be few and far between when she started working under the watchful eye of her mother.

She pulled her mobile from her handbag and rang his

agency. Within minutes she had arranged to meet him at the same hotel in three hours' time. She rang the hotel.

'Excuse me, is Room 231 available?'

'When would Madam like to stay?' replied a rather bored man.

'Today. Now. I'm unexpectedly in town and need a room straight away.'

'Yes, it is, Madam. But only for one night. Will that suffice?' He sounded no more interested than a few moments earlier. 'As it's such short notice, I will need your credit details straight away to secure the room.'

'Perfect, I'll be with you shortly.' She gave him her credit number and decided she needed a drink before heading off.

She found a place boasting a romantic courtyard and walked in, making her way to the back of the bar. She sat down in a tiny space surrounded by old brick walls draped with climbing summer flowers. The waiter took her order and she waited, enjoying the sun warming her newly exfoliated skin. Her thoughts turned to Sam, his beautiful face filling her head. What am I doing? Will he even be pleased to see me? She had shut out the memories of that night for so long they were now faded, the specifics blurred by time. She did remember how good he had made her feel, and she was hungry to feel that way again. Would he even remember her? He had said she was special, but how could you know after spending only a few hours with someone, no matter how intense those hours had been?

A familiar confusion started to drift into her head like a fine mist. She didn't understand sex, love or men. She didn't understand her reaction to Sam. Jesus, why did life have to be so complicated? Was this love, lust or obsession? She knew men were a topic of fundamental importance, yet she could only learn more by paying for the knowledge by the hour. Within such narrow parameters, the true answers to her questions would be impossible to unearth. The very voyage of

discovery she longed for could threaten the fabric of her life, and turn solid foundations into dust, only for her to discover they had been the foundations she needed to build a happy life for herself all along.

The waiter brought her drink and set down a small bowl of olives beside it. She thanked him and took a large gulp. Why could she not simply accept the lessons history had provided and believe the life set out before her was the best one she could live? The evidence was compelling enough. She was surrounded by happy, well-adjusted women. Her mother was the living embodiment of the Movement and she had even experienced life on the other side; however, Cara couldn't simply accept the choices her mother had made. She was tired of living a life prescribed by others, she wanted to choose her own path.

Cara downed her drink, placed the money on the table and left with her head held high, determined to discover her own truth.

By the time she heard the knock on the door, the effects of her third glass of wine were giving her the confidence she so badly needed. The agency had agreed to withhold her name, so she knew Sam would be surprised to see her.

She tottered towards the door and opened it. He was exactly how she remembered him. His thick chestnut hair in loose waves surrounding those beautiful, mesmerising, brown eyes. She realised he was standing there in the doorway, staring at her, saying nothing.

'Hi, Sam. Would you like to come in?' She was suddenly very worried he wouldn't.

He stepped forward. He still hadn't spoken. She closed the door behind him, sealing the room around them.

'I hope you don't mind, Sam. I've just finished my degree and it's been a tough three years -'

'So, you decided to have a little R&R with me did you, Cara?' His tone was not friendly.

'No, it's not like that. It's been a tough three years because I couldn't stop thinking about you, wanting you. The only way to put you out of my head was to bury myself in books. But my course is over now, and all my feelings have risen to the surface again. I had to see you. This was the only way.' She sat down heavily on the bed. 'This is a terrible mistake. I'm sorry, Sam. Leave if you want to. I understand. I wasn't sure how you'd react, but I had to take the risk.'

Sam sat down beside her on the bed; his eyes had softened, and his body relaxed a little.

'No, I'm sorry, Cara. But it was quite a shock. I'm glad to see you though. I've thought about you a lot. I've still not met anyone else like you.' He looked at her, then held her face, tilting it towards his.

'You look wonderful,' he said, then leant in and kissed her. As his lips met hers the world dropped away, the boundaries of her skin melted, and she felt herself flowing against and into him, like a sea lapping against an invisible shore.

Cara saw him every day during her final two weeks of freedom, despite the enormous risk she was taking. When it was time to say goodbye again, she couldn't do it. They were lying on his bed together. He had a flat in Camden, overlooking the lock. His job paid well, and it was tastefully, if sparsely, furnished. The first time he had taken her home she had been surprised to discover a large, smoky grey cat snoozing on his sofa. It had opened one sleepy green eye, taken her in, and closed it again. Apparently, Gulliver was not fazed to find a strange woman in Sam's flat. This realisation had not pleased her one bit. Now Gulliver curled himself around her legs whenever he saw her, purring contentedly as she scratched him under his chin.

'I don't want this to end, Sam,' she said, looking out of the bedroom window at the cloudless blue sky.

'Neither do I. Does it have to?'

'Perhaps for a short time while I save up a deposit for my

own place. Then, if we're very, very discreet, we can see each other whenever we like. But I'm not sure how I'm going to find enough excuses to satisfy my mother while I'm living at home. We're travelling to and from work together for God's sake. It's going to put too much of a strain on everyone.'

'But why do you need your own place? This can be our place. It's big enough for two. Why don't you move in with me?' He brushed the fingertips of his right hand down her arm.

'You don't know very much about the Completist Movement, do you? Which surprises me, given that 80% of your clients are Completists.'

'It shouldn't surprise you,' he said, lifting himself onto his side to look down into her face, 'I don't really talk much to my clients.'

Cara winced. She tried not to think about how Sam made his living, and she didn't want to be reminded of the details.

'But you must know how we live. You read the news, pass us in the street.'

'Of course, I'm not completely ignorant! I know you lot have turned your back on men and run your own companies and make your own money.'

'That's correct. But did you know that, if I got caught having this affair with you, I would immediately be thrown out of the Movement and I would never see my mother or sister again!'

'Really? Jesus, I had no idea what a huge risk you were taking. I'm honoured,' and he kissed her so tenderly Cara temporarily forgavc him. When the kiss was over, she continued to wonder at his failure to realise what she had to go through to be with him. The lies she'd told, the complicated plans she'd been forced to make. In truth, Cara was staggered at Sam's ignorance. Was he atypical or did all men know so little about how and why half the female population chose to live the way they did?

He lay back down and they both lay there, staring at the ceiling.

'What shall we do about lunch?' Sam said, breaking the silence.

When it was time to say goodbye, Cara held Sam close, trying to embed his essence into her skin, breathing his smell deep into her lungs. 'You know I won't be able to see you now, don't you? If I do get an opportunity, I will take it, I'll leap at it! You have to know I'll be thinking of you every day. Working hard to earn enough money for my own place, so we can be together again. Will you wait for me, Sam? Will you give us a shot?'

'Cara, when I saw you again, I knew you were the only woman I wanted to be with. So, yes, I will give it a shot you daft woman. I'll have to make do with Gulliver for a while. He doesn't quite match up to you, but he's the next best thing.' They smiled at one another, each one waiting for the other to say goodbye. Cara stood on her tiptoes, kissed him on the cheek and walked away. She couldn't look back.

CHAPTER 47

Emmeline cleared the mugs and plates from Table Six. She took the dirty crockery into the kitchen, then returned to the table, giving it a wipe down while checking whether her other customers needed any attention. The couple at Table Four were deep in conversation, and the mother at Table Three was busy encouraging her six-year-old to have another mouthful of beans and toast.

She had been happily working at the café at the end of their road for nearly a year now. Her boss was a good man to work for. He was funny, generous and unflappable, even when there was a rush on. His regulars loved him. He had owned The Café on the Corner, or The Corner Café, as his customers preferred to call it, for over ten years. It was cosy and kitsch. Mismatched floral crockery competed valiantly with elaborately framed pictures of fluffy kittens and playful puppies.

Frank served traditional English Fayre and adhered to a strict timetable. Breakfast could be ordered from 8.00 a.m. until 10.00 a.m., then it was called Brunch until midday. After the cuckoo clock had struck 12, you could only order from the lunch menu until 3.00 p.m. when High Tea would kick in. He

never took an order after 4.30 p.m. and he closed on the dot of five; encouraging Emmeline to chivvy any customers loitering over their tea and cakes to hurry up and finish. The occasional newbie sometimes took offence, but his regulars just laughed and shouted well-meant abuse at Frank, who would remind them they had kettles at home, so they should fuck off and use them.

Emmeline liked feeling physically tired at the end of the day. The routine helped her order her thoughts, and she was beginning to get her life back on track. Her mother had found herself a job as an office cleaner. It had been impossible to find anything more rewarding. No-one liked Outsiders. She had to leave the house far earlier than Emmeline, so they never saw each other in the mornings, but they always had their evenings together. Emmeline loved coming home to find her mother pottering about the place. She relished having someone who was so pleased to see her, who would sit enthralled at her silly stories about particularly charming or difficult customers; and the nuggets of nonsense Frank muttered a hundred times a day.

The weekdays passed pleasantly until Friday night, when Emmeline would nip into the local shop to grab a bottle of red for herself and a chilled bottle of white for her mum. They would sit and drink and put the world to rights, until they collapsed into their respective beds, their heads fuzzy from the alcohol, but lighter for sharing their fears with one another.

Emmeline was glad her mother knew about her drinking. She needed to come clean in order to help herself. Ironically, her mother's admission she had also turned to the vine to numb her pain, improved the situation for both of them. It was easier to be strong to save someone else than it was to save yourself. Neither of them believed they were alcoholics, but they both recognised they were on the brink.

Her mother had suggested to Emmeline that a routine and a physically demanding job, might help her. She had spotted

the 'Staff Wanted' postcard in the Café window and convinced her to apply. Emmeline repaid the favour by finding her the cleaning job and persuading the boss to give her mum an interview. He had begrudgingly agreed. Her mother was still a good-looking woman; he was a few years older than her and still unmarried. Her mother's impressions of his clumsy attempts at flirtation often had them clutching their sides with laughter.

Emmeline opened the front door and launched her usual greeting into the air. There was no reply. She peered into the room; it was empty. She shouted again, this time directing her voice upstairs, and heard her mum scrabbling around in her bedroom. She appeared at the top of the stairs in her dressing gown, her hair dishevelled, looking sheepish.

'Mum? What's going on?' Emmeline couldn't decide whether to feel anxious or amused.

'I've got company,' her mother mouthed, stabbing her finger in the direction of her bedroom and dissolving into silent giggles.

'You dirty bitch!' Emmeline mouthed back at her, a big grin on her face.

Before they could continue their silent conversation, a man's voice shouted from the bedroom.

'Sophie, what are you doing, are you coming back? Or should I get up and say hello to Emmeline?'

Emmeline liked the sound of his voice. Merriment and mischief were weaved through his sentence, and she hoped her mum would tell him to get up.

'Good idea, Harry. We'll be downstairs in the kitchen.' Her mother scurried down the stairs towards her, fastening the ties of her dressing gown as she went. She shoved Emmeline into the kitchen and jumped up and down in front of her like a schoolgirl.

'So? Come on. Who is Harry and where did he come from?'

'Oh, Emmeline, don't be cross with me. He's the driver of the bus I catch to work. There's hardly a soul on it at that time in the morning, so we've been gradually getting to know one another over these last few months. I had a coffee with him the other day and he really made me laugh. He's so funny, Emmeline, and quite handsome. Well, I think so.'

'Why on earth did you think I'd be cross? I think it's great. I'm really happy for you!' She gave her mum a huge hug then stopped abruptly as Harry entered the room.

He was wearing a pair of faded blue jeans and a pale blue hoodie which set off his wavy blonde hair and blue eyes. He looked like he'd stepped off a surfboard, rather than a bus.

He lolloped over to them, shoving his arm out at Emmeline.

'I'm Harry, and I'm very pleased to meet you.'

Emmeline shook his hand. It was huge. She couldn't help but reflect his beaming grin back at him. His happiness was infectious.

'Very pleased to meet you too, Harry. Can I offer you a drink? We only have red or white I'm afraid.'

'I tell you what. I know you girls like to spend Friday evenings together, and I don't want to intrude. Why don't I bid you both farewell and leave you to it?'

Sophie and Emmeline glanced at one another.

'No, Harry, we'd like you to stay,' said Emmeline replying for the both of them.

'In that case, I'll put on my trainers, nip down the road and grab a few beers. OK?'

'I wondered whether you might be more of a beer man. See you in a minute then.' Emmeline grinned at him.

As soon as the front door closed Emmeline turned to face her mother.

'I like him, Mum. He seems like a stand-up guy.'

'Now we need to find someone for you.' Her mother's eyes twinkled.

Emmeline turned to fetch the wine she had bought. She didn't want anyone, and now she'd have to share her mum with someone else.

'Maybe, Mum, maybe. We'll see. Glass of the usual?'

'Yes please, Trouble.'

Emmeline sighed quietly. Her mum was too happy to notice her changed mood. She would have to snap out of it. She didn't want to piss on her party.

Harry made it easy for Emmeline. He had a quick wit and easy banter. He soon had them both laughing at tales of mothers leaving babies on his bus and of 'the mirror-men', who would always take the same seat so they could watch women in skirts as they went up the stairs to the top deck.

By the end of the evening, Emmeline was rooting for their relationship, even if it meant she would have to become more self-reliant. It was about time she stood on her own two feet.

CHAPTER 48

Cara's phone rang. It was the first call she had received since starting her new job. She answered nervously, hoping it wouldn't result in someone asking her to do something she had no idea how to do.

'Cara Ingleton,' she said. She could see the call was coming from reception. Who the hell was coming to see her? She didn't have any meetings booked. A sharp pain shot through her stomach. Please don't let it be him. She started praying silently to herself.

There's a delivery for you, Miss Ingleton. A rather nice one, actually.'

'Thank you, I'll come down and get it.'

Cara didn't feel much better. What if he'd sent something to her, something blatantly romantic? How the hell was she going to explain it away when everyone on reception had witnessed it?

'Here you go, Miss Ingleton,' the girl said, emerging from the cubby hole behind the reception desk. She was holding a huge bouquet of flowers. 'They're lovely, aren't they? And they smell divine.' She handed them over with a broad grin.

'Thank you, and please call me Cara.'

‘I’m Kat. You should get those in water as soon as possible!’

‘Thanks, Kat. Will do.’

Cara stood in the opulent toilets on her floor, droplets of perspiration forming on her forehead. She put the flowers down and opened the envelope attached to their protective cellophane. At least he’d had the sense to ask them to put his message in an envelope. She noticed her hand was shaking.

’Congratulations, Cara. It’s great to see all our afternoon study sessions paying off! Thinking of you. Lots of love, Samantha x’

She exhaled; unaware she had been holding her breath. Cara was impressed. He’d put a lot of thought into the message, and she loved its double meaning. So, I now have an old college friend called Samantha. I wonder whether I might meet up with her to catch up from time to time. After all, looking at these lovely flowers, we are very close.

She scrutinised her reflection in the mirror. The colour was beginning to return to her cheeks. She dabbed her forehead with one of the little cotton pads Femmeur provided in all the toilets. They sat alongside the discreet box filled with every type of sanitary protection on the market. Satisfied, she picked up the flowers and headed back to her desk.

‘Wow, Cara, they’re lovely!’ Saturday said, swivelling her chair to follow the flowers across the office floor. Saturday sat behind Cara and was a senior graphic designer and Head of Product Design. She was in her late thirties and, unusually for a Completist, wore very outlandish clothes, albeit dark ones, because, as she had explained to Cara within minutes of their first meeting, this was what people expected her to look like, and Saturday liked living up to people’s expectations. She had winked at her and then carried on with her work.

‘They’re from Samantha, one of my closest college friends. Sweet of her, and a complete surprise. She’s not normally this thoughtful.’ Cara laughed. She was pleased at herself for

adding such a personal detail about her imaginary friend, it added credibility to the charade.

'You'll want to get those in water,' Saturday commented as she swivelled her chair back to face her screen. 'You'll find some vases in one of the cupboards in the kitchen.'

She had agreed to meet her mother in the ground floor foyer at 5.30 p.m. every evening unless one of them had to work late. Her mother raised her eyebrows questioningly as she approached.

'They came today. Aren't they lovely? They're from Samantha, a close college friend of mine. She certainly took me by surprise. I hadn't had her down as a 'sweet gestures' kinda girl.' Cara smiled confidently at her mother.

'They are lovely. What did the message say?'

'I'll show you when we get home. It's rather awkward to retrieve it from my bag at present.'

Cara hid her face behind the flowers. She didn't like deceiving her mother, but she had told so many lies over the last few weeks, it was becoming a habit.

Gemma was waiting for them when they got home. She smelt every flower, as Cara carefully arranged each bloom into the only vase they owned. Her mother rarely treated herself to flowers, and she could never remember her receiving any. The vase was too small to contain all of them, so Cara made a separate arrangement for her bedroom in an old milk jug. Gemma asked to see the card, and she noticed her mother looking over Gemma's shoulder as she read the message out loud.

'Where does Samantha live?' Gemma asked. 'It would be nice to meet her. Maybe she could come to supper one day?'

Cara was prepared for the question. She had spent most of the afternoon putting flesh on Samantha's bones, as she took in every petal of each bloom. She had a feeling she would be seeing her at least once a month until she got her own place. 'I'm afraid it's unlikely. Samantha lives in Coventry. But I

know she comes to London every now and again, so next time she's down, I'll ask her.'

After dinner, Cara announced she was exhausted and retired to her room. She sat on her bed and altered the contact details in her mobile. She renamed 'Local Taxi Firm', 'Samantha', and typed in her message: 'Well done! And thank you, they're lovely. I'm sure Samantha and I will be able to meet in a few weeks for drinks after work. I'll let you know as soon as. Thinking of you too xxxx'. She pressed send, and waited for the delivered icon to appear, then deleted the message.

CHAPTER 49

Emmeline watched her mother's relationship blossom with awe. She had never seen her behave like this with her father. She had a constant grin on her face, and the number of times they touched one another was staggering. Harry would absent-mindedly rest his hand on her mother's bottom while she was cooking, and she would touch his arm or give him a peck on the cheek for no apparent reason.

Emmeline accepted the new status quo easily enough. Harry was a nice man, and he obviously doted on her mother. She had never seen her happier. When they were together, even the structure of their tiny house seemed to swell, puffing out its chest with pride at the joy it contained. Emmeline wished the house could physically, rather than metaphorically, swell. There was one thing detracting from this domestic bliss: Harry was a big man. He filled the small downstairs room and Emmeline resented the invasion of their compact space. However, she tried hard to remind herself this was a small price to pay, given the obvious benefits to her mother's well-being and hence her own.

After many weeks of witnessing a healthy, happy relationship, Emmeline started to wonder if she should let go of her

own fears. She knew where they were lurking, and she also knew she hadn't had the courage to examine them; to diminish them through familiarity, as Francesca would have put it. She had chosen instead to drown them in alcohol, to get herself through each day at Imperial when she had to face lectures with professors, all of whom had been men.

Whenever she had approached a lecture hall, her chest had tightened and she had struggled for breath, leaning against the corridor wall, breathing slowly and deeply, as she tried to regain enough composure to step across the threshold. She was never the first to arrive or the last to leave and hadn't shown up to a single one to one with her mentor. There had been many days when her physical reaction to attending a lecture had been so overwhelming, she had returned to her room, defeated.

She knew her fears had already cost her the degree she was more than capable of getting and relegated her to a life of serving food and drink to virtual strangers; albeit protected in a safe bubble by her kind, generous boss. Was she going to let it steal away the chance to experience the kind of happiness her mother was currently feeling too? She had never before toyed with the idea of a relationship with a man. Her glittering career had always been her first and only love. Perhaps its disappearance was creating a void in her which needed to be filled.

Emmeline had considered contacting Francesca again; but the idea had died within seconds, when she realised neither her, nor her mother, could now afford her exorbitant fees.

There was one man who had caught her attention. He had come into the café the day before for a take-away coffee and she had been drawn to him, rather than repelled by him. He had a calm demeanour and his voice was gentle and low. He had thanked her with a small smile and a slight nod of his head. When his eyes met hers, there had been a moment of

connection. She had caught herself holding onto his cup a millisecond longer than necessary.

It was Friday morning. As she brushed her hair, she leaned in closer to the mirror. She no longer made much of an effort with her appearance. She was always clean and tidy, but her eyebrows weren't plucked into the perfect arcs she noticed on so many of the female faces she saw each day. Her nails never sported a jaunty colour that matched the top she had chosen to wear. Any hint of jauntiness would be difficult to achieve, considering her clothes were now predominantly black, interspersed with the odd grey or blue item, when she was feeling particularly cheerful.

She remembered how she would wear crop tops before Mr E, unafraid to expose her youthful skin to the sun and stares of others. After, was different territory. The only skin she now exposed was on her forearms, hands and face. She brushed her hair back into a ponytail and secured it with a black tie, which apparently possessed the power to reduce the likelihood of split ends. Opening the bathroom cabinet, she scanned the shelves for tweezers and found some nestling behind the dental floss. She yelped as she extracted the first hair. Seeing her skin become angry and red, Emmeline gave up on the whole idea. This was a job for the evening, not minutes before she had to leave the house.

Outside, a slight crispness in the air signalled the end of the summer and warned of cooler days to come. She stepped up her pace, regretting her lightweight jumper. Frank was already busy prepping for the breakfast rush as she opened the door with her key. He would never open the doors before 8.00 a.m., so she locked the door behind her.

He looked up from the bacon and smiled. Then he paused and looked at her again. 'Is that a hint of lipstick I see on that beautiful face of yours?'

Emmeline blushed. 'Might be, might not,' she said, grabbing the cutlery tray and heading towards the first table.

‘Let’s suppose it is, because then I would be able to say, it suits you, Emmeline. You should wear it more often.’ Emmeline had turned away from him to set the tables, but she was smiling. Frank was good at picking up her signals, and he had clearly decided against teasing her.

‘So, what’s the guess for today?’ Emmeline asked, changing the subject. They played this game every morning, each estimating the number of customers they would be serving throughout the day. The loser always made the winner a cup of tea after they locked the doors on the dot of 5.00 p.m.

‘I have a feeling you will be making me tea today,’ Frank responded. ‘I’m feeling particularly lucky. So lucky, I’m planning to buy my annual lottery ticket.’

‘My, my. I had no idea you would be so rash as to put your faith in Lady Luck.’

‘That, my dear, is the joy of long-term relationships. You discover new things about one another,’ he said pointing at her with the bread knife.

Emmeline laughed. ‘So, what’s your guess?’

‘My premonition is 183. What’s your stab in the dark?’

Emmeline turned to look at him, raising her eyebrows. ‘My educated guess, would be 152, possibly 153, should a stray passer-by be foolish enough to enter.’

‘So, what’s it to be then, 152 or 153? Come on, Emmeline, a cup of tea is at stake here.’

‘153. I most definitely sense foolishness is in the air today.’

Frank made a note of their guesses on a napkin and put it in the usual place under the counter. ‘Right,’ he said, checking his watch, ‘Let the game begin.’

The man was their fifth customer of the morning. Emmeline was making a pot of tea when he walked in. She hoped she could finish before Frank felt obligated to step in and serve him. She placed the pot of tea on a tray with two pink cups and saucers, a blue milk jug and a yellow sugar bowl. ‘I’ll be with you in a moment,’ she said, as she brushed past him.

She returned to the counter as quickly as possible, wiping her hands on her apron. 'Sorry about the wait. What can I get you this morning, take-away latte?'

'Well remembered,' he replied, flashing her a timid smile. 'Can I also have a croissant please, it is Friday, after all.'

'Of course.' Emmeline smiled at him and busied herself with his order. She desperately wanted to chat with him, ask him if he had moved into the area, anything. Her cheeks burned. How could she have turned into such a pathetic tongue-tied idiot? She had been known for her ready, and often acerbic wit at school, and now she was struggling for words. With a weak smile, she handed him his coffee and a paper bag containing his croissant.

'Enjoy,' she said, as he took them from her.

He gave her that smile and nod again. She turned and sighed. Frank sidled over to her and touched her arm. 'We can do some practice flirting after closing tonight if you like?' he said, his tone devoid of any judgment or mockery. She turned to him and smiled. 'You are sweet, Frank. And, as usual, very perceptive. But I think I've lost the art for good, if I ever possessed it in the first place.'

'Why don't you take five? I can hold the fort.'

'It's alright. The day has barely begun. Bit too early for a fag break!'

At least all was not lost. Frank had to make her a cup of tea at five past five. They had served 163 customers. He was dignified in defeat. As he brought the cups over to the table where she sat, smoking her favourite cigarette of the day, he suddenly stopped.

'Goodness, it turns out, this really is your lucky day,' he said looking out of the café window. She turned to follow his gaze then quickly turned away.

'Shit,' she said, looking at Frank, a terrified expression on her face.

'No time for our little practice session I'm afraid, you're

going to have to wing it. I'll drink this perfect cup of tea. I suggest you get out of here and see what your grinning man is doing lurking outside the café at ten past five on a Friday night!'

'I'm not sure I can,' Emmeline whimpered, a sudden tightness gripping her chest.

'Of course, you can. Just breathe. You have nothing to lose. If you completely fuck up, he'll go elsewhere for his latte. And I think the business could stand the loss. Now piss off. I'll see you tomorrow morning.' He waved her away with his hand and picked up his favourite gold-rimmed teacup, indicating the topic was not up for further discussion.

Emmeline inhaled deeply. Here goes nothing, she thought. Pushing aside her panic, she stood up. She left with her head held high, looking straight ahead. She saw him cross the road from the corner of her eye and turned her head towards him. He was smiling.

'Hi. I'm sorry to pounce on you. I was wondering whether you'd like to drink a coffee which was maybe made by someone else? With me, I mean. Don't worry if you've got to be somewhere, it's just that this was the only way I could ask you in private. I'm Jack, by the way.'

She liked the way he had stumbled over his words. 'Hi Jack, I'm Emmeline. I was on my way home, but I guess I could make a diversion. Sorry. I mean, yes. That would be nice.' She groaned internally at her cack-handedness.

'Great! I don't suppose you know anywhere nearby? I'm new to the area and I haven't explored my surroundings yet.'

'There's a place around the corner. It's not as good as Frank's, but it's not bad.'

'I'm pleased I stumbled upon the best café in the neighbourhood and not just because of the coffee.'

Emmeline smiled shyly at him. His flirting was as bad as hers. It made her feel more confident.

'So, what brings you to this salubrious part of town?' she asked, as she led the way to the other café.

'I've started a new job, and you get more for your rental buck in this neighbourhood. I searched for places closer to work, but I didn't fancy living in a shoebox. At least here you get enough room to swing a cat. Not that pets are allowed.'

She laughed. 'Good to know you're not averse to a bit of animal cruelty!' It was his turn to laugh.

They ordered their coffees and sat down at a table for two in the corner.

'This is definitely not as good as yours,' he said, sipping his latte.

'Good to know,' Emmeline replied. 'So, what's the new job, if you don't mind me asking?'

'Fireman,' he replied.

'Really? I didn't know firemen wore suits to work!'

'No, not really. But don't all women like firemen?'

Emmeline laughed. 'I have personally never wasted a second of my life thinking about them, so I'm probably the wrong girl to answer that question!'

'OK, I'm a vet, specialising in cute, cuddly animals.'

'Oh, in that case, will you marry me?'

'It would be an honour and a privilege,' he said, grinning at her.

Half an hour later she was messaging her mum to say she would be late home. She didn't want her worrying. When she received her response, she confirmed everything was more than OK and she would explain everything later.

She didn't want the date to end. The conversation flowed and she was relaxed and happy to be in his company. They ordered another coffee and both drank it very slowly, until the last gulp was cold. She glanced at her mobile.

'I'm sorry, but I'm going to have to go. Mum will have supper waiting.'

'Lucky you. It's leftover pizza for me.'

‘Don’t you cook, then?’

‘I do, but a trainee Marketing Executive doesn’t command a very high salary. However, if you’ll allow me to, I’d love to cook you supper one night?’

‘I’d like that,’ she replied, ‘but maybe after a few more coffees?’

‘No problem. Can I buy you one tomorrow?’

‘I work on Saturdays. But you could pick me up afterwards?’

‘Deal!’

Her mum rushed to the front door before she even had time to close it behind her.

‘What’s going on, Emmeline?’ she asked.

‘I’ve been on a date!’ she said.

‘Jesus. Harry, Emmeline’s been on a date!’

‘Time to crack open the champagne, then. Double celebration!’

‘Mum?’ Emmeline said, looking at her mother’s beaming smile. ‘It’s evidently my turn to ask what’s going on!’

‘Come into the kitchen, Emmeline. We’ve got something to tell you.’

A few seconds later Emmeline was in shock.

‘Mum, that’s wonderful news!’ She finally managed to stutter, confronted by their beaming faces as they stood in joyful unison, Harry’s arms wrapped around her mother’s waist. So, this was what happy ever after looked like. Her mother was to become a Chosen One again. The name had never felt so apt. She found herself looking at her mother’s left hand. She held it towards Emmeline and wiggled her engagement finger at her.

‘Isn’t it lovely? Harry told me he’s been putting money aside since he was 20, hoping that, one day, he would meet the right person and marry them.’

The unexpectedly large diamond glinted in the kitchen lights, a little lighthouse of hope casting its beam into Emmeline's eyes, guiding her back to the safety and comfort of her prescribed destiny.

'It's absolutely amazing, Mum. Truly stunning.'

Harry had reluctantly let go of her mother to open the champagne, and they heard the pop of the cork as the bottle released its frothy happiness into three champagne glasses specifically brought, no doubt by Harry, to make sure the romance of the occasion wasn't diminished by their cheap tumblers.

He handed a glass to each of them. 'I'd like to propose a toast,' he said, holding his glass aloft. 'To my darling Sophie and her beautiful daughter. The two most precious women in my life.'

Emmeline wanted to cry. His sincerity reached inside her, searching out her pain and holding it tenderly, like a mother soothing a troubled child. She lifted her glass, her hands trembling, and took a sip as they did.

'When are you thinking of getting married?' Emmeline asked, trying to keep her voice calm and even.

'Harry and I would like to do it sooner rather than later, and keep it simple. We thought next month, before winter properly arrives. We only want a Registration, no big ceremony. You, me and Harry.'

'Oh, right, sounds good. Will Harry move in with us then?' Emmeline held her breath. She suddenly wondered whether they would expect her to move out.

'Initially, love,' her mother said beckoning her to follow her into the lounge area. Her mother sat down on the sofa and Emmeline instinctively chose the armchair, leaving the space beside her mother for Harry. 'Harry is going to put his flat on the market and I'm going to look for a better job once we're married. It shouldn't be a problem when I'm Mrs Jackson. You know how things work. Then we'll look for a new place

together. And, of course, we fully expect and want you to live with us.'

Emmeline was surprised at her reaction. A few seconds ago, she had been frightened of being made homeless; yet now she didn't feel like she had a home to lose, despite her mother's offer. The dynamic had changed; sitting opposite the two of them, she was the outsider. She would start looking for a place of her own.

CHAPTER 50

Cara stood outside a bar she had never been to before. She had left work early and visited a non-Completist clothes shop to buy a new outfit; and despite the disdainful service she had received from the shop assistant, she had emerged in a curve hugging turquoise dress which complemented the fading tan she had worked so hard to acquire that summer. In addition to being a venue they had never visited before, the bar was also conveniently close to Sam's apartment, although she didn't want to appear presumptuous. She checked her mobile, he was late. Not late enough to make her angry, but late enough to make her anxious; then she saw him and her heart started to race. He was the most beautiful man she had ever laid eyes on. He came towards her, grinning from ear to ear.

'Hi, Samantha. So lovely to see you again,' she said, noticing his eyes scanning her body appreciatively. Cara smirked as she shook his hand.

'Good to see you too, Cara. I've missed our study sessions. Do you really want to go for a drink? You know it's only a ten-minute walk to my place from here. Wouldn't you rather do

some revising? It's important to keep abreast of new developments, you know. You never stop learning!'

'Oh, I didn't realise there had been any new developments in my chosen field of expertise. I'd hate to get behind with my lessons. Lead on, study partner.'

They barely spoke to one another as they walked side by side without touching. Cara knew she was different from the women she was walking past; years of carrying herself in a certain way might attract unwanted attention, despite her new outfit. It simply wouldn't do to be seen with a man unless he was a business contact. As they marched up the back stairs, avoiding the communal lift, their sexual tension filled the space around them. As soon as the front door closed, they lunged towards one other, kissing each other greedily; hands tearing at buttons and belts, until they had created the necessary openings for what they both had in mind.

Sam pushed her onto the sofa and was on top of her before she could kick her heels off. She wrapped her legs around his waist as he entered her, sweeping away the weeks of frustration with each thrust. They came together a few minutes later, then they both laughed.

'God, that feels so much better. You wouldn't believe how many times I've fantasised about this moment.' Sam sat up and looked at Cara's body, her right breast exposed, the fabric of her dress bunched up around her waist.

'You look like a beautiful, wanton slut. It's making me hard all over again.' He glanced down at his crotch, encouraging her to follow his gaze. She needed no encouragement; and with a little more elegance, they both stripped off their remaining clothes and slipped naked together beneath the duvet.

A few hours later Cara was in Sam's shower, washing him off her skin. She dried herself and went into the lounge to start gathering up her things. Sam had his dressing gown on and was pouring them some wine.

'Sweetheart, I don't have time. I have to get home. I don't want Mum to get suspicious.'

'Have one glass, Cara. You were meant to be meeting Samantha for drinks, she'll expect your breath to smell of booze.' Sam handed her a glass and she took a swig and handed it back to him. 'Good thinking Detective! I love you. I'll see you as soon as I can.'

'Jesus, this is tough, Cara. These past six weeks have dragged by. I'm not sure I can live like this for the next year, or however long it's going to take for you to save a deposit.'

'Please don't do this, Sam. Not now. It won't be long. I've already looked into things. They're building a new set of Starter Pods in Haringey. I've already put my name down for one. It won't be long.'

'A Starter Pod? I thought you'd be able to do better than that!'

'Fuck you, Sam. My salary isn't as much as a sex worker's, but to be able to get one of those in under a year, is pretty good going.' She had chosen her words carefully; two could play at the belittling game.

'Facilitator, if you please. And I'm sorry. I know you're doing your best. I just miss you.' Cara instantly regretted her retaliation.

'I miss you too, with all my heart, mind and vagina. I'll try to meet up with you again in a couple of weeks. Chin up, and keep fantasising!' She blew him a kiss and opened the door.

Sitting on the bus home, she checked her mobile. She realised she wouldn't be able to meet Sam in a couple of weeks as she would be on her period, and she knew it would frustrate them both if they couldn't fully enjoy the experience the next time they met. It would have to be the week after. She sent him a message to let him know. His response surprised her. "Cara, become a Chosen One. If you're serious about our future together then why put us through this? It's going to

have to happen one day. You need to make a choice. You need to choose me."

Cara sat staring out of the window, trying to imagine life without her mother and sister. Then she tried to imagine a life without Sam. Each option was bleak. She looked further into the future. Gemma would grow up and leave home. Her mother would grow old and spend her days with her friends, doing whatever retired people do; and she would be climbing the corporate ladder. Creating a home for herself, a life; perhaps even saving for a baby. She would probably see Gemma and her mother once a month. She would have to satisfy her sexual urges through a Facilitator; and while she was being fucked, she would dream of Sam sliding his fingers into her while kissing her lips, nibbling her breasts and whispering obscenities in her ear. She already knew the decision she was going to make; it was simply a matter of when.

CHAPTER 51

The café was busy, there were only two free tables left. There had been a steady flow of customers since they opened the doors and Emmeline hadn't been able to update Frank on her mother's engagement. She was loading a tray with tea and homemade scones when the café fell silent. Emmeline looked up and saw that two Completist women had come in. They were middle-aged, and one was rather plump while the other was a little too thin. They ignored the hushed customers with their prying eyes and made their way to one of the empty tables. As they took their seats the conversations resumed, but the previously noisy chatter had become a background hum, interspersed with the chink of teaspoons on china. Emmeline glanced at Frank. He was staring at the two women. She delivered her tray to Table Five and was about to greet her new customers when Frank left his post behind the counter and walked over to them.

'Taylor, is that you?' she heard him say.

'Frank! Well, I never. How lovely to see you!' the plumper woman replied. 'Camille, this is Frank, a very dear old friend of mine, who I haven't seen in, goodness, it must be over ten years! How are you?'

‘I’m fabulous, thank you. You’re in my café. I’ve been here for about the same time, for my sins. I must have got it shortly after you joined the Movement. It’s so good to see you!’

‘You too, Frank. This is my wife, Camille. We met shortly after I became a Completist and we haven’t looked back since, have we?’

Camille smiled at Frank.

‘What can I get you ladies?’

‘Some tea and a couple of slices of that delicious looking chocolate cake, as long as you made it! Frank makes the most gorgeous cakes, Camille. You won’t regret it.’

‘Your wish is my command. Two enormous slices of cake coming up.’ And he strode back to the counter, a broad grin on his face.

‘I’ll get it Frank. I know you’re up to your ears.’ Emmeline said as she hurried over to him. ‘Can you believe how rude everyone was when they came in?’ she whispered as she grabbed a teapot from a shelf.

Frank shook his head in disgust. ‘Un fucking believable,’ he muttered.

Emmeline delivered the tea and cake, giving them both a warm smile. The café crowd had now adjusted to the two interlopers, and the background noise had increased. The two women were halfway through their cakes when the café quietened for a second time.

Two policemen had walked in and approached the women. The taller of the two addressed Taylor.

‘Madam, we’ve had a report that you are in breach of the Segregation Act of 2095, in that you have conversed with and hence re-established a social connection with someone outside of the Completist Movement. I am therefore placing you under immediate arrest.’

Frank put his knife down on the countertop and calmly walked over.

‘Good afternoon, officer. I’m the owner of this establish-

ment, and I think there has been a misunderstanding. This lady did not initiate the social contact, I'm afraid I did. She's an old friend of mine who I haven't seen or spoken to since she joined the Movement over ten years ago, and I was so pleased to see her again, I forgot myself. So, you see, there was absolutely no intention on behalf of this dear lady to make contact with me, she rather had it thrust upon her.'

'That's as may be,' the officer replied, 'but any breach of the Act is a strict liability offence, therefore, the context in which the breach happened is irrelevant, as is the intention of the offender.'

Emmeline looked at the two women. They had turned pale and Taylor was looking at Frank, terror in her eyes.

'Now, please step aside,' the police officer continued, 'And Madam, please come with me.'

Taylor rose from her chair like an automaton, until her trance was broken by Camille's desperate voice.

'Please, Officer, this is an awful mistake.' She had stood up and grabbed Taylor's arm.

'This is outrageous!' Frank shouted. The second officer stepped towards him.

'Calm down, Sir. And Madam, let go of the offender and stay exactly where you are. If you both have anything further to say you can make a statement at the Hackney Police station. If either of you say another word, you too will be arrested for obstructing a police officer in the execution of his duty.'

The other police officer was already marching Taylor towards the door and, in an instant, she was gone, bundled into the back of a police car, leaving Frank hugging the sobbing Camille.

Frank glared at his customers.

'Which one of you called the police?' he said. There was an edge to his voice that Emmeline had never heard before. Everyone shook their heads and shrugged their shoulders.

'One of you did, otherwise that debacle would never have

happened. What's wrong with you, whoever you are?' he said scanning their faces for any hint of guilt. 'What has this country become? Where's our tolerance gone? For the love of Jesus, she was having some tea and cake! No-one was attacked, no-one was hurt, and it wasn't even her fault, it was my fault! Her only mistake was walking into my café, which is now closed. So off you all go. I apologise to all of the people who didn't call the police, and who now can't finish their afternoon tea. But before you all start complaining, remember that lovely woman is going to face the rest of her life in prison.' Frank's voice broke, his eyes filling with tears. People were starting to get up and leave, but some sat and stared at him. He turned towards them. 'I said, get out! Now!'

Emmeline hurried over to the door, locking it behind the last, muttering customer and pulling down the blinds.

Frank took Camille into her arms and dissolved into tears. 'I'm so sorry, Camille, I'm so sorry.'

Emmeline didn't know what to do for the best. Then she went to the back of the café and grabbed the bottle of whisky and three glasses. She placed them on the table and started to pour healthy measures.

'Good thinking, Emmeline,' Frank said, wiping his eyes. 'Sit down, Camille. Drink this. Do you smoke?' he asked offering her a cigarette. She shook her head. 'Do you mind if we do?' She shook her head again.

Frank took a large swig and lit up. 'This is utter bullshit,' he muttered. Camille reached for her glass and lifted it to her lips. Her hand was trembling. Then she looked at them both.

'The worse of it is, we fought so hard against the Segregation Act. We knew it would cause divisions between us and the rest of society, and it has.'

'Damn right it has. It's had a massive impact. Before the Act was introduced, this society tolerated most people, including people who weren't heterosexual. But now, every lesbian is a Completist, because the government classified

them as Outsiders in 2098, and all the gay men have been forced underground. It's always the same old story. Segregate one group for wanting to choose a different way of life from the majority and you put a marker in the ground. Soon, a secure society becomes an insecure, paranoid one. I remember the seismic shift in attitude once the Act came into force. Suddenly, anyone perceived as deviating from the norm was a threat. One act of retribution designed to punish Completists, a pathetic kneejerk reaction from a bunch of alpha males with bruised egos, and the veneer of tolerance in this country was erased overnight. Threaten the pack and they close ranks.'

'I can't believe she's going to have her life destroyed for acknowledging an old friend.' Camille said, taking another large gulp of her whisky.

'I feel ashamed,' Emmeline said, 'I had no idea about all this.'

'My sweet girl, you weren't even born. You didn't know what things were like before. How could you? The fact that you're ashamed is enough.' Frank patted Emmeline's hand.

'I'm so sorry too, Camille. Is there really nothing that can be done?' Emmeline said.

'I'm going to speak to the Founders. We're strong now. Our new mission is political equality, and we're making headway. We must be able to lobby Parliament. I'm going to do everything I can. I don't have a choice. The thought of life without Taylor is unimaginable.'

'I'll help in any way I can. Just let me know what you need.' Frank said.

'What I need right now is another glass of that whisky.'

Camille refused Frank's offer to drive her home, preferring to call a Completist taxi firm. It was after 5.00 when she left.

Frank was very low, and Emmeline suggested they have another drink together. He smiled at her, but shook his head.

'I appreciate the gesture, but I'm going to retire hurt for the evening.'

'At least let me clear up and get everything ready for the morning.'

'You're a good girl. Thank you. By the way, congratulate your mother on her engagement for me, will you?'

'How did you know?'

'Harry came in for a coffee on your day off, earlier this week. He showed me the ring. Oh, and if you're looking for a place of your own, I have a room in the house I own around the corner coming up for rent. It's a lovely room, and it's yours if you want it.'

Emmeline gave him a hug. 'You're a kind, wise man, Frank. You mustn't blame yourself for what happened today. It's not your fault. You wouldn't intentionally hurt anyone. You've been more of a father to me than my own father or Harry ever could be.'

Frank kissed her softly on her forehead and sighed.

'I don't feel like a good man right now. Night, my little angel.'

CHAPTER 52

Emmeline stood, hands on hips, surveying her new room. Jack stood beside her. She was pleased. The walls were painted, the bed made, the boxes unpacked, and everything was in its place. She knew it wouldn't be for long, but for now, it was perfect.

'Looks pretty good, doesn't it?' said Jack.

'It's beautiful. Thank you so much for all your help. I couldn't have done it without you!'

'I'm sure you could've, but it might have taken you a little longer,' he said nudging her arm.

'I have an expensive bottle of red waiting for us downstairs, and we have the lounge to ourselves. The others invited us to join them for a drink, but I declined. I hope I made the right decision?' Emmeline asked.

'Let me see, red wine, and home alone with the woman I love. Sounds awful, but I'll cope.' Jack turned to her and took her in his arms. He kissed her softly. 'Do you fancy watching a film?'

'Funny you should say that. I heard the new Amy Styles film has been released to view. Fancy that?'

They settled down on the rather worn, but comfortable

sofa, and clinked their glasses. 'Here's to three months of getting to know the most wonderful person that has ever made me coffee!' Jack said, looking into her eyes.

Emmeline smiled and raised her glass to her lips. She trusted those eyes. Jack had been so patient with her, so understanding. He had let her talk about her fears, until he became a safe haven; his arms a harbour wall, sheltering her from the wild world beyond.

Halfway through the film he leant over and kissed her, tenderly at first, then with a passion and urgency he had never shown before. She was ready. He swept her up into his arms and carried her upstairs, and Emmeline willingly gave her all to her man. The man who had convinced her love did exist. The man who might even be her happy ever after. The happy ever after she'd never imagined she'd want.

He left after breakfast the next morning. When he started getting ready, Emmeline was a little hurt; she had planned a day of relaxation together, maybe a pub lunch with her new housemates. They hadn't discussed it because she had assumed he would spend the whole weekend with her.

'I'm sorry to go so soon,' Jack said. 'I've got to help another mate out today. He's asked me to go and look at a car with him, and it's halfway up the country.'

Emmeline smiled. She knew she looked disappointed, and Jack was evidently feeling awkward. 'I really am sorry. I should have told you. It was thoughtless of me. I really don't want to go, especially after last night. But that wasn't planned!'

'Honestly, don't worry. I'll see you tomorrow, for your usual, shan't I?'

'Wouldn't miss it for the world. I love you.'

'I love you too.'

CHAPTER 53

Emmeline reached over to stop her alarm. Her eyes wandered around her newly decorated room. The smell of the Wild Rose paint still lingered in the air. She was happy.

She sat up, shoving her feet into her slippers. Her mum and Harry had given her a brand-new bed as a moving in present. It was blissful and made getting up for work that little bit harder. She stretched her arms above her head, shuddered and stood up. She had half an hour before she started at the café. Plenty of time to get washed and dressed and walk around the corner.

Emmeline trotted along the pavement, pulling her coat around her against the fresh November wind. She decided she would take the longer route to work, past Jack's house. She had never been this way before, but she needed to be close to him, despite knowing he would soon be walking into the café to collect his morning coffee. As she approached his red front door, she crossed over to the other side of the street, looking up towards his bedroom window. She was hoping she might catch a glimpse of his silhouette, maybe give him a cheery wave, if their eyes met. Her heart stopped at the same time as

her feet. Jack was standing by the window. He didn't see her, he was too engrossed in kissing a woman; he was holding her face tenderly, the way he had held hers. Her feet started moving again. She had to get away. She found herself in front of the café unable to open the door. She started pounding on the glass, her chest so tight she was sure she would stop breathing. She felt herself go, sinking down into a different world, a safe space, where there was nothing. The next thing she knew she was lying on the café floor, her head resting on several tea towels, her left hand in Frank's.

'Ah, there you are. You dipped out on me for a moment. Gave me quite a shock.' He was trying to sound light-hearted, but his expression gave him away. The creases on his forehead competed with the forced smile lines of his mouth.

'How are you feeling? Do you think you can sit up? If not, I can call an ambulance.' His free hand started to stroke her forehead, gently sweeping away the hair from her face.

Emmeline stared up at him. She felt weak and shaky. She tried to sit up, grasping his arm for support. He helped her to her feet and then to a chair.

'Listen. You don't look at all well. Sit there quietly. I'm going to make you a sweet tea and some toast and honey. Try to stay with me, Emmeline.'

She heard him rushing around the kitchen, then, as he was waiting for the toast to brown and the kettle to boil, he went over to the café door and sellotaped a notice to it, drawing down the blinds and returning to the kitchen, summoned back by the whistle of the kettle and the clunk of the toaster.

He sat down opposite her. 'Please, try to drink this and take a nibble on the toast. You need to get those blood sugars up.' He pushed her favourite teacup towards her, and spooned a heaped teaspoon of sugar into it, stirring it purposefully. He examined Emmeline and was prompted to spoon some more sugar into her cup. 'I know it'll be disgusting, but you can trust me, I'm a café owner.'

Emmeline did as she was told. 'That's better, you've turned from ghost white to alabaster; we're making progress.' He patted her hand.

Emmeline smiled weakly at Frank. 'Thank you,' she whispered, as she continued to sip her tea and nibble her breakfast.

Frank sat silently watching her. He seemed to be waiting for the right hue to appear on her skin before speaking.

'What brought this on? You've been so happy lately, positively exploding with vitality.' He spoke quietly, worried her answer would be difficult for her to say and for him to hear.

'It's Jack, Frank. He's seeing another woman.' She could barely get the words out. She felt disconnected from the world and from her own body.

'Oh, Sweet Mary Jesus, the prick. How could he? How could he do this to you, after knowing everything you've been through?' Frank pushed his hand through his mop of a fringe, eyes searching the air above his head, expecting Sweet Mary to actually provide an answer to explain away this crime against his beloved Emmeline.

'Are you sure it was him?' His voice was louder now, angry.

'I walked past his house this morning. I saw him kissing a woman in his bedroom. It was Jack. He was standing by his window. Holding her face, like he holds mine.' Her voice was surprisingly steady. She felt incredibly calm. Her body had blown a fuse to protect her brain from overloading. Now she was being reset, and her emotional circuits were still down.

'I should've known he couldn't be trusted when he joked he was a fireman then a vet. Ridiculous outmoded gender stereotyping.'

Her mobile phone buzzed. It was Jack. He was asking her if everything was alright. He was outside the café for his coffee.

She turned the phone towards Frank.

'He's outside, is he? Shall I go and get the kitchen knife

and cut his dick off? It would be my absolute pleasure.' Frank wasn't smiling.

She reached over to take his hand.

'Thank you, but I'd much rather have another cup of tea and some more toast. And then I think we should get on with our day.'

Frank squeezed her hand. As he started to walk towards the kitchen, he stopped and kissed her on the top of her head. Emmeline decided there and then that this kiss would be her last.

CHAPTER 54

Kate reached for the sugar jar; her third coffee, and it wasn't even ten. Cara was up to something. First, the flowers, from a girl she had never mentioned before, then the extra care she took over her appearance whenever they met; but what really had Kate convinced, was the radio silence on Cara's return. No newsy updates, no titbits of gossip, nothing.

Conversation between them had become stilted; they were dancing around each other with words, boxers jabbing at the air, testing their opponent, waiting for them to drop their guard. They hadn't even discussed plans for her birthday. It was hard to believe her daughter would be 22 in eight days time.

She would have to speak to her soon. She didn't know why she had avoided it for so long. Yes, yes, she did. She was frightened. Frightened of what her daughter would say to her. Terrified.

They met, as usual, in the foyer at 5.30 p.m. and smiled at one another. 'Good day?' Kate asked politely.

'Not the best.' Cara replied. 'You?'

'Ditto. Lots of things playing on my mind. I couldn't

really concentrate.' Kate waited for a response. Cara didn't say a word. That was it, the last straw. She wouldn't put up with this shit anymore.

They spent the journey home on the bus in silence, the space between them thick with unspoken words.

Back home, Kate made her way to the kitchen as Cara took off her coat and headed towards the stairs.

'Cara.'

'Yes, Mum?' Cara sounded strained.

'Come and have a cup of tea with me. We need to talk.' It wasn't a request. Reluctantly, Cara sat down in her usual spot.

Kate bought the teas over and sat down with a sigh.

'What's going on? I know you're hiding something from me, and my mind is imagining the worst, so tell me. Please. It can't be worse than the thoughts in my head.'

'What would be the worst thing I could say to you right now, Mum?' Cara looked directly into her eyes for the first time in weeks. Her own were filling with tears.

Shit, maybe she was wrong. Maybe Cara was sick. She reached out her hand to hold Cara's.

'Are you ill?' she asked in a whisper.

'No, Mum. I'm not ill.'

'What is it then?' She braced herself for the reply.

Cara's face was ashen. 'I want to become a Chosen One.'

Kate crumpled. Her daughter had fallen in love. She felt angry and betrayed. This couldn't be happening. The stupid fool. You idiot, Cara, you don't know what you're doing! Kate, get your shit together, convince her to stay. Come on, you can do this. Kate straightened her back.

'I knew it. Samantha is a Sam. Right?'

'Yes.' Cara looked down, momentarily the chastised little daughter, then raised her head, meeting Kate's stare.

'When did it start?'

'Sam's the Facilitator you arranged for me,' she said.

Kate jerked back in her chair, anger surging through her. 'This has been going on for nearly four years?'

'No, Mum. Listen to me,' Cara's voice was louder now. She leant forward; her eyes fixed on hers. 'I felt incredibly connected to him after that first night. I wanted to see him again, but I knew I couldn't, so I went to Chester to forget him. I replaced him with my studies. Ironically, I've got him to thank for doing so well!'

'Well, let me shake that man's hand,' Kate replied, sarcastically.

Cara ignored her and carried on. 'Once my course was over, he came flooding back into my head. So, I arranged to see him again, the first week I was home. I was hoping to feel nothing. Hoped I could leave it all behind and get on with my life. But it was incredible.' Cara's face lit up. Kate's heart sank. 'I know I can never make you understand, but I love him. I can't imagine a life without him in it.' Kate could see that Cara was pleading with her now, begging her to understand, to forgive her for choosing Sam over her.

'How dare you say I could never understand. I understand perfectly. I adored your father, until the beatings started. But do you know what finally ended our marriage?' Kate's eyes had turned black. 'He had sex with another woman shortly after you were born. Obviously, I wasn't satisfying his sexual needs, so he simply turned his back on us, his family, and went to find some other vagina to fuck.'

It was Cara's turn to sit back in her chair.

Kate stared past her daughter. Come on, Kate, calm down. Make her understand. 'I don't want the same thing to happen to you. That's why I joined the Movement. This was never going to happen to me again, nor to any daughter of mine. But here you are, putting yourself in front of the firing squad.' She reached over and grabbed Cara's hands. 'Cara, men can't be trusted. They'll always use a woman, and when they have no further use for her, they're gone.' Jesus, she needed a

cigarette. She got up from the table, striding towards the larder. She reached for an old biscuit tin from the top shelf and pulled out a packet of cigarettes and a lighter. Lighting one, she took a deep drag, and sat down again, grabbing a saucer from the draining board.

'I didn't know you smoked,' Cara said, staring in astonishment.

'I don't as a rule, just on very special occasions. Want one? After all, the choice you've evidently made will kill you emotionally, so why not damage yourself physically as well.' Cara shook her head at the packet being thrust towards her.

'Mum, I can't know how much my father hurt you, and I can't imagine how I'd feel if Sam did the same thing to me. Especially as I'd have given up the two people I love the most to be with him. It would probably be even worse for me because of the sacrifice...'

'Cara, I had to give up my family too.' Kate interjected, leaning towards her, holding her attention with the fire in her eyes 'I had to leave behind my mother and sister when I joined the Movement.'

Cara stared at her as if she were a stranger.

'I didn't know you had a sister,' she said.

Kate slumped back in her chair. 'She's my twin. We're not identical. She's eight minutes older than me. We were inseparable when we were growing up, a bit like you and Gemma, only you're more of a second mum to Gemma, Sophie was my best friend.' She stubbed out her cigarette, and angrily wiped away an unexpected tear. 'Neither Sophie nor my mother could understand why I wanted to become a Completist. They didn't know about the violence. At first, they pleaded with me, then they were angry. They thought I was rejecting them over a stupid affair. But I wasn't rejecting them, Cara. I was rejecting the pain and sorrow men had caused me.'

She paused. Should she go on? Should she tell her everything? Something in Cara's eyes gave her the reassurance she

needed. 'In the end I had to tell them about the beatings and the other reason I no longer wanted men in my life. I needed them to see I wasn't turning my back on them, but it still destroyed everything.'

Cara was listening intently; she was barely breathing. Kate felt her hand on hers, urging her to continue. Could she trust her? Would she believe her?

Kate sighed and continued. 'It wasn't solely your father's violence and infidelity, Cara. My father started sexually assaulting me when I was eight years old.'

Cara gasped. 'Oh, Mum. Oh my God. That's disgusting. I had no idea.' Cara looked completely horrified; at that moment, Kate loved her daughter with all her heart. She believed her, there wasn't a shadow of doubt in those precious eyes. Cara's faith spurred her on.

'My mother and sister never suspected. He was very clever at covering his tracks. It started when he insisted on separate bedrooms. Sophie was given the room next to theirs and I had the one at the front of the house. He told me if I said anything to anyone, he'd kill Sophie. I believed him. There was no tenderness in what he did with me, it was brutish, violent. It only stopped when he died of a heart attack. I was 15. After that, I was desperate to leave home. Seeing my mother and sister grieving for him made me feel sick. Every time I went to my room, I could still feel his weight on me, still feel him probing my body, threatening to beat me whenever I cried out.' Kate shuddered, her stomach churning, sweat trickling down her breastbone.

'I left home as soon as I turned 16. I think they were relieved. Their shared grief for my father, and my lack of any, alienated me even further. My mother had turned him into a saint, and I was full of rage. Even in death, I had to keep my father's filthy secrets, to protect my mother and sister, keep his memory intact.' She shook her head in disgust. 'I only told them because of their reaction, when I told them I was

becoming a Completist. Sophie couldn't take it, tears were streaming down her face, and my darling mother blamed me. I lost it, and out it came. Sophie stepped back from me as if I was a leper. There was a moment of complete silence, then my mother started screaming at me to get out, and Sophie ran to her, not me. And the look she gave me. I'll never forget it. That was the last time I saw my mother. I did meet Sophie one day on the bus. It was the day before you started school. She hated me.'

'What did she say?'

'Thankfully, she didn't speak to me. But I could feel her hatred, it radiated from her.'

For a moment, they sat looking at one another, then Cara stood up and stepped towards her. Kate rose to meet her, and they wrapped their arms around each other; two women, trying to heal a gaping wound. Kate held her daughter tightly, breathing her in; her baby, her beautiful girl. Then her embrace softened as she eased her body away from her daughter's. Perhaps it was time to let go.

'I don't know about you, but I could do with something stronger than tea. Is there any wine in the fridge?' Cara said.

'Good idea. Gemma won't be back from Mandy's for another hour or two.'

Cara poured them two large glasses and sat back down. 'Can I ask you a question?'

'Fire away.' They were both calm now, the air between them clean and fresh.

'How were you able to fall in love after what your father did to you?'

Kate gave a wry laugh. Cara was trying so hard to understand. Looking so earnest. Caring so much. 'David was kind to me. He took things at my pace. I felt respected, understood. When we finally started to be intimate, it was so far removed from my experience with my father, I didn't link the two in my head. I did love your father very much and I trusted him with

my life. I was sure our relationship was much more than physical intimacy. I couldn't understand why he couldn't wait a few months. Let me get over your birth. My pregnancy was trouble-free and we sailed through it, together. I thought he was looking forward to being a father as much as I was a mother. I began to think we could make our marriage work.'

Kate shook her head before continuing. 'I found them after my hospital appointment was cancelled. My gynaecologist was unavailable, and they were too short-staffed to offer me an alternative. I'd had a very difficult birth. I was hoping to return from hospital with the green light to resume our sex life, only to find he had already resumed his.'

Cara sat back in her chair, putting her hands on her cheeks, as if her head had become too heavy to support itself. 'I wish I'd known about this before. I often wondered why you joined the Movement, giving up any chance to feel what I feel for Sam. But now I understand. You've suffered so much.'

'Does it change your decision?' Kate held her breath. Please say it does, my lovely girl, please.

'I'm sorry, Mum, but I don't believe Sam is like my father. He's a gentle soul. And even though he meets hundreds of women every year, he only wants me. Perhaps that's our saving grace. If men are so obsessed with sex, perhaps his job will keep him faithful. I don't know what the future will bring. And the thought of causing you more pain is awful, but it's not my fault. We live in a divided society, and we're forced to make impossible choices. But we still have to make them, and try to live with the consequences.'

Kate panicked. Oh God, Cara was wrong, so wrong. She couldn't make her see, make her understand. What else could she tell her? There must be something more she could say...

'But what about Gemma, Cara? I'm not sure she'll ever be able to forgive you. She doesn't understand romantic love, and probably never will.'

Cara's face crumpled. Kate dared to feel hope.

‘I don’t know how to tell her.’ Kate was screaming inside her head. Then don’t. Stay with us. We truly love you. We’ll never desert you. Come on Cara, come on. Don’t tear us apart.

‘I can’t tell her yet. I’m exhausted. You’ll let me tell her, won’t you?’ Cara pleaded.

Kate knew she had lost, she nodded. ‘But don’t leave it too long. I’m not sure how I’m going to pretend there’s nothing wrong when I know you’re about to leave me forever.’

Cara reached across the table and grabbed her mum’s arm, there was panic in her eyes. ‘Oh, Mum,’ she sobbed, ‘I’m so sorry.’

Kate stroked Cara’s hand. ‘I love you and always will. But you are making a big mistake, and I won’t be there to pick up the pieces unless you re-join the Movement. For your sake, I hope you never have to.’

CHAPTER 55

Emmeline approached her mother's new, olive-green front door. She was glad her mother's life was going so smoothly. They had moved into the new place a few weeks before Christmas. Emmeline had spent Christmas with them, trying to share their joy, hiding her devastation as best she could. She had already bought Jack his Christmas present and had been imagining Christmas Day cozied up with him on the sofa, while her mum and Harry prepared lunch together in the kitchen. Instead, she had sat alone, watching a film, listening to her mum laughing with her husband as they stirred the gravy together.

And now it was the 10th of March. It was her 21st birthday in a couple of weeks and Emmeline was determined not to waste any more of her life wallowing in self-pity. She was dreading this evening, but was sure, after everything she had been through, her mother would understand. She knew she would be upset. It had been a difficult decision to make; but her mind was made up.

She rang the doorbell.

'Come in, Trouble. What an unexpected pleasure to see you on a week night.' Her mother ushered her into the

kitchen, where Harry was waiting to hand her a glass of red. He offered her a cigarette, which she gladly accepted.

'The place looks better and better every time I see it. Love the colour you've chosen for the walls.'

'Thanks, we're really pleased with it too, aren't we Harry?' Harry beamed. 'I've made your favourite, vegetable lasagne and chips!'

'Thanks, Mum. How long until it's ready?'

'I just need to reheat the lasagne. But I thought we'd have a catch up first.'

'Great. Shall we sit in the kitchen or the lounge?'

'Let's stay in here. The lounge is in a bit of a mess. We're halfway through painting it.'

They sat around the kitchen table and a hollowness crept through her.

'You alright love? You've gone very pale.' Her mother reached over and touched her hand.

'Not really, Mum. I've got something to tell you and I'm not sure how you're going to react.' Emmeline noticed her voice was quiet and small.

'I won't know until you tell me, so don't keep me in suspense. You're making me feel anxious.' They both reached for another cigarette. Emmeline offered her packet to Harry to repay his earlier generosity.

'You're alright, Emmeline. I'll have one of mine.' He smiled at her, but she could see he was also bracing himself.

Emmeline sighed. All the words she had carefully rehearsed had fled from her brain, and she was struggling to know how to begin.

'It's alright, Emmeline, there's nothing you can say that I can't handle, that we can't handle.' Her mother placed a hand on each of theirs, a mark of their new family solidarity.

'You know what Jack did to me destroyed the fragile trust I had in men, don't you, Mum? Present company and Frank

excepted, of course.' Harry smiled. Her mother nodded her head.

'The way I see things, the aftermath of what happened to me at school stole my future from me, and Jack crushed my faith. No woman has ever hurt me. You've been a great mum. Your love and attention more than made up for Dad's neglect. And as for Charlie, we never connected. He was a pain in my side and the reason my father never spent time with me.'

Harry and her mother looked confused, but held their silence, waiting for Emmeline to get to the point.

'I've had enough of being hurt and disappointed. I want to regain control of my life. I want to go back to college and get my degree -'

'But that's brilliant news! I couldn't be happier. Why the long face?'

'Mum, you didn't let me finish. I want to go to Chester.'

Her mother looked puzzled. 'But that's a Completist college, Emmeline,' she said, her face darkening.

'I know, Mum. I'm going to become a Completist. I don't want to risk any more men messing up my life. All I ever truly wanted was to get a good degree in Engineering and build big, beautiful structures. I've never imagined myself in a wedding dress, or holding a baby in my arms. Whenever I used to daydream, it was about receiving an award for the amazing avant-garde work I'd spearheaded.'

No-one spoke. She saw her mother's expression and she was suddenly afraid. She had often experienced her anger, but never her hatred. Her mother's face had never looked so ugly: her features, a grotesque caricature of the woman she knew.

'Mum?' She held her breath, waiting for the explosion to hit her.

'I can't believe what I've just heard. Truly, I can't. You want to join that group of bitter, twisted women, who blame all their woes and failures on men?' She didn't wait for, or want, a response. 'This is ironic. My own daughter doing

exactly what my little sister did to me, turning her back on me. After all we've meant to one another. Kate and I used to be as close as I thought we were. Jesus, Emmeline, how the fuck can you do this to me when I've already lost Charlie? I never imagined you'd break my heart. You've always had my back. We're a team, aren't we? You didn't see me running to join those witches when I got divorced. No, I stuck it out, I coped. I worked through my problems and look at me now. I didn't turn my back on my entire life, on my beliefs, on love!'

Emmeline was trying to resist the urge to get up and run. She was stunned.

'Have you got nothing to say for yourself!' her mother shouted.

'I don't understand. I didn't know you had a sister who joined the Completists. I knew you didn't like the Movement, but you never said you hated it. You believed they were cowards, as I recall. But surely you can see this isn't about not loving you, this is about surviving. No... not surviving, that's the wrong word. This about having a chance to thrive.' Her mother was staring at her. Emmeline's words were bouncing off a stone wall. She tried again to make her understand.

'I don't feel safe as a Chosen One, I can't function properly. I love you, Mum, I always will. But don't blame me for the choices I've been forced to make, I had no say in this crazy shit. But I do understand why the Movement needed to happen. Why women needed to have this choice. Can't you see that too? I'm sorry about your sister, but I bet she suffered at the hands of men. I know you and Dad got divorced, but that's not as bad as being nearly raped, then cheated on, and having a father who didn't give a shit.' Emmeline was angry at her mother's complete lack of understanding, and the tone of her voice was hardening. 'I'm sorry you think I'm weak. But most of all I'm sorry you can't understand why I have to do this. I guess it's difficult to empathise with someone when your experiences don't

mirror theirs. Although, I did expect a little more compassion.'

Her mother's response to her indignation was rage. Emmeline stared at her. She's going to explode. She's literally going to burst. This is all about her, what she's been through, she doesn't understand how I feel. Jesus, I'm done, I'm out of here. Emmeline heard Harry say something but then her mother's voice smashed into her head.

'Get out, Emmeline. You've made your decision!' she screamed. 'I don't know who you are anymore!'

'Come on, Sophie love. Don't be like this, don't end things like you ended them with Kate.' Harry's tone was quiet and conciliatory.

'Oh, fuck off, Harry! You can't begin to understand what's it's like to have your sister and now your daughter turn their back on you.'

Emmeline had already left the room. She couldn't bear to hear anything else her mother had to say. She had wanted her memory of her to be left intact, but it was smashed beyond repair, lying in shards on the kitchen floor.

As she walked away from all she knew, she was surprised at the relief she felt.

CHAPTER 56

Sam lifted her up in his arms and swung her around the lounge.

'I can't believe you've done this for me. This is the best day of my life. Thank you, Cara. There'll never be a single day when you regret your decision. We're going to be so happy. I'm going to make sure of it.'

'Put me down, you idiot,' Cara laughed, and as he placed her back on solid ground, she kissed him as if her life depended on it.

When they were lying together in his bed, Sam softly stroking the skin on her arm, Cara turned her head on the pillow to look at him.

'I can't tell Gemma, I can't. I'm going to take a day off work, pack up my stuff and leave tomorrow. Do you mind? I know it's the coward's way out, but I'll write her a long letter. Mum will explain. She understands, she's been in love.'

'You're the one going through this, you handle it the way you want to.' He kissed her tenderly on the forehead. 'We can buy a new place together. We should be able to get somewhere really nice with our joint salaries. We can use the money you've

saved to buy all new stuff for it. Make a fresh start. Begin our lives together properly.'

'Oh, Sam. What a brilliant idea. How exciting! A spot of house hunting might take my mind off things.'

'You know, I meant what I said earlier. I'll do everything I can to make you happy, and from the last hour, I seem to be able to do quite a few things that put a smile on your face!' He winked at her.

She looked at him, realising she was doing exactly what her mum did to her. She was sizing him up.

'What's the matter? Did I not please Madam earlier?'

'It's not all about the sex though, is it, Sam?'

'Don't be silly. I love the way you cook too!' Cara thumped him on his arm.

'You big dick!' she said.

'I know. But it's a cross I have to bear,' and he placed her hand on his groin.

'Jesus, Sam. Aren't you exhausted?' she said, surprised to feel him harden beneath her fingers.

'You're blessed to have a man with amazing staying power!' he said, rolling on top of her and holding her hands above her head.

She wanted to believe him, to trust him.

....

The following day was the hardest day of her life. Once she had packed her suitcase and placed the letter on the kitchen table, she found herself going back upstairs. She opened Gemma's bedroom door and looked at the posters on the walls and the piles of textbooks on her desk. She stared fondly at the array of discarded clothes and underwear littering the floor; then her eyes rested on the photograph on Gemma's bedside table. It was a picture of the two of them, taken by her mother, the day they went to Hyde Park and took a rowing boat out on

the Serpentine. They were looking into each other's eyes and laughing. Cara started to cry. She shut the door and went downstairs. She picked up her suitcase, opened the door, and stepped outside. Closing the door behind her, she took her house key off her keyring and posted it through the letterbox.

CHAPTER 57

Joining the Completists was like emigrating to a new country. Emmeline arrived at the nearest branch office, laden with all the documents that encapsulated her entire existence. She was prepared for the erasure of her old life. It was strange to think her mother would know nothing more about her, not even where she was or what she was up to. She could even choose a new name. Apparently, many Completists did, using their defection, as the COs liked to call it, to start afresh. They likened their decision to transgender people, whose old name belonged to a different person. They discarded their names, as they discarded their former lives: naked and free: a rebirth. Emmeline realised she had no need to go through this metamorphosis. There was nothing wrong with *her*, she merely had the wrong mother. She would now belong to the world she should have been born into.

The process was remarkably quick and she left the office a few hours later, with an interview set for Chester the following week. The young woman who had transferred her explained that her education and living expenses would be covered if they accepted her, on the understanding that 20% of her first five years of salary went to the Movement and, if she gradu-

ated, she was guaranteed a job in a Completist company. Apparently, everyone paid the same percentage, no matter how much they earned, and she would be told exactly what this money paid for and the benefits it would bring to her life. It was a virtuous circle because Completists tended to buy goods and services from other Completists, so their wealth stayed within the system and led to more money being ploughed back into supporting the members.

Emmeline felt truly liberated. She had never appreciated how crushing it was to live under the gaze of men. For the first time, she understood why Completists held their heads high and looked directly ahead. It was a sign of freedom. She headed off to the Transition House with a spring in her step. She was going to meet a woman called Christine. She had been involved in the Movement from the very beginning.

Emmeline was a little anxious about meeting her. What if she didn't like her? She knew she wouldn't be under her roof for long; nevertheless, it would be nice to see a friendly face.

When the door opened, she was relieved to see an elderly woman with short greying hair, who looked like she spent her days cooking apple pie. Christine smiled warmly and shook her hand.

'Welcome, Emmeline. Come on in and I'll show you your room. Emmeline followed her up the stairs and Christine opened the first door they came to. The room was bright and airy. It smelt of fresh linen and Emmeline noticed a Completist pin on the pillow, with a yellow rose next to it.

'I'll give you a few moments to get used to your new surroundings,' Christine said, smiling gently. 'When you're ready, come on down and we'll have some tea and cake.'

Emmeline sat down on the bed. She picked up the rose and smelt it. Its perfume was sweet and delicate. She wondered if she should wear the pin immediately and brushed over its metal surface with her fingertips. Every Completist she had ever seen wore their pin on their right side, over their heart.

She got up and looked in the mirror on the wall opposite the bed. After carefully attaching the pin to her jumper, she scrutinised her reflection. She saw an entirely different person. This was it. She was in. She was a Completist. So many things had happened to her that day, but wearing this pin made everything real. She couldn't wait to rediscover the cheerful, carefree version of herself again. She wanted her back so badly. She longed to laugh, to have conversations unconcerned about hidden agendas and double meanings. She wanted to feel safe, protected.

She heard the kettle singing from the kitchen and decided to head downstairs and grab herself some cake. Would Christine be a chocolate cake person, or would it be a wholesome carrot cake? When coffee and walnut was placed on the table, she was a little disappointed, until she tasted it.

'Best coffee and walnut cake I've ever had,' she said, beaming at Christine.

'Thank you, Emmeline, it's always been a favourite of mine. Now, how can I help? Would you like me to contact your old landlord, for example?'

She had already squared everything with Frank before she left; however, Emmeline was surprised and relieved when the conversation focused on practical help and the history of the Movement. Christine didn't ask her why she had joined, but she did give her the number of a counsellor. Emmeline heard nothing to cause her concern. On the contrary, she returned to her room, feeling she was in safe hands, supported but not controlled. She sat, cross-legged on her bed and glanced through the information she had been given. There was a flyer for a Facilitator Service which made her smile. Christine had not explained this particular benefit, and at first Emmeline was confused; however, the copy soon clarified exactly what was on offer. She didn't think she would be needing this particular number but placed the flyer carefully back in the paper wallet. She paid more attention to

the booklet on mental health. She knew it was strictly forbidden to have any contact with family members and friends outside the Movement and was well aware of the consequences. She had already learnt from Camille how hard the Movement had fought against the Segregation Act, recognising the psychological problems it would cause. Emmeline felt a wave of melancholy wash over her. It was awful that she would never see her mother again, but the person she was missing the most was Frank. She pushed the memory of his tear-stained face and the warmth of his final embrace into the recesses of her mind. She didn't want to cry. Not today.

Emmeline had been a Completist for six days when she visited the university campus. She was delighted to see the grounds full of trees, each one surrounded by dozens of daffodils. She was shown into a bright, modern room, where three cheerful faces beckoned her to take a seat in front of them. Since Emmeline had made her decision to join, her head had, once again, been filled with the dreams and passions she had set aside for so many years. The disabling self-loathing, pain and resentment Mr E had ignited in her had been transfigured into a beautiful anger, driving her forward with renewed determination.

This was all she wanted. She must have successfully communicated her passion and demonstrated her abilities, as they immediately offered her a place. She would have to tread water for a few months until the next autumn intake, but they gave her the details of a number of engineering firms who took internships, explaining she would be offered a placement at one of them and would be paid on a needs basis. All she had to do was complete a financial form showing her outgoings and her pay would cover them. Emmeline was impressed. She had

some savings, so she knew she would be able to make ends meet.

A week later, she was standing at another front door, her suitcase by her side. She rang the bell and a young woman in her mid-twenties answered.

'Hi, you must be Emmeline. Come in, come in. I'm Laura. I'm the only one in at present, all the other girls are at work. So am I, actually. I'm the housekeeper. It's my job to keep the place clean and handle all the administration, so the rest of you can get on with your jobs without any distractions.' Laura was petite and neat. Her blonde hair was pulled pack into a loose ponytail and she wore only the merest hint of make-up. Her skin was clear and her eyes a deep blue. She could have stepped out of an alpine meadow.

'Seriously?' Emmeline said, laughing out loud.

'Oh yes. Every Completist house is run like this. Oh, and don't worry, all my wages are included in your rent, and they're subsidised by the Movement. Didn't they explain that to you?'

'Shit, this gets better and better. They probably did, but it's been information overload over the past fortnight. Perhaps I zoned out at that point!'

Laura laughed. 'The transfer process must be quite overwhelming. I'm the daughter of a Completist, so I've never been through it. I couldn't imagine how I'd handle things in your shoes. You're on the second floor. It's a lovely room, views over the park. I hope you like it.'

Emmeline followed Laura, listening to her talk about the other girls. She smiled at her enthusiasm as Laura gave her a thumbnail sketch of each of them. 'I sense you'll fit right in. And Zoe's off to Chester in September too. So, you never

know, you might have a ready-made roomie when you move up there.'

After a full inspection of the immaculate shared lounge, kitchen and bathrooms, Emmeline was left to settle in. It didn't take her long to unpack. She hadn't brought many personal effects with her. She did have a single photograph of her and Frank outside the café. They were each pointing a finger behind them at the café windows, smiling ridiculously. There had been nothing to celebrate, other than the fact they had finally got around to cleaning them; nonetheless, Frank had declared this moment of clarity should be captured for posterity, in case it never happened again. It was their expressions Emmeline loved. Mock pride and mirth, Frank had called it.

She had asked for the photograph the day she had told him she was leaving. He had ruffled her hair and placed one final soft kiss on the top of her head, as he stood up to retrieve the café album from a nearby bookshelf.

Now she arranged the photo carefully on top of the chest of drawers, next to her mirror and her small collection of make-up brushes.

She sat down on her bed and took in her new home. Last stop before Chester. She felt light and excited. Truly happy. She hoped the other girls would be welcoming and decided to make the most of her free time before studies robbed her of it. Chester was going to be tough, and she was determined to graduate this time.

CHAPTER 58

Sam had left for work and Cara sat on the sofa, mobile on lap, scanning job sites. It had been six weeks since she had left home, and this was the only space in which she existed. She had been wiped off the Completist system and had discovered her transfer would remain unregistered until she married. She was an Outsider now, in limbo. She was alone and uncared for, immediately discarded by this new society. She had even started to believe Sam regarded her as a lesser human being without her prestigious job and fat pay packet. As a disenfranchised person, she was shocked at how difficult it was to get a decent job, despite her qualifications and experience in one of the top UK companies. The message was clear, embrace the life of a Chosen One by marrying, or we will not embrace you. The irony was not lost on her. She had chosen to be a CO, but they were turning their back on her until she was chosen by a man.

She hadn't wanted to marry Sam so soon. Marriage was not even a concept she fully understood. She knew what it was; they had learned about it at school. She also knew her mother had been married to her father; but they had never

discussed her wedding day, neither the logistics nor how she had felt.

To add insult to injury, Cara had been unable to make any new friends. It was difficult to meet people when there was no need to step outside your own front door. She had no friendly girlfriends to fill her in on how to go about arranging a wedding and, more importantly, to find out how she should feel about it.

Cara sighed. She really had no choice. The more she dipped into her savings to pay her share of the bills, the less money they would have to spend on their new place. There wouldn't even be a new place if she didn't get herself a decent job. She went to her search panel and typed in "Wedding Planner". She was shocked at the number of hits her search yielded. She reached for her wine and entered the portal of "Bliss Ltd – it's the day you deserve". Cara wanted to gag, but she had to start somewhere.

After a couple of hours of research Cara put her mobile down and her feet up on the sofa. She now realised what a big deal this was to the COs. A wedding day was obviously the pinnacle of a woman's achievement, if the money and effort they were prepared to spend was any indication. She was also surprised at how everything was centred around the woman. The man was a mere accessory, dressed in clothes to complement the bride, while the dresses were extraordinary. She didn't see a single one which could ever be worn in the real world. A wedding day was pure fantasy. A day on which a woman could take the starring role in her very own play. Cara could only imagine weddings had evolved in this way to make up for the lack of importance or status women had in their everyday lives. Sites constantly referred to this day as the bride's special day, as if normal life for them was very ordinary, humdrum.

The only thing Cara wanted from a wedding was access to

this new world she had chosen, and the ring. She did like the look of the engagement rings; and had learned the bigger the diamond, the greater the love of the man you were marrying. Sam had better get her a sizeable one. She was already seeing it as compensation for the sacrifices she had made to be with him: sacrifices she had foolishly not anticipated nor considered having to make, in the name of love.

Cara wondered how the COs viewed having children. She searched again and discovered there were similarities, as Completists made a big fuss over pregnancy too. However, as Cara swiped through more pages on her mobile, she noticed distinct differences between how the COs and Completists celebrated this event. They both focussed on the joy a baby can bring the mother, but Cara noticed how the CO companies selling baby products used emotive language, emphasising a baby's vulnerability, and its reliance on its mother. The Completists were far more pragmatic, focussing on the practical difficulties a single mother would face, and directing them towards products and services which could help make their lives easier.

Cara was not surprised. She had learnt a CO's primary role was to care for the children, while the husband provided financial support for the family unit. It made sense when, in the recent past, economic inequality had allowed a man to earn more money than a woman for the same job. It was evident to Cara that her teachers had been right. For men to maintain their disproportionate stake in the economy and enjoy the increased wealth and freedom of choice it yielded, they had to make the role of mothering appear to be more rewarding than it actually was. It was a way of distracting women from wanting what men had.

A baby was a woman's compensation, just like the engagement ring. The marketing gurus' message was clear: COs were lucky to have the vitally important role of staying at home looking after the little ones. How did these women

continue to buy into this myth, when they were surrounded by so many Completists demonstrating the opposite and when so many of them were too poor to stay at home and struggled to juggle work with childrearing? She was beginning to realise how her previous life was blocked from their view by a veil of silence: hidden in plain sight by powerful, male-led media giants. She was left to conclude these women were either wilfully blind to their own manipulation, or very much in love with a man, as she was. Cara took another large swig of her wine. For the first time in her life, she was powerless and controlled, and she didn't like it. She needed to change her situation. She would get her power back, in this warped world, by asking Sam to marry her as soon as he got home.

Cara didn't have to wait long. He only had two bookings that evening. She got him a glass of wine ready and sat down again, nervously flicking through the various programmes on her mobile, trying to find something to occupy her racing mind.

The door opened. He shrugged off his coat and plonked himself down beside her.

'Hello, beautiful,' he smiled, leaning in for a kiss.

'Hello, gorgeous. All good?'

'All good thank you. You alright?' He had noticed her agitation.

'I've been thinking...'

'Oh God, what about?' he said in mock horror.

'Sam, my darling man. I think we need to get married as soon as possible.' He laughed.

'What's so funny?' Cara was genuinely perplexed.

'That was romantic!'

'What are you talking about?'

'The man is meant to ask the woman. It's a big deal.'

'Oh. I didn't know, did I? How could I?'

'It's meant to go something like this,' and Sam was

suddenly kneeling on one knee in front of her. She stared at him. He took her hand.

'My darling, Cara. Would you do me the honour of being my wife?'

Cara laughed. 'Yes, I would. Thanks for asking.'

Sam laughed again. 'I guess that's how it goes when you want to spend the rest of your life with an ex Completist!'

Cara ignored him. She was in unchartered territory where she had no idea how she was meant to behave.

'So, what happens next? I think I know. I've been doing a lot of research this evening. You're meant to buy me an engagement ring, aren't you? I've found a few pictures of the ones I like.'

Sam resumed his place on the sofa beside her.

'Come here,' he said, and he hugged her. 'We'll go shopping for one tomorrow, I promise.'

'Great, then can we go to a registry office and get married, please. I need to start living again.'

'Don't you want a big wedding day then?'

'You mean wear a ridiculous dress and pay a fortune to have a party for our families and friends? Seems a little pointless when I have no-one to invite and, for some bizarre reason, none of your family speak to you because of what you do.'

'I guess you're right. We're both Outsiders, in our own ways, aren't we? I'm not sure they provide a walk-in service. But we'll find out.' He looked sad, deflated. He was staring beyond her, his hands limp on his lap.

'We could have a party down the pub with your mates and their partners,' she suggested, taking his hands in hers and squeezing them. It is a big deal becoming Mr and Mrs Brown. We should mark the occasion. We can both go shopping for something nice to wear. And maybe we could hire the private room they have, get a DJ in for the night?'

'Maybe,' he said. 'I'm tired, I think I'm going to have a shower and go to bed.'

‘OK. I’ll join you soon.’ Cara watched him trudge towards the bedroom, gulping back his wine as he went. She reached for her mobile and searched for ‘engagement ring shopping’. She didn’t want to disappoint Sam by behaving inappropriately again.

CHAPTER 59

Sam had obviously woken up determined to make this a memorable day. He gently kissed Cara on the forehead and, as her eyes opened, she saw his smiling face.

'I've been out and bought us freshly baked croissants, freshly squeezed orange juice, plus your favourite coffee.'

She sat up in bed and saw the breakfast tray beside her.

'You're so sweet. So thoughtful. I love you.'

'I love you too, future Mrs Brown.'

They sat together, content and happy, slathering butter and marmalade on the warm pastries.

'If it's alright with you,' Sam said, 'I'd like to go to a little jeweller in the City. I used to pass it on my way to work, before my current job. I always dreamed about bringing the right girl there one day to buy her a ring, and you're certainly the right girl.'

'Oh, Sam. I'd love it. I'm so sorry about yesterday evening, I evidently ballsed it up, big time.'

'It's not your fault, and it doesn't matter. We're going to have a lovely day. And with any luck, I'll be carrying you over the threshold tonight.'

‘Are you going to get me drunk then?’ she laughed.

‘No, idiot, it’s a tradition. The groom carries the bride into their home on their wedding night.’

‘Wow. Sounds fun.’ Cara gave him a sticky kiss. She was actually thinking it sounded weird; however, she had ridden roughshod through every tradition so far, so she was determined to avoid destroying yet another.

Cara was convinced the jeweller had been open for business since the reign of Elizabeth I. The shop’s diamond-cut glass windows twinkled invitingly, luring them into a small, dark interior, framed by dense, dusty beams. The man who served them seemed as old as the building; nonetheless, he was gracious and kind, and certainly knew his diamonds. Cara chose a three stone, square cut, diamond ring set in platinum. She discreetly moved away as they whispered about the price. Over breakfast, they had decided Sam wouldn’t wear a wedding ring, his clients might not appreciate it. Cara walked out of the shop with her left hand in front of her, a huge grin on her face. She tilted her hand to let the stones catch the light.

‘Look how it sparkles, Sam. Isn’t it beautiful?’

‘You do realise my knob will probably fall off with all the extra work I’ll have to take on to pay for that.’

Cara threw her head back and roared with laughter. A woman passing on the other side of the road, quickened her pace.

‘We’re off to the registry office right away. I’m not having you change your mind now!’

It was far easier than either of them had imagined to get married. There were only a few forms to fill in and the place was empty. The registry staff were excited and glad to see them. It was a surprisingly warm and intimate experience. As they stood in front of the smartly dressed smiling woman conducting the ceremony, they felt like the most important people in the world. When Cara repeated her vows, the room

slipped from view and she only saw Sam's eyes staring into hers, a gentle smile on his perfect lips.

Everything had been worth it.

CHAPTER 60

On the morning of Emmeline's graduation, she was intensely grateful to have Zoe as a friend. They had hit it off the first evening they had met and, as Laura the housekeeper had predicted, she had found a ready-made roomie.

Zoe's family were lovely and had welcomed Emmeline into their lives with a generosity that astounded her. They clapped and hollered when Emmeline was on the stage receiving her degree, filling the void where her family should have been. Emmeline did have one guest. She searched the audience and soon found Frank's face in the sea of women. She had had to get him special dispensation to attend and had thought long and hard about contacting him; weighing up the risk of being caught with her visceral need to have him present. The Guardians had reluctantly given it, as he was not a blood relative and had confirmed he was gay. In their eyes, he was virtually an honorary woman; and if Emmeline was willing to take the risk to have him there, who were they to deny her request. They had taken every precaution possible, and there he was, smiling through his tears. How she loved that man.

Many glasses of champagne later, Zoe and Emmeline staggered to their college room for the last time, giggling.

'I can't wait to get out of here and move into our own place,' Zoe slurred as her head hit the pillow. Neither of them could be bothered to undress or wash away the first make-up they had applied all year. 'And you heard she who must be obeyed. You're staying with us until we find a place. She won't take no for an answer.'

'How very rapey of her!' Emmeline replied. They both dissolved into giggles and drifted off into a deep, drunken sleep.

It took longer than they had anticipated to pack the car up and head off the next morning. Zoe begged Emmeline to be her second pair of eyes. She was sure she was still drunk and couldn't be trusted behind the wheel.

They arrived at Zoe's house in Hampstead with fully functioning hangovers.

'My, my girls. You look as fresh as dewy daisies,' Zoe's mother said sarcastically, as she eyed the two of them standing dejectedly in the doorway. 'Will you be retiring to your beds for a while?'

They emerged in their pyjamas at 4.00 p.m. to find burgers and chips waiting for them downstairs.

'Mum, you're a genius. Perfect hangover cure. Thank you.'

'Enjoy. You're looking at our entire week's meat ration. So, what interviews have you both got lined up?'

'Jesus, Mum. Can't this wait until tomorrow? But if you must know, we've both got three interviews. Don't worry, your little darlings will be in full-time employment and out of your hair in no time. Now, could you please pass the ketchup, and leave us to enjoy this very special treat.'

It took several days for Emmeline to feel on top form again. She scrutinised her reflection in the full-length mirror in Zoe's room. Satisfied that she looked like a professional who was going places, she picked up her bag and headed for the door.

'Good luck,' she heard Zoe shout from the bathroom. 'Knock 'em dead!'

'Good luck to you too, my constipated friend. Remember, our success will get us out of here!'

'I'm hearing you loud and clear. Now go! I have things I need to concentrate on.'

Emmeline smiled, ran down the stairs and grabbed Zoe's car keys from the hallway table. It was Femmeur today, the one she really wanted. They had recently launched a property development business and were known for their innovation, so might be prepared to commission adventurous builds. She wished she could fool her stomach into believing this interview was not that significant because it was doing summersaults. After her seatbelt had fastened her into place, she sat for a moment, breathing deeply and slowly. She adjusted the rear-view mirror and spoke to her reflection, 'you've got this, Emmeline. This job is yours.' Her reflection gave her a determined nod, and she set off.

She reached their impressive offices in good time, parked Zoe's car in the space they had allocated her and made her way to the flower-filled foyer, their delicate scent pervading the air.

'I'm here for an interview with Miss Ingleton,' she explained to a very smiley young woman, who took her coat and offered her refreshments. She watched her coat being swallowed up by a glossy black wall; the door, that had opened at the touch of the receptionist's hand, closed effortlessly, the edge melting into its neighbour, obscuring its very existence. Emmeline took a seat on a velvet chaise longue to contemplate her imminent meeting. The place had a good vibe to it, and she felt her shoulders relax. She had liked the headshot on the

Femmeur website of Miss K. Ingleton. She had one of those faces which made you wonder whether you had met before.

CHAPTER 61

Kate thanked Jane Knowles for coming and stood up to show her out. She returned to her desk and scanned Emmeline Ferguson's C.V. Emmeline had been born a year after Cara, and had attended Chester. She felt the familiar twinge of pain in her gut. It had been over three years since she had seen her elder daughter, although she thought of her every day; wondering whether she was happy, whether she was thinking about them too. Gemma had wanted to go to Chester before Cara left without saying good-bye. She had tried to explain Cara's actions, to ease Gemma's pain; but Gemma could not forgive her sister. She had gone to Nottingham in the end, and was doing well. Nevertheless, Cara's departure had created a void in them both: one they could never seem to fill. Kate ran her fingers through her hair and refocussed her mind on the document in front of her.

Kate was particularly interested in this candidate. Emmeline had joined the Movement at the same time as Cara had left it. It was against protocol to ask her why, however; it was going to be difficult to stick to the rules and remain entirely objective. She was too interested in her past, rather than her future. Kate told herself it was merely the surname that had

piqued her interest, it was the same as Sophie's. She got up and headed to reception.

As soon as she laid eyes on Emmeline she knew. She stood rooted to the spot, looking at a diluted version of her older sister. She was glad she had seen her before she had called out her name, as Emmeline was gazing out of the window, oblivious to her presence. She held her hands in her lap like Sophie and the profile of her nose, with its slight tilt upwards, made her heart leap. She forced her feet to walk out of reception and stood in a hallway between empty glass meeting rooms, taking long deep breaths, her eyes closed. She saw Sophie's face, and those eyes, accusing her of destroying their mother and ripping her own soul in two. She must have got pregnant shortly after she had left. Or could she be imagining this? No, the resemblance was unmistakable.

When her breathing had returned to normal, she wiped her hands on her skirt, placing the palm of her right hand on her cheek, to check it was dry enough to shake Emmeline's hand. She turned and walked back into reception, calling her name.

Emmeline stood up and smiled at her. Her hair was straighter and darker than Sophie's, but she had her mother's eyes as well as her nose. She was tall and slim and moved easily across the floor towards her.

'Very pleased to meet you, Emmeline,' Kate said extending her right hand. Emmeline took it and Kate noticed a puzzled look flash across her eyes.

'Pleased to meet you too, Miss Ingleton.'

'Call me Kate, Emmeline.'

'Kate,' Emmeline repeated, her voice expressionless. Suddenly Emmeline looked at her, as if seeing her for the first time.

'Kate!' she said. There it was, the connection. So, Sophie had mentioned her. This should be interesting.

‘Come with me,’ she said softly, giving her a reassuring smile.

Kate closed the door of her office and turned to look at Emmeline. ‘Before I do what I have an overwhelming urge to do, I need to ask you whether you’re Sophie’s daughter?’

Emmeline nodded. Kate approached her with open arms. ‘May I?’ she asked. Emmeline nodded again, and Kate put her arms around her, pulling her into her body, holding her close. Emmeline was trembling. Kate held her closer. Then she stepped back, smiling.

‘This is a turn up for the books! I think we should sit down, don’t you?’

Kate steered Emmeline towards her sofa and sat down beside her. ‘Are you alright?’ she said, handing her a tissue.

‘I’m fine. I think. Actually, I’m not sure how I feel,’ Emmeline said, ‘but it’s not bad,’ she added, hurriedly.

‘What a relief! I wasn’t sure your mother would have painted me in the best light.’

‘She didn’t! I only found out about you when I announced I was joining the Movement, a few months before I started at Chester.’

‘I’m guessing your mother didn’t take your news well?’

Emmeline laughed dryly. ‘Understatement of the year.’

‘I know what it feels like to be on the receiving end of Sophie’s hatred. But you know it comes from the pain of rejection, don’t you? As well as a stubborn refusal to see someone else’s point of view!’ Kate smiled at her young guest.

‘I guess you could call Mum stubborn. Although I had always thought of her as resilient, until then. History repeating itself didn’t exactly make it easy for me to follow in your footsteps.’

‘Did she tell you why I joined the Movement?’ Kate asked, holding her breath.

‘No, only that you had turned your back on her. She’s still

very bitter about it. But if you don't mind me asking, I'd love to know.'

'Look, this is huge for both of us, and it's complicated. Why don't we meet outside the office for a meal one evening, and we can have a proper chat?'

'I'd like that.'

'Let's put a date in the diary now. How about Thursday evening? It'll give us both a couple of days to think about things, and then we'll take it from there.'

They arranged to meet at a restaurant close to Emmeline's house, and Kate rescheduled the interview with an impartial colleague.

'Emmeline, it's been amazing meeting you, it really has. And I very much look forward to Thursday evening. I'll send you a message with my personal contact details.' Kate resisted the urge to hug her again, and simply held out her hand. Emmeline took it, and Kate laid her other hand on top of Emmeline's. 'You must never feel guilty about the decision you made, Emmeline. I've yet to meet a Completist who didn't have a good reason for joining, and I'm sure you're no exception.'

Emmeline gave her a sad smile, and they walked back towards reception. As Kate returned to her office, she wondered how Emmeline would react when she told her everything; but the truly pressing question was, what the hell had happened to her?

CHAPTER 62

Emmeline had reserved the table for two by the window. She checked her mobile. It was 7.25 p.m. Kate should be here any minute. She was anxious to hear about her life and why she had chosen to become a Completist.

Since their meeting, Emmeline had thought about her own mother. Had she ever truly connected with her? While she had been far more present than her father, this was more a mark of her father's absence than of her mother's attention. She had often talked it through with Zoe, when the line between one day and the next was blurred by wine. Zoe viewed her mother more as a friend than a parent, which made Emmeline realise just how ordinary her relationship with her own mother had been. Her mother was simply an over-protective and controlling parent. Standard issue. Too pre-occupied with her own troubles to focus on her daughter. As a result, Emmeline had kept things from her, preferring to confide in Tess about the strange challenges adolescence threw in her path. She had never doubted her mother's love, but her mother did what society expected of her, rather than seeing and reacting to Emmeline as a person. Perhaps this explained

the relief she had felt when she left her mother's house, over three years ago.

'Evening, Emmeline.' She turned towards the voice and saw her aunt standing by the door of the restaurant. A young waitress ushered her to their table and handed her a menu.

'Can I get either of you ladies a drink?'

'I'd like a large gin and tonic please,' her aunt said, 'How about you, Emmeline, care to join me?'

'It would be churlish not to. Make that two.'

'Shall we get our choices out of the way, then we can settle in for the evening,' her aunt suggested. They both glanced at the menu, scanning the typed words for something familiar.

'Is the lobster spaghetti good here?'

Emmeline raised her eyebrows.

'I know, it's super expensive. But I only eat lobster once a year, so I want to make sure it's going to be good, oh and this is on me.' Emmeline smiled her thanks.

'I've never had it, it's a bit out of my financial league, and I'm not sure I'm entirely comfortable eating it either.' Emmeline tried to keep the judgment from her voice.

'Fair enough. You do know they plough 50% of the profits back into replenishing stocks? It's taken over 100 years, but apparently the seas are nearly as full as they were before they introduced the ban on the private consumption of seafood.'

'That's good to hear,' Emmeline responded politely, 'but I think I'll stick to the vegetable lasagne.'

'I'll join you, then,' her aunt said, giving her a sheepish grin. 'Tell me about yourself, Emmeline.'

She hadn't spoken about her life in any detail since she had confided in Jack, although Frank was privy to the main highlights. It was liberating to speak freely to an enthralled audience. Her aunt only took her eyes off her when their waitress delivered the wine and food. She looked genuinely grief-stricken when she heard about the assault and nodded her

head in solidarity when she came to describe her relationship with Jack.

They had just finished their lasagne when Emmeline started to describe the evening she told her mother she was joining the Movement. She saw pain in her aunt's eyes when she described her mother's reaction, and noticed her fumble in her handbag for a tissue. 'I'm sorry, Kate. I didn't mean to upset you.'

'You haven't upset me, my dear niece. I'm remembering when I did the same thing.' She dabbed at her eyes and gave her a weak smile, her eyes darting to the next table to check whether her tears had been observed; but the two elderly women were engrossed in their own conversation, one head vigorously nodding in agreement.

'Look, you know the rest, you read my C.V. It's your turn, tell me about you.' Emmeline suddenly felt guilty about her indulgent monologue, and she desperately wanted to know about her aunt.

'I think we should both order a very gooey dessert before I start. Shall I get us another glass of this, it went down rather well, didn't it!' Emmeline watched her aunt look over her shoulder to catch their waitress's attention. The young woman hurried over.

They both ordered the hazelnut and chocolate torte. 'It's good to see you have my excellent taste in desserts,' her aunt said, laughing, but then she stopped and looked at her, as if sizing her up.

'I'm going to start with two pieces of good news. The first is, you've got the job at Femmeur, if you want it, my colleague was very impressed with you. And the second is, you have two cousins.'

'That's quite an opener! I'm delighted about the job offer, of course I am. But I'd rather know about my cousins. The job offer is great, but cousins, that's big.' Emmeline sat forward, encouraging her aunt to continue.

'Obviously, they're both girls! Gemma is my younger daughter and she's currently in her second year at Nottingham. I'd love you to meet her. She'll be thrilled. Unfortunately, you'll never meet Cara, my elder daughter. She's almost exactly a year older than you. She fell in love with a Facilitator and became a Chosen One at the same time as you joined the Movement. Life's a weird motherfucker sometimes, isn't it?'

Emmeline didn't know how to react. It was a huge amount of information to take in. She suspected her aunt was trying to cover her pain with profanity.

'I'm so sorry. How did you feel?'

'Not great, Emmeline. But we understood each other, and we parted loving one another.' Emmeline reached over and touched her arm. 'I miss her so much. Sometimes the pain is unbearable, and Gemma feels it too. She worshipped her sister. I tried my best to explain why she left, but you try making sense of romantic love to a girl who has absolutely no interest in men.'

'I know how difficult it must have been for Gemma. Romantic love never made sense to me either, when I was growing up, and I was raised as a Chosen One!'

'Love, eh? Sex dressed up in pretty paper,' her aunt said, shaking her head.

'Except the paper can be torn off all too easily. And by then it's too late. You've been dazzled by the packaging to such an extent you don't even recognise the poisoned gift you've been given.' Emmeline replied, staring into her wine glass.

'Spoken like a true Completist.' Her aunt raised her glass to Emmeline. Before she could raise her own the waitress approached with their desserts. Her aunts' eyes widened in appreciation as she took in the creation nestling in an artful swirl of chocolate.

'So why did you join the Movement? I'm guessing, by your reaction to Jack, the same thing happened to you?' Her aunt finished her mouthful, and sighed.

'It did. I was married to Cara's father, and he had an affair while I was still recovering from her birth. Although he did have the decency to stop hitting me while I was pregnant. But that wasn't the only reason.' Her aunt paused, searching Emmeline's face. Seemingly satisfied with whatever she found there, she continued, lowering her voice to such an extent that Emmeline was forced to lean in to catch what she was saying.

'Your grandfather started sexually assaulting me when I was eight. Sophie only found out when she wouldn't accept my decision to join the Movement. She was begging me to change my mind, saying I could get over David's violence and infidelity, that I was overreacting. So, rather than take that secret to the grave, as I had intended, it came blurting out, to justify my actions. That's what I tell myself. But perhaps I wanted to make them hurt the way I did. I resented Sophie for never having had to go through what I did. And my mother, for failing to protect me from her husband. I lashed out.'

Emmeline kept quiet. She could sense her aunt had more to say.

'Cara believed me when I told her. She never doubted me for a moment. My mother and sister did not. Any empathy they had for me transformed instantly into loathing. I thought about it afterwards, and I truly believe this is what marks the difference between growing up as a Completist as opposed to a Chosen One. The Completists view men as guilty until proven innocent, but the Chosen Ones are always prepared to give them the benefit of the doubt.'

Emmeline sat back, stunned by her aunt's revelation. She wasn't sure what to say. 'I don't think women are born distrusting men, or that men are born distrusting women. I think it's nurture rather than nature. And what you've just said backs that up.'

'Maybe. But wouldn't it be great to go back in time to the beginning of everything and see how men and women were with each other? Did the men willingly accept women needed

protecting when they were pregnant and vulnerable, or did they see it as a burden from the get-go? A curse laid at their door which they resented. Men forever having to take care of women, whether they liked it or not.'

'That would be fascinating to know,' Emmeline said, warming to the topic, relieved to be shifting from the intensely personal to the conceptual. 'The latest theory is that men lash out at women because they're subconsciously jealous of their power to create life. Along with the fact they have to impress us to get us to mate with them. This makes them feel inferior so they compensate by keeping the economic power to control and limit us, levelling out the playing field, as they would see it.'

'God knows! All I know is we've gone badly wrong. Women shouldn't feel forced into a movement in order to live the way they want to. Why can't we find a way to live which suits both sexes, without this bullshit need to control and compete?'

Her aunt's voice was now a great deal louder and the elderly women looked over in their direction. Emmeline gave them a small smile of apology. Her aunt appeared oblivious. Emmeline was not convinced by her aunts last observation. 'But doesn't that ride in the face of evolution? How can we evolve into the best version of ourselves if we don't weed out the weak, the ones who are unwilling to change and adapt?'

'And I presume you mean men when you say, "the weak"?'

'I guess I do. After all, it's women who are moving forward, and the men who are holding on to the old ways.'

'I'm too tipsy to carry on with this conversation,' her aunt said laughing. 'Shall we order some coffee?'

Emmeline nodded, and then reached over and touched her aunt's arm. 'Kate, I want to say how humbled I am to have you as my aunt. To have made such a success of your life, against all the odds, is quite something. I know our decisions have torn our families apart. But you didn't let your pain overwhelm

you. You saw a way to leave the pain behind, and you took it. You've created a new world for yourself, and you have two beautiful daughters and an amazing career to show for it.'

'Thank you, Emmeline, and right back at you,' her aunt said looking into Emmeline's eyes, a half-smile playing on her lips. 'But the pain continues, doesn't it? The two worlds still collide, and women must still choose which world to live in. We still have to make impossible choices and enormous sacrifices. It would appear we can never have it all.'

CHAPTER 63

It only took two months as Mrs Brown, for Cara to find a position heading up the Graphics Department in Product Development for a large multinational company. The world had opened up for her, now she was truly a Chosen One. They had moved into their dream house, eight months later.

She had even made a couple of girlfriends, although she was never sure they entirely trusted her, and she certainly didn't understand them. Sam had warned her not to mention his profession and she was glad she had heeded his advice. It was very clear that normal COs would never put up with their husbands sleeping with other women, regardless of whether they were being paid to do it. Cara didn't have a problem with Sam's occupation when they met. He was simply a service provider, and she was confident he loved her; however, lately she was beginning to wonder if his work might threaten their marriage.

Jealousy and insecurity seemed to pervade every aspect of a CO's life. They were particularly jealous of other women, but only if they were more beautiful or more successful than they were. Her two friends were on the same pay grade as she was

and all of them were equally attractive, so perhaps that's why she had been welcomed into their circle of trust.

Every Friday after work they would have a drink at a wine bar around the corner from their office. Lisa was always talking about her sex life, and the evening her friends met Sam for the first time, was no exception.

'Where are you two going this evening?' Lisa asked, as they settled themselves at a corner table at the back of the bar which had just been vacated by two city-types in charcoal-grey pinstripes.

'Sam's taking me to the theatre. We thought we'd both enjoy the new play that's opened at the Haymarket.'

'Lucky you. Andrew never takes me anywhere these days. We've only been married for four years, but I feel like we've turned into my parents already!'

'What do you mean?' Cara asked.

'Everything's a little dull. During the first year, we were at it like rabbits, now I'm lucky if we manage it four or five times a year.'

'Oh, don't worry, Lisa. That's quite normal!' Anne said. 'The passion dies and is replaced with companionship. I prefer it. You become good friends, not simply lovers.'

'You're friends with your hubby, are you?' Lisa asked, sounding rather surprised.

'I would say so. Aren't you?' Anne replied, nervously fingering her gold-looped earrings.

'No. I don't think we are. We don't seem to have much in common, and I can see his eyes glaze over whenever I try to speak to him about something that's bothering me. My friends are women.' Cara wished Lisa would chill out. It was the weekend and she really did not want to spend her time listening to Lisa bitch about her husband.

'What about you, Cara? Would you say Sam was your friend?' Anne asked, obviously trying to redirect Lisa's attention onto her.

Cara glared at Anne for dragging her into the conversation. How could she admit that Sam and her still couldn't keep their hands off one another? They would hate her, wouldn't they? 'I've only been married for 18 months, so I guess we're still in our honeymoon period,' she laughed, 'although things in the bedroom are slowing down a bit!' She was lying, but she was learning the rules of the game.

'Make the most of it,' Lisa said. 'Anyone for another drink before we return to domestic bliss?' They both downed their drinks and pushed their empty glasses across the table towards Lisa. As they watched Lisa push her way through the crowd of office workers, Anne raised her eyebrows and shook her head. 'If she's that unhappy, why doesn't she just leave him. I'm getting a bit tired of hearing about her marriage.' Cara nodded at Anne, looking towards the door for any sign of Sam.

Lisa was still at the bar when he strode in. He looked around and Cara waved at him. The crowds seemed to part as he made his way towards them. Anne's mouth opened as he extended his hand towards her.

'Very pleased to meet you, Anne. I've heard so many good things about you from Cara.' Anne blushed.

'Lisa's getting a round in. Shall I ask her to get you a drink?' Cara said, getting up from her seat.

'Don't worry. I'll share yours. We'll have to go soon, I'm afraid.'

Lisa returned, her eyes widening as her gaze settled on Sam.

'You must be Lisa. Cara didn't tell me how attractive you both were.'

Lisa laughed. Her hand touched her long hair.

'Cara's a lucky girl!' Lisa said, giving him a warm smile.

Anne raised her eyes at Cara. Should she be jealous? Was Lisa trying to chat up her husband?

'Why thank you, Lisa. What a lovely thing to say. Difficult

though it is to leave you lovely ladies, if we don't head off soon, we'll be late for our table.'

'Dinner and the theatre. Is this a special occasion?' Lisa asked.

'No. I just wanted to treat my wife. She deserves it, after all, she puts up with me.'

'I can imagine that's quite a tough job!' Lisa said, looking at Anne and laughing.

They said their goodbyes and left them finishing their wine. Cara could sense they were already talking about them as they left.

'You're quite the charmer, aren't you?' she said, linking her arm through his.

'Goes with the territory. Don't forget, I make my living by telling women what they want to hear.'

Cara briefly wondered how many times he had told her what she wanted to hear. She felt uneasy, but then she looked into his twinkling eyes and banished the thought from her head.

The play wasn't as good as the reviews had promised, it was meant to be a comedy about relationships, but the jokes rolled over her. It was difficult to appreciate irony when you lacked any true understanding of what was being made fun of. She found herself daydreaming. Would she categorise her husband as a friend? She hadn't really considered it before Anne's comment. They didn't really spend that much time together. She worked all day and Sam was out for most of the evening. The only day they had to themselves was Sunday, and that was mainly spent in bed. What were they, without sex? Had she mistaken lust for love? Was their mutual desire for one another their only connection?

Her upbringing had been the Garden of Eden and now she was surrounded by snakes.

CHAPTER 64

Cara heard the front door close, which was usually her cue to get up. However, this morning she continued to lie in bed, wondering what her morning ablutions would bring. 'It's fine for you,' she said, gazing out of the window, 'flitting around in your white, fluffy frocks, up there in the blue. What about me, stuck down here in the United Kingdom?' She laughed at the irony of her country's name, swinging her legs out of bed. She opened her underwear drawer, dashed into the bathroom and peed on a stick, then carried it into the lounge, cradled in her hand like an injured bird.

The sofa held her as she stared at the result. She looked up and around at the beautiful room. Everything was neat and tidy. The cushions were plumped to perfection, and the carefully chosen curtains were artfully tied back, folds of silk caressing the polished oak. The objects which had once brought her such comfort now mocked her with their military precision, as she contemplated the impending chaos of her life. She closed her eyes, opened them, and stared at the test again. The beaming face was still grinning at her. She wanted to smile back but could only muster a sigh as she put her hand on her

belly. She had always wanted a child; however, whenever she had raised the subject with Sam, he had convinced her it was not the right time.

When her mother had told her she was pregnant with Gemma, they had both been delighted; but Gemma had been planned and saved for. She remembered the first time she held her and gazed into her tiny wide-open eyes. She was the most precious gift her mother could have given her. She shook the thought from her head; even after three years, the loss of her little sister was as painful as the day she had left home.

She wondered whether to tell Sam straight away or wait until she had seen the doctor; although she knew why she wanted to delay the moment. The longer she waited, the more real the baby would become, and the harder it would be for him to convince her not to have it. This shouldn't be a situation she manipulated. Her gut feeling could be wrong. He might be delighted.

Sam would be back with their morning coffees soon. She got up and checked her appearance in the gilded mirror above the console, running her fingers through her hair. She turned at the sound of his key in the door. He came in brandishing their drinks.

'I'm pregnant,' Cara suddenly said, forcing a smile and looking at Sam intently, anxious not to miss the slightest nuance in his expression which might hint at how he truly felt. She needn't have bothered. His reaction was plain to see. He was crestfallen.

'Not what I was hoping for.' Cara sat down on the sofa; its stuffing deflated beneath her.

Sam rushed over and sat down beside her, taking her hands. She tried to resist.

'Cara, I love you, you know I do. But I don't think this is the right time for us. We've only just begun our lives together. I think we should keep things as they are. I'm so happy, aren't

you?' His voice sounded panicked, his words tumbling from his mouth.

'I am happy. But I didn't plan this, it was an accident. I must have forgotten to take a pill or something. And we've been married for over three years.'

'If it's an accident, why don't we think about an abortion? If it's a boy, we'll be allowed to. They're actually encouraging it. There aren't enough women to go around.'

She shivered with disgust. 'And what if it's a girl? We won't be allowed to abort a girl. So, we'll have to become parents, whether you like it or not. If you can cope with that scenario, why abort a boy!'

'At least I've got a 50% chance of getting what I want.' Sam said sulkily.

'What's that supposed to mean? I can't believe you! You said you wanted children before we got married. Was that a lie?' Cara's disappointment was turning into anger.

'No, no, of course not. But it doesn't feel like the right time.'

'I don't believe it's a matter of timing. You're afraid of something aren't you? What is it? Are you afraid I will love the child more than I love you?' She was trying to remain calm, to coax the truth from him.

'I don't think so, but it is connected to it, I guess.' She could tell he knew what was going on inside his head but didn't want to say the words out loud.

'Sam, you're not making any sense, tell me. Please, this is important.' Cara looked at him, willing him to tell her the truth. Sam sighed like a condemned man.

'Look, it's probably stupid, but I read a magazine article. It said lots of marriages start to fail as soon as kids arrive. I don't want us to become one of them.'

'Listen, Sam. I know raising children puts pressures on a marriage, it's hard work. But it can also be hugely rewarding. Did you also read *why* they started to fail?'

'Yes, I did. And the main reason is because the woman loses her libido and their sex life goes down the toilet.'

'So, you don't want children in case it affects our sex life, when you get more arse than a toilet seat?'

Sam looked like a guilty child. He stared down at his hands. They no longer had her fingers intertwined with his. Cara had snatched her hands away from him seconds before. 'That's not fair, Cara,' he said, quietly. 'Sex with you is completely different. You're mine, I love you.'

Cara dismissed his words, remembering his sulks on the rare occasions she had turned down his advances. 'You obviously lied when you said you wanted children, because there will never be a good time, will there? If that's what you believe, it doesn't matter if we have children now or when I'm 30. The end result, according to that article, will be the same. You jerking yourself off in front of a porn film, while I lie exhausted, fast asleep in bed.'

Sam continued to look at his hands.

'Why did you say you wanted children? I thought I was marrying someone who wanted the same future as me, a future which included raising a family together, and growing old together.'

'It felt like the right thing to say at the time.' Sam let out another huge sigh.

'Why, because it's what I wanted to hear? Or was it one of the ways to get me to marry to you?'

'I honestly didn't think about it. I may have even meant it at the time, I hadn't read the article then. Anyway, it's not only the article. I have friends of friends who now have children and they all say the same thing. The sex slows down, drastically, and their relationships become a never-ending cycle of working, nappy changing and arguing about whose turn it is to get up in the night.'

It was Cara's turn to stare at her hands. Memories from her childhood clouded her mind like disturbed river-silt. The

voice of her teacher explaining how the true obstacle to equality was the sexualisation of women. How this would never change until sex was a way of cementing a lasting bond between two consenting people, rather than something a man does to possess a woman.

She pushed herself off the sofa as if she were nine months pregnant, not nine days.

'I'm going to spend some time by myself. I need some thinking space. I'll check into a hotel.' She looked at her husband, half expecting him to leap up and hold her. To make sense of this ridiculous scene. Tell her he couldn't live without her, all of her, and the baby she was carrying.

He didn't try and stop her. To her horror, he leant back on the sofa, put his feet on the coffee table, and turned on the wall monitor, selecting some anodyne film on his mobile. He turned the volume up as she clattered around the bedroom, throwing her belongings into a suitcase.

He didn't even turn his head to say goodbye.

CHAPTER 65

Cara checked into a budget hotel and instantly regretted her decision. Why had she chosen this dump? Was she punishing herself? She should have booked a luxury suite. She was raging. How could he behave like that? It wasn't as though this was a stupid row about keeping the house tidy. She was pregnant with his child, for fuck's sake; the supposed love of his life, and he didn't seem to give a shit. What was he expecting her to do, come back home, her tail between her legs, the child aborted, saying he was right and she was sorry?

She sat on the bed and wondered what to do next. She wanted her mum and Gemma. She didn't feel like she could ask Anne or Lisa for help. She had no-one.

She heard her mother's voice, saying, "Cara, men can't be trusted. They will always use a woman, and when they have no further use for her, they cast her aside." God, she hoped she wasn't right. Perhaps she would return tomorrow and he would sweep her up in his arms, and tell her how sorry he was, that he was excited to go on this next part of their journey together; however, she couldn't visualise the scene. The screen had gone blank.

Cara grabbed her mobile. She had heard about a Completist Gender Verification Clinic in Soho who would help COs. These clinics existed to double-check the Completist's Gender Selection Process had worked while the pregnancy was in the early stages. She didn't want to go to a CO clinic, as they would pressurise her into an abortion if she was carrying a boy. They had only been opened recently, to support the government's new policy of increasing the number of female births. She knew which street the clinic was on, so she ordered a taxi to pick her up the next day. She couldn't search for their contact details; that information wasn't available to her, so she would have to turn up and hope for the best.

At 9.00 a.m. on Monday morning, she was lingering nervously on the pavement outside the building, having called in sick. She could do this. She pressed the door buzzer and a voice came over the intercom.

'Hello, I really need your help. I'm an ex-Completist and I've just found out I'm pregnant. My husband doesn't want the baby.' The door lock was released and she went in.

The young woman who greeted her was lovely. She listened to her story and told her they would fit her in. Half an hour later, Cara was lying on a table with her stomach exposed; another woman, about her age, was fiddling with a machine beside her.

'This isn't going to hurt at all. We've developed a non-invasive technique. It's like a scanner, only smarter! And don't worry; it's 100% safe. The only thing you'll feel is a slight warmth on your abdomen. The whole process takes less than five minutes.

The woman smiled at Cara and began. Cara wondered how five minutes could pass so slowly. By the time she handed her the printout with the result, she was dressed and sitting in a comfortable chair. She had waited in silence, too anxious to

make small talk while the machine quietly whirred in the background.

She studied the printout she had been given. She was having a boy.

As soon as the woman saw she had read the result she said, 'I'm sure you're aware the government are offering COs entirely free and immediate abortions to any woman carrying a boy.'

Cara stood up. 'I do know. That's why I came to you. I thought I'd need some thinking time, and I was worried I'd be forced to do something I might regret. I've heard some awful rumours. But I don't need any time to think. I'm very happy with my little lad,' she said. The very idea of killing him, treating him as though he had never existed, appalled her. The woman smiled at her.

'I'm glad you're happy, but do think of the consequences. If your husband really doesn't want this child, and you have it, it will put you in a very difficult position if it results in divorce. You'll become an Outsider and you won't be able to re-join the Movement. It's something to bear in mind. We hear Outsiders have a tough time.'

'You hear correctly. To be honest, I would re-join the Movement in a heartbeat if they allowed sons. I don't want to do this alone. I'd give anything for a cuddle from my mum right now.' Cara felt tears pricking her eyes.

'Will I do as a temporary substitute?' the woman said, opening her arms to her.

Cara accepted the invitation of this compassionate stranger and her tears arrived in earnest. She was overwhelmed with sadness. The woman stroked her back as she held her and Cara wondered why Sam had been unable to offer her this comfort, why he had turned his back on her so easily.

When she finally left the clinic, she wandered around the streets searching for a café. The morning rush of office workers

scurrying to their respective buildings had abated, but the streets were still busy. Cara kept her head down, something she still found counter-intuitive after so many years of doing the opposite. Having selected a small café in a road parallel to Wardour Street, she sat in a window seat and stared out at the world, a world that had become threatening and uncertain, and Cara knew, if she divorced Sam, it would turn its back on her.

As she munched through her scrambled eggs, she came up with the semblance of a plan. If she went back to Sam, it was likely he would pressurise her into getting rid of the baby, something she now knew she couldn't do. She would have to go back, in case he had suddenly transformed into father of the year; but assuming the worst case, where could she go? Could she stay in their house and ask him to leave, or should it be the other way around? She didn't want to divorce him.

Where had her burning love for him gone? How had their deep connection been so easily severed? The love she already felt for her unborn child was far deeper than anything she had ever felt for Sam. Had she been a complete fool? Mistaking physical attraction for the real deal? If that was the case, it wasn't her fault; it was her upbringing. What chance did she have of understanding love? Completists were taught that an emotional connection between partners, as a prerequisite to marriage, only evolved in the 18th century, as an antidote to the exploitation and degradation of humanity caused by the emergence of modern capitalism. The COs she'd met certainly didn't see it like that. To them, true love was heaven on earth; a complex concoction of behaviour and feelings, which made sense of the chaos and randomness of life. Cara wasn't sure she had ever felt like that about Sam. Then, it hit her. Was she avoiding divorce, not because she couldn't bear to lose Sam, but to avoid the hardships of being an Outsider and raising her son alone? It was all so confusing. Cara simply didn't understand what she was meant to feel or how she was meant to behave. It was bullshit. The search for true love was as

pointless as a quest to find the Holy Grail. Maybe Sam was in the same boat. He had thought he was in love with her, when he was only duped by lust, and always had been. For all she knew, he might be as clueless as she was. She swallowed the last mouthful of egg and took a gulp of tea.

It didn't really matter that she was confused about how her relationship was unravelling and the reasons for it. One thing was crystal clear, she was having this little boy; and if she had to lose the other man in her life because he couldn't cope with the competition, so be it. But where could she go if Sam threw her out?

Then she remembered her Aunt Sophie. Perhaps she'd help her? After all, she hated the Movement, and would be glad she'd left it. Cara had done to her mother what her mother had done to her aunt. Cara would be her aunt's avenging angel; although Cara's heart had only ever been full of love where her mother was concerned.

The more she thought about it, the more it made sense. She would go back to Sam today, and, if necessary, head for the Central Bureau of Citizens first thing tomorrow morning. As she left the underground and walked towards their house, her longing to find Sam ready to embrace them both, grew. That would be her dream scenario. That would show he did love her, that he couldn't envisage living without her, that he needed her, baby and all.

When she opened the front door, Sam wasn't home. The monitor was broken, shards of glass littering the floor, and there were two empty bottles of wine on the coffee table. Then she noticed the letter.

"Dear Cara,

I once asked you to choose me over your mother and sister. I'm asking you to do the same again. Choose me over this baby. If you love me, you'll make the right choice."

She threw the letter on the floor. 'The right choice for whom, Sam!' she shouted, striding into the bedroom to pack

up her things. Cara felt sick, heartbroken. Before she left, she picked up the letter and wrote her reply.

"Dear Sam,

I live in my skin. It holds everything that I am. My sinews, my gristle, my muscle, my soul. And now it holds our baby. But you just see my skin."

CHAPTER 66

The woman sitting opposite Cara looked bored. She must hear stories like hers all the time. Cara stared at the woman. She pitied her: to become so desensitised to human pain and suffering must surely diminish a person.

'Let's see now,' the woman said, trying to inject a little enthusiasm in her voice. 'Here we are, I have a Sophie Ingleton who had a twin sister called Kate. She was married, then divorced, and now she's married again. She's now Mrs Jackson. Would you like their address? I will need you to sign the disclosure form, to confirm you've requested the information, and I'll need to scan your identity chip.'

Cara could only manage to nod at the woman. She had found her, but would her aunt take her in?

Soon afterward, Cara stood outside the address she'd been given, staring at the green door in front of her. Plucking up the courage to press the bell. Sophie was now her only hope. Cara had managed to get hold of Sam. It had been a difficult phone call. He had not changed his mind. He was convinced a baby would destroy their relationship. She had begged him not to instigate divorce proceedings, but when she confirmed she was keeping the baby, he had turned

to stone. It had been like speaking to a stranger. He had made it clear it was Cara who was choosing a bundle of cells over him, so she couldn't love him the way he loved her. It was her decision to bring this baby into the world, so she could do it by herself, as an Outsider. He had also made it clear he wouldn't leave his home; and, as the baby was a boy, he was pretty certain she wouldn't get enough money from the divorce settlement to rehouse herself somewhere decent. He had discovered it was contrary to public policy to support single mothers of boys, and he was evidently glad. Sam had been betrayed, and he had the government on his side.

Her determination to continue with the pregnancy had faltered as she listened to him. She had wondered why she was giving up everything for something that resembled a tadpole. But then she remembered that tadpole was her son, and he was relying on her to keep him safe.

She finally rang the doorbell. The door opened and there was her aunt. She was a haggard version of her mother: more like eight years her senior, rather than eight minutes. Sophie had initially smiled at her, but now she was staring, looking puzzled and anxious. Cara started to panic. 'I'm so sorry to come to your home unannounced, but you're my aunt and I'm your niece, and I would really appreciate it if you would invite me in so I can tell you why I'm here. It's quite a complicated story!' Cara realised she was speaking far too quickly, and she fell silent. The colour had drained from her aunt's face. Cara held her breath.

'Of course,' Sophie finally said, her voice robotic. She stepped aside and Cara tentatively entered the hallway.

'Harry! Can you come down, love? We've got a visitor.'

'Coming!' Within seconds Cara saw a tall, lean man, with a mop of blonde hair come galloping down the stairs, pulling on a clean sweatshirt. He stared at her, 'Blimey, you look a lot like our Emmeline. You could almost be her sister.'

She saw her aunt glare at her husband. 'Probably because this is Emmeline's cousin, Harry. This is Cara.'

'I'm sorry. This must be a huge shock for you. Do you want me to come back at another time? I really didn't mean to upset anyone.'

'Come on through, Cara. I'm sorry too. It is a shock, a huge shock, but it doesn't mean you're not welcome. The last time I saw you, you were a babe in arms. Sit down, I'll put the kettle on. Harry, do you want a cuppa?'

'Do you know, love, I think I'm going to crack open a beer. Perhaps you might like something a little stronger too?'

'You're right, Harry. I wasn't thinking straight. Cara, would you like a glass of wine?'

'That's really kind of you, but I think I'll stick to the tea.'

Harry poured Sophie a large glass of white. Sophie handed Cara her mug of tea and then Harry offered them both a cigarette. Cara declined.

'So, to what do we owe this pleasure?' Harry asked, sounding genuinely enthusiastic.

'To cut a very long story short, three years ago, I became a Chosen One.'

Sophie raised her eyebrows and looked at Harry. 'I fell in love with a man and we got married. I'm pregnant with his son, and he wants nothing to do with the baby, or me, if I choose to have it. And I do choose to have it. So here I am, homeless, pregnant, and about to become an Outsider. I really need a friend at the moment, and I can't go and see my mum, it would be too dangerous for her. So, I'm doing the next best thing, seeing her sister.'

'She talked about me, did she?' Sophie asked, ignoring Cara's plight.

'She only told me about you when I told her I wanted to become a Chosen One. She said you'd been very close and you weren't happy about her defection.' Cara was choosing her words carefully.

‘I’m sure she put it in stronger terms than that!’ Sophie laughed bitterly. ‘What happened to her? All I know is she had you. You were only a few weeks old when she left David. I fell pregnant with Emmeline a few months later. She was born in March too.’

Cara saw Sophie look at Harry, and he reached across the table to hold her hand. ‘Do you have any sisters?’ she continued.

‘Yes, her name is Gemma, she’s five years younger than me.’

‘Did you get on?’

‘Oh yes. I loved her to bits from the moment I saw her. Mum said her relationship with you was the same when you were younger.’

Sophie drew a deep breath and then let it out. Cara saw Harry give her hand a squeeze.

‘I guess it was, Cara. I guess that is why I hated her so much for leaving me. That, and the lies she told about my father to justify it.’

Cara kept her mouth shut. She didn’t think arguing about whether her mother had been sexually abused would get her the help she needed.

‘So, what is it you’re asking for? Our friendship, our support, a home?’ Cara couldn’t work out whether Sophie was prepared to offer her any of those things. While she didn’t sound hostile, she could tell Sophie was finding the situation difficult.

‘If it’s at all possible, I’d really like a room to sleep in, while I try to work out what I’m going to do. I have a good job, at least until the divorce papers are issued. And I could pay you some rent money. I wouldn’t say no at the chance to become friends, either.’

Sophie looked at her, and Cara saw her eyes soften. Did she miss her sister? Did she understand the situation she was facing? Cara held her breath.

'You can move in with us while you figure things out. I'm not going to charge you rent. You'll need any spare cash for the baby. You can have Emmeline's room. She won't be needing it anymore. She left to join the Completists. Life's a weird motherfucker sometimes, isn't it?'

Cara laughed. 'My mum uses that phrase too,' she said, as relief swept through her body.

'I know. Where do you think she got it from?'

Cara sighed in relief: her immediate problems were now solved. 'Thank you, Sophie. And you too, Harry. You can't imagine how relieved and grateful I am to be made to feel welcome. I promise I'll try to keep out of your hair as much as possible.'

Cara saw Harry squeeze Sophie's hand again. She could tell Sophie still wasn't sure she had done the right thing, but Cara was glad her heart was ruling her head. She silently thanked Emmeline.

CHAPTER 67

Emmeline smiled at the four other women who had all got up to greet her. The office was freshly painted, the furniture brand new.

'Welcome to Femmeur Installations, Emmeline. We've heard good things about you. I'm Charlotte, and I have the honour of heading up this new venture. This is Frankie, who is one of the most talented architects in the world, and this is Natasha, another brilliant engineer like yourself. And last, but by no means least, this is Anita. She's our Project Co-ordinator. She keeps us in line, on time and in budget!'

'I'm so pleased to be here.' Emmeline responded, walking forward to shake each of them by the hand. They were a motley crew. Charlotte was slim, elegant and smartly dressed, whereas Frankie's hair was stuck up in a messy bun, her grey linen suit baggy and dishevelled. Natasha looked more like her, smart but still casual, with loose, straight hair that shone with health. Anita was tiny, but hewn from steel. Emmeline wondered how many hours it took in the gym each week to get muscles like hers.

'This is your space, Emmeline. Natasha helped me kit it out. I hope you've got everything you need. But if you want

anything else, let me know. And please, make it your own. Rearrange it, get rid of any stuff you don't want. You can see we've all put our own personal stamp on our areas!' Charlotte was looking straight at an electric guitar, hanging above Frankie's desk.

'Thank you. It looks perfect.'

'Have a cup of coffee and settle in for half an hour, then we'll get together and explain what it is we're trying to achieve over the next 12 months. We already have our first major project, which is top secret, and very exciting. We're designing and building the new HQ for the Movement. It's a prime site in Central London, and it's going to get us a great deal of attention. We need to make sure it's the right kind of attention. But most importantly, our client has to love it. But we'll talk about the project later. The kitchen is over there.' Charlotte pointed to a grey door on the other side of the floor.

'Thank you, I can't wait to start. Does anyone else want a coffee or tea?' They all shook their heads, gesturing to the full mugs on their desks.

'Just missed the last round I'm afraid,' Natasha said, 'but I'll wander over with you, so you know where everything is.'

When they were in the kitchen, Emmeline lowered her voice, 'That is Charlotte Burke isn't it?'

'It is indeed,' Natasha responded. 'God knows how much they paid to poach her from Target Construction. She's as amazing as anything you've read about her, and a genuinely nice person too. Frankie's C.V. is also incredible. She designed the new O2 Arena after the old one was declared unsafe five years ago. Hardly surprising, it had been standing for over 140 years.'

'Oh my God. The Mirage is one of my favourite new buildings in London: so unique. It's amazing how it makes its presence felt but blends in with the environment so it's virtually invisible. Incredible structure.'

'That's Frankie's calling card. Now you see it, now you

don't. She's done some amazing rural work. Her structures are the closest thing you can get to manmade nature.'

'To be honest, Natasha, it's all a bit intimidating. I feel like an imposter.'

'Believe me, you're not, Emmeline. We've all seen your college work. It shows real promise. And some of your structures appear to defy the laws of physics. You've earned your place here, so don't worry.'

'Thanks, Natasha. I had no idea I'd be working with such brilliant people. They were very secretive about the team at my interview.'

'Well, count yourself as one of us. Now I'll leave you to settle in.'

Emmeline stood at the coffee machine, trying to remember which buttons to press and in what order. She was sure Kate must have pulled a few strings to get her the job. She was due to meet her for lunch in the rooftop restaurant, and she was going to make damn sure she paid.

After the meeting, Emmeline was clear about her part in the project. She decided she needed to retire to the breakout room; a quiet, gently-lit, soundproof glass office filled with climbing plants. She had brought her own pad and started to sketch. She was so absorbed in her work she didn't hear the soft knock at the door. It opened and Kate walked in.

'Hard at it already?' she laughed.

Emmeline jumped. 'Jesus, you scared me,' she laughed.

'Sorry. But when you didn't show for our lunch date, I decided to come and find you.'

'Oh, Kate. I'm so sorry. I completely lost track of time.'

Kate peered over her shoulder. 'Looks interesting.'

Emmeline shut her pad. 'Oh, just a few scribblings, but thanks. And a huge thanks to you if you had any part to play in getting me here. This is an amazing place, and the team are incredible. I'm so excited!'

Kate laughed. 'And hungry, I hope.'

'Very. But I must insist I pay.'

'That's very sweet of you, Emmeline, but your first lunch at Femmeur is on the house. So maybe next time.'

As they tucked into their salads and sweet potato fries, Kate invited her to come to tea the following Saturday and meet Gemma.

'Please say yes. She's back from Nottingham for the weekend, and she's so excited to meet her cousin.'

'I'd love to. Zoe and I are flat-hunting during the day, but our last viewing is about 4.00 p.m. so I could make it for around 6.00ish?'

'Perfect. We'll look forward to it.'

CHAPTER 68

Gemma was nervous. While she really wanted to meet Emmeline, it was stirring up memories of Cara, and she still couldn't think about her without tearing up. They were bound to talk about her and she didn't want to cry in front of a stranger.

People kept telling her that time would heal her pain, but it only increased the length of time she was able to put it aside. Whenever she remembered her sister, her feelings were as visceral as the day her mother told her she would never see her again. Gemma could never forgive Cara for not saying goodbye. She would never understand how Cara's feelings for a man she barely knew could trump the love they shared for one another. The only way she could make sense of it was to assume Cara did not love her. This realisation wounded her; it made her feel stupid and small for caring so deeply, for having made Cara the most important person in her life, for trusting her. Gemma still loved Cara; but her love was smothered by feelings of anger and resentment, buried beneath a bitterness she could not escape. The only thing that might have helped was to be forever denied her, because she could never ask her why she had left. It was as if Cara had died but was still living

in another dimension out of her reach. She wished she had been run over. She could have grieved normally then. Knowing she was potentially still out there in the world, living and laughing without her, was too much to bear.

The doorbell rang and Gemma started. She checked her appearance in her bedroom mirror, took a deep breath, and headed downstairs. She heard Emmeline's voice. She sounded happy, pleased to be in their home. As she entered the kitchen, she saw her and stopped in her tracks. There was no mistaking the family resemblance.

'Emmeline, this is Gemma,' her mother said.

Emmeline smiled at her warmly. 'Hi Cous, this is all a bit weird, isn't it?'

Gemma stood rooted to the spot. 'Sorry,' she managed to stammer, 'this is quite difficult. I am excited to meet you, but...'

Her mother strode over to her and gave her a hug. Gemma immediately burst into tears.

'I'm so sorry,' she sobbed. 'I didn't want to behave like this, only you look a bit like her and...'

'Gemma, I completely understand. I cried when I met your mum. She looks a lot like my mum, and I miss her terribly too.'

Gemma saw Emmeline's face start to crumple and she broke free from her mother's arms and went to hug her.

They stood clinging to one another like lovers reunited after a decade of estrangement. Gemma didn't notice her mother standing alone, wiping her eyes with her hand as she watched their pain flow out of and into each other. For a moment, Gemma felt like she was holding Cara, and then her mother's arms wrapped around them both.

'I'm not sure I have enough tissues,' her mother eventually said as the intensity between them diminished. 'I bought plenty of wine, but we may have to resort to toilet paper, I'm afraid.'

Both girls laughed and the circle was broken.

Her mother dashed off to the downstairs toilet and came back into the room triumphantly brandishing a new, plump roll. She gave each girl a wad, and they both blew their noses simultaneously. The noise made them laugh again, and they were soon seated around the kitchen table, wine glasses in hand.

'Here's to love lost and love found.' Gemma said, raising her glass.

They all smiled sadly at one another and clinked their glasses.

'Now tell me how the flat-hunting went,' her mother asked Emmeline excitedly.

CHAPTER 69

Sam hadn't wasted any time. Cara received the divorce papers six weeks after she had found out she was pregnant. She was sitting in the kitchen having breakfast with Sophie when there was a knock at the door.

'Do you want me to get it?' Cara asked.

'Would you? I'm in the middle of a cigarette.'

Cara opened the door to a clean-shaven, stocky young man.

'Are you Cara Brown?' he asked smiling.

'That depends on who wants to know,' she replied.

'Cara Brown, I am serving you with divorce papers,' he said, thrusting a brown envelope into her hands.

She closed the door and headed back to the kitchen.

'Great start to the weekend!' she said, as she threw the envelope on the kitchen counter. Sophie looked puzzled.

'Sam found me sooner than I'd hoped.'

'Ah, the dreaded divorce papers have landed. I'm sorry, love. You'd better make an appointment with a lawyer. Mine was alright, and she was cheap, if you want her number?'

Cara accepted, beggars couldn't be choosers. She made the call to Avril Raynehart the following Monday. She got an

appointment for the same evening, which didn't fill her with confidence.

Avril looked as worn out as the carpet in her tiny office. She managed a half-smile as Cara took the seat opposite her and started to explain her circumstances. When she had finished, Avril looked up from her notebook and put her pen down.

'Mrs Brown, you're not going to like what you're about to hear, but the law is clear when it comes to women leaving their husbands to have a son. The government views any divorce, regardless of the circumstances, as an act of desertion by the wife. This is a factor the courts are obliged to take into consideration when deciding the financial settlement. The fact you chose to leave Sam will also go against you, reducing the amount you're likely to receive from the split of the matrimonial assets. The amount will be further reduced because you are choosing to continue with your pregnancy. Think of it as a punitive levy. I would estimate you are unlikely to get more than 30%. As you are having a boy, maintenance will be governed by the amendments to the Child Maintenance Act which came into force at the same time as the government's policy on encouraging the abortion of male foetuses. To put it bluntly, Sam will not have any liability to pay child maintenance. Any maintenance you receive will have to be negotiated outside of the courts and will be on a purely voluntary basis. Sam will be able to stop any payments he chooses to make, and you will have no recourse to the courts if he does.'

Sam's research had been correct. Cara had thought she was prepared for bad news, but this legislation shocked her.

By the time she got home she was raging at the injustice of it all.

'I can't effing believe what Avril told me,' Cara said, as she stormed into the kitchen.

'Can I get you a strong mug of camomile tea?' Sophie laughed.

‘Seriously, this is no laughing matter. She reckons I’ll get 30% of the assets and no child maintenance because I am daring to have a boy, against the wishes of my government. This is bullshit! It’s blatant coercive social engineering!’

‘You could look at it that way, or you could argue it’s the state protecting its citizens from behaviour which threatens to destabilise society. Insisting the wellbeing of the whole has to be put above the wellbeing of the individual.’

‘Would you put it that way?’ Cara asked, thinking this did not sound like something her aunt would trot out.

‘Yes, I guess I would. Look, Cara, you knew what you were letting yourself in for. You knew you were swimming against the tide. I’m honestly surprised at your reaction. What else were you expecting?’ Cara sat down, stunned by her words.

‘Listen, I don’t have a problem with protecting the status quo, but why is it only the women who are forced to modify their lives and behaviour? The man’s life remains largely unaffected. Sure, he has to pay maintenance for his daughters and existing sons, but he doesn’t lose his job, or face any social stigma. If anything, people feel sorry for him. After all, a man would never get rid of a wife, unless her behaviour made him desperately unhappy, so it’s always going to seem like the wife’s fault!’

‘Look, it isn’t ideal, nothing is. But remember, it was the Completists who brought this about. If they didn’t exist there would be enough women to go around and the divorce laws would have stayed as they were.’

‘You sound like a Completist! Except you’re blaming all the woes of our society on those women, rather than men!’

Sophie glared at her. ‘I think we’ll have to agree to disagree on this one.’

Cara changed tack. ‘I’m dreading going into work tomorrow. My boss will be informed, now the papers have been served.’

Sophie gave Cara a sympathetic smile. ‘I think you should

prepare yourself for the worst. The divorce will go through reasonably quickly if you agree a settlement, and I think you now realise that fighting for more will be a futile exercise, so at least you'll get your money quickly. But don't worry if there's a couple of months when you're short of cash before it arrives, Harry and I will support you.'

Cara stood up and went to hug her. 'I'm sorry about what I said earlier,' she said quietly into her shoulder as she held her.

'Me too. I was too harsh. Don't think I don't know how you're feeling, because I do. And for what it's worth, I think you're making the right decision to keep your son.' Sophie stroked her hair, like her mother had in the past.

The next day, Cara was called into her manager's office as soon as she had taken her coat off. He told her she had to leave immediately and would be paid her months' notice. She didn't argue.

Two security guards watched her pack up her desk. Not a single colleague approached to wish her well, not even Lisa and Anne. How different her departure would have been had she stayed married to Sam. Her desk would have been covered with cards, as she waddled out of the office to begin her year's maternity leave. If she had been carrying a girl, she would have received her full salary for the whole year, while her little lad, would have only entitled her to three months money and a tenth of her pay for the remainder of the time. Today, thanks to Sam's selfishness, she was leaving with no prospect of a job and only a month's money to put in the bank.

She took a taxi to her new home. Sophie and Harry were both out at work. The previous night, Sophie had promised to arrange an interview with the cleaning company she had worked for, but Cara wasn't holding out much hope. With divorce papers registered and served, she was already an Outsider, and would now be closely monitored by the state. She was obliged to declare her status to any prospective employer, putting her through the humiliation of explaining

that she was pregnant with a boy and that her husband no longer wished to stay married to her, then swallow their inevitable judgment. A pregnant woman was not going to be their first choice for a job which involved manual labour. She had her applications ready for several menial office jobs, but wondered whether it was even worth sending them. Reality was kicking in, and she didn't like it.

She sat on her bed, staring at the wall opposite. Her hand wandered to her belly.

'What am I going to do, little man? How am I going to be able to care for you, and give you a decent life?' She felt powerless again. She didn't want to be an Outsider. She curled up in the foetal position and pulled the duvet over her head.

'Cara, you home already?' Sophie shouted up the stairs. Cara stirred at the sound of her voice. She uncurled herself and padded downstairs.

'They sacked me today,' she said, as she wandered into the kitchen.

'I'm sorry, love. That was fast. Are you alright? You look like you could do with a nice cup of tea and a slice of cake.'

'Thanks,' Cara said as she flopped down into a kitchen chair. 'I'm not sure I can go through with this.'

'What do you mean? Through with the pregnancy, through with the divorce?'

'I don't know. I want this baby to be born. And I certainly do not want to stay married to Sam. But I can't live like this, it's shit.' Cara rested her head on the table and closed her eyes.

Sophie sat down opposite her, placing a mug and a large slice of chocolate cake on the table.

'Cara, look at me. Let's look at your options. You abort the baby, get divorced and marry again when you meet a great guy, like my Harry.'

'Why would I have to abort the baby to remarry?' Cara had raised her head, in an effort to appease Sophie by looking like she gave a shit.

‘Come on, Cara, get real. Another man’s child wouldn’t put off all men, but it will put off most.’

‘Not keen on that option, Sophie. Any more suggestions?’

‘You keep the baby. Use up all your financial settlement trying to make ends meet, because you’ll only be able to get a low paid job, and live alone for the rest of your miserable life.’ Sophie took a mouthful of cake.

Cara started to feel angry. She sat up straight. ‘Here’s another option. I give birth, get my son adopted by a childless, loving couple from a country unaffected by this madness, and then go back and join the Movement. I’ll miss my son terribly, but he’ll be alive, I’ll have a great job, a healthy salary, and lots of like-minded friends.’ She stared defiantly at Sophie, who calmly took another bite.

‘And never have the chance to love again?’ she said.

‘Absafuckinglutely, Aunt Sophie. What is a man’s love worth anyway? As far as I can see, it’s a one-way street. Their way, or no way.’ Cara was fully animated now, she leant forward, her arms on the table, hands folded in front of her.

‘I get why you feel this way, Cara. Everything is raw and your hormones are all over the place. But love doesn’t have to be like that. Harry doesn’t dictate the terms of our relationship. He loves me for who I am.’ Sophie delivered her last line like a devout Christian talking about Jesus Christ.

‘Are you sure, Sophie? How would Harry feel if you got pregnant with a son?’

‘He’d be delighted. He always wanted children. It would be tough at our age, but we’d manage.’

‘You don’t think he’d persuade you to abort the baby, in case it affected your relationship?’

‘No! Harry’s not selfish like Sam. If I wanted the baby, he would support me.’

‘Well, those responses would have been mine less than four months ago. Now, look at me.’

‘Cara, I always think love is like religion. It’s built on faith

and a belief that things will work out for the best. You've known love, and isn't it the most amazing feeling you've ever experienced? There's nothing like it. I don't care what the Completists say about the satisfaction they get from their brilliant, fulfilling careers. They give up that feeling. The feeling of being loved, adored and desired by another human being.'

'Is that true?' Cara countered. 'They have different kinds of love. The loyal love of a friend. The unquestioning love of a child. And these kinds of love are more likely to stand the test of time than the elusive romantic love between a man and a woman.' Cara was utterly convinced by her own argument. To her mind, she had spoken an unassailable truth.

'I'd have to disagree with you about the love of a child standing the test of time. My daughter left me, and my son has never bothered to track me down. And you, you also left your mother. All love is fragile Cara, no matter what form it takes.'

'I still love my mother and my sister, very much. And I would visit them, but it's too risky with the Segregation Rules. Did you know the Movement wanted their members to be able to see their families? It was the government who insisted that all ties were cut. The Completists don't see Chosen Ones as a threat. The way I see it, love as a Chosen One sucks, because they prescribe who and how I love. Did you know the government class every gay woman as an Outsider? Which is why they've all become Completists. We let women love women.' Cara sat back in her chair, satisfied she had dealt Sophie a sucker punch.

'That's as may be,' Sophie said, 'but you don't let women love men, or women love their sons. And,' Sophie added, her voice rising in tone and volume, 'as for still loving your mother and sister, I'm sure you do. But you didn't love them enough to put them above your own needs, did you? The same way Emmeline and Kate didn't love me enough.'

'Like you didn't love your son enough, and made it clear

to Emmeline and Kate you hated them for joining the Movement,' Cara snapped back.

Sophie winced. When she spoke again, her voice was calmer, more measured. 'Yes, I have to accept that. I knew what the consequences of divorcing Peter would be and I went ahead anyway. Perhaps you should accept the consequences of your decisions. You don't like the ones facing you now. So be honest. Decide what is going to make you happy and go with it.'

Cara stared at her tea. 'So, we're all selfish bastards at heart.' Her voice was also calm, the rage quelled by the sound of her own anger.

'I guess we are. But that's survival, isn't it?' Sophie said quietly.

'Maybe. But before now, I didn't have to kill anyone to live the life I wanted.' She looked at Sophie with huge sadness in her eyes.

'Then don't. Have the baby and give it up for adoption. Then go back to the Movement. I think that's what you really want, isn't it?'

CHAPTER 70

If Cara had been carrying a girl, she would have faced life imprisonment for attempting to arrange a foreign adoption; however, she soon discovered there was a queue of childless couples as keen and willing to adopt baby boys from the UK as the government was to get rid of them. The politicians had never declared this practice as policy, but everyone was willing to turn a blind eye, leaving the organisations who helped people find parents for the UK's unwelcome sons to get on with their job.

Cara wished she could meet the other women going through what she was. It would have been a comfort not to have to do this alone; but one of the ways the organisations kept their end of the unspoken bargain was to isolate the mothers involved from one another. No-one needed to know the scale of the problem. It did not raise the UK government's standing within the international community.

Cara chose a couple from Norway who had applied to the UK Adoption Service. They were a young, professional couple, and the woman ran her own nursery. Her name was Kari. Her husband, Sven, was a history teacher at The University of Oslo. Cara liked the fact it only took an hour to fly to

the city; and, despite the proximity to the UK, it could have been another planet in terms of its politics. She knew Completists were achieving some success in other countries where women suffered from economic inequality, but Norway had always been ahead of the curve in that respect. Somehow, they had managed to get things right without the need for radical movements which set one section of society against another. She even considered moving to Norway herself so she could keep her son, but the idea of leaving her family behind for a second time was too difficult to contemplate. It had been hard for her to negotiate the CO world without taking on a completely new culture and language.

As she lay awake, stroking her son through her skin, feeling him kick and swirl inside her, she imagined them taking walks together, strolling hand in hand through snowy landscapes. She would hear his laughter, as she pushed him down undulating slopes on his sledge, and the soft thump of his arrival in a snowdrift at the bottom. They were daydreams, but they eased her pain.

Since their blood-letting, Cara and Sophie had become much closer. Cara recognised it could have gone the other way. The truth had a tendency to alienate people, but they had both recognised it for what it was. Cara had accepted she had put her love for Sam above her feelings for her sister and mother and was determined to rectify the situation; and her aunt had realised it was her inability to forgive her sister and daughter that was maintaining the emotional chasm between them.

'I have to sign the official adoption papers next week,' Cara said, as she helped Sophie make the dinner. Cara was chopping onions, so Sophie didn't comment on her tears until she saw her shoulders start to shake.

'Hey, are you alright? Isn't this what you wanted? Are you having second thoughts?' she asked, pulling Cara away from her work and turning her towards her.

Cara wiped her eyes with the back of her arm.

'Oh, Sophie. I can never imagine the moment when they take him from me. It's too much for my brain to handle. Giving my little lad to total strangers. How am I going to do it? I already love him so much.'

Sophie held her for a moment, then called Harry to join them. Cara was confused.

'Sit down, Cara,' instructed Sophie. 'Harry and I have been talking and we've got something we'd like to discuss with you.'

Harry looked at Sophie, searching her face for confirmation it was the discussion he thought it was. Sophie nodded.

'What's going on?' Cara asked the pair of them.

'We'd like to adopt your baby.' Sophie said quietly.

'What?' Cara wasn't sure whether she had heard her correctly.

'We didn't want to say anything before, we didn't want to make things more complicated. But we've been thinking about it for a few months now. I told you Harry has always wanted children. And I miss my Charlie. To be honest Cara, I'm done losing people. I don't want to lose another member of my family. I know it'll be difficult. He would never be able to know you were his mother. But at least you would know where he was and that he was with people who would cherish and care for him. We might need a little financial help from you, to cover the childcare costs so we could both still work...' Her voice trailed off; she was evidently waiting for her to react.

Cara looked from one to the other and saw the hope in their eyes. 'Oh, my goodness. Yes, yes, I would love that!' She reached out and grabbed their hands, holding them tightly in her own. 'You don't know how much this means to me. Thank you both, thank you so much.'

Sophie smiled at Harry. He was grinning as broadly as she was. 'Can you believe this, Harry? You're going to get a son,' but Harry couldn't speak. Large tears were rolling down his

cheeks. He beamed at Sophie and squeezed Cara's hand so tightly she let out a little yelp.

Harry released her hand immediately, a look of horror in his eyes. 'It's alright, Harry. No damage done.' Cara laughed.

'Thank you, Cara, for giving me the greatest gift a person could give another,' he spluttered. 'I haven't been so happy since Sophie agreed to marry me.'

'Do you know, Harry, if all men were like you, we wouldn't need the Movement. I can't think of a better man to raise my little lad. You're kind, you love and respect Sophie, and I know you'll love my son. Talk of the devil, he appears to approve, he's going crazy in here. Feel.'

Cara grabbed both their hands and placed them on her stomach.

'There you go, Harry. A ready-made centre-forward. Feel the strength of his kick!' Sophie laughed.

Harry started to cry again.

'Right, that's enough of that, Mum and Dad. Let's get the dinner going. I'm starving, and centre-forwards are not made on air alone.'

Cara slept soundly for the first time in a long while that night; her hand resting on her son's body, as he slept peacefully inside her.

CHAPTER 71

For the last two months of her pregnancy, Cara used some of her settlement to move into a cheap but clean hotel, so they could hide their family connection from the Adoption Agency. She used her married surname for all the paperwork; she had delayed updating her identity chip. The decree absolute had only come through a couple of months earlier, and she had three months to attend an Identity Bureau before she would be in breach of regulations. The Adoption Agency was used to dealing with matters at the last minute, and this had been an easy case to administer. Their Visit Report had been glowing. It was obvious the child would be going to a loving and stable home. They weren't inclined to dig any deeper.

Cara found the days lonely. She tried to get out and exercise, and she spoke to Sophie every evening, but she had too much time to herself to focus on what she was about to do.

When her due date came and went, she made an appointment with her midwife to see if there was something she could do to speed things up. While she was dreading his birth, the thought of waiting even longer, only to lose him, was driving her mad.

The midwife was kind. She understood her frustrations, her own daughter had been 10 days overdue; however, intervention sooner than 14 days after the due date was no longer recommended. She warned her not to try any of the suggestions she might find on the internet. Nothing was scientifically proven to work: the baby would appear when he was ready.

He decided to make his appearance the same day. When she got back to the hotel, Cara was restless and began to tidy and double-check her hospital bag. By the evening she was having contractions every half hour. At 3.00 a.m. she could no longer bear the pain and made the call to Sophie.

'Hi, Sophie. I'm taking myself off to the hospital now. I've been having regular contractions for the last two hours and they're getting really painful.'

'Can you wait another 20 minutes so we can come and pick you up?'

'I don't think I can. Don't worry, I'll see you there. I've got to go now, I'm about to have another one.'

'We'll be there as soon as we can. Try to keep calm!'

By the time Cara was told about their arrival it was nearly over, but knowing they were near, gave her renewed strength for the final push. Sophie had wanted to be with her for the birth, but they hadn't wanted to arouse suspicion and potentially jeopardise the adoption.

As she waited for the next contraction, she imagined them both sitting in the waiting room. Harry would be holding Sophie's hand, and they would both be desperate for a cigarette. She felt less alone now, less afraid. Thank God she had been assigned a wonderfully kind midwife. She would be forever grateful to her.

Joe was born at 4.56 a.m. Sophie was called for ten minutes later. Those few minutes with him lying on her chest seemed to last a lifetime. She stroked his tiny body, tears

streaming silently down her cheeks. 'I love you,' she said over and over again. Then Sophie came into the room.

'Happy Birth Day,' Cara said as she handed him over. Her aunt took him and nestled him into her arms, his blue eyes stared up at her face. Cara ached to be the one looking into those eyes, searing her face into his memory; so, if they ever met again, there might be an inner connection he would be able to feel, if not explain.

'Hey, little Joe. Welcome to the world. It's a bizarre old place, but I've got you, you'll be fine.' Sophie looked into Cara's tired, bloodshot eyes and squeezed her hand.

'Thank you, love. I'm so glad you found me. You know we'll love him as our own, and good luck with everything.' Then, as she went down to kiss her goodbye, she whispered, 'Perhaps one day this madness will end, and you'll be able to visit us. We'll all be waiting for you.'

Cara was looking over Sophie's shoulder, trying to catch a final glimpse of her perfect son. She caught his eye and tried to convey her endless love for him in the split second she had before Sophie stood back up and squeezed her hand in a final farewell.

Cara's eyes never left him until the door closed. The midwife, who had respectfully kept her distance, came over and patted her hand.

'Let's get you stitched up and washed, shall we?' she said.

A few days later, Cara sat waiting for her turn. Her name was called and she went into the side room indicated by the lady at reception. She handed over her dossier of paperwork to the woman sitting behind the desk, who smiled at her as she took the documents for processing.

'I'm Joan Smith. This won't take too long, Cara,' she said. She typed her maiden name into the computer, and stopped.

‘Welcome back, Cara. Your mother and sister are going to be delighted to see you again, I’m sure.’

‘I do hope so. That’s all that’s keeping me going right now.’

‘I can imagine. I have a friend who was in the same situation as you, and it took a while for her to laugh again. But you know we’ll help in any way we can; you only have to ask.’

Cara smiled at the woman. It was good to be back.

FOUNDERS MEETING

Libretta's car swept up the drive of Marilynn Johnson's house. It had been 13 years since Marilynn had hosted an annual conference, but that day was embedded in her memory. Libretta shuddered as she recalled how her dogs had mauled a journalist to death that afternoon. She had never seen his torn body. It was not a gruesome image that was making her skin crawl, but the memory of how easily her colleagues and friends had condemned a man to death. At least Marilynn's hunch had been right. No-one had known about his whereabouts, so they had all managed to stay out of jail and out of the public eye.

The main item on today's agenda was the recently released Mental Health Report. The Movement had been documenting the state of their members' minds for over 50 years. In the beginning, many issues were directly related to the treatment they had suffered at the hands of men, but this last report confirmed an undeniable new trend, which needed to be addressed.

This time, as she crunched her way to the front door, she noted with satisfaction she was the first to arrive. Margaret opened the door and she sensed a chill in her greeting. She

guessed Marilynn must have told her she had been against releasing the dogs.

She was politely shown into the Library and informed that Marilynn would be down shortly. She sat at the head of the table and poured herself a glass of water. As she raised the glass to her lips, Marilynn came swishing into the room, her signature silk skirt rippling around her legs. Despite being in her seventies, Marilynn was as glamorous as ever, and she still moved like a gazelle. Libretta, on the other hand, walked like a 73-year-old; it wouldn't be long before she would have to step down as CEO of her company and Chair of the Movement.

'Morning, Libretta, you look a little tired, are you alright?' Marilynn sounded genuinely concerned for her old friend. She had forgiven Libretta's squeamishness long ago.

'I think the 15-hour days are starting to catch up with me!' Libretta laughed.

'I do know how you feel. I wonder if we should put succession planning on today's agenda? I was talking to Sylvia the other day, and she was wondering the same thing. We're all getting a little long in the tooth. Perhaps it's time for us to retire and let some new blood in. What do you think?'

'I think we could pose the question today, after the main discussion is finished. There is still so much to do. And a few invigorated youngsters might be exactly what's needed.'

'The Report makes interesting reading, doesn't it? Poses all sorts of questions for our future, should be an interesting debate.' Marilynn moved a chocolate cake a few centimetres to the right, to align it neatly with the sandwiches. Satisfied, she stood up and checked the clock. She was about to make a comment about other members cutting it a bit fine, when the door opened and the seats around the table began to fill up. Libretta smiled as each person took their place and, at 11.00 a.m. sharp, she called the room to order.

'Morning, one and all, and welcome to Marilynn's beautiful home once more. As you know, the main item on the

agenda is the latest Mental Health Report. I'm not going to go through its main points, as you have all, no doubt, read it in detail.

I firmly believe it's time to lobby Parliament to remove The Segregation Act from the statute books and demand the release of all those Completists who are currently serving a life sentence for the most trivial transgressions. I'm sure we all recall the case of Taylor and Camille Andrews in 2136, which ended with them both taking their own lives. A moment of extreme sadness for all our members.

Libretta turned to their host, who was always given the first opportunity to speak. 'Marilynn, what are your thoughts?'

'It's clear from the Report that the strain of family estrangement is weighing heavily on a large number of our members. Over 60% of those not raised as Completists have made use of our Mental Health Services to try and manage their pain and anger at being denied access to those they still love. While the Report makes it clear these women understand why this situation exists, and appear to hold no grudge against the Movement for the Segregation Act, both these factors can exacerbate their pain, as they have no outlet for their anger.

We all know we had little choice but to agree to these awful terms in order to get The Self-Determination Act passed. But a great deal of water has run under the bridge since then. We know attitudes continue to change. Chosen Ones profit from the economic equality the Movement has achieved. Moreover, as we gradually gain more political power, some ministers are finally listening to us. These changes mean it is likely our request for statutory reform will fall on sympathetic ears. For this reason, I think we should lobby Parliament with immediate effect.'

'Thank you, Marilynn. Who would like to speak next?'

A number of hands were raised, but following Movement

Protocol, Libretta asked Kerry Greer to speak, as she was the most senior.

'I agree with Marilynn, but perhaps not for exactly the same reasons. I see distinct advantages for the Movement if our members feel able to safely socialise with COs, outside of a business environment, which should happen naturally once they are able to reunite with their families and friends. Members would be able to explain how we live and why we choose to live as Completists. This could undermine the insidious propaganda still put out by the government. In addition, it may help us recruit more members.'

'An interesting point, Kerry. And very much worth bearing in mind. Sylvia, you wanted to say something?'

Sylvia peered through her glasses, whose lenses had thickened over the years, along with her waistline. 'I'm for it too. But for a different reason. I worry about creating another batch of Castoffs. The first generation of Castoffs, as the COs call them, have grown up into our worst enemies. And frankly, it's hardly surprising. I don't mean to be blunt, but we have to acknowledge their fathers were abandoned by their wives and forced to raise their sons, a role they never wanted. These men have heard their fathers bitch about their lost mothers and the Movement with no-one to intervene and dilute their criticism. I know the last time we discussed Project Manhood, the evidence indicated men were hard-wired to seek control and power, but I think the actions of these men, some of whom are now Members of Parliament, show us nurture exacerbates these traits. Perhaps the right kind of nurturing could minimise them. We have had a number of members who transferred out of the Movement only to return several years later, leaving sons behind. This is a relatively recent phenomenon. But I wouldn't want to see another generation of Castoffs being raised to despise all women and the ideals Completists stand for. Contact with their mothers should minimise this risk.'

'Another good point. If no-one else has anything new to add, we should take a vote.' Libretta surveyed her audience, checking for consensus. 'Right, all those in favour of lobbying Parliament to repeal The Segregation Act raise your hands.' Every hand went up. 'Thank you. Now we have to plan how we are going to do it!'

Kerry Greer spoke. 'I may have the solution. My family owns the largest pharmaceutical company in the UK. Some of you may know that we are the only manufacturers of the prostate cancer drug, Testicuclean, which is 100% effective. What you won't know, and please do not discuss this outside this room, is that we are about to launch a new drug which halts the onset of dementia and Alzheimer's. As you know, heart disease has been radically reduced since the population were forced to eat a largely vegetarian diet, and most cancers are now curable, but the one thing we haven't managed to defeat, thus far, is dementia. The average life expectancy in 2020 was 80 years old, it is now 100. In 2020, 1 in 14 people over 65 had dementia, now 50% of the over 65's suffer from this condition. This is a huge drain on the public purse and our own. My suggestion is that I threaten to refuse to make this drug available to the COs unless they agree to repeal The Segregation Act.'

There was a spontaneous round of applause. 'Congratulations Kerry, what an incredible achievement. I think we have indeed found the solution! That's a brilliant suggestion! Let's raise our teacups to Greer Pharmaceuticals and their brilliant CEO, Kerry Greer.'

The delicate chink of fine bone china had never before been such a hopeful and joyous sound.

PART THREE

CHAPTER 72

Kate was preparing lunch when she heard Gemma shouting. The knife she was using clattered to the floor as she rushed to the front door. Cara was standing in front of her. Her beautiful, baby girl was back. She pushed past Gemma and took her into her arms. It was wonderful to feel her again; to feel her heart pounding against her own. 'My darling girl. I can't believe it! Are you back for good?'

She stepped back and drank in Cara's face, noticing the fine lines around her eyes, the dark circles beneath them.

'I am. I've re-joined the Movement. Will you have me back?' Cara asked, anxiously searching her face for a sign of her fate.

'Of course, we will, won't we, Gemma? You daft child! Only Gemma's moved into your old room, so you'll have to make do with the smaller one. Come in, come in!'

She put her arm around Cara's shoulders and led her into the kitchen. Her daughter was wearing loose-fitting top and trousers, but Kate was too overwhelmed with happiness to heed the alarm bell ringing in her head.

'I can't believe it's really you. Would you like a cup of tea...

no. What am I thinking? Let's crack open the champagne! Gemma, would you get the glasses please.'

Cara sat down in her usual place at the table. Kate struggled to ease the cork out of the champagne bottle, but finally managed to pour the liquid into the three glasses. Her hands were shaking. Gemma had sat down on the kitchen worktop. Kate could feel her watching her intently, avoiding eye contact with her sister. She'd come around. How could she not? Her sister was back from the dead. She carried two glasses over to the table, setting one in front of Cara. She sat down next to her and they waited for Gemma to join them.

Gemma chose to sit beside her mother, rather than in her usual chair, next to Cara's. Kate understood Gemma's pain, but she was too happy to deal with it now. She lifted her glass. 'To a reunited family!'

Cara clinked her glass gently against her mother's and then held it towards Gemma, who was yet to raise hers. She saw Cara looking into her sister's eyes, imploring her to join the toast. Gemma held her gaze, raised her glass and brushed it against Cara's, giving her a nod. She did not smile.

They each took a sip and put their glasses down. Kate looked at Cara, then at Gemma. She took a deep breath and sighed. 'Perhaps tea would've been better,' she said. 'I'm so delighted to see you, but you've obviously had a rough time. You wouldn't be sitting in front of us, otherwise. What happened?'

'You were right, and I was wrong,' Cara's voice trembled as she spoke. 'Sam turned out to be like my father. He loved sex more than he loved me.'.

'Did he hurt you?' Gemma asked, her face clouding with anger. Kate's heart quickened as Gemma's protective instincts kicked in.

'No, Gemma. Not physically.'

Kate watched her younger daughter's face transform as she allowed her anger to subside and let her heart fill the space.

Kate held her breath. Gemma reached out her hand to touch Cara's.

'You were a complete cow and a fucking wanker for not saying goodbye,' Gemma said quietly.

'I was a fucking wanker, wasn't I? And I couldn't bear to see your pain, which makes me a cowardly cow.' Gemma gave her a small smile, and sighed, shaking her head.

'Welcome home, fuckwit. It's good to see you.'

'It's phenomenal to see you,' Cara replied.

'Don't be so melodramatic,' Gemma said standing up and walking around to the other side of the table to sit next to her.

'That's better,' Kate said. 'Let's try again, shall we? To a reunited family!'

'To a reunited family!' Gemma and Cara said in unison, and all three glasses clinked together.

'So, did Sam cheat on you?' Gemma asked as they placed their glasses down.

'No, it was worse than that. He wanted me to abort our baby in case it got in the way of our sex life.'

'Oh, Cara, I'm so sorry.' Kate said, grabbing her left hand as Gemma grabbed her right.

'It's alright,' Cara said, looking from one to the other, 'I didn't go through with it.'

They both looked at her, simultaneously coming to the same conclusion.

'The child was a boy then,' Kate said flatly.

'A beautiful, perfect little boy,' Cara replied her voice breaking. Kate wanted to hold her in her arms, and absorb her pain; but she felt numb. Instead, she got up and reached for the box of tissues. She sat back down and handed her one.

'You left him with Sam?'

'No, Mum. I wasn't going to leave my precious boy with that cunt when he didn't even want him in the first place,' Cara snarled as she blew her nose. 'I left little Joe with your sister and her new husband. They've adopted him.'

Kate dropped Cara's hand and sat back in her chair. She sucked in her breath.

'Mum, it's a long story. When Sam made it clear he didn't want the baby, I went to a Completist Gender Verification Clinic to find out what sex it was. If Joe had been a girl, Sam would have had no choice but to accept the situation. Did you know our government is actively encouraging Chosen Ones to abort boys or put them up for adoption with foreign countries?'

'I knew about their policy to encourage boys to be aborted, but I didn't know they facilitated overseas adoptions,' Kate replied, sitting forward in her chair.

'It doesn't surprise me. It's not something they're proud of. No one actually said it was legal, but it was far too easy for me to arrange to have Joc adopted by a Norwegian couple.'

'But you said Sophie had adopted him?'

'She has. But she didn't tell me she wanted him until I was about to sign the adoption papers.'

'So, she didn't really want him?' Kate could feel her anger vying for control.

'It wasn't like that, Mum. She wanted me to be sure about what I was doing. Give me a chance to change my mind and keep him. But she knew I didn't want to live as an Outsider with a child. It was only when I broke down and said I couldn't bear the thought of him in another country that she told me they'd been talking for months about adopting him. I jumped at the chance.'

'Christ, this is too much to take in.' Kate stood up and retrieved her hidden stash of cigarettes, picturing her sister holding her first grandchild, a child she would never meet.

'Don't judge me, Gemma,' she said, casting her a warning look. 'The last time I had one of these was when your sister told me she was going to become a Chosen One.'

'I'm not judging, Mum. I feel like having one myself!'

She offered Gemma the packet. 'You're alright, I think they might be off.' Gemma said, winking at Cara.

'And how would you know about that?'

'I don't. But after nearly five years, it's an educated guess!'

Kate lit a cigarette and inhaled. 'You seem to have a point Gemma,' she said, coughing. She grabbed her glass, gulping down some champagne, while stubbing out the cigarette in disgust. Then, after glancing at the ashtray for a second, she decided she needed the hit and immediately lit another.

'So, Cara. How the hell did Sophie end up adopting my grandson?'

Cara waved away the cloud of stinking smoke. 'When Sam made it abundantly clear he wanted nothing further to do with me or the baby, I had nowhere to go. I had no friends who were close enough to turn to. Chosen Ones tend to shun women raised as Completists. And as soon as you divorce, you are virtually locked outside the system. You lose your job, all state benefits, plus, in any divorce, it's the woman who's committing an act of desertion, even if it's not her decision, which means less money.'

'Wow,' Gemma gasped. 'That's twisted.'

'It sure is,' continued Cara. 'So, there I was. Homeless, friendless and about to have my income cut off. That's when I remembered Sophie. I wondered if she might be willing to help. She might see it as karma and welcome me, if for no other reason than to spite you, Mum.'

'And was that why she took you in?' Kate was concentrating on her every word.

'I think it was, at first. But as we got to know one another, it became very clear she still loves you. She never said as much, but she seems angrier with the Movement than with you. Although she's still holding onto the pain of your abandonment, as she sees it.'

Kate bent her head down and pressed her fingers into her

brow, rubbing her skin hard for a few seconds, trying to force this information into her brain. She raised her head.

'Did you like her?'

'I did. It was hard not to. She's a lot like you. She's had a hard life, Mum. She divorced from her husband, lost her son to him, spent a few tough years as an Outsider and lost her own daughter to the Movement. But luckily, when Emmeline left, she was already married to Harry, who's the best man I've ever met. They're genuinely happy together. She's a complete romantic, refuses to give up on love. And Harry is too. Aside from being with me, Joe is in the best place he could be. Strange how her daughter decided to become a Completist at the same time I became a Chosen One. Even stranger to think I have a cousin who I could track down and meet, now I've rejoined the Movement.'

'You won't need to track her down. She works at Femmeur and she comes around for dinner about once a fortnight.'

'What? To use your favourite phrase, life is a weird motherfucker sometimes. How did you end up knowing Emmeline?'

'That's a long story too. She came for an interview at Femmeur. I had a funny feeling about her, and I knew, as soon as I saw her, she was Sophie's daughter. She's lovely, Cara. I think you two will get along, don't you Gemma?'

'She's really nice. I'm very fond of her. We often have lunch together at work.'

Kate watched Cara's eyes narrow, could she be jealous? She decided to change the subject.

'Do you have any photos of Joe?'

'No, not a single one. We pretended there were no family ties when we organised the adoption. It was easy with different surnames. I moved out of the house and lived in a hotel while it was being arranged. I only saw Joe for a couple of minutes after he was born. And then I placed him in Sophie's arms and he was gone.' Cara was close to tears again.

‘Come here, my baby girl.’ They stood up and Kate wrapped her in her arms. ‘You’re home now. And by all accounts, Joe has a loving home too. You never know, maybe one day, the men of this country will come to their senses and we’ll figure out a way we can all live together again. You can be reunited with Joe, and I can meet my grandson and my sister.’

‘Maybe, Mum, maybe,’ Cara said quietly, and she buried her head into her shoulder. She was back where she belonged.

CHAPTER 73

It was clear Cara was grieving for Joe. Each morning, Kate could hear her groan with pain as she woke up. She had never heard a sound like it. It reached into her and tore at her soul. Kate also noticed Cara touching her belly absent-mindedly throughout the day; and when wet patches appeared on her daughter's top, Kate's heart bled for her. The sadness would return to her daughter's eyes, as she realised Joe had gone.

There was nothing else for it. Her daughter needed to be distracted. She would speak to Libretta. Within days, Cara was offered a job in their Marketing Department. The only opening was a more junior position; however, Cara accepted her demotion willingly, and Kate knew she would be putting in the hours and would soon make up for lost time.

As the weeks passed, Cara's groans subsided, and Kate started to hope her daughter would eventually be able to find some peace. It was good to have her family back together, even though it could be challenging at times. The morning Cara was due to start work it was as if she'd gone back in time.

'Hey, you two!' she shouted up the stairs. 'You both ready?'

'Sorry, I'm coming right now!' Cara replied.

'About time,' Kate said, smiling as they both exited their bedrooms and came storming down the stairs. 'Honestly, it feels like getting you both ready for school all over again.'

'Mum, we're all grown up now. We choose to leave everything until the last minute, don't we, Cara?' Gemma laughed as she reached for her coat.

'Let me grab the keys. I think I left them in the kitchen.'

'Come on, Mum,' they both said mockingly, 'we're going to be late!'

As they stood on the bus, Kate smiled at her daughters.

'You OK, Mum?' Cara asked. 'You've got your inside face on.'

'It's so lovely to be all going to work together, to be together again.' Cara squeezed her hand, then looked straight ahead.

When they walked through the doors at Femmeur, Kate reminded them they were all going to meet at the Rooftop Restaurant. 'I think we should invite Emmeline too. It's high time you met your cousin, Cara.'

'Mum, it's my first day in a brand-new job. Can't it wait?' she responded, testily.

'I hardly think it's brand new. You know most of the people in your department, and you can do this job with your hands tied.'

'Fine. I look forward to it,' she said unenthusiastically.

'Don't be like that,' Gemma chastised. 'She's lovely, and she's really excited to meet you.'

'Great,' Cara responded flatly, but she winked at Gemma as she spoke.

'It's settled then. I'll call Emmeline and we'll all meet at 1.00 p.m. See you later, girls.'

Emmeline jumped at the invitation. Kate arranged to meet her at the lift in the restaurant. She had a feeling Emmeline might need a little moral support.

The morning flew by, and Emmeline was waiting for her when the lift doors opened. They spotted Gemma already seated at a corner table, and she waved at them.

'Cara not here yet, I see,' Kate remarked to Gemma as they sat down.

'She messaged me and said she might be five minutes late. Probably wants to make an entrance, you know Cara!'

Emmeline laughed. 'Don't be mean, Gemma. She's probably a bit nervous. I know I am. It's all a bit surreal. Two parallel universes finally converging. Is that her?' Cara was walking towards them, her eyes resting on Emmeline, who stood up to greet her.

'It's lovely to meet you, Cara. Who would've believed it? You look like your mum.'

'Thanks, I think,' Cara said.

'Don't be so rude,' Kate said, laughing.

Cara didn't seem to know whether to shake her hand or hug her. The moment passed, and they both sat down without touching.

'How's everything going?' Kate asked her daughter, brightly.

'I can report to the Head of HR that I'm settling in nicely, thank you,' Cara replied. 'Everyone has been lovely, such a contrast to my last place of work!'

'Did the COs give you a tough time?' Emmeline asked.

'They sure did. Were you ever anti-Completist, Emmeline?'

'Do you know, I don't think I was. I remember envying your way of life when I was growing up. I didn't think much of my father or my brother. And I kept imagining how much happier my mother and I would be if they weren't around.'

Cara nodded her head. 'I'm sorry, Emmeline. But Harry is lovely, isn't he? And your mum seems really happy now.'

'I'm glad. Are they both still smoking like troopers?'

'Actually, they were trying to cut down. They didn't want to smoke around Joe.'

Kate noticed the tender expressions on the girls' faces at the mention of his name. 'So, what's on the menu today?' she said, changing the subject.

The rest of lunchtime was spent making idle chitchat. There was too much to say, and the Rooftop Restaurant was not the place to say it.

'Emmeline, why don't you come to dinner on Sunday night, then we can have a proper catch up,' Kate suggested, as they all made their way to the lift to return to their desks.

'I'd love that. Hope you all have good weeks, if I don't bump into any of you before Friday.'

'You too, Emmeline,' replied Cara, giving her a warm smile.

Kate returned to her desk feeling happy and smug. She knew they'd get on. Kate was so happy to have her family reunited. There was only one fly in her ointment, and that was Cara's state of mind. The awful first groans of the morning had stopped, but, too frequently, Kate saw her daughter drift off to another place. Her eyes would fill with tears and she would go up to her room. Kate had tried to talk to her about it, but she just said she was missing Joe. She would never share more than that. Kate wished she could make her pain go away.

CHAPTER 74

Cara was in the kitchen, helping to prepare dinner. She basted the roasted vegetables one last time as Kate toasted the pine nuts.

'Are you alright, my lovely girl? You're very quiet.'

'I'm fine. I'm overthinking this evening, that's all.'

'What do you mean?'

'I don't really know. There is no common truth, is there, only common ground, if you're lucky. Everyone has their own truth, so searching for *the* truth is futile. You can only try to understand your own. But even that is like shifting sands, reinvented, revised, remodelled. The brain's way of surviving trauma, fear and failure. I guess I'm anxious about discovering Emmeline's version of the truth.'

Kate sighed. 'I'm confident, whatever she has to say, we will find common ground rather than judgment. She's an intelligent, open-minded person. You'll see.'

Cara smiled. 'I'm sure you're right. People may fuck with your brain but you fuck with yourself more than anyone else!'

Kate gave Cara's shoulder a reassuring squeeze. Where had this come from? It was like cooking with Gustave Flaubert as your sous-chef.

‘I’ll get it!’ Gemma shouted, as the doorbell rang. Kate noticed Cara’s body tense.

They heard Gemma chatting to Emmeline as they made their way down the hall, and Emmeline came in to the kitchen flourishing a bouquet of flowers and a bottle of red.

‘Thank you, Emmeline. You really shouldn’t have, but I’m glad you did! And red is perfect. We’re having roasted vegetables and pasta, and we certainly have enough time for a quick drink before it’s ready.’ Kate heard her overly cheerful greeting and realised her elder daughter’s nerves were rubbing off on her.

‘I’ll do the honours,’ Cara said, taking the wine from her mother and searching for a corkscrew. ‘Weird to think they used to have metal screw tops or synthetic corks, until people realised natural corks were better for the environment.’ Cara was making small talk.

‘Weirder to think we nearly destroyed the ocean when plastic was invented,’ Gemma added, oblivious to the tension in the air.

‘True,’ Cara said, as she poured the wine into four glasses and handed them around. ‘Here’s to still mopping up the mess of our ancestors! Cheers!’

They clinked their glasses and took their places at the table. Kate noticed Emmeline held back, only sitting down when everyone else was seated.

‘Look, I want to break the ice.’ Cara’s words came thick and fast. ‘What I mean is, this situation is odd, not bad, just odd. It’s like we swopped mothers, and not any old mothers, twin sister mothers. I’ve hardly spoken about my time as a Chosen One. Poor Gemma and Mum are too scared to bring it up because of Joe. But I think we should talk candidly. Ask every question, express every fear, and talk about the state of the nation!’ Cara looked at the faces around the table.

‘I think that’s a good idea,’ Kate agreed. ‘But let’s not do it on an empty stomach.’

'Let me do it,' Gemma said, getting up to serve dinner. Emmeline turned to Cara. 'You're right. If you hadn't said it, I would've. And in the spirit of honesty, I have to admit I was jealous of you spending so much time with Mum and Harry. I miss her so much.'

Cara laughed. 'I was jealous of you! When Gemma and Mum spoke about how nice you were, it made my insides shrivel. I felt usurped, as if my kingdom, my safe space, had been stolen from me.'

'Rest assured, your throne is very much your own!' Emmeline said, snorting derisively at her inadvertent rhyme.

'You know your mum misses you terribly. She really regrets how things ended between you. She asked me to track you down when I re-joined the Movement, and tell you she loves you very much.'

Emmeline's eyes filled with tears.

'Jesus, girls. Tears before the first mouthful! You know crying cuts your appetite,' Kate said. Gemma placed bowls of steaming pasta in front of them.

'Sorry, Kate. It's your bloody daughter's fault!'

'Sorry,' said Cara, 'but I think it's going to be one of those evenings. Did you buy more tissues at the supermarket, Mum?'

'Cara, honestly! And yes, I did. I got the economy pack.' Kate winked at Gemma.

'Good. Safe in that knowledge, I'd like to ask you a question, Mum. And by the way, this is delicious. How did you feel when you got to know Emmeline? Did you feel like her existence in some way made up for my loss?'

'Wow, Cara. Bring out the big guns, why don't you.' Kate put down her fork. 'I guess I did. I remember seeing Gemma and Emmeline together the first night she came here, and thinking they both might help each other heal, and maybe me too.'

'And did she?'

‘She did as far as I was concerned,’ Gemma said looking directly at Cara. ‘I was so angry with you, Cara, I had forgotten that I loved you. Emmeline’s defection made me understand your transfer a little better...’

‘And Gemma’s anger made me understand my mother’s anger a little better too,’ Emmeline interjected.

‘I remember having a screaming row with Sophie. And her pain made me appreciate what I’d done to you both.’ Cara said.

There was a moment's silence.

‘Do you think my mum will ever forgive me?’ Emmeline asked Cara.

‘She already has. And being able to forgive you meant she was finally able to forgive Mum too.’

‘Really?’ Kate said, reaching for the tissues.

‘Really, Mum. The only thing she still rails against is the system. The one thing that stands in the way of being able to tell you herself. That stands in the way of all of us being a family again.’

‘Let’s fuck the system over then, shall we?’ Kate said wiping her eyes.

‘What do you mean, Mum?’ Gemma asked. They were all looking at her intently.

‘I’ve had a brilliant idea. We’re still allowed to go abroad on holiday, despite the on-going climate crisis. Each person is allowed to fly out of the country for one week each year. We’ve never been abroad. Why don’t we all go on holiday together, to a place where people are just people, somewhere like Greece!’

They all looked at one another with puzzled expressions on their faces.

‘When I say, all, I mean all of us, including Harry, Sophie and Joe,’ Kate clarified. Now they were looking at her as if she had lost her mind.

‘But how can we arrange it when we can’t communicate with them?’ asked Gemma, reaching for the parmesan.

‘Not can’t. Not supposed to. And like little sheep, we live by the rules laid down for us, because we’re afraid of the consequences if we don’t. They’re not our rules and I say to hell with them!’

‘They’re pretty big consequences, Kate,’ Emmeline said, remembering Taylor’s arrest in the café when she was working with Frank.

‘Hear me out, Emmeline. What’s the real risk of being caught? They used to send teams over to check on Completists in the early days, but realised it was a waste of resources. Most families ended up estranged, so wouldn’t have met up, even if it were possible. I think they also scaled down the surveillance when Europe got wind of what was going on and threatened economic sanctions. I know it’s still a risk. We all know how they like to make examples of people who break the rules, just to put the fear of God into us, but it tends to be on home turf these days, and incidences are becoming less and less frequent. To be honest, there’s probably more chance of our plane crashing than a dark car with blackout windows, pulling up outside our villa to arrest us.’ Everyone had stopped eating. There was a mixture of fear and excitement in their eyes.

‘I don’t mean to continue to piss on the party, but under The Segregation Act, don’t all Completists have to give details of any foreign holidays to the government? They must run them through a database or something, specifically to detect any secret foreign liaisons. Mum has the same maiden name as you, and it’s not a particularly common one. Won’t that pique their interest?’

‘I hadn’t forgotten, Emmeline, and it’s a good point. But I’m pretty sure the last time I looked at the Offenders Database we hold on every Completist in jail for breach of that

sodding Act, not one had been caught abroad since the first decade. We could look at flying to a different island from them and then hiring a car and meeting them at the villa? I'm sure there are loads of boats connecting them all.'

'Mum, you're in the best position to assess the risk. You've got access to all the data. I think we should leave it to you to make the call as to whether extra precautions need to be taken,' Cara said, looking at the others for confirmation. Gemma and Emmeline nodded. Kate gave Cara a grateful smile and continued.

'It would only take one letter. We could book a villa large enough for everyone, making sure it was far enough in advance for Sophie to be able to book flights without a problem. We could put all the details down in the letter and Cara could post it through their letterbox. That's the only risky part of it. But Cara could dress as a CO, and I don't think the neighbours would bat an eyelid. They would still have the memory of her imprinted in their brain as a person who used to live around there. Unless Sophie has a good friend among them, who knows her business?' Kate turned to Cara and waited for her response.

'I can't remember anyone visiting while I was living there. And anyway, Harry and Sophie would have kept what was going on a secret, to protect Joe. Mum, you're a genius!'

'It has been said,' Kate replied smugly, taking a large swig of red.

'But how will we know they're coming?' Gemma asked.

'We won't, until they get there. And even if they don't, we can still have a good time. But from everything that's been said around this table tonight, I think they'll do everything possible to come, don't you, Cara?'

'I do, Mum, I really do. This might work. I want to go. I'd do anything to see Joe again. What about you Gemma, you've got the least to gain from the trip?'

'If Mum thinks we can get away with it, I'm in,' Gemma said, reaching over to squeeze her sister's hand.

They all looked at Emmeline. 'Hell, yes!' she said, giving them a broad grin.

CHAPTER 75

Sophie padded sleepily downstairs in her dressing gown and noticed the bright white envelope lying on the door mat. It was Saturday, and her turn for a lie-in. She picked it up. It felt heavy. She examined the envelope for clues as to the identity of the sender but there was nothing written on it. She opened it, unfolded the letter, and immediately recognised the handwriting. Sophie was now wide awake and stood, wide-eyed, carefully reading every word.

'Harry! Harry, where are you!' she shouted at the top of her lungs.

'Sophie, I'm here in the garden, are you alright?'

Sophie ran into the kitchen. 'What is it, love?' he asked when he saw her face. 'I was showing Joe the daffodils.'

'Sit down, Harry. I've got something to show you.' She handed him the letter; her hands were shaking.

As he read, she watched his face intently. He was halfway through when he looked up at her, his expression a mixture of surprise and confusion. He continued to read, then put the letter down on the table.

'What do you think, Harry? Can we do it? Do you want to do it?' she asked, the words rushing from her mouth.

'If you want to do it, we'll do it. We'll find a way, my love. I'm guessing you'd go in a heartbeat?'

'Oh, Harry, I would, I really would. It's time. It'll be difficult for Cara to see Joe for a week and then have to say goodbye again, but he's too little to know what's going on.'

'It will be difficult for you to have to say goodbye to them both all over again too, Sophie.'

'I know. It'll break my heart. But this time, at least I will be saying goodbye properly.'

'In that case, I'll book the flights today. Do you know this will be my very first trip abroad? I never had enough money for a holiday before, I was too busy saving up for your engagement ring!'

'You're a lovely, lovely man, Harry Jackson.' She went over to him and wrapped her arms around his neck, staring over his shoulder at Joe. He was smiling as if he knew something good was happening.

'Hello, little man. You're going to see your mummy and meet my daughter, Emmeline; your cousin, Gemma, and your Aunt Kate. We're going on a family holiday!' Joe smiled up at her, as he fiddled with the zipper on Harry's hoodie.

'I wish we could let them know we're coming,' said Harry.

'I know. But I don't want to risk messing this up. They wouldn't have gone to such trouble unless they were pretty certain we'd be there. Do you know who I'm most nervous to see again?'

'Of course, I do. Kate.'

Sophie kissed the top of his head and released her arms from around his neck. 'Is it too early for a glass of something?'

'It's never too early for that, my love. Wine or beer?'

'Considering I haven't even had breakfast, I think a beer will have to do.'

'Shall we take these into the garden so we can have a cigarette?' Sophie suggested. 'Alcohol is too wet without one, don't you think?'

They ambled into the garden and lay Joe in his pram.

'What's the weather like in Greece in September? Is it still hot?' Sophie wondered out loud.

'I'll go grab my mobile and we'll find out.' Harry perched his cigarette on the side of the ashtray and went inside.

Sophie smiled at Joe, then frowned. For a moment, she'd forgotten about her father. She shivered in the weak spring sunshine.

CHAPTER 76

Zoe stared at the mountain of clothes on Emmeline's bed. 'You're never going to get all those in that,' she said, pointing to Emmeline's suitcase.

'I know,' Emmeline replied despondently. She sat down on her bed. 'Help me!' she laughed. 'I've never been abroad. I haven't a clue what to pack.'

'Well, I have. Many times. So, watch and learn, my friend. You're staying in a villa, right? On the coast?'

'Correct.'

'So, the main thing you'll be wearing is a bikini. And when you're not sunbathing, a pair of shorts and a T-shirt. You're going for seven days. Two bikinis, one to wear, while one is being washed and dried. Four T-shirts, two pairs of shorts. Will you be going to a restaurant to eat?'

'I don't know. Maybe.'

'One casual dress and a jumper to put over your shoulders and wear later on in the evening when the temperature drops. Which dress, which jumper?'

Emmeline pointed at her favourite dress and jumper.

'Seven pairs of knickers, and two bras. One pair of trousers and a long-sleeved top for sitting around the villa in the

evening. Et voilà. Apart from one pair of sandals to go with your dress.' She scooped up the pile of unwanted clothes and dumped them on the floor. 'This lot can go back in your wardrobe. Don't forget to choose a comfortable outfit to travel in. Maybe something warm and cosy, it's going to be cold tomorrow. Think about wearing trainers. You never know, you might find the energy to go exploring.'

Emmeline surveyed the remaining items. 'That was easy!'

'Everything is, when you know what you're doing! Now have you got suntan lotion and after-sun cream? Oh, and mosquito repellent.'

'Check. Bloody hell, Zoe. I can't believe I'm doing this!'

'What, going on holiday? Why? It's quite normal you know. I can't believe you haven't ever had a holiday abroad. I mean I get the flying bit. I've only flown twice in my life. It's hard to justify flying, for a holiday. But I guess you've built up a few carbon credits by now.'

Emmeline checked herself. She had forgotten that Zoe didn't know the real purpose of the trip. She normally shared everything with her; but Kate had cautioned her against telling anyone, and Zoe had been raised in a Completist household. She would, at the very least, be frightened for her.

'You're right. I'm being stupid. I guess I'm nervous about flying, that's all.'

'Don't be. It's so safe. All you need to do is remember to suck a boiled sweet as you take off and land, it helps regularise the pressure in your ears, so you don't suffer any discomfort.' Zoe was taking her holiday consultant role very seriously and had started to fold and pack the clothes neatly into Emmeline's suitcase.

'Oh, and don't wear or take any jewellery. You'll walk through a tunnel to the departure lounge which will scan you, your I.D. chip and your luggage, and it does not appreciate metal. I got into all sorts of trouble when I forgot to take my ring off. They confiscated it, and it was one of my favourites.

Not a great way to start a holiday. What time is Kate picking you up?'

'The crack of dawn! Our flight leaves at 6.30 a.m. This time tomorrow I'll be in Zakynthos!'

'Early night for you then. I'm so jealous. This time tomorrow I'll be at my desk pouring over my inbox, sipping my first coffee of the day.'

Emmeline checked her alarm call for 4.00 a.m. three times as she tried to fall asleep. Her mother's face kept appearing in her head. What if they didn't come? What if Cara had been lying, and her mother hadn't forgiven her? What if her mother didn't want to come because she didn't want to see Kate again? She tried to quieten her mind. She went through her revised designs for the new Headquarters, and gradually submitted to sleep.

Cara was having the same problem. The only face she saw was a tiny baby's. She lay in bed stroking her stomach repeatedly murmuring, soon Joe, soon. Mummy will see you soon; as if her mantra would make him materialise in Greece with or without Sophie and Harry. She had to see him, to hold him, to smell him.

Kate was struggling with words, the right ones to convince Sophie about what had happened to her at the hands of their father. As she rehearsed speeches in her head, she started to remember how his hands had felt, the smell and heat of his breath on her neck, the pain between her legs. She couldn't do it. She shoved him from her brain, replacing him with imagined images of little Joe, her grandson. He would be seven months old now; she remembered when Cara had been that

age, struggling to sit up by herself and determined to get mobile. Cara had been such a pretty baby. Her soft, blond, wavy, baby hair had made her look like a pre-Raphaelite cherub. She remembered she had bought her a pair of angel wings when she was toddling. Cara had refused to take them off and they had been ruined when she insisted on wearing them in the bath, but she had kept them. Kate drifted off to sleep cradling an imaginary Joe in her arms.

Gemma was so excited she lay in bed willing the night away. Images of crystal-clear blue lagoons surrounded by craggy cliffs filled her head. She finally fell asleep at midnight with the sound of gentle waves lapping against her pillows.

Sophie nudged Harry who was snoring gently beside her. He grunted as he regained consciousness.

'I can't sleep,' she whispered, as Harry shifted his body towards hers and opened his eyes.

'Everything will be fine, Sophie,' he murmured. 'Remember, we're going because we all love one another. Love will find a way through. It'll make things right.'

'You darling man,' she said as she reached out her hand to stroke his cheek.

He smiled and gently pushed her on her side so her back was next to him. He pulled her body close to his and idly stroked her arm. Sophie listened to his breathing become shallow and regular, her own eyelids growing heavy. Kate's face faded from her mind as she finally let sleep take a hold of her.

CHAPTER 77

Kate was staring out of the taxi window as they made their way from the airport to their holiday rental. Its tyres weaved around the pockmarked surface of the rudimentary roads; the suspension absorbing most of the shock whenever they accidentally hit a pothole. After several more minutes, it made a sharp left and pulled up outside a property that matched the photo Kate had been sent. They had chosen a quiet spot, away from the main tourist town of Laganas. When they opened the car doors, they were welcomed by the sound of cicadas and the smell of pine drifting on an already warm breeze. The villa was surrounded by a garden, littered with olive, lemon and fig trees.

'It's beautiful!' exclaimed Cara, resting her eyes on the light grey rendered walls and the covered first-floor terrace, beckoning them to take a seat and enjoy the view.

Kate paid the taxi driver and put the code into the key box by the front door. She was relieved they were the first to arrive, anxious to get established before Sophie turned up. They all wandered into the huge, red-tiled lounge, dragging their suitcases behind them.

'Look at the fireplace!' said Gemma. 'It's meant to be

reasonably fresh at night, so we could have a real fire if we wanted to, couldn't we? How cool would that be?'

'Or too warm, perhaps,' Cara joked. Gemma groaned.

'Bagsie first choice of bedroom,' Gemma shouted and, dropping her suitcase, ran up the stairs.

'No way,' Cara retorted, as the other two girls raced after her.

Kate walked onto the terrace. She looked out at the calm, blue sea spread out before her, its surface glinting in the morning sunshine. An island took centre stage in the distance. She breathed in and started to believe everything would work out. Reluctantly, she turned her back on the peaceful view, to umpire the bedroom wars which were breaking out above her.

'Gemma, you can't have a bedroom with a double bed in it, unless you want to share with me or your sister. There are only two, and I'm giving the bigger one to Sophie and Harry, as they will have Joe sleeping with them.' Kate kicked herself and glanced anxiously at Cara who was about to speak, but bit her lip. 'So, what's it to be?' Kate continued in a gentler tone, 'a double or that lovely single room with the beautiful view overlooking the gardens, where you can have a little privacy.'

'Fine,' Gemma said begrudgingly, as she went to collect her suitcase.

'Now, you two. There is one double and one twin-bedded room left. I don't care which room I have, so it's up to you. Do you want to share a room?' Cara and Emmeline glanced at one another. They looked like ten-year-olds. 'We do,' they said in unison. 'We'll take the twin room, Mum,' Cara said. 'You can have the double all to yourself.'

'Why thank you. Glad we're all happy. I don't know about you lot, but I'm going to unpack, then make a cup of tea and explore the rest of the house and garden.'

'Sounds like a plan, Kate,' said Emmeline; and the two girls trotted down the stairs to retrieve their suitcases.

The larger double was the only room with an en-suite, and

Kate was glad she would be able to offer it to her sister. It would start things off on the right foot. Kate had paid for the accommodation. It was clear from both Cara and Emmeline's description of her sister's life, that she was financially more comfortable than Sophie. She was determined to pay for the majority of the food and wine while they were there as well, but only if they were happy with the arrangement. She didn't want them to feel like the impoverished relatives.

Her own room was simply furnished. The walls were white, and the bed had a heavy metal frame pushed against one wall. The sheets were cream and crisp, but their starchiness was softened by a mosquito net, which was draped elegantly over the bed. The floor had the same red earthen tiles and there was a multi-coloured cotton rug on it by the side of the bed, nudging the bedside table. The room had two windows, and she opened the window on the far side to be greeted by a jungle of trees and shrubs. Flashes of brightly coloured flowers broke up the lush green of palm fronds and the more muted greens of the various shrubs and trees she didn't recognise. She walked to the other window and opened that too. The mosquito net billowed and she smelt the faint odour of an olive grove. She started to unpack her clothes into the small chest of drawers and wardrobe. She had brought one simple, but smarter dress with her, in case she could persuade everyone to go to a restaurant one night. She felt at peace.

Half an hour later they were all together on the terrace drinking tea.

'It doesn't taste the same as in England,' Gemma said, glancing at her cup with suspicion.

'It's the milk,' said Emmeline. 'They have different cows in Greece.'

'And how would you know?' asked Cara, raising her eyebrows at her cousin.

'I don't. I'm bullshitting you!'

They laughed and Gemma punched Emmeline on the

arm. Then the room fell silent as they all heard a taxi pull up outside. They looked at one another, with terror and excitement in their eyes. Cara was the first to her feet; Kate was the last.

Her daughter flung open the front door. Sophie was standing by the taxi with Joe in her arms. Kate's eyes immediately locked onto her sister. She looked tired from the journey. Kate wanted to run towards her, throw her arms around her, but she moved back from the doorway to watch Cara, whose eyes were fixed on her son. He was rubbing his, evidently disgruntled at having been woken up too soon. He started to take in his surroundings and spotted Cara. Kate held her breath, then the spell was broken.

'Cara, how lovely to see you. We made it!' Kate looked at Harry, and immediately knew she was going to like the mop-headed man who stood beaming at her daughter.

'It's amazing to see you all too!' Cara replied, stepping towards her son.

'May I?' she said, to both Sophie and Joe, as she held her arms open.

'Of course, Cara. Joe, this is your Auntie Cara. She wants a cuddle, is that alright?' Joe put his arms out towards Cara and she took him from Sophie. Kate could sense she was resisting the urge to hold him tightly to her, to feel as much of him against her as possible. Instead, she held him on her hip, making sure he could see Sophie and smoothed his wavy hair away from his eyes.

'Hello, Joe. Welcome to your home for the next week, we're going to have such fun, you and I,' and she placed a gentle kiss on the top of his head. Kate was proud of how Cara was keeping calm for Joe's sake. She could only imagine the turmoil behind her controlled façade. Kate transferred her gaze to her sister. Cara had been right. Sophie looked ten years older than she did. Her fine brown hair was greying and her face was far more lined than her own. Sophie glanced over in

her direction and their eyes met. Sophie offered her a nervous smile and Kate returned it, nodding her head in welcome. Kate turned towards Emmeline. She was standing on the front doorstep, staring at her mother; looking like a timid faun at the edge of a thicket, waiting for Sophie to give her a sign it was safe to come out into the open. Sophie obliged by opening her arms and, seconds later, Emmeline was in them, crying. Kate prayed she would receive an equally warm reception.

Kate jumped, startled by Gemma draping her arms around her waist.

'Are you alright, Mum?' she asked.

'I'm fine, Gemma. But honestly, I don't know what to feel. It's all a little surreal.'

'Tell me about it,' replied Gemma. 'Cara can't take her eyes off Joe. Sophie and Emmeline have morphed into a single organism, and Harry's about to burst into tears.'

As if on cue, Cara walked over to him. 'Hi, Harry,' she said, kissing him on the cheek. 'It's lovely to see them like this, isn't it?'

'It breaks my heart, Cara. The world shouldn't be this way.'

'My dear, Harry, the world isn't, it's the UK that's fucked up, but we have our own world here for a whole week. And I, for one, am going to adopt the Buddhist philosophy and live in the present moment for the entire time.'

'Good shout, Cara,' said Harry, perking up a little.

Emmeline and Sophie had finally hugged themselves out and Kate watched Emmeline walk towards Harry and Cara.

'Harry, how are you?' she said, with mascara all over each of her cheeks. Cara looked at her cousin and laughed.

'What?' Emmeline asked.

Sophie, now alone, walked towards her and Gemma. Kate could feel her body tense as she approached. Gemma tightened her grip around her waist.

'Hello, Kate. It's good to see you again.' Sophie said softly.

Kate smiled at her sister, her eyes searching Sophie's for any hint of hostility. There was only an ache to reconnect. Kate still wanted to touch her, hug her, but she stood her ground. This needed to be taken slowly. 'You must be Gemma. Cara has told me so much about you. All very, very good, I hasten to add.'

'Hi, Aunt Sophie, pleased to meet you.' Gemma held out her hand, and Sophie shook it.

The others were approaching.

'This is my husband, Harry.'

'Hello, Harry,' Kate said. 'So nice to meet you. Cara says you're one of the good ones!'

Harry laughed. 'I don't know about that. It's easy to be good with a woman like Sophie at your side.'

Kate smiled and turned towards Joe and her daughter.

'Mum, this is Joe.' Cara said, turning Joe towards her.

'Hi there, Joe. You're such a beautiful boy. You look like your mummy.' Kate smiled at Cara, and then at Sophie, swallowing the lump in her throat. 'Right, enough of this madness. You both must be gasping for a cup of tea, come in. There's a wonderful view from the terrace.'

'That would be lovely. Unless there's a glass of chilled white wine in the fridge and a cool beer for Harry?'

'Shit, of course. Help yourselves. We are on holiday, aren't we? I think I'll join you.'

'Mother,' said Gemma mockingly. 'It's not even lunchtime! Can I join you too?'

'Cara, Emmeline, would you like a glass of wine?' Sophie asked.

Emmeline nodded, but Cara shook her head. 'You all go ahead. I'll be babysitter for the rest of the day and then get smashed this evening, after he's asleep!'

'Would you, Cara? It would be lovely to be able to totally relax,' Sophie said. 'You've no idea what a handful he is!' Kate saw panic flash in her sister's eyes as soon as the

words had left her lips. She immediately turned to Harry for solace.

'No, unfortunately I don't,' Cara replied quietly; then, recovering herself, added, 'but I'm willing and ready to find out!' and she gave Sophie a reassuring grin.

Apart from their encounter on the bus, it had been over 26 years since they had last seen one another. Sophie's appearance had initially shocked her; however, she could now see the young woman she had left behind so many years ago. She saw it in her smile, her gestures and her eyes. Her sister was still intact.

Sophie looked more like their father, and the resemblance had grown with age. Kate now realised how some of her anger towards him had transferred itself to Sophie. She was ashamed to admit, even to herself, that there had been fleeting moments when she had wished Sophie had been the one to take after their mother; then perhaps she would have drawn his attention, and Kate would have been given the bedroom next to theirs.

She heard Joe chuckling and turned her head towards the sound. Cara was sitting on the rug in front of the fire playing peek-a-boo, popping her head above a cushion and then peeping out from the sides. Each time she said 'boo', Joe giggled, and his chubby body jerked with surprise. *Shit, she's a natural. She needs to get pregnant as soon as possible. Leaving Joe is going to kill her.* She noticed Sophie looking at Cara too; they exchanged a smile and wandered towards the terrace, sat down and started to talk.

'Thank you for coming, Sophie,' Kate said as they sat looking out over the clear, blue sea towards the horizon.

'Didn't you think I would, then?' Her sister said, lighting a cigarette and offering the packet to her.

'Actually, after Cara told me about her time with you, I was pretty sure you'd come if you could.' They both lit their

cigarettes and simultaneously put them to their lips and inhaled. They looked at one another and laughed.

'Look at us being all twiny,' Sophie giggled.

'I've missed you,' Kate said, quietly.

'I've missed you too,' Sophie replied, her eyes conveying the regret of all the years apart.

'I really like Harry,' Kate said, lightening the mood.

'I got lucky there. I've never met a man with a kinder heart. I know it's a cliché, but he really does bring out the best in me. I'm calmer and kinder now, more tolerant. Your Gemma is also lovely, a little shy perhaps, but that's to be expected around people she's only just met.'

'Gemma's a thinker. She's got a wicked sense of humour, you'll see, she'll soon warm up. So, tell me what's been going on with you, Sis.'

Sophie spoke about how she had met Harry, their new house, the day Cara turned up on their doorstep, and how their relationship developed. Kate told her about her career, the home she had created, and how she had met Emmeline. They knew they were both keeping to safe topics, gradually coming together, each successful exchange rebuilding the trust between them. They also knew there were difficult conversations ahead but, for now, they were happy to sip their wine, chatter about their lives and admire the view, warmed by the September sun.

CHAPTER 78

Cara had woken up with a start at 3.00 a.m. Emmeline remained fast asleep beside her. Cara wondered how she could not hear Joe crying. She didn't know what to do. Should she go to him? She realised she was being ridiculous as his crying stopped almost immediately. Sophie would have reached over a sleepy arm to soothe him back to sleep. She knew it would always be Sophie he would seek out to comfort him whenever he felt afraid, lonely or confused. She wouldn't even be a memory, unless they made this an annual event; and, even then, she would only ever be the fun auntie he spent one week a year with.

Joe did look like her, but his resemblance to Sam was unmistakable. Did Sam ever think about her or their son? He could track him down if he really wanted to. It was so unfair he could see him whenever he wanted, but she couldn't. However, Sam clearly didn't care about him. She had sacrificed her entire life for their son; yet he was the one who could watch Joe grow up. He could choose to have a relationship with him. She started to imagine them playing in the park together, laughing and wrestling. Him, proudly watching Joe, as he blew out his birthday candles. Him delivering expensive

presents for Christmas, dressed as Santa Claus. She sat up. She needed to sit in front of the inky dark sea; otherwise, she was going to scream and wake the whole house up.

As she entered the lounge, she noticed she wasn't the only one who couldn't sleep. Her mother was sitting, silently, staring into the darkness. As Cara approached, she turned her head.

'It's been an odd day hasn't it. Did Joe's crying wake you?'

'It did.' Cara sat down with a thump on the baggy sofa. 'It's so difficult, Mum, seeing Joe again, knowing he'll never be mine, never know me as his mother.'

'You should start seeing someone when you get back home.'

'It's not a psychiatrist I need, it's my son.'

'I was looking at you with Joe today, and you're a natural. You should seriously think of having another baby when we get back. I think it would help.'

'What, dog gets run over so get another puppy?' Cara's tone was hard and mocking.

'I didn't mean it like that. You know I didn't.' Her mother looked hurt, the pale moonlight softening the few lines that had started to appear on her face. She looked young, vulnerable.

'I know. I'm sorry.' Cara reached out and touched her arm. 'Did you hear the rumour circulating about lobbying Parliament to abolish The Segregation Act?'

'I did. But it's only gossip, Cara. They've tried before. It's wishful thinking.'

'I'm not so sure. Haven't you noticed the number of support groups popping up for Completists in my situation? Add us lot to the original members who are still pining after their sons, and you have quite a significant problem.' Cara sat back and placed her feet on the coffee table.

'Ah, the infamous Castoffs,' her mother said. 'Did you know Fran had to leave a son behind?'

'No, I didn't.'

'Maybe you should have a chat with her. She wouldn't mind. She's my closest friend. She'd talk to you in a heartbeat if it would help.'

'I might just do that. I've always liked Fran. I remember staying with her when you had Gemma. She was lovely to me.'

'She enjoyed having you. We both nearly lost it when we saw the way you looked at Gemma when you first held her in your arms.'

'Oh, Mum. If I ever do have a little girl, Joe won't be able to hold her in his arms. He'll think he has a new cousin if we ever do this again, not a sister. It's all so wrong.' Her mother stroked her leg, reassuringly.

'I know it seems black, but don't blame the Movement, Cara. Place the blame where it lies. If Sam hadn't been so upset about your sex life being disrupted, you'd still be with him, raising Joe together. He could even have stayed married to you, for appearance's sake, so you could have raised Joe alone. But no. He abandoned you both, and made it impossible for you to raise your son, except in poverty. It's still a male-dominated world, Cara. It's Sam and the government who screwed you over, not the Movement. They're the ones who created polices to punish women who leave their husbands, no matter what the circumstances. It was the government who forced the Movement to accept The Segregation Act in exchange for our right to live without men.'

'Seriously, Mum. It's too early, or late, for a lecture on politics. But don't worry, I know who's to blame, and it's not you or me; we just suffer.'

Her mother stood up. 'I'm going to try to get some sleep. Please think about what I said about trying for a baby. I love you.' She kissed her daughter on the head, and Cara stared into the nothingness beyond the terrace.

CHAPTER 79

The next day, Sophie was the first up with Joe. There was a chill in the air, and she was sitting on the sofa in the lounge, the doors to the terrace firmly shut, reading to Joe from a big book of nursery rhymes and children's stories. Kate recognised it from their childhood.

'Morning Soph,' Kate said as she yawned and stroked Joe's head. 'You know, I think you're so brave taking on a little one. You must be exhausted! Can I get you a coffee or some breakfast?'

'A coffee would be lovely. It is difficult, but Harry's very good, he's not like Peter was.'

'And how was that?' Kate asked from the kitchen, as she made the coffee.

'Selfish, self-absorbed, egotistical, take your pick. He was very good at doing what he wanted to do and not very good at thinking about other people. He did end up with some kind of relationship with Charlie, because he adored him, and I forced him to help. But he had no real relationship with Emmeline because he wasn't interested. He was too busy playing football with his mates.'

Kate came back into the lounge and handed Sophie a mug.

She had lain Joe on his back and given him a toy to play with, which he was carefully scrutinising.

'I'm sorry, Soph. Is that why you left him?'

'Pretty much. Although in truth, he left me once Emmeline arrived. We should never have had children.'

'Sounds like Peter was a bit like Cara's Sam, although Sam's "football" was played in bedrooms across London.'

Sophie nodded her head. 'How about you, Sis? How's life been without selfish, violent, cheating bastards in it?'

Kate laughed. 'Pretty good, funnily enough. Although it was really difficult at first, coping with men's reactions to me as a Completist. I get it. After all, we're basically flicking the V at them every time we come out of our offices or homes. But often they misinterpret the way we look straight ahead as arrogance, rather than a sign of liberation, which is what it is -'

'I never knew that! I thought it was arrogance too, that you lot believed we were so beneath you, you couldn't even look at us.'

'No, not at all! It truly is a sign of liberation. We no longer feel the need to look at men, to see if they are noticing us, because we're not defined by their attention or lack of it.'

'Oh, I see.' Sophie took a sip of her coffee and winced. Kate realised she'd forgotten to add sugar. 'I guess that's true. Girls and women are always slyly checking out the opposite sex to see if they're being noticed, it's what you do, isn't it?'

'Yes, it is. Until you become a Completist.' Kate got up to fetch the sugar from the kitchen, continuing to talk as she went. 'I'm sure men must register the constant attention of women too, even if they're not always aware of it. It must flatter their egos. To be ignored by a woman probably ruffles their feathers a bit. Being on the receiving end of bruised egos, day after day, isn't always easy, but you get used to it.' She handed Sophie the sugar bowl.

'Thanks, Sis. You were saying yesterday how much you enjoy your job. It sounds like you've done really well. I'm

assuming, as you could afford to have Gemma, that you're making a good living?'

'I am. I'm very comfortable. And we don't have to pay for childcare like you have to. It's an overhead each firm accepts as a cost of doing business. Every Completist firm also provides free initial medical attention, and no-one needs to find the money for private education because our schools and colleges are so good. Ironically, all the women who joined at the same time as I did have also made a killing on their houses. We were forced into buying properties in the scummier areas of London, which basically became Completist ghettos. We gentrified the areas and now the house prices have shot through the roof.'

'So, you've never looked back then?' There was the tiniest hint of anger in Sophie's tone.

'Of course, I have. I lost my entire family. I lost my mum and my best friend,' Kate's voice softened and she reached for Sophie's hand. 'Thank God we started to get close again, after Dad's death.' Kate paused and looked at her sister; it was the first time either of them had mentioned their father.

Sophie picked up her cigarettes and beckoned to the terrace. She put Joe's mobile in front of him and he started happily bashing a rattle, sending it whizzing into the air, to loop around and dangle in front of him again.

Her sister offered her packet and Kate took a cigarette.

'Look, you've said the D word,' Sophie said. 'I've been dreading this. I've gone over and over it in my head, and I've never figured out how we can move past it. I'm not saying you're a liar anymore, because you wouldn't make it up. It's not in your character. But my brain won't accept it as my truth. Does that make sense? I simply can't see our father that way. To me, he was a kind, funny, normal Dad. To think of him touching you, hurting you, I can't do it.' Sophie shuddered, and lit her cigarette.

Kate felt surprisingly calm. 'I do understand. Why do you

think I kept my mouth shut for so many years? I saw how he was with you and Mum. But in my room, he was a stranger. A different man altogether. Did you know he used to say it was my fault? I looked too much like Mum when she was young and pretty, so he couldn't help himself.'

'Don't Sis. I can't go there. I can't hear those things. I'm sorry, I know it's really unfair on you, but you can talk about all that shit with a therapist, a stranger. I don't need to hear it. But as I said, I'm not calling you a liar and I do understand why you thought the Completist way of life could bring you peace. And I'm really glad it has.' Sophie's tone was sincere and warm.

Kate smiled at her sister and touched her arm. 'Thanks Soph. You're right, you don't need to hear it, and I don't need to say it, not to you, not now. The very fact you've acknowledged it as my truth is enough. By the way, is Mum still with us?' Kate braced herself for Sophie's response.

'No. She died shortly after Charlie was born. She was hit by a bus. Walked straight in front of it, and never regained consciousness. It was horrible.'

Kate gazed out at the sea. A ripple of sadness ran through her body. 'Did she ever tell you we were conceived on the day The Movement started the Uprising?'

Sophie laughed. 'She did! She said Dad was so upset at the news, she felt obliged to be nice to him!'

Kate took a long drag on her cigarette. 'I hated the way she used the word nice as a euphemism for sex. All I can say is I wish she'd been "nice" to him a little more often.' Kate stubbed out her cigarette, and the conversation was halted by a squeal of frustration from Joe. 'Ah, I think Joe has beaten that rattle to death and has realised he's been abandoned!'

'Let's hope Cara wakes up soon. She's so good with him. I'm getting a little jealous!' Sophie exclaimed, and the two sisters smiled at one another and returned to the lounge arm in arm.

CHAPTER 80

The sky was a cloudless, Greek Island blue on the morning when Gemma convinced Emmeline and Cara to visit a little cove about 20 minutes' walk from their villa. There were only a few dozen people lying on the golden sands, their cars and scooters scattered randomly on the scrubby headland above the beach. Gemma had only managed to drag Cara away from Joe because Sophie had asked to spend some time alone with him. As they started out, Gemma began to wish her sister had stayed at the villa, as all she did was bitch about how selfish her aunt was, denying her precious time with her child when she would have him all to herself for the rest of his life.

The thigh-trembling descent shut Cara up and they were now claiming their reward, seated on their towels, facing out to sea. Gemma was transfixed by the undulating vastness before her, and they all listened in silence to the waves breaking rhythmically on the wet sand, only to be immediately dragged back into the ocean: the never-ending cycle of separation and unity.

She was overwhelmed by the beauty of the water, a thousand diamonds glinting on its surface beyond the breaking

waves. When Cara broke her meditation with some anodyne comment about the biceps on a reclining Greek man, she flashed her a scathing look. She saw Emmeline glance in the direction of the man, she suspected more to humour her sister than out of genuine interest.

'He keeps smiling at me,' whispered Cara.

'Look straight ahead and ignore him,' suggested Emmeline.

'We're not in the UK now, Emmeline. We don't have to behave like Completists, we're just women here,' Cara said, playfully throwing a handful of sand at her cousin.

'Sorry, force of habit. But why do you care anyway? You're not interested, are you?' Emmeline asked, brushing the sand off her towel.

'Have you seen his body, his face, his smile? Who wouldn't be?'

'Me,' said Emmeline laughing.

'And me,' Gemma said, looking defiantly at her sister.

'Honestly, you both don't know what you're missing.' Cara flashed a coy smile at the tanned man to her left, splayed out on a brightly coloured beach towel. His face broke into a broad, white grin.

'Gemma might not, but I certainly do,' Emmeline retorted, 'and I can reassure you, Gemma, you're not missing much.'

'Ah, but that's not true is it, Emmeline?' challenged Cara.

'Is this conversation really necessary?' Emmeline snapped.

'It's fine, Emmeline. If my sister insists on educating me on the joy of sex, let her. There is a small part of me that's interested. But not interested enough to want to do anything about it.' Gemma reluctantly tore her gaze away from the waves to look at Cara.

'I'm not about to discuss the ins and outs of lovemaking, excuse the pun,' Cara said smirking. They both looked pityingly at her, but she carried on regardless. 'I miss being close to

a man's skin. They smell different, they make you feel...' Cara paused; Gemma and Emmeline waited expectantly. 'They make you feel alive, in a way nothing else does,' she finally said. Gemma looked at Emmeline, they were evidently both distinctly underwhelmed. 'Sorry, that's the best I can do I'm afraid. You'd understand if you'd experienced it for yourself.' Cara was becoming a little agitated by their vacant expressions.

Emmeline laughed. 'Sorry Cous. I do know what you mean. It's true. There's no other comparable feeling. But while it's a nice sensation, personally, I don't miss it. Or perhaps, the truth is, I don't let myself miss it. There are too many negative feelings associated with sex, for me at least.' Emmeline looked down at the sand, fiddling with the fringe on her towel.

'I've seen the aftermath for both of you. I'm in no hurry to follow in your footsteps. I'm not sure I even want to go to a Facilitator, ever,' Gemma announced emphatically.

'I get it, Gemma, I really do. And I think I'd be the same if I was in your shoes. But it's like a drug for me, an addiction I want to be free of. But when temptation is staring me in the face, I feel it calling me.' Cara gave the man another smile, then turned her head back towards them.

'So, Greek God over there is calling you, is he?' Emmeline laughed.

'He is. And do you know, I might answer his call. We're on holiday. I couldn't stomach a Facilitator again, not after Sam. This could be my last chance to feel a man close to me again. I'm not saying I want to sleep with him, but what harm could a little flirting do, maybe a last kiss?'

'You do you, girl!' laughed Emmeline.

Cara turned and smiled again at her Greek God, and he beckoned her to come over.

'See you later, girls,' Cara said as she got up.

Gemma sighed as she watched her sister walk across the soft sand, dragging her towel behind her. 'Seriously! She's

totally ruined the vibe, this was meant to be our day together, the three of us. I want to go now.'

'Oh, come on, Gemma. We can't leave her. Let's go for a walk along the beach, maybe go for a swim if the water's warm enough. By the time we get back, she'll be bored of Adonis and back sitting with us.'

They walked to the edge of the cove, then turned back. They could see Cara in the distance, she had not left his side.

'Swim?' Emmeline suggested.

When they emerged from the water, the sun was not strong enough to keep the goose bumps away and they ran across the sand towards their towels.

As they wrapped themselves up, they glanced towards Cara, who was deep in conversation with Adonis, laughing when he laughed. Gemma turned her head away. She just didn't get it. Men left her cold. Sometimes she wished she understood what all the fuss was about, if only to understand her sister better. This aspect of Cara had been the one thing they had never been able to share.

'I'm done. Let's walk back. It'll dry us off and warm us up,' suggested Gemma.

'OK, I'll go and tell Cara.' Emmeline returned several minutes later, unamused.

'Cara said she'll follow on later. Apparently, he has a scooter and is going to give her a lift to the villa when they're ready to leave. I'm not sure your mum will be best pleased to see Cara turn up riding pillion with whatever his name is. But that's Cara's look out. She said she wouldn't be long.'

They pushed up the winding path to the unmade road, groaning with the effort, grasping the twisted trunks of the scrubby trees for support.

At the top of the cove, they took a moment to admire the view and their climb. Looking down, Gemma saw Cara and Adonis stand up and start packing their stuff into his duffel

bag. ‘Looks like Cara might get home before us.’ Gemma said, pointing to the couple below.

‘Best get going then. With any luck we can meet up with her outside the villa, go in together, and no-one will be any the wiser.’ They pulled on their shorts and T-shirts, rolled up their towels, and started walking.

They were approaching a bend in the road, when they heard the scooter coming up the hill. They turned towards the sound, in time to see Cara grinning at them, one hand looped around the Adonis’s waist, the other waving at them triumphantly as she sped by.

‘Lucky cow,’ Gemma said. ‘I’m bored of this walk now. My legs hurt, I’m tired and all I want is to get home and get showered.’

‘Me too. But we’ve done the big hill now, it’s pretty much downhill all the way from here.’

As they turned the corner, the twisting road, with its potholes and gravel verges sloped gently downwards towards home. Gemma couldn’t see the scooter or hear its engine.

‘Wow, they must have been going some to be out of view,’ she said. Emmeline didn’t reply. She was staring at something in the distance, something she didn’t like the look of.

Gemma followed her gaze; Emmeline’s face frightened her.

‘Can you see that, halfway down? After the large olive tree, by the side of the road?’ Emmeline asked.

‘Yes, I can. Oh, God, it looks like a scooter on its side.’

As they stood, staring at the spot, something on the road moved. They saw Adonis stagger to his feet and stumble towards a heap, crumpled by the side of the road. They both started running.

Gemma had never run so fast in her life. By the time she reached Cara, her chest was burning, her throat dry and sore.

She knelt beside her. Patches of her skin had been sloughed off her arms and shoulders by a million tiny pieces of gravel. Gemma reached for her sister’s head, it felt heavy in her

hands, like a baby's. As she turned her face towards hers, she knew she was dead. Her sister's eyes were vacant, unseeing, staring beyond her. Gemma heard someone muttering, no, no, no over and over again, then realised it was her. As she gently placed Cara's head on her lap, her hand touched a patch of something warm, soft and wet. There was a gaping hole in the left-hand side of her skull, and then Gemma saw the rock.

Her scream filled the valley and reverberated off the rocks until it was lain to rest, absorbed by the ancient olive groves. Her scream gave the answer to a question Emmeline no longer needed to ask. Gemma sobbed into her sister's flayed chest, smelling blood and tarmac, as Cara's lifeless eyes stared into the Mediterranean sky.

Emmeline had been watching Gemma, unable to tear her own eyes away from the horror in front of them. She was in a daze, transformed into a statue, frozen with shock. Then she heard groans coming from behind her. She instinctively turned towards them; and there was Cara's Adonis, sitting, hunched over his knees, his head between his hands. He was covered in blood. She went over to him.

'Are you OK?' she asked. She felt like she was sleepwalking.

He raised his head, his nose bloody and red. 'We hit hole in the road, I did not see it. She flew off....' Emmeline stared at him. She saw a little boy. A scared, sad little boy. She reached into her bag, found her mobile and called Kate.

CHAPTER 81

Kate was holding Joe in her arms when she heard her mobile and wandered inside to answer it. She had been showing him the garden from the front terrace, pointing out the figs and lemons, describing to him what each fruit felt like in your mouth.

'Kate,' Emmeline said. Her voice sounded strange, strained, too quiet.

'What it is?' Kate could already feel the fear creeping across her body like an eclipse.

'It's Cara. There's been an accident...' Kate tumbled into Emmeline's hesitation, freefalling, dreading its end. 'She's dead.'

Kate stepped back, leaning on the solid wooden sideboard for support. Joe was suddenly unbearably heavy. She stumbled to her knees and laid him down on the floor. He took one look at her face and burst into loud sobs. Sophie came running down the stairs.

'What is it, Sis, what's the matter?'

Kate couldn't speak, she handed her the mobile. 'Who is it?' Sophie shouted into the speaker. 'What's going on?'

Kate could vaguely hear her sister talking and someone else; it sounded like Emmeline's voice. She was sure she had been told her daughter was dead, but it couldn't be true, it was some kind of sick joke; but who could do something like that? It was Emmeline wasn't it, who had told her? She looked at her sister's strained face. Then she heard her yell up the stairs and Harry came running down.

Kate felt Sophie grab her arm and yank her up from the floor. She started shouting at Harry. He looked terrified, but he picked up Joe and left the room. Then her sister started screaming at her. She tried to focus on what she was saying, it seemed important. She was asking her to go somewhere.

She managed to stumble through the door into the daylight. Sophie was looking at her, wanting her to do something, but she was a long way off and Kate couldn't be bothered to reach her. Her sister kissed her head, and then her arms pushed her gently downwards. Then she was crouching in front of her, and she heard her words. 'Don't worry, I'll look after things. I'll look after our girls. You stay here for a bit. I'll be back soon.'

Kate watched her sister get smaller and smaller, until she disappeared from view. She had an overwhelming urge to see Joe, to hold him, to keep him safe. She hauled herself up and went back into the house. Joe was mithering to himself as Harry paced up and down talking to God knows who about she cared not what.

'Can I have him, Harry? It's OK. I won't drop him.' She sat down on the sofa cradling him in her lap. She leaned over Joe and smiled at him. He had Cara's eyes. He reached up to grab a lock of her hair. 'Hello, little man. I'm sorry if I frightened you earlier. It's all right, everything will be fine. Mummy will be home soon.' It was such a natural phrase to placate him with, and it was true, in his world. This would always be his truth. He would never know how wonderful his real mum

was, how much she had sacrificed for him. She stroked his fat little cheek and leant down to kiss his forehead. Unless of course they were wrong. Cara might not be dead. She might be in a coma. That was it. She would be fine; everything would be fine.

CHAPTER 82

Sophie removed the untouched mug of tea from the table beside Kate, who was kneeling on the floor in front of Joe, building him a tower of bricks, talking to him as she carefully placed one brick on top of the next. Joe was the only one Kate had spoken to since Cara died, unless she needed something specific from one of them. She was trying to reach her sister, to break through her grief, but she'd shut down, gone into her own little world with Joe as her only companion.

She felt Harry's familiar touch on her shoulder and turned towards him.

'Still no better?' he whispered, nodding towards Kate.

Sophie shook her head. 'I don't know what to do. I keep trying to tell her about the arrangements for taking Cara home, and she nods and smiles at me, but I'm not sure she's taken in a single word. It's not like her. She's always been the stronger one, the one who keeps her shit together, but I think this has broken her.'

'You're doing everything you can, love. Emmeline and Gemma will get her home safely. I've just rung the taxi firm, they're picking them up at 9.00 a.m. tomorrow.'

Sophie turned and hugged him. 'I don't know what I'd have done without you these past few days. The way you've handled everything. You've been amazing.'

'Thanks, love. But to be honest, I've welcomed the distraction. I still can't believe she's gone. I don't want to believe it.'

They both turned to look at Kate, oblivious to them, focussed on Joe and the tower she was building. Sophie shook her head and turned away. 'Where are the girls?' she asked.

'I think they're out on the veranda.'

Sophie walked towards the sliding doors and peered out. They were sitting together and laughing. Sophie quietly slid open the door and listened. Gemma was recounting some amusing anecdote about her sister and Emmeline had her arms around her. She carefully closed the door.

Sophie lay in bed, unable to sleep. She turned towards Harry and started to whisper to him, hoping Joe would remain fast asleep beside them. 'Harry, I'm worried. I don't know how Kate's going to cope when we have to say goodbye tomorrow. She's obsessed with Joe. I mean, I get it. He's half Cara. Leaving each other was going to be difficult enough, but after this.'

'I know. It's going to break my heart, so God knows how Kate's going to cope.'

'I don't think it'll even register with her that she is saying goodbye to us as well. It's so sad. I wanted to be able to say goodbye properly this time. I feel so sorry for her. Oh, Harry, it could have been Emmeline.'

'We both know she'd never have spoken to that man.'

'I know. But Kate had only just got Cara back. God, Harry, I don't know how I would cope in her shoes.' Harry gathered her to him. She laid her head on his chest and heard his heart beating, safe in his arms.

Gemma was in Cara's bed. She could still smell her sister on the sheets. It didn't bother her; it gave her comfort. She decided to steal the pillowcase and take it home.

'Emmeline,' she whispered in the dark, 'are you asleep?'

'No, Gemma, I'm still awake. Can't you sleep?'

'Not really. I'm so cross with her. I don't want to be, but I keep thinking over and over again, why did she have to start talking to that guy? I mean, it's barely been a year since Sam totally screwed her over, you'd think she'd have been put off men for life. But there she was, getting all excited over a bare chest and a handsome face. She should have stayed safe with us. She was an idiot!'

'You know, my darling little Cous, I've been thinking a lot about it all, and I wonder if Cara would ever have been truly happy as a Completist. She seemed born to be with a man and raise kids. She was very attracted to men, and did you see her with Joe? I try and avoid him if I'm honest. I don't appear to have a maternal bone in my body. And as for men, they leave me cold.'

'So, what are you saying, Emmeline? Are you honestly trying to make me feel better by saying she's better off dead because she would have had an unhappy life ahead of her?'

'Of course not! What I'm saying is, you shouldn't blame her for flirting. It's who she was, she couldn't help herself. Nothing more.'

'Sorry, Emmeline. I didn't mean to snap at you. You've been so kind to me. I'm not sure what I'd have done without you. Mum's gone into her own little world of grief with Joe. She doesn't seem to be registering the fact I exist.'

'I know, but we're leaving tomorrow. And Joe will be staying with Sophie and Harry. And I'm not going anywhere, Gemma. We'll get through this together.' She held out her hand to Gemma in the dark and squeezed it, three times.

Kate lay on her back under her mosquito net. She had both windows open, and, from her bed, she could see the stars. They blazed brightly here. She had never seen so many. Their sheer number made her feel insignificant. She could understand why they had always fascinated and enthralled mankind. Was Cara up there, among them, flesh transformed into cosmic energy, forever part of the universe, forever outside her grasp? She remembered the day she had been born, and the moments after David had left her at the hospital to go home for the night. She had picked her up and held her in her arms, staring at the wonder of her. She had never felt love like it; it flooded out of her, covering her daughter in its warmth. She knew her love would never die. It would never be challenged or weakened. She had known then, as she stroked her tiny hands, that no matter what her little baby grew into, and whatever she did, she would love her. Her pain would be her pain, her joy would be her joy; but now she couldn't feel her anymore, and the space she had taken up inside her was empty.

CHAPTER 83

Kate stood, shoulder to shoulder, with Gemma and Emmeline in a quiet, side waiting room of the small airport, staring out at the runway. The luggage was being loaded onto the plane they would board. Kate watched, motionless, as Cara proceeded slowly up the conveyer belt towards the hold. Her daughter was in a white box sitting on what looked like a wooden pallet. She glanced at the others, Gemma had tears streaming down her face, and Emmeline had a look of disbelief and horror on hers. Kate was a stone. Her eyes returned to the two men loading her daughter onto the plane. They walked beside the box until it was nearing the hold, then they stopped at the conveyor belt as one man jumped up and disappeared into the plane's belly. The belt started again; and, as the box tipped forward at the top, the other man started to guide her inside; but the box got stuck, so the man shoved it hard from behind. Kate flinched. Take your hands off her! Where's your respect, for God's sake. Then she was gone.

Gemma stuck her hand in her pocket and pulled out a tissue. She blew her nose. 'I'm going to sit down,' she said, turning to face the rows of metal chairs and walking towards

three vacant seats. Kate followed her. She didn't know what else to do.

'We'll be boarding soon,' Emmeline said, to no-one in particular.

'Are you OK, Mum?' she heard her daughter ask. She turned her head and responded with a small smile and a half nod. Gemma reached over and squeezed her hand; it remained limp and unresponsive.

'You OK, Emmeline?' Gemma asked.

Kate glared at the back of Gemma's head. Jesus, why doesn't she shut up? I can't bear it, I truly can't, this is too much, too much; how can she even talk?

She saw Emmeline smile at Gemma. 'I'm fine. I'm a bit shocked. I don't know what I expected, but it wasn't that.'

'I know what you mean, it was kind of brutal wasn't it. She was a piece of cargo...' Gemma couldn't finish her sentence.

Kate stood up abruptly. 'Right, anyone for coffee?'

Gemma and Emmeline looked at her, startled by the sound of her voice. She looked at them, waiting for a response.

'Yes, why not. I'll come and help you carry them,' Gemma said.

'No, please don't. I mean, it's not necessary. I can manage by myself, thanks.'

Kate wandered off aimlessly. She wanted some peace, some quiet. She wanted Cara back. Had she even given her sister and Harry a goodbye hug? She couldn't remember. All she could recall about this morning was Joe reaching his arms out to her and crying as she got into the taxi.

FOUNDERS MEETING

Libretta sat in the back of her car as they waited for the security guard to let them pass. He leant into the car and pointed his scanner at Libretta. Satisfied, he nodded, and the tall, steel gate slid open. Libretta gave him a curt smile. She had long thought that Kerry's security arrangements smacked of paranoia. They had already had to negotiate the outer perimeter security gate, and this second line of defence against the outside world always annoyed her. Finally, Kerry Greer's enormous Hampstead mansion, came into view.

Libretta was shown into the room Kerry reserved for more intimate meetings. There was a large oval table surrounded by comfortable, leather armchairs; the polished surface of the gleaming wood reflecting the light from the chandelier above it. A few moments later, Kerry entered the room, her signature pearls moving in rhythm with her body as she strode towards Libretta. 'Good to see you, Libretta. I trust you had a safe journey?' She didn't wait for a reply. 'Everything is in order. The others are waiting in the Blue Room. Shall I call them in?'

'Thanks, Kerry. Good of you to host us,' Libretta said. Kerry gave her a gracious smile and pressed a buzzer under the table top. Within a few minutes all the armchairs were occu-

pied. Libretta stood up and tapped her teacup. The room fell silent.

'Thank you all for coming to this emergency meeting, and a huge thanks to Kerry for organising this at such short notice. I have some wonderful news. The government have agreed to repeal The Segregation Act!'

Kerry started to clap, and the others joined in, their faces a mixture of surprise and delight.

'I think we should organise a massive celebration. Is everyone in agreement?' Every grinning head in the room nodded.

'Excellent, I'll get my PA to start the ball rolling and we'll aim to have some initial ideas with you by the end of the week. While I have you all, I also wanted to discuss another topic. Should we now consider allowing members to have sons and, if so, how should they be raised?

I know it's an important question and I've rather sprung it on you, but it's entirely relevant. Many of our members will be anxious to reconnect with the sons they left behind. The Castoffs. God, I hate that name. We've been closely monitoring this group, and the harsh but necessary decision by the Movement to force women to leave behind their sons has resulted in anguish and pain for our members, and for those boys. Their pain has been turned into extreme misogyny by the bitter fathers who were left behind to raise them.

There's also been quite a few Completists who've transferred out of the Movement, only to return to us, leaving their sons behind. I know they'll now be able to see them, but only if their fathers co-operate, and I emphatically do not wish to see history repeat itself. Who would like to kick us off? Kerry, any thoughts?'

Unsurprisingly Hermione's hand shot up. 'I wondered if you might have something to say on this point.' Kerry gave a nod of agreement that Hermione could speak before her.

Hermione drew a deep breath, as if determined to be

heard. She looked around at her colleagues, straightened her back and started to speak clearly and loudly. 'We couldn't have a more compelling set of data than the information we've captured through monitoring the Castoffs. It's been an important part of Project Manhood's work. Unless we all want a country whose population is entirely female, and I'm sure there are a few of us who do, we have to find a way of raising the next generation of men so they empathise and support the Movement and its aims. If we don't, we leave the fate of this country in the hands of some of the greatest misogynists to have ever existed. These Castoffs are zealots. And the articulate ones, who've managed to gain political power, are very, very dangerous and damaging to the Movement. I believe we must act and allow our members, or those who wish to, to have sons. We will devise a training programme for these boys and monitor them closely throughout their childhood, eliminating any who show a strong desire to control and dominate, and integrating the rest into our society. When the time comes, they will marry Completist women, and together they can raise a new generation of men. Eventually, as we continue to grow and prosper, this will become the new world, and we will have created it.'

There was a general nodding of heads. A few women were looking at one another with unexpected admiration for Hermione. Libretta was one of them.

'I, for one, am not opposed to this in principle. I have kept abreast of your research on the Castoffs and it makes frightening reading. I would like to clarify one of your comments though. When you say we should eliminate any boy who shows a strong desire to control and dominate, what do you mean?'

All eyes turned from Libretta to Hermione. The room waited.

'I think we've already established we're not squeamish when it comes to getting rid of males who could harm the

Movement, so I'm suggesting exactly that. Not overtly, but covertly. No member will know if their son has been flagged as potentially undesirable. And, in any case, I hope they will be few and far between. We would arrange for them to have accidents. We can hardly let them live with the COs, that will perpetuate the very problem we're trying to eradicate. Better to eradicate their genes, surely?'

The room was silent. No-one would ever have guessed that softly-spoken Hermione would turn out to be their most ruthless member. Libretta spoke again. 'What happens if the training programme fails, and we have thousands of undesirable young boys? What then, Hermione?'

'We'll have to ensure the programme doesn't fail, Libretta. It's not difficult to encourage people to be compliant, to accept an ideology. There are certain tried and tested techniques which are virtually fool proof. It may not surprise you to hear that I've been working on a proposal. Could I suggest I present it to you the next time we meet? I'm certain you will be reassured.'

'And I'm certain we would all be very interested to hear what you have to say! All those in favour, please raise your hands.'

'To clarify, Libretta, we're voting on hearing Hermione's proposal, not on the principle of whether we agree to raising sons in the Movement. Is that correct?' Marilynn searched the room for reassurance that her question was not a stupid one; she was gratified at the number of supportive smiles.

'That's correct, Marilynn. I certainly don't think we can vote on the principle until we hear what Hermione has to say. Now, if I may have a show of hands of all those in favour of Hermione preparing a proposal for our consideration at our next meeting, please.

Carried unanimously. Thank you, Hermione. Can I suggest we all reconvene in a fortnight's time. I believe Sylvia has kindly agreed to host the next meeting, if you can organise

things within that time frame, Sylvia?' Libretta looked over in her direction and she nodded her head. 'That's settled then. I'll crack on with arrangements to celebrate the repeal of The Segregation Act, and we'll reconvene on 18 September to finalise them and hear Hermione's proposal. But one last thing. I propose the discussions regarding the raising of sons be erased from the minutes. All those in favour, raise your hands. Motion carried.'

Libretta was the first to leave. She sat in the back of her chauffeur-driven car, her eyes staring vacantly at the scenery she passed, her mind racing. She had an uneasy feeling in the pit of her stomach.

ALSO BY SARAH WILDE

Want to know what happens next?

Welcome to *The Sacrifice*, the second book in *The Completists* trilogy.

CHAPTER 1

Libretta tapped her teacup and brought the room to order. Conversations were deferred, cake crumbs pressed from plates onto fingers, and corners of mouths dabbed.

'Ladies, now we've decided on how we're going to celebrate the repeal of The Segregation Act, it's time to hear from Hermione. I think I can safely speak for us all, when I say we're intrigued and excited to hear her proposals on how we're going to raise sons within the Movement, if we decide to proceed with this monumental decision. Hermione, over to you.'

Hermione stood up and strode to the front of the room. Libretta smiled. Was that a new suit she was wearing? They were in Sylvia's London townhouse, the third floor of which had been converted into her home office, complete with stylish boardroom and magnificent views over Hyde Park. Hermione looked very much at home in her surroundings.

'Thank you, Libretta. Firstly, I must warn you, my recommendations are controversial. They have to be, to ensure we don't create a new generation of Castoffs. As I explained when we last met, we're embarking on the creation of a new breed of

men, who regard women as their equals, save for physical parity. True partners for Completist women, who will share our vision of how the world could and should be. Our research over the last 50 years suggests men are not inherently geared to dominate and control women. Therefore, I've devised a programme which, if meticulously followed, will ensure the sons of the Movement will work with their future partners to build and protect this new world against anything or anyone that threatens it.' Hermione looked around the room. She had everyone's attention.

'Firstly, we must have control over the genetic input for this first generation. The Movement will create a gene bank of men who already display the characteristics we're seeking. Intelligent, liberal thinkers who understand and empathise with us. It shouldn't be difficult to identify suitable individuals, but we may have difficulty in convincing them to become sperm donors. And here is the first point of controversy. I propose we flatter these men into participating. We don't explain our vision, we merely convince them it's unhealthy for the UK to have such a disproportionate number of women. We tell them we never foresaw how many women would become Completists, and that it is unacceptable that the Movement's success will be to the detriment of the UK population as a whole. Therefore, we want to give members the choice to have sons. It will be easy for them to understand our members wouldn't choose fathers who didn't support their principles. We will emphasise how unique they are, as they alone possess the qualities our members admire. We can make it abundantly clear that they would have no financial, or other obligations for any offspring. In fact, I believe we should compensate them generously for participating in this "humanitarian venture".'

'Sorry to interrupt, Hermione, but what happens if we don't get enough of these men to agree?' Kerry Greer was always keen to get to the crux of the matter.

‘Then we cast our net wider, become a little less picky. But with that comes the increased risk of breeding undesirable males, and naturally they’d have to be eliminated from the Programme in order to avoid creating more Castoffs.’

‘And there we have it, do we not, ladies?’ continued Kerry. ‘The key issue. I’m sure Hermione is about to reveal an excellent programme of education to ensure all these boys grow into men our future members would want to build lives with. But what are we going to do with those who don’t make the mark?’ Kerry looked around the room at her friends and colleagues.

They all turned to Hermione, waiting for her response.

‘There’s a huge amount of irrefutable research which shows one can predict, with a surprising degree of accuracy, how a human being is likely to develop from a young age. One can tell whether they will become leaders, followers, free thinkers or conformists. We’ll be able to identify undesirable boys at around the age of four. I propose covertly eliminating these four-year olds. If you turn to Appendix 1, you will see the methods I’m proposing to achieve this. But let me reassure you all, I don’t believe we’ll ever have to instigate such methods, especially if we’re able to genetically select from a highly vetted pool of donors. Research also shows that the traits which lead men to discriminate against women are mainly learned responses. Predominantly, sons learn from their fathers. This first generation will not have fathers.’

‘Doesn’t research also show that serial killers and psychopaths are often made by overbearing single mothers?’

‘This is incorrect, Kerry. Many do come from single parent families, but the mother often has a history of substance abuse which leads her to neglect and abuse the child. This point leads on to the other important factor for the first generation. We need to pick our mothers just as carefully, and train them to raise these boys. Amazingly, no society in the history of mankind has ever offered comprehensive parental instruction.

The usual procedure is for society to intervene only when things go badly awry and the well-being of the child is already at risk. I'm suggesting the opposite. We should open up the Programme to our members of child-bearing age, and then put them all through a rigorous selection process. Those who make the grade will undergo a thorough training programme and be given continual support while they raise these boys.'

'Can I suggest we look carefully at the education programme and then open up the floor to questions?' Libretta said, sensing the unease in the room. 'Appendix 1 is obviously disconcerting, to say the least, but we cannot objectively assess the risks until we fully understand the process.'

Hermione gave Libretta a look of gratitude, and the room settled down. Over the next hour the room listened to how the sons of Completists would be raised. When she finally sat down, it was the newest and youngest member of the group who spoke. Serena Robertson was the first, and only, guardian to have been elected by members, in the hope her involvement would bring a fresh perspective to the group. 'As you all know, I was born and raised a Completist. I'm of child-bearing age, but I've never considered having a boy, because it was never an option. At the beginning of Hermione's presentation, I questioned whether I would want to be subjected to such close scrutiny while I raised a child, seeing it more as interference than support. But now, after hearing the details of the whole programme, I think the risks of anything going wrong are minimal. And to be a part of such a ground-breaking and brave initiative, would be an honour. Not only could it mean finally achieving harmony and respect between the sexes, but it could even result in a more peaceful, productive future for the whole of mankind. I see it as a stealth revolution, which, within a few generations, could change the world forever. Unless we're prepared to stand up and say the Movement is about the eradication of men, then what other choice do we have?'

There was a moment of silence, broken by Libretta.

'Thank you, Serena. I think you've neatly summarised our dilemma. We shouldn't forget why this Movement was started. It was not to destroy men. It was to protect women and demonstrate that we should be viewed as equals and treated as such. The Movement was born out of the unwillingness of men to share their economic power, and this inertia still exists. Replacing the old by breeding the new is likely to be the only way we'll ever achieve the equality we all crave. If there are any of you who want to dominate men, or even eradicate them, you should question your motivations. But I for one, will be voting in favour of the immediate implementation of this programme. Not without reservations, but with hope and faith.' Libretta paused and then, looking at each of them in turn said, 'With Sylvia's permission, I propose the group makes use of the many delightful rooms in this house to discuss, with whoever they wish, the concerns or otherwise regarding the Programme, and then reconvene in this room, in an hour's time, to take a vote.'

Want to carry on reading?

Visit Amazon and search for *The Completists* by Sarah Wilde or alternatively visit www.wildetales.com.